# DATA MINING METHODS and APPLICATIONS

# OTHER AUERBACH PUBLICATIONS

**Agent-Based Manufacturing and Control Systems: New Agile Manufacturing Solutions for Achieving Peak Performance**
Massimo Paolucci and Roberto Sacile
ISBN: 1574443364

**Curing the Patch Management Headache**
Felicia M. Nicastro
ISBN: 0849328543

**Cyber Crime Investigator's Field Guide, Second Edition**
Bruce Middleton
ISBN: 0849327687

**Disassembly Modeling for Assembly, Maintenance, Reuse and Recycling**
A. J. D. Lambert and Surendra M. Gupta
ISBN: 1574443348

**The Ethical Hack: A Framework for Business Value Penetration Testing**
James S. Tiller
ISBN: 084931609X

**Fundamentals of DSL Technology**
Philip Golden, Herve Dedieu, and Krista Jacobsen
ISBN: 0849319137

**The HIPAA Program Reference Handbook**
Ross Leo
ISBN: 0849322111

**Implementing the IT Balanced Scorecard: Aligning IT with Corporate Strategy**
Jessica Keyes
ISBN: 0849326214

**Information Security Fundamentals**
Thomas R. Peltier, Justin Peltier, and John A. Blackley
ISBN: 0849319579

**Information Security Management Handbook, Fifth Edition, Volume 2**
Harold F. Tipton and Micki Krause
ISBN: 0849332109

**Introduction to Management of Reverse Logistics and Closed Loop Supply Chain Processes**
Donald F. Blumberg
ISBN: 1574443607

**Maximizing ROI on Software Development**
Vijay Sikka
ISBN: 0849323126

**Mobile Computing Handbook**
Imad Mahgoub and Mohammad Ilyas
ISBN: 0849319714

**MPLS for Metropolitan Area Networks**
Nam-Kee Tan
ISBN: 084932212X

**Multimedia Security Handbook**
Borko Furht and Darko Kirovski
ISBN: 0849327733

**Network Design: Management and Technical Perspectives, Second Edition**
Teresa C. Piliouras
ISBN: 0849316081

**Network Security Technologies, Second Edition**
Kwok T. Fung
ISBN: 0849330270

**Outsourcing Software Development Offshore: Making It Work**
Tandy Gold
ISBN: 0849319439

**Quality Management Systems: A Handbook for Product Development Organizations**
Vivek Nanda
ISBN: 1574443526

**A Practical Guide to Security Assessments**
Sudhanshu Kairab
ISBN: 0849317061

**The Real-Time Enterprise**
Dimitris N. Chorafas
ISBN: 0849327776

**Software Testing and Continuous Quality Improvement, Second Edition**
William E. Lewis
ISBN: 0849325242

**Supply Chain Architecture: A Blueprint for Networking the Flow of Material, Information, and Cash**
William T. Walker
ISBN: 1574443577

**The Windows Serial Port Programming Handbook**
Ying Bai
ISBN: 0849322138

## AUERBACH PUBLICATIONS

www.auerbach-publications.com
To Order Call: 1-800-272-7737 • Fax: 1-800-374-3401
E-mail: orders@crcpress.com

# DATA MINING METHODS and APPLICATIONS

Edited by
**Kenneth D. Lawrence**
**Stephan Kudyba**
**Ronald K. Klimberg**

Auerbach Publications
Taylor & Francis Group
Boca Raton    New York

Auerbach Publications is an imprint of the
Taylor & Francis Group, an **informa** business

Auerbach Publications
Taylor & Francis Group
6000 Broken Sound Parkway NW, Suite 300
Boca Raton, FL 33487-2742

International Standard Book Number-13: 978-0-8493-8522-3 (Hardcover)

**Library of Congress Cataloging-in-Publication Data**

Data mining methods and applications / editors, Kenneth Lawrence, Stephan
   Kudyba, and Ronald Klimberg.
      p. cm.
   Includes bibliographical references and index.
   ISBN 978-0-8493-8522-3 (alk. paper)
   1. Data mining. I. Lawrence, Kenneth D. II. Kudyba, Stephan, 1963- III.
Klimberg, Ronald K.

   QA76.9.D343D38347 2008
   005.74--dc22                               2007034116

**Visit the Taylor & Francis Web site at**
**http://www.taylorandfrancis.com**

**and the Auerbach Web site at**
**http://www.auerbach-publications.com**

# Dedications

To the memory of my dear parents, Lillian and Jerry Lawrence,
whose moral and emotional support instilled in me a life-long
thirst for knowledge.

To my wife, Sheila M. Lawrence, for her understanding,
encouragement, and love.

**Kenneth D. Lawrence**

To my family, for their continued and unending support
and inspiration to pursue life's passions.

**Stephan Kudyba**

To my wife, Helene, and to my sons, Bryan and Steven,
for all their support and love.

**Ronald K. Klimberg**

# Contents

## SECTION II APPLICATIONS OF DATA MINING

## SECTION III OTHER AREAS OF DATA MINING

# Preface

This volume, *Data Mining Methods and Applications,* is a compilation of blind refereed scholarly research works involving the utilization of data mining, which addresses a variety of real-world applications. The content is comprised of a variety of noteworthy works from both the academic spectrum and also from business practitioners. Such topic areas as neural networks, data quality, and classification analysis are given with the volume. Applications in higher education, health care, consumer modeling, and product purchase are also included.

Most organizations today face a significant data explosion problem. As the information infrastructure continues to mature, organizations now have the opportunity to make themselves dramatically more intelligent through "knowledge intensive" decision support methods, in particular, data mining techniques. Compared to a decade ago, a significantly broader array of techniques lies at our disposal. Collectively, these techniques offer the decision maker a broad set of tools capable of addressing problems much harder than were ever possible to embark upon. Transforming the data into business intelligence is the process by which the decision maker analyzes the data and transforms it into information needed for strategic decision making. These methods assist the knowledge worker (executive, manager, and analyst) in making faster and better decisions. They provide a competitive advantage to companies that use them. This volume includes a collection of current applications and data mining methods, ranging from real-world applications and actual experiences in conducting a data mining project, to new approaches and state-of-the-art extensions to data mining methods.

The book is targeted toward the academic community, as it is primarily serving as a reference for instructors to utilize in a course setting, and also to provide researchers an insightful compilation of contemporary works in this field of analytics. Instructors of data mining courses in graduate programs are often in need of supportive material to fully illustrate concepts covered in class. This book provides those instructors with an ample cross-section of chapters that can be utilized to more clearly illustrate theoretical concepts. The volume provides the target market with contemporary applications that are being conducted from a variety of resources, organizations, and industry sectors.

*Data Mining Methods and Applications* follows a logical progression regarding the realm of data mining, starting with a focus on data management and methodology optimization, fundamental issues that are critical to model building and analytic applications in Section I. The second and third sections of the book then provide a variety of case illustrations on how data mining is used to solve research and business questions.

# I.  Techniques of Data Mining

Chapter 1 is written by one of the world's most prominent data mining and analytic software suppliers, SAS Inc. SAS provides an end-to-end description of performing a data mining analysis, from question formulation, data management issues to analytic mining procedures, and the final stage of building a model is illustrated in a case study. This chapter sets the stage for the realm of data mining methods and applications.

Chapter 2, written by specialists from the University of Rhode Island and East Carolina University, centers on the investigation of three major strategies for forming neural networks on the classification problem, where spatial data is characterized by two naturally occurring classes.

Chapter 3, from Kent State University professionals, explores the effects of asymmetric misclassification costs and unbalanced group sizes in the ANN performance in practice. The basis for this study is the problem of thyroid disease diagnosis.

Chapter 4 was provided by authorities from Rensselaer Polytechnic Institute and addresses the issue of data management and data normalization in the area of machine learning. The chapter illustrates fundamental issues in the data selection and transformation process and introduces independent component analysis.

Chapter 5 is from academic experts at Saint Joseph's University who describe, apply, and present the results from a multiple criteria approach for a team selection problem that balances skill sets among the groups and varies the composition of the teams from period to period.

# II.  Applications of Data Mining

Chapter 6 in the applied section of this book is from a group of experts from the University of Alabama, Baylor, and SAS Inc., and it addresses the concept of enhancing operational activities in the area of higher education. Namely, it describes the utilization of data mining methods to optimize student enrollment, retention, and alumni donor activities for colleges and universities.

Chapter 7, from authorities at the University of Rhode Island, focuses on a data mining analysis using clustering of an existing prescription drug market that treats respiratory infection.

Chapter 8, from professionals at the University of Arkansas and Roger Williams University, focuses on the simple neural network model for two group classifications by providing basic measures of standard error and confidence intervals for the model.

Chapter 9 is provided by a combination of academic experts from the New Jersey Institute of Technology and a prominent business researcher from Health Research Corp. This chapter introduces how data mining can help enhance productivity in perhaps one of the most critical areas in our society, health care. More specifically, the chapter illustrates how data mining methods can be used to identify candidates likely to develop chronic illnesses.

Chapter 10, from an expert the University of Southern California, investigates a domain specific approach to data and process quality using data mining to produce business intelligence for the purchasing and account receivable process.

Chapter 11 in the applied section of this book is provided by a leading consultancy organization, Accenture, which focuses on better understanding consumer behavior and optimizing retailer interaction to enhance the customer experience in retailing. Accenture introduces data mining and the concept of an intelligence promotion planning system to better service customer interests.

# III. Other Areas of Data Mining

Chapter 12, provided by a data mining consultant from Advanced Analytic Solutions, discusses some of the authors' actual experiences across a variety of data mining engagements.

Chapter 13 is provided by experts from the University of Nebraska and the University of Montevallo. The chapter reviews the general developments of fuzzy sets in data mining, reviews the use of fuzzy sets with two data mining software products, and compares their results to an ordinal classification model.

Chapter 14 is from a researcher at Georgia Southern University who presents the results of applying latent semantic analysis to the article keywords from data mining articles published during a six-year period. The resulting model provides interesting insights into various components of the data mining field, as well as their interrelationships. The chapter includes a reflection on the strengths and weaknesses of applying latent semantic analysis for the purpose of developing such an associative model of the data mining field.

Chapter 15, from authorities from the New Jersey Institute of Technology, Rutgers University, and Saint Joseph's University, focuses on the development of a discriminate classification procedure for the categorization of product successes and failures.

## Acknowledgments

We would like to express our sincere thanks to John Wyzalek and Catherine Giacari of Auerbach Publications/Taylor & Francis Group for their help and guidance during this project and to our families for their devotion and understanding.

**Kenneth D. Lawrence**
**Stephan Kudyba**
**Ronald K. Klimberg**

# About the Editors

**Kenneth D. Lawrence, Ph.D.,** is a professor of management and marketing science and decision support systems in the School of Management at the New Jersey Institute of Technology. His professional employment includes more than 20 years of technical management experience with AT&T as director, Decision Support Systems and Marketing Demand Analysis, Hoffmann-La Roche, Inc., Prudential Insurance, and the U.S. Army in forecasting, marketing planning and research, statistical analysis, and operations research. He is a full member of the Graduate Doctoral Faculty of Management at Rutgers, The State University of New Jersey, in the Department of Management Science and Information Systems. He is a member of the graduate faculty at the New Jersey Institute of Technology in management, transportation, statistics, and industrial engineering. He is an active participant in professional associations at the Decision Sciences Institute, Institute of Management Science, Institute of Industrial Engineers, American Statistical Association, and the Institute of Forecasters. He has conducted significant funded research projects in health care and transportation.

Dr. Lawrence is the associate editor of the *Journal of Statistical Computation and Simulation,* and the *Review of Quantitative Finance and Accounting,* as well as serving on the editorial boards of *Computers and Operations Research* and the *Journal of Operations Management.* His research work has been cited hundreds of times in 63 different journals, including *Computers and Operations Research, International Journal of Forecasting, Journal of Marketing, Sloan Management Review, Management Science, Technometrics, Applied Statistics, Interfaces, International Journal of Physical Distribution and Logistics,* and the *Journal of the Academy of Marketing Science.* He has 254 publications in the areas of multi-criteria decision analysis, management science, statistics, and forecasting; and his articles have appeared in more than 24 journals, including *European Journal of Operational Research, Computers and Operations Research, Operational Research Quarterly, International Journal of Forecasting,* and *Technometrics.*

Dr. Lawrence is the 1989 recipient of the Institute of Industrial Engineers Award for significant accomplishments in the theory and applications of operations research. He was recognized in the February 1993 issue of the *Journal of Marketing* for his "significant contribution in developing a method of guessing in the no data case, for diffusion of new products, for forecasting the timing and the magnitude of the peak in the adaption rate. Dr. Lawrence is a member of the honorary societies Alpha Iota Delta (Decision Sciences Institute) and Beta Gamma Sigma (Schools of Management). He is the recipient of the 2002 Bright Ideas Award in the New Jersey Policy Research Organization and the New Jersey Business and Industry Associates for his work in auditing and use of a goal programming model to improve the efficiency of audit sampling.

In February 2004, Dean Howard Tuckman of Rutgers University appointed Dr. Lawrence as an Academic Research Fellow to the Center for Supply Chain Management because "his reputation and strong body of research are quite impressive." The Center's corporate sponsors include Bayer HealthCare, Hoffmann-LaRoche, IBM, Johnson & Johnson, Merck, Novartis, PeopleSoft, Pfizer, PSE&G, Schering-Plough, and UPS.

**Stephan Kudyba, Ph.D.,** is a faculty member in the school of management at the New Jersey Institute of Technology where he teaches graduate courses in data mining and knowledge management. He has authored the books *Data Mining and Business Intelligence: A Guide to Productivity, Data Mining Advice from Experts,* and *IT, Corporate Productivity and the New Economy,* along with a number of magazine and journal articles that address the utilization of information technologies and management strategy to enhance corporate productivity. Dr. Kudyba also has more than 15 years of private-sector experience in both the United States and Europe, and continues consulting projects with organizations across industry sectors.

**Ronald K. Klimberg, Ph.D.,** is a professor in the Decision and System Sciences Department of the Haub School of Business at Saint Joseph's University, Philadelphia. Dr. Klimberg received his B.S. in information systems from the University of Maryland, his M.S. in operations research from George Washington University, and his Ph.D. in systems analysis and economics for public decision-making from Johns Hopkins University. Before joining the faculty of Saint Joseph's University in 1997, he was a professor at Boston University (ten years), an operations research analyst for the Food and Drug Administration (FDA) (ten years), and a consultant (seven years).

His research has been directed toward the development and application of quantitative methods (e.g., statistics, forecasting, data mining, and management science techniques), such that the results add value to the organization and are effectively communicated. Dr. Klimberg has published more than 30 articles and made more than 30 presentations at national and international conferences in the areas of management science, information systems, statistics, and operations management. His current major interests include multiple criteria decision making (MCDM), multiple objective linear programming (MOLP), data envelopment analysis (DEA), facility location, data visualization, risk analysis, workforce scheduling, and modeling in general. He is currently a member of INFORMS, DSI, MCDM, and RSA.

# Editors and Contributors

## Editors-in-Chief

**Kenneth D. Lawrence**
New Jersey Institute of Technology
Newark, New Jersey, USA

**Ronald K. Klimberg**
Saint Joseph's University
Philadelphia, Pennsylvania, USA

**Stephan Kudyba**
New Jersey Institute of Technology
Newark, New Jersey, USA

## Senior Editors

**Richard T. Hershel**
Saint Joseph's University
Philadelphia, Pennsylvania, USA

**Richard G. Hoptroff**
FlexiPanel Ltd.
London, United Kingdom

**Sheila M. Lawrence**
Rutgers University
New Brunswick, New Jersey, USA

**Daniel E. O'Leary**
University of Southern California
Los Angeles, California, USA

**Harold Rahmlow**
Saint Joseph's University
Philadelphia, Pennsylvania, USA

## Contributors

**Tom Bohannon**
Baylor University
Waco, Texas, USA

**Kevin J. Boyle**
Saint Joseph's University
Philadelphia, Pennsylvania, USA

**John C. Brocklebank**
SAS Institute
Cary, North Carolina, USA

**Rich Burgess**
SAS Institute
Cary, North Carolina, USA

**Pias Chaklanobish**
Research and Development Center
SAS Institute India
Pune, India

**Chad Cumby**
Accenture Technology Labs
Chicago, Illinois, USA

**Juee Dadhich**
Research and Development Center
SAS Institute India
Pune, India

**Cali M. Davis**
University of Alabama
Tuscaloosa, Alabama, USA

**Mark J. Embrechts**
Rensselaer Polytechnic Institute
Troy, New York, USA

**Andrew Fano**
Accenture Technology Labs
Chicago, Illinois, USA

**Adrian Gardiner**
Georgia Southern University
Statesboro, Georgia, USA

**Rayid Ghani**
Accenture Technology Labs
Chicago, Illinois, USA

**Louis W. Glorfeld**
University of Arkansas
Fayetteville, Arkansas, USA

**Tom Grant**
SAS Institute
Cary, North Carolina, USA

**J. Michael Hardin**
University of Alabama
Tuscaloosa, Alabama, USA

**Michael Y. Hu**
Kent State University
Kent, Ohio, USA

**Ronald K. Klimberg**
Saint Joseph's University
Philadelphia, Pennsylvania, USA

**Marko Krema**
Accenture Technology Labs
Chicago, Illinois, USA

**Stephan Kudyba**
New Jersey Institute of Technology
Newark, New Jersey, USA

**Jyhshyan Lan**
Kent State University
Kent, Ohio, USA

**Kenneth D. Lawrence**
New Jersey Institute of Technology
Newark, New Jersey, USA

**Sheila M. Lawrence**
Rutgers University
New Brunswick, New Jersey, USA

**Tom Lehman**
SAS Institute
Cary, North Carolina, USA

**Scott J. Lloyd**
University of Rhode Island
Kingston, Rhode Island, USA

**Paul Mangiameli**
University of Rhode Island
Kingston, Rhode Island, USA

**Alexander Mechitov**
University of Montevallo
Montevallo, Alabama, USA

**Helen Moshkovich**
University of Montevallo
Montevallo, Alabama, USA

**Illya Mowerman**
University of Rhode Island
Kingston, Rhode Island, USA

**Himadri Mukherjee**
Research and Development Center
SAS Institute India
Pune, India

**Lokesh Nagar**
Research and Development Center
SAS Institute India
Pune, India

**Jerry Oglesby**
SAS Institute
Cary, North Carolina, USA

**Daniel E. O'Leary**
University of Southern California
Los Angeles, California, USA

**David L. Olson**
University of Nebraska
Lincoln, Nebraska USA

**Dinesh R. Pai**
Rutgers University
New Brunswick, New Jersey, USA

**Eddy Patuwo**
Kent State University
Kent, Ohio, USA

**Theodore L. Perry**
Health Research Insights, Inc.
Franklin, Tennessee, USA

**Richard D. Pollack**
Advanced Analytic Solutions
Newtown, Pennsylvania, USA

**David West**
East Carolina University
Greenville, North Carolina, USA

**Doug White**
Roger Williams University
Bristol, Rhode Island, USA

**Ira Yermish**
Saint Joseph's University
Philadelphia, Pennsylvania, USA

**Guangyin Zeng**
Rensselaer Polytechnic Institute
Troy, New York, USA

**G. Peter Zhang**
Georgia State University
Atlanta, Georgia, USA

# TECHNIQUES OF DATA MINING

**1**

# Chapter 1

# An Approach to Analyzing and Modeling Systems for Real-Time Decisions

John C. Brocklebank, Tom Lehman, Tom Grant, Rich Burgess, Lokesh Nagar, Himadri Mukherjee, Juee Dadhich, and Pias Chaklanobish

## Contents

# 1.1  Introduction

## 1.1.1  A Problem for Organizations

Many IT (information technology) organizations have smaller budgets and staffs than ever before. Organizations are asking themselves how they can meet growing demands for new business applications and network processing. For a growing number of these organizations, the answer has been to outsource business functions to an application service provider (ASP). Also called application hosting, this arrangement provides access to state-of-the-art applications to companies that prefer to have those applications managed by subject matter experts. The organization can choose the applications it needs and get the benefits of the applications' functionality almost immediately — without having to license and set up the software and without having to hire system administrators to maintain it.

## 1.1.2   A Solution for Organizations

SAS® Solutions OnDemand offers the benefits of traditional hosting — such as low risk and fast "time to solution" with minimal investment — plus the benefits of a cohesive, broad-spectrum program.

With the power of SAS software as its underpinning, SAS Solutions OnDemand offers analytic power that enables an organization to accomplish goals such as the following:

- Predict future outcomes of interest.
- Understand complex relationships in data.
- Model behavior, systems, and processes.

Specifically, SAS Solutions OnDemand can offer benefits that include:

- Strategy reports that provide clear focus on emerging opportunities
- Data mining results that reveal subtle but significant patterns in huge volumes of data, providing new insights for making better business decisions
- Personalization that creates unique and tailored customer segments to support highly targeted activities, such as e-mail campaigns and test marketing
- Demand forecasting that helps anticipate upcoming needs for such issues as product inventory, staffing, and distribution readiness, so that organizations can make proactive decisions to serve those needs
- Data warehouse services that organize and assess the quality of the incoming data before constructing a dimensional warehouse from which organizations can perform their own ad hoc analyses

In summary, SAS Solutions OnDemand delivers the widest portfolio of analytic algorithms, mathematical data manipulations, and modeling capabilities.

## 1.1.3   Chapter Purpose

This chapter explains the software-as-a-service concept (specifically showing the benefits of SAS Solutions OnDemand) by explaining the key hosting components that an organization would need: warehouses, data quality, and analytics effectiveness. The chapter begins with an overview of those components and ends with a real-time analytic deployment case study.

## 1.2 Analytic Warehouse Development

### 1.2.1 Entity State Vector

An *entity state vector* (ESV) is a single database table that contains the minimum and sufficient information needed to describe an *entity*, at a point in time, by a single row of data. Examples of an entity include a student, a customer, a household, a supplier, a product, or a vendor. The goal of building an ESV is to enable the organization to spend more time on solving business problems and considerably less time working on data management issues.

ESVs are particularly useful in analytic modeling activities because many modeling tools are designed to work with data in the form of one row of data per entity. After the data elements that are useful in predicting entity behavior have been determined, the ESVs can be used in batch processes for activities such as mail or call center lead-generation, based on analytic output.

ESVs can also be modified in real-time, with updated or new information generated by transaction-oriented systems, to support real-time decision making. For example, a customer might not be a candidate for a product. During an interaction with that customer, new information is gathered, and the ESV is updated in real-time. Through the use of predictive models and on-demand scoring, the customer has now been identified as having a propensity for the product (that is, an inclination to buy).

Think of an ESV as the most extreme, denormalized expression of the entity. Because all requisite data is in a single table, an ESV is also the least complex way to think about that entity. In contrast, working with data structures that consist of multiple tables and confusing field formats can add time to the process of solving business problems. For example, an ESV eliminates the need for investing time in learning how to efficiently join tables, handle missing values, and then working with categorical variables and a mix of indicator variable formats.

Very large ESVs can be processed in a very short period of time through the use of such tools as the SAS® Scalable Performance Data Server® (SPD Server) and SAS® Enterprise Miner™. Using these tools together makes building predictive models a relatively easy and fast process.

Although building an ESV before the need arises minimizes the time required to provide predictive modeling solutions for implementing real-time decision making, the task of building an ESV is not necessarily a trivial process. Organizations would not want to do that for each new business problem that arises.

### 1.2.2 "Wide" Variable Set Used for Analytics

After building the ESV, it can be used for model development. The analyst who is conducting the model development need not be an IT data management expert. The ESV makes performing the analysis easy, and a pre-built ESV greatly reduces the time required to perform the analysis. The ESV is designed to be a tool for analysis across many different platforms. Careful consideration should be put into the ESV design phase. An analyst should be careful not to rule out variables that might influence a business problem.

That is, from an analysis perspective, it is better to have more information than less information. Ruling out information that is later deemed irrelevant is better than producing a poor analysis because of incorrect initial data. It is the goal of the analysis to identify which data points are most relevant and have predictive properties. Thus, it is a good idea if the ESV is "wide" in terms of the number of data points in its design. Adding variables to the ESV can be time-consuming, while ignoring them takes no time at all.

### 1.2.3  "Minimum and Sufficient" Variable Set for On-Demand and Batch Deployment

After a predictive model has been built and is ready for deployment, only those variables needed to run the model are required. When scoring entity data through use of a predictive model, only the fields found in the score code are needed. The fields required for scoring can be considered the minimum and sufficient set of variables needed to drive the model. Because all the information needed to drive a model is in the ESV, running a scoring model is easily accommodated by running the model using a *view* of the ESV that contains only the minimum and sufficient set of variables. A view is a program that calls an existing dataset to create a new dataset. A view is accessed exactly in the same way as a standard dataset, but it does not consume the disk space that the data would require. If there are multiple models to score, each model can have its own view of the ESV. This technique minimizes the processing time needed to score large volumes of entity data. Combining a minimum and sufficient view of the ESV with an ESV built by using the SAS® Scalable Performance Data Server® (SPD Server) minimizes the processing time to score large sets of entities.

Creating an entity ID index on top of an ESV enables the analyst to quickly find the data that is associated with a single entity. In some real-time, on-demand scenarios, information newer than what currently exists in the ESV can be used to update the contents of the ESV and to re-score the entity in real-time through on-demand scoring.

For example, if in a Web application a customer supplies new information about himself or herself, the current information about that customer can be updated in the ESV and the next best offer for that customer can be determined on-the-fly by running the combination of predictive models and a rules-based engine that drives the Web application to present the next best offer. The process of updating the customer information in the ESV, re-scoring the customer's propensity for a set of products, and passing those results through a rules-based engine can be added to the Web application. The process can be easily made into a stored procedure, so that on-demand execution of a rules-based engine functionality can be added on a system-by-system basis (for example, call center, Web application, and customer service representative), independent of the systems architecture of each of those systems.

## 1.3 Data Quality

### 1.3.1 Importance of Data Quality

Analytic data warehouses are vital to today's organizations. Millions of records can now be loaded into analytic data warehouses in real- or near-real-time from transactional or operational systems. Analytic models built from the data warehouse play a critical role in the organization's ability to react quickly with the most up-to-date information. The speed at which an organization reacts often determines whether the results from modeling efforts can be used to achieve the desired results. Applications such as fraud detection, credit scoring, cross-selling, and up-selling depend on having the latest customer information available for modeling purposes.

#### 1.3.1.1 Relation to Modeling Results

As both the speed of updating data warehouses and the need for real-time (on-demand) modeling have increased, data quality has also had to keep pace. No longer can organizations afford to spend days or weeks combing through the data to look for anomalies before building models. Yet even a few "bad" observations can spoil the best efforts of a model to predict the targeted behavior. The old saying "garbage in, garbage out" (GIGO) is even more true today as the time between model results and the action taken by the organization has grown shorter.

#### 1.3.1.2 Examples of Poor Data Quality and Results of Modeling Efforts

Inaccurate data can lead to inaccurate results. This seems fairly obvious but the effects of poor data quality can be as small as sending the wrong campaign to a few customers or as large as miscalculating the model scores for the entire customer base. The first scenario might occur if systematic changes in scoring algorithms or data extraction occur after the models are built. The latter situation might occur if corrupted data is used to build the model. The risk of either situation occurring can be reduced by instituting data quality rules.

## 1.4 Measuring the Effectiveness of Analytics

### 1.4.1 Sampling

SAS Solutions OnDemand analytic projects often process many terabytes of data. Even with the power of SAS®9 and today's very advanced computing resources, it is not realistic from a development standpoint to perform analytic discovery, reporting, or modeling on such large data sources where many iterations are made in order to fine-tune a process. Jobs that are run on datasets of this magnitude would put unnecessary loads on operational systems, and jobs would take excessive processing time to complete. A better practice is to use sampling to provide data from which to perform development analytics.

## 1.4.2 Samples for Monitoring Effectiveness

SAS Solutions OnDemand has a methodology for creating and maintaining a sample of data, so that a sample population base is maintained across history and new members are added to the sample as the overall population grows. Such a data sample preserves a holistic view of the customer and works well for such analytic exercises as determining triggers that cause a change in needs and goals for customers — as a whole or individually. This sample data source is ready for use by several analytic methods, such as reporting, analytic modeling, and forecasting.

The sampling process is designed to work at any entity level and also preserves hierarchies in the data. The following example considers data as sampled where a Household/Customer/Account hierarchy is implied and where sampling is carried out at a 5 percent sample rate. The technique illustrated below uses simple random sampling as the base, but more advanced sampling methods could be used.

The process begins with a population defined by the historical data sent to SAS Solutions OnDemand when a project starts. Every household is assigned an equal chance or probability of being selected into the sample. As new households come into the population, they are assigned a uniform random number in the interval 0 to 1, using the RANUNI function (SAS Institute Inc., *SAS Language Reference: Dictionary*). The assigned random numbers are permanent and are stored in an output dataset in a column called PERM_RAND_NUM. Only household records that receive a PERM_RAND_NUM at or below 0.05 are kept in this table. As new customers and accounts are added to the households already included in the sample, these accounts (plus all the data corresponding to these new customers and accounts) are added to the sample. The maintenance process depends on keeping assigned households in the sample after they enter it.

## 1.4.3 Longitudinal Measures of Effectiveness

SAS Solutions OnDemand analytic projects often deal with historical data. The data is normally received at regular update frequencies (such as daily, weekly, or monthly) and lends itself well to longitudinal analyses, such as forecast model applications.

### 1.4.3.1 Lifetime Value Modeling

Lifetime Value (LTV) analysis has quickly become the way many companies view their customers. LTV analysis combines profitability and churn data, and returns

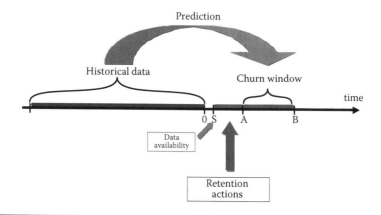

**Figure 1.1    Churn model timeline.**

actionable customer information. LTV measures allow companies to address items such as customer loyalty and customer profitability. Maximizing customer value for existing customers and developing new customers into profitable, long-standing customers are typical applications of LTV analyses.

This section illustrates at a high level how SAS Solutions OnDemand combines survival analysis and customer margin into LTV measures. The discussion behind the methods can be found in more detail in Allison (1995) and Lu (2003).

Typical data mining methods are effective in predicting customer churn events. However, using these methods for predicting when a customer might churn is not practical. Survival analysis is a powerful tool designed to make these types of predictions. LTV analysis and deployment consider historical data to predict the likelihood that customers will churn during a specified time period. Retention or intervention strategies are implemented to prevent customers from leaving the customer base. Figure 1.1 shows this process through a timeline.

## 1.4.3.1.1    Gathering Inputs

As with any analysis, it is necessary to set up and prepare data before running the analytic procedures. Often, the data represents an incomplete view of customer lifetime histories. Using the data information that is available, the LTV analysis requires variables that report customer tenure and active status.

The first step is to create two variables: TENURE and STATUS. Both variables are needed to view LTV through a survival analysis framework. Survival analysis looks at historical data and uses the data to predict probability of survival for future periods. Survival in this context can be thought of as the opposite of churn.

TENURE represents the length of time each customer has been with the organization. This variable should be built at a level of granularity on which the organization can act. That is, if business decisions are based on monthly data, then TENURE should be built based on the number of months the customer has been with the organization.

STATUS represents whether the customer currently is active with the organization or has churned. Those customers who have left the organization are referred to as *observed cases*. Customers who are still active with the organization are known as *censored cases*. To be eligible for inclusion in the SAS software procedures used later in the analysis, each customer must be assigned as either a censored case or an observed case. STATUS is an indicator variable that receives a value of 1 for observed cases and 0 for censored cases. Censored data is common for survival analysis when complete customer history is not available. The concept of censoring and how it is used in the context of survival analysis is discussed in much more detail in Allison (1995) and Lu (2003).

A key component of most analyses is determining a final subset of variables for which the analysis can be run without losing generality of model fit. Models can suffer from being "over-fit" when too many inputs are fed into the model. Often, these variables, or combinations of these variables, mislead the analyst into believing that specific signals in the data exist when in fact they are really artifacts of "over-fitting" the model. Therefore, it is important to identify a minimal variable set that still holds the relevant information for the LTV analysis.

The two main SAS procedures used for analyzing survival analysis are the LIFEREG and PHREG procedures (SAS Institute Inc., SAS/STAT User's Guide). PROC LIFEREG produces parametric regression models for censored data using maximum likelihood estimation. PROC PHREG uses semi-parametric estimates based on partial likelihood estimation. When the shapes of the survival and hazard functions are known, PROC LIFEREG generally produces better estimates.

The LIFETEST procedure in SAS helps with variable reduction in Survival Analysis. Figure 1.2 illustrates a call to PROC LIFETEST that produces rank test statistics for all covariates specified in the model through the TEST statement.

```
proc lifetest
     data=work.ltv_model_final
     method=lt
     plots=(s,h)
     notable;
     time DURATION*STATUS(1);
     test INPUT1
          INPUT2
          INPUT3
             more input variables
             ;
Run;
```

**Figure 1.2  Sample PROC LIFETEST code.**

**Table 1.1  Sample PROC LIFETEST Output**

| Variable | Test Statistic | Standard Deviation | Chi-Square | Pr>Chi-Square |
|----------|---------------|--------------------|------------|---------------|
| INPUT1 | 870522 | 66172.5 | 173.1 | <.0001 |
| INPUT2 | 258.3 | 21.9608 | 138.4 | <.0001 |
| INPUT3 | 53923525 | 8816451 | 37.4084 | <.0001 |
| ETC. | ... | ... | ... | ... |

Table 1.1 shows output where chi-square test statistics are reported, along with their corresponding probability values. For the survival analysis, SAS Solutions OnDemand keeps all variables that have a probability value that is less than or equal to a certain threshold (usually 0.05).

### 1.4.3.1.2   Incorporating Results into Future Analytical Monitoring Efforts

The previous subsections illustrated methods for using longitudinal data for LTV analysis under a survival setting. After the LTV analysis is complete, the analyst can segment the population and make characterizations about each segment. For example, for each segment, it is simple to report summary statistics on many variables. The LTV analysis requires forecasting expected revenue and then calculates LTV. Both expected revenue and projected LTV estimates are excellent measures when characterizing the segments and should help define areas where potential marketing and intervention strategies would apply.

Suppose the segment characterization has identified a segment that has high expected attrition rates as assigned by the survival analysis, but that also shows high net present value. This segment is an excellent candidate for an intervention strategy because there is a base of profitable customers who appear as though they will leave soon.

After deploying the attrition intervention strategy, it is important to measure its effect in an effort to learn from the outcome. One possible technique is to report the number of customers who responded to the intervention strategy (perhaps a discount offer was mailed). Counting the proportion of the population who responded is straightforward. Another measure to assess is whether the intervention strategy was able to lower the expected attrition rate that was given by the survival models. It is very important to be able to assess the effects of analytic modeling efforts.

### 1.4.3.1.3   One-to-One versus Segmented Approaches to LTV Modeling

Some retail operations prefer to view LTV from a segment perspective rather than for each individual customer. Customers can be segmented through business rules rather than through analytic models. For example, segments can be constructed based on the product or products, or on the media that first initiated the engagement. Consider a 10 percent off promotional coupon offer that attracted several new additions to the customer base. It is straightforward to track this population base and determine the Net Present Value. Inferences could also be made based on populations of similar offers that would provide expected LTV estimates and attrition rates for the segment. Because the cost of customer acquisition is often so high, the retail operation group often plans to provide additional incentives to encourage the group to make additional purchases and remain in the customer base rather than leaving. A pre-post analysis can be generated to study the effect of the intervention strategies and their effect on future revenue and attrition rates for the segments.

## 1.4.4 Automated Detection of Model Shift

SAS Solutions OnDemand uses the SAS® Model Manager for model deployment. SAS Model Manager includes automated methods to detect when a model has become outdated because of changes in the data that feeds the model. Over time, customers' characteristics change, as do their needs, creating another challenge for the analyst. It is important to ensure that models are always current and relevant for the times when they are deployed.

SAS Model Manager reports two types of output for evaluating model shift: (1) the characteristic report and (2) the stability report. SAS Model Manager provides model life-cycle reports that include model assessment reports such as lift and the receiver operating characteristic (ROC). These reports, which are useful for detecting model shifts in the data, can be based on the data for differing points of time, as defined by model rebuild periods.

### 1.4.4.1 Characteristic Report

The SAS Model Manager characteristic report is one of two data consistency reports. The characteristic report is an input data source report that does not depend on any model. It examines the consistency of the composition of input datasets that are submitted to models over time. The characteristic report also detects and quantifies shifts in the distribution of input variable values over time. Input variable distribution shifts can point to significant changes in customer behavior that might be due to new technology, competition, marketing promotions, new laws, or other influences.

For example, suppose a model that runs weekly uses an input variable called CUSTOMER_AGE. Also suppose that a marketing promotion generates a surge of new customers between the ages of 18 and 21. An organization can use the characteristic report to detect the change in the distribution of CUSTOMER_AGE in the current dataset, as well as measure the extent of the shift. Knowing the extent of the new data shift helps the organization decide whether or not to adjust its model.

To find data shifts, the characteristic report compares two variable value distributions: (1) the training dataset that was used to develop the model and (2) a current dataset. If large enough shifts occur in the distribution of variable values over time, the original model might not be the best predictive or classification tool to use with the current data.

The characteristic report uses a deviation index to quantify the shifts in a variable's value distribution that can occur between the training dataset and the current dataset. To create the characteristic report, the deviation index is computed for each predictor variable in the dataset.

Numeric predictor variable values are bucketed into ten bins for frequency analysis. Outlier values are removed to facilitate better binning and to avoid scenarios that can aggregate most observations into a single bin. After calculating deviation index values for each input variable, the characteristic report sorts them in descending order.

If the training dataset and the current dataset have identical distributions for a variable, the variable's deviation index is equal to zero. A variable that has a deviation index value that is greater than 0.1 but less than 0.25 is classified as a *mild deviation*. A variable that has a deviation index value greater than 0.25 is classified as a *significant deviation*. Section 1.5.4.2 shows a characteristic report example (see Figure 1.10).

## 1.4.4.2 Stability Report

The SAS Model Manager stability report is the second data consistency report. The stability report evaluates changes in the distribution of scored output variable values as models score data over time. The stability report uses the same deviation index function as the characteristic report. However, the stability report detects and quantifies shifts in the distribution of output variable values in the data produced by the models, instead of quantifying shifts in the distribution of input variable values in the data submitted to the models.

While the characteristic report indicates changes to the scope and composition of the submitted datasets over time, the stability report evaluates the impact of the data variations on the model's predictive output during the same interval. The characteristic report does not require model interaction, but the stability report requires output data from the model to generate the output variable deviation statistics.

The deviation index for the stability report is calculated the same way as the characteristic report. Too much deviation in predictive variable output can indicate that model tuning, retraining, or replacement is necessary. Section 1.5.4.2 shows a stability report example (see Figure 1.11).

# 1.5 Real-Time Analytic Deployment Case Study

## 1.5.1 Case Study Exercise Overview

Orion Sporting Goods (OSG) is a large retail distributor that has traditional brick-and-mortar stores, direct catalog mailings, and an Internet presence. OSG has been in existence since 1998. The data available for this exercise covers the period from 1998 through 2002. Currently, OSG is evaluating certain changes in marketing methods to increase sales. In the spirit of data mining exercises, where the analyst needs to have data available with the outcome present in order to build models, SAS has structured the data such that the period of January 01, 1998, through June 30, 2002, is used to characterize outcomes in the last half of 2002.

There has been a great deal written on data mining techniques; this material is specific to building predictive models from end-to-end (Berry and Linoff, 1997). Rather than discussing those topics again, this section includes some techniques that can be used to help increase the signal for the predictive models. This section also focuses on how to manage model portfolios and takes a deeper look at model deployment. Model deployment is presented from both the batch process viewpoint and the real-time, on-demand viewpoint.

Material that was presented in several of the previous sections presented in this chapter is revisited through a case study to provide more specifics.

### 1.5.1.1 Case Study Problem Formulation

On July 1, 2002, OSG started several promotional activities to try to increase its sales to customers who have registered for the Orion Star Card:

- ■ OSG sent a 10 percent off coupon to all OSG Star Card customers; the coupon could be used in any purchasing channel (retail, catalog, or the Internet).
- ■ OSG sent a general mail offering double points toward Gold status for any purchase made before December 31, 2002.
- ■ OSG implemented a new personalized recommendation engine for the Internet channel.

The recommendation engine that had been developed for the Internet channel tailors customized product recommendations to the customer through a three-phased approach:

1. When the customer visits the Internet channel, he or she is greeted with a set of generic product recommendations based on top-selling items at the time or items that OSG is currently marketing heavily. Closeout items are also good recommendation candidates in this first phase.

2. As the customer navigates the Internet channel, the content he or she views is recorded. The information about the content that is viewed is sent to the recommendation engine. The recommendation engine then produces product recommendations that are based on the most logical set of next actions based upon recent customer history shopping patterns.

3. The customer then adds the product or products to his or her shopping cart, at which point the customer has identified himself or herself. Customer-specific recommendations are given, based on a mixture of the customer's historic patterns and overall customer trends, where the historic trends translate to product-specific model propensities.

The following subsections focus on the analytic methods that can be used to evaluate the effect of the 10 percent discount offer and also show how analytic method results are used in a recommendation engine scenario.

### 1.5.1.2 Case Study Industry-Specific Considerations

As discussed previously, OSG has three sales channels: brick-and-mortar locations, catalog, and the Internet. The brick-and-mortar locations account for the majority of OSG's sales but they offer a challenge because specific customers cannot always be associated with transactions unless they use their Orion Star Card when making the purchase. For this study, only transactions associated with a particular customer ID are considered. This limits the population for model building; however, the results from the models can be extrapolated to the general population without too much fear of bias.

Another effect that is not measured in this analysis is the concept of *true response*. The models are built with the assumption that marketing promotions drive the customers to make a purchase. However, some customers would have made a purchase without receiving the promotion. A relatively new concept in response modeling is measuring the true response by adjusting for customers who, without any type of promotion, make a purchase. There are some interesting methods for removing this type of bias from statistical models but they are not included in this chapter.

## 1.5.2 Analytic Framework for Two-Stage Model

After considering the business goals of the OSG discount offer, SAS Solutions OnDemand evaluates the data that is available and develops an analytic plan that allows for an analytic pre-post assessment of the offer. SAS approaches this exercise through a classic two-stage model retail framework.

Using a binary target indicator variable that defines whether the customer has made a purchase anytime between January 01, 1998, and June 30, 2002, the process begins with the building of a decision tree model. Under this framework, the decision tree provides a supervised method of segmentation. This method is also known as *target-driven segmentation*. The decision tree is configured so that the resulting tree splits form groups of homogeneous segments, where variation is reduced within segments. Each segment is assigned a purchase response rate as determined by the output tree structure.

Next, within the resulting tree segment populations, a logistic regression response model is developed, per segment, to further define the customer's probability of purchase. Finally, regression models are developed to model the retail spending for the purchasers.

This same framework is then applied to those who responded to the 10 percent discount offer, to view the offer's effect.

### 1.5.2.1  Data Specifics

The data with which SAS Solutions OnDemand starts the entire process is a star schema dimensional model that is assembled as a set of fact and dimension tables. The dimensional model serves as the input for the entity state vector (ESV) data mart. The OSG data is at the customer level, which is also the granularity of deployment. As such, the state vector is at the customer level and will be referred to as the CSV. The merits of converting this data into the analytic-ready ESV data were discussed previously. Figure 1.3 shows the dimensional data layout of the

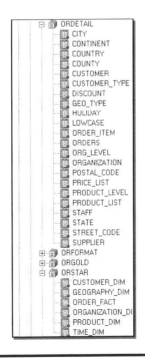

**Figure 1.3  OSG data model.**

OSG dimensional structure. Note in the figure that ORGOLD contains the same data as ORSTAR; however, it is specific to the Gold customer base. ORFORMAT is a format library that contains variable formatting information.

The CSV data available from the Orion Star Schema database lends itself to the creation of hundreds of variables for input to modeling procedures. Retail modeling applications typically create variables that measure recency, frequency, and monetary values for each customer. These variables can often be supplemented or transformed to measure a degree of momentum. To illustrate the standard tools (segmentation, logistic, and linear regression) used in response modeling, these variables were created through a CSV for this case study.

### 1.5.2.2  Data Mining Techniques

In general, there is more than one way to approach a business problem. Formulation of the business problem is crucial to a successful data mining exercise. The business problem must be well-articulated so that the objectives are clearly defined. Formulating the business problem in this way makes the process of determining the appropriate data mining technique much clearer.

There has been much written about which data mining techniques apply to which data sources (Berry and Linoff, 1997; Han and Kamber, 2000; Wang, 2003). Rather than contributing more to that conversation, the focus here is on specifics that are applied during the case study.

#### 1.5.2.2.1  Navigational Output as Model Input

Section 1.5.1.1 provided a preliminary setup for the recommendation engine process, where product-specific recommendations are rendered, based on the specific navigation patterns defined at the customer visit level. To identify patterns in the data, the data analyst would be justified in conducting an affinity analysis. In this case, the analyst might decide to derive events that lead to a purchase event and might also use the output rule set to drive the online product recommendations.

SAS Solutions OnDemand has taken this approach a bit further here by taking the output from the affinity analysis to help create input variables that complement the predictive models built for this case study.

#### 1.5.2.2.2  Time Series Data as Model Input

SAS Solutions OnDemand uses a technique for summarizing time series data into a single row per customer. The pieces of output from the summarization are used as potential model drivers for analytic models. This application works very well when dealing with transactional type data and, as a retailer, OSG does collect transactional sales data. Consider CSV data where variables such as a monthly time frame,

**Table 1.2    CSV with ARIMA Output Appended**

| Customer_ID | AR1_1_price_r | AR1_2_price_r | AR1_3_price_r | AR1_4_price_r | AR1_5_price_r | AR1_6_price_r |
|---|---|---|---|---|---|---|
| 1 | -0.021951725 | 0.202328829 | 0.1458229895 | 0.062872108 | -0.204703755 | -0.070255612 |
| 3 | -0.074998324 | 0.2819491421 | -0.021936608 | -0.071478206 | -0.098111865 | -0.061302199 |
| 4 | 0.2993925781 | -0.129000972 | 0.4796193388 | -0.078369784 | -0.02254435 | -0.097919631 |
| 5 | -0.036138599 | -0.028298238 | 0.0534255447 | -0.03379453 | -0.056778286 | -0.109845742 |
| 6 | -0.075176924 | -0.020970636 | -0.054915342 | 0.0332126946 | -0.068669525 | -0.0723183 |
| 7 | 0.0301608723 | 0.144375431 | -0.114136676 | 0.2281391903 | -0.02724272 | -0.122566605 |
| 9 | -0.035405139 | -0.043384365 | 0.1558001621 | 0.0130882432 | 0.1595654866 | -0.034028217 |
| 10 | 0.1082619411 | -0.017607865 | 0.0787760379 | -0.087641563 | -0.06394841 | -0.073678582 |
| 11 | -0.036065654 | 0.0055300573 | -0.044445906 | 0.568268119 | -0.031680209 | -0.055403377 |
| 12 | 0.0034588282 | 0.0037789679 | -0.127654072 | -0.135217476 | -0.091408721 | -0.152337153 |

and the amount purchased per month are present to identify the customer. Very simply, the analyst could consider taking the mean of the amount purchased per customer and add that value to a list of potential model inputs. In an approach that is a bit more advanced, the analyst could fit a regression line to the data for each customer and collect the intercept and slope as potential inputs. In either case, these are attempts to summarize a time series into a single row of data. In this case study, SAS takes a more sophisticated approach by applying advanced time series models to the data and recording summary statistics to be used in modeling activities. AutoRegressive Integrated Moving-Average (ARIMA) models are generated and output for autoregressive terms and moving average parameters are appended to the CSV. Table 1.2 shows a few rows from the CSV with ARIMA output appended.

## *1.5.3   Data Models*

SAS Solutions OnDemand has created a CSV dataset for the OSG analytic activities. The CSV serves many analytic purposes and can be viewed as a cube structure that houses several different data dimensions. The rows of the CSV are defined by two dimensions: (1) customer and (2) time. Each customer receives one row of data for each month if he or she is an active customer. This data design provides a quick way to subset the data for a specific period of time on which to run analytic models. Because time is preserved as a dimension, the data holds historical information about the customer. Thus, the CSV is ready for time-series analysis as designed. The columns of the CSV represent dimensions such as geography, demography, and purchase.

The CSV becomes a post-analysis recipient of analytic output, which also makes it a deployment mechanism. Product-specific models are generated that produce, per customer, the propensity to purchase the products over a future time frame. The customer-specific propensities are then appended to the CSV. The recommendation engine considers this information and bases product recommendations appropriately.

### *1.5.3.1   Data Discovery Insights*

SAS Enterprise Miner provides two nodes that perform affinity analysis: (1) Path Analysis and (2) Association Analysis. The Path Analysis node expands on the

**Table 1.3    OSG Top Products**

| | Top_Products |
|---|---|
| 1 | Petanque Balls Chromium 8-pack |
| 2 | Bulls Eye Stuart/Tungsten 24 Gram |
| 3 | Hurricane 4 |
| 4 | Lucky Tech Intergal Wp/B Rain Pants |
| 5 | Comfort Shelter |
| 6 | Family Holiday 4 |
| 7 | Pacific 95% 23 Gram |
| 8 | Expedition10,Medium,Right,Blue  Ribbon |
| 9 | Rain Jacket |
| 10 | Big Guy Men's Air Tuned Sirocco Shoes |

scope of the Association Analysis node by examining sequential events that are several items long. That is, where the Association Analysis node reports unidirectional rules involving two items or two sets of items, the Path Analysis node reports rules of several items where the rules are directional. The Path Analysis node is especially useful for examining clickstream data, such as that recorded in Web logs.

In this study, SAS Solutions OnDemand has determined the top-selling products for OSG using simple frequency analysis. Among the top products are those given in Table 1.3.

Next, the Path Analysis node is used to look at the events and sets of events that led to product purchases. Using the transactional purchase data, the process is explicitly searching for product purchase events that lead to purchasing any of the top items at OSG. Then, for each top purchase product, an output dataset is produced that contains the top sequential purchase activities that lead to the purchase event. Table 1.4 shows common paths that lead to the purchase of the Bulls Eye Stuart/Tungsten 24 Gram product.

Now, using the Path output information, the goal is to complement product-specific models for the Bulls Eye Stuart/Tungsten 24 Gram product. Consider the first rule above: Wyoming Men's T-Shirt with V-Neck → Aim4it 18 Gram Softtip Pil → Bulls Eye Stuart/Tungsten 24 Gram. An indication variable for each customer who showed purchase patterns for the first two items of this rule is created. That is, those customers who purchase a Wyoming Men's T-Shirt with V-Neck

**Table 1.4    Top Product Path Output**

| Item 1 | Item 2 | Item 3 | Rule Size | Rule Confidence[%] |
|---|---|---|---|---|
| Wyoming Men's T-Shirt with V-Neck | Aim4it 18 Gram Softtip Pil | Bulls Eye Stuart/Tungsten 24 Gram | 3 | 42.8571 |
| Aim4it 80% Tungsten 22 Gram | Aim4it 16 Gram Softtip Pil | Bulls Eye Stuart/Tungsten 24 Gram | 3 | 37.5000 |
| Bulls Eye Stuart/Tungsten 24 Gram | Aim4it 80% Tungsten 22 Gram | Bulls Eye Stuart/Tungsten 24 Gram | 3 | 8.8235 |
| Aim4it 18 Gram Softtip Pil | Bulls Eye 15 Gram 80% Tungsten So | Bulls Eye Stuart/Tungsten 24 Gram | 3 | 8.1967 |
| Pacific 95% 23 Gram | Aim4it 16 Gram Softtip Pil | Bulls Eye Stuart/Tungsten 24 Gram | 3 | 8.1081 |
| Aim4it 16 Gram Softtip Pil | Bulls Eye 15 Gram 80% Tungsten So | Bulls Eye Stuart/Tungsten 24 Gram | 3 | 6.8182 |
| Aim4it 16 Gram Softtip Pil | Aim4it 80% Tungsten 22 Gram | Bulls Eye Stuart/Tungsten 24 Gram | 3 | 5.7692 |
| Aim4it Spinning Top Medium Shafts | Bulls Eye Stuart/Tungsten 24 Gram | | 2 | 4.8724 |
| Aim4it 80% Tungsten 23 Gram | Bulls Eye Stuart/Tungsten 24 Gram | | 2 | 4.4776 |
| Wyoming Men's Polo-Shirt | Bulls Eye Stuart/Tungsten 24 Gram | | 2 | 4.4118 |

**Table 1.5    CSV with Product Specific Propensities Added**

| Customer ID | Hurricane_4 | Comfort_Shelter | Family_Holiday_4 | Bulls_Eye_Stuart_Tungsten_24Gram |
|---|---|---|---|---|
| 1 | 0.3396034964 | 0.0493555856 | 0.6687259966 | 0.3735357152 |
| 3 | 0.6152319334 | 0.6840289252 | 0.5145901495 | 0.3474179312 |
| 4 | 0.6395043948 | 0.5419705596 | 0.1197459368 | 0.4233176324 |
| 5 | 0.2820073195 | 0.530101043 | 0.4947471835 | 0.2162388369 |
| 6 | 0.3866088355 | 0.3808029566 | 0.3636914759 | 0.3825139033 |
| 7 | 0.0788897542 | 0.0038608583 | 0.7115288939 | 0.920640287 |
| 9 | 0.8906405149 | 0.5128496105 | 0.9118745015 | 0.2989465861 |
| 10 | 0.9329743283 | 0.5966671159 | 0.172543977 | 0.7445140531 |
| 11 | 0.7919859652 | 0.2608813756 | 0.4537132673 | 0.2165215543 |
| 12 | 0.874982227 | 0.8777286545 | 0.9807314495 | 0.7091462075 |
| 13 | 0.2202323453 | 0.8555536852 | 0.3801774654 | 0.9542102711 |
| 16 | 0.1183232782 | 0.2578593554 | 0.6507987295 | 0.9657019223 |
| 17 | 0.3695351427 | 0.8592262165 | 0.8645557877 | 0.3167702203 |
| 18 | 0.6742128179 | 0.9014260992 | 0.0386555768 | 0.720361099 |

and then purchase an Aim4it 18 Gram Softtip Pil received a value of 1. Otherwise, the customers received a value of 0. The same logic was applied for the other rules shown above, and the end result is an enhanced set of relevant indicator variables to help predict Bulls Eye Stuart/Tungsten 24 Gram purchases. It would also be possible to consider a strategy for assigning rule confidence or support measures (Berry and Linoff, 1997; SAS Institute Inc., SAS Enterprise Miner Documentation) to each customer, based on the output shown above.

Finally, a set of Path-based indicators that help drive product-specific propensity models is generated. The customer-specific propensities are then added to the CSV for the purpose of making intelligent product recommendations as shown in Table 1.5. See Section 1.5.5 for an explanation of how this data is used to make customer-specific product recommendations.

### 1.5.3.2   Target-Driven Segmentation Analysis Using Decision Trees

Segmentation algorithms are often a good first step after the dependent and independent variables have been constructed and after the data has been structured properly for modeling purposes. Decision tree procedures that use a dependent or target variable can be used to do the following:

- Assign probabilities to segments. These segment probabilities can be used to determine who to promote or not to promote.
- Split the population into more homogeneous groups, to which other modeling algorithms can be applied.
- Identify independent variable interactions.
- Identify nonlinear relationships between dependent and independent variables.
- Identify data quality issues not previously discovered.
- Provide good overall insight into the relationship between independent and dependent variables.

Some companies might use segmentation models for all their statistical modeling needs. Segmentation models have some key advantages over other modeling techniques, including:

- Segmentation models are intuitive and easy to explain to other departments in the organization, such as marketing.
- The customer selection process for segmentation models is relatively easy for the IT department to code.
- Segmentation models give the organization a manageable number of "subpopulations" that can be tracked over time.
- Segmentation models make it easy to determine the most profitable segment and to examine drivers for that segment.

One big disadvantage to using a segmentation model as the final model is that every customer in a segment gets the same model score (probability). This approach often does not provide the flexibility needed by the marketing or advertising departments within an organization.

Best practices have often found that combining decision trees with other forms of modeling produces the best results. Decision trees are used to break the population into like groups, and then more granular modeling techniques can be used to assign individual probability scores.

Figure 1.4 provides an example of an SAS decision tree that is built on OSG data. The target variable is the binary *buy* versus *no buy* variable. This model can be used as a predecessor for other techniques, as a benchmark, or both.

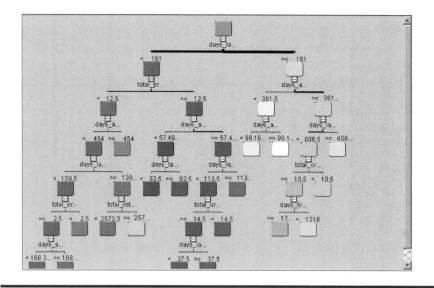

**Figure 1.4   Decision tree split output.**

### 1.5.3.3   Logistic Regression Response Model

Logistic regression is the most widely used and accepted modeling tool employed in building response models. Logistic procedures use the independent variables to formulate the probability of an event (typically binary). This probability can then be used to rank individuals within the population.

Determining the *usefulness* of the logistic regression model can be accomplished in many ways. Below, the concepts of *score distribution*, *model lift*, and the use of the ROC curve are discussed as ways to measure the value that is gained using a statistical model instead of using random selections from the population.

Score distributions generate the distributions of the posterior probabilities or predicted values. The score distribution chart plots the proportions of events and nonevents on the vertical axis across the various bins in a lattice defined by the various models and the various datasets. This approach can be used as one of the tools for analyzing the model performance.

Figure 1.5 compares score distributions for competing regression and tree models. The horizontal access is based on the posterior probability range (0 to 1, from left to

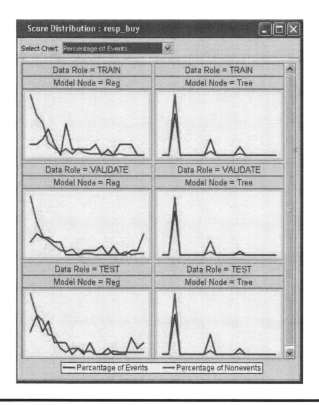

**Figure 1.5   Score distribution chart.**

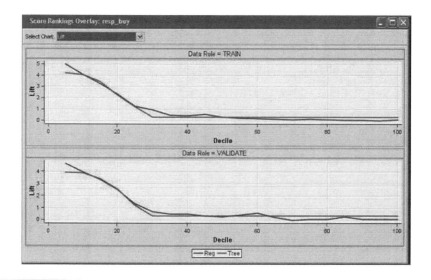

**Figure 1.6    Lift chart.**

right) and the vertical access shows the proportion of events and non-events. A well-performing model will show clear delineation between the two distributions, with the event proportions weighing more heavily toward 1 on the posterior probability range.

*Lift* is the most common statistic used to measure the effectiveness of models in many marketing applications. The purpose of target modeling is to identify a subgroup of the entire population to get a better response rate on the selected subgroup members. In general, lift is calculated as the target response divided by the average response.

In this example, lift is calculated by dividing the population into deciles into which a population's members are placed according to their probability of response. The highest responders are put into decile 1 and so on. The lift chart in Figure 1.6 shows the lift curve for two different models. Note that the deciles in Figure 1.6 are represented as 0, 10, 20, …, 100.

The ROC curve, which is defined as a plot of sensitivity as the *y* coordinate versus its *1-specificity* as the x coordinate, is an effective method of evaluating the quality or performance of target models. Sensitivity is defined as the number of true positive decisions divided by the number of actually positive cases. Specificity is the number of true negative decisions divided by the number of actually negative cases.

Figure 1.7 shows the ROC curve from the SAS Enterprise Miner Model Comparison node for the two models. The performance quality of a model is demonstrated by the degree that a ROC curve pushes upward and to the left. This region is also referred to as the area under the ROC curve (AUC). It can take any value between 0 and 1. The area ranges from 0.50 for a purely random model to 1.0 for a perfect classifier. In the fitted models in Figure 1.7, the AUCs are equal to 89 percent and 81 percent, respectively.

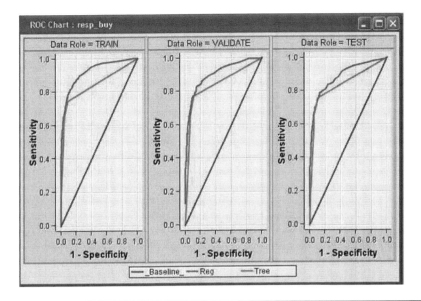

**Figure 1.7    ROC chart.**

### 1.5.3.4    Regression to Model Return

The final step in this modeling process is to provide the OSG Marketing Department with a tool to assess the profitability of the promotion. Marketing can then apply the costs that are associated with the campaign to determine which customers or customer segments are profitable, and by how much.

The profit table is a useful tool for measuring the value of a predictive model. The table shows the profit from each segment and the corresponding probability of response. For target mailing, OSG can use the segments that have a higher probability of response to get the better response with few number of target customers. Table 1.6 shows the actual total profit gain from each segment and the corresponding customer percentage. The graphs show that the top 57.23 percent of customers constitute 85.94 percent of the total profit.

### 1.5.3.5    Product-Specific Models with Path Indicators

Section 1.5.3.1 discussed enriching the CSV with information to produce product-specific models. The data elements required to create these models, in addition to the base CSV, are product-specific target indicators and the PATH rule indicator variable inputs. After the models are produced and registered with SAS Model Manager, the CSV receives the product-specific propensity scores for the Internet channel deployment through the recommendation engine.

**Table 1.6    Segment Profit Table**

| Segment | Frequency | Total Profit | Prop_resp_buy1 | Total Profit Share | % Cumulative Profit | % Customer | % Cumulative Customer |
|---|---|---|---|---|---|---|---|
| 2 | 31806 | $36,543,258.34 | 0.88 | 0.59 | 58.74% | 46.98% | 46.98% |
| 24 | 6940 | $16,103,808.76 | 0.73 | 0.26 | 85.94% | 10.25% | 57.23% |
| 56 | 4740 | $2,477,509.04 | 0.67 | 0.04 | 89.94% | 7.00% | 64.23% |
| 29 | 4506 | $1,238,754.52 | 0.63 | 0.02 | 91.74% | 6.66% | 70.88% |
| 31 | 6665 | $619,377.26 | 0.57 | 0.01 | 92.25% | 9.84% | 80.72% |
| 43 | 1600 | $1,238,754.52 | 0.56 | 0.02 | 94.93% | 2.36% | 83.09% |
| 82 | 93 | $433,564.08 | 0.54 | 0.007 | 95.63% | 0.14% | 83.23% |
| 13 | 9768 | $1,858,131.78 | 0.54 | 0.03 | 98.28% | 14.43% | 97.65% |
| 58 | 1209 | $619,377.26 | 0.53 | 0.01 | 99.27% | 1.79% | 99.44% |
| 101 | 77 | $123,875.45 | 0.50 | 0.002 | 99.47% | 0.11% | 99.55% |
| 57 | 96 | $247,750.90 | 0.45 | 0.004 | 99.51% | 0.14% | 99.69% |
| 83 | 87 | $130,069.22 | 0.33 | 0.0021 | 99.72% | 0.13% | 99.82% |
| 100 | 121 | $173,425.63 | 0.28 | 0.0028 | 100.00% | 0.18% | 100.00% |

**Table 1.7  Top Product Paths**

| Item 1 | Item 2 | Item 3 | Rule Confidence(%) |
|---|---|---|---|
| Scania Mitten, Women's/Junior/Men's | Sheet Sleeping Bag, Red | Hurricane 4 | 100.0000 |
| Polyester 3-Persons | Jl Rainlight Essential Pants | Hurricane 4 | 37.5000 |
| Mattress with 5 channels 196x72 | Comfort Shelter | Hurricane 4 | 26.6667 |
| Outback Storm Kitchen | Lucky Tech Intergal Wp/B Rain Pants | Hurricane 4 | 18.7500 |
| Mayday W'S Sports Pullover | Comfort Shelter | Hurricane 4 | 18.7500 |
| Lucky Tech Classic Rain Pants | Comfort Shelter | Hurricane 4 | 14.2857 |
| Basic 10, Left , Yellow/Black | Tent Summer 195 Twin Sleeping Bag | Hurricane 4 | 11.4286 |
| Expedition Zero,Medium,Right,Charcoal | Outback Sleeping Bag, Medium,Right/Blue/Blac | Hurricane 4 | 10.0000 |
| Basic 10, Left , Yellow/Black | Expedition Zero,Medium,Right,Charcoal | Hurricane 4 | 6.5217 |

An assessment of the impact of the Path rule indicator variable inputs finds that several of the product-specific models were influenced positively as a result of adding these inputs. Consider the Hurricane4 product that listed as a top-selling product (Figure 1.7). Using the Path node in SAS Enterprise Miner, SAS Solutions OnDemand considers the following output when creating Path rule indicator variable inputs. Indicator variables were created for the top three rules shown. An indicator variable called Hurricane4-Path1 is added to indicate whether the customer has followed the purchase pattern of Scania Mitten, Women's/Junior/Men's → Sheet Sleeping Bag, Red. Hurricane4-Path2 indicates the purchase pattern of Polyester 3-Persons → Jl Rainlight Essential Pants; and finally Hurricane4-Path3 indicates the purchase pattern of Mattress with five channels 196x72 → Comfort Shelter. The rule confidence on the other rules was too low to consider for variable input addition.

For the Hurricane 4 product-specific propensity model, a decision tree model was built and declared as the champion model. Table 1.8 is output from the decision tree model showing variables that were found to be influential in the model. The decision tree outputs a variable importance dataset that shows the two inputs for Hurricane1 and Hurricane2 as influential signals in the model. For more information about the calculation of Importance, see the SAS Enterprise Miner Documentation (SAS Institute Inc.).

### 1.5.3.6  LTV

Section 1.4.3.1 laid the groundwork for conducting an LTV analysis through a survival analysis setting. The analysis for Section 1.5.3.2 yielded a segmentation schema that was characterized to better understand the segments. A segment was identified where the members were found to be longstanding customers for OSG who had shown recent slowing of purchase activity. This segment was selected for further review through the LTV analysis. The analysis results enable OSG to understand which of these longstanding customers are getting ready to leave and also to predict the impact if they leave. For several of the customers in this segment, an intervention strategy was planned and the results of the intervention would be measured through future data collection.

The key components for this analysis are forecasted revenue figures and survival probabilities. SAS Solutions OnDemand has taken the monthly historic data on

**Table 1.8  Decision Tree Model Variable Importance Output**

| Variable | Label | Number of Rules | Importance |
|---|---|---|---|
| PWR_days_last_purchase | Transformed Days Since Last Purchase | 9 | 1 |
| Hurricane4-PathA | Hurricane 4 Path Indicator A | 1 | 0.99156 |
| PWR_total_profit | Transformed Total Profit | 7 | 0.83474 |
| LOG_days_avg_ between_purchase | Transformed Average Days between Purchase | 6 | 0.83241 |
| PWR_total_cost | Transformed Total Cost | 4 | 0.77952 |
| PWR_total_qty | Transformed Total Quantity | 3 | 0.66872 |
| PWR_days_first_purchase | Transformed Days Since First Purchase | 4 | 0.65009 |
| Hurricane4-PathB | Hurricane 4 Path Indicator B | 2 | 0.56866 |
| PWR_total_retail | Transformed Total Retail Spend | 3 | 0.5491 |
| SQRT_total_orders | Transformed Total Orders | 2 | 0.54529 |
| SQRT_total_products | Transformed Total Products | 1 | 0.42384 |
| Days_as_customer | Days as a Customer | 1 | 0.36919 |

retail spend for each customer and built a Winter's Method forecast model to predict the last half of 2002 using SAS® High-Performance Forecasting (Brocklebank and Dickey, 2003). Note that the data used to generate the forecast models started in 1998, but was reduced for Table 1.9 to show only a subset of the data, so that more than one household could be displayed. PROC LIFEREG was used to produce monthly probability of survival estimates for each customer for the last half of 2002. LTV estimates are produced that condition the predicted revenue values by taking the factor of the survival probabilities. An intermediate dataset that shows the predicted values, survival probabilities, and the conditioned LTV estimates appears in Table 1.9.

Taking the sum across customers produces the expected six-month LTV estimate for each customer, as shown in Table 1.10.

## 1.5.4  Model Management

There are many dynamic elements involved in analytical models, including changing market conditions, changes in the model population, inclusion of new

**Table 1.9    LTV Prediction Table**

| Customer_ID | Month | Actual | Predict | survival_prob | LTV |
|---|---|---|---|---|---|
| 107 | JAN2002 | 53.11 | | | |
| 107 | FEB2002 | 78.89 | | | |
| 107 | MAR2002 | 25.34 | | | |
| 107 | APR2002 | 74.13 | | | |
| 107 | MAY2002 | 34.18 | | | |
| 107 | JUN2002 | 31.87 | | | |
| 107 | JUL2002 | | 42.575191493 | 0.693435296 | 29.523140515 |
| 107 | AUG2002 | | 5.063196274 | 0.677734721 | 3.4315039141 |
| 107 | SEP2002 | | 80.914054569 | 0.654835042 | 52.985358322 |
| 107 | OCT2002 | | 4.2810292469 | 0.62590929 | 2.6795359764 |
| 107 | NOV2002 | | 93.042191022 | 0.5919452 | 55.075884886 |
| 107 | DEC2002 | | 60.169784101 | 0.553848053 | 33.324917774 |
| 439 | JAN2002 | 79.94 | | | |
| 439 | FEB2002 | 49.09 | | | |
| 439 | MAR2002 | 12.49 | | | |
| 439 | APR2002 | 11.74 | | | |
| 439 | MAY2002 | 0.00 | | | |
| 439 | JUN2002 | 18.12 | | | |
| 439 | JUL2002 | | 64.054948513 | 0.993789838 | 63.657157303 |
| 439 | AUG2002 | | 95.854681449 | 0.978928161 | 93.834847034 |
| 439 | SEP2002 | | 66.030004027 | 0.957220700 | 64.07070221 |
| 439 | OCT2002 | | 73.143486154 | 0.929778772 | 68.007260736 |
| 439 | NOV2002 | | 49.253433267 | 0.897488059 | 44.204368222 |
| 439 | DEC2002 | | 63.032815542 | 0.861188279 | 54.283121937 |

products, etc. At the base of the analytical model are the scoring rules, which are based on customer behavior. All the behavior changes have a direct influence on the overall effectiveness of the predictions. This is why the monitoring of the analytical model performance over time is needed. Because data shifts over time cause a model to become less relevant and predictive, models must be constantly reevaluated to determine when the model should be refreshed or recalibrated.

Model maintenance includes benchmarking the consistency of submitted input data, the consistency of scored output data, the predictive performance of a selected

**Table 1.10    LTV Output Table**

| customer_id | ltv |
|---|---|
| 107 | 166.98 |
| 439 | 290.49 |
| 535 | 162.25 |
| 614 | 99.45 |
| 660 | 223.76 |
| 893 | 176.92 |
| 1169 | 86.72 |
| 1277 | 115.81 |
| 1310 | 300.11 |
| 1382 | 154.33 |

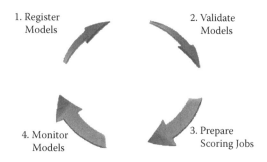

1. Register
Models

2. Validate
Models

4. Monitor
Models

3. Prepare
Scoring Jobs

**Figure 1.8    Model life cycle.**

model at a given point in time, the predictive performance of a selected model across time, and the predictive performance of multiple models using the same input dataset.

After an analytical model is in production, SAS Model Manager provides a central, secure, shared, and searchable repository of the model. SAS Model Manager promotes models through life-cycle phases such as development, testing, production, and administering scoring tests. It facilitates tracking model performance and applicability and enables auditing and accountability. Model management is a cyclic process, as illustrated in Figure 1.8.

The following sections show how OSG can use SAS Model Manager as a cross-functional hub to facilitate management and decision making during the life cycles of predictive models.

### 1.5.4.1    Cataloging, Updating, and Maintaining Models

SAS Model Manager uses a hierarchy of folder types to store modeling projects and their associated model files, metadata, and reports. The major types of folders are Project folders, Version folders, and Model folders, all of which facilitate the cataloging, updating, and maintenance process for each model. Figure 1.9 shows the project folder for the Bulls Eye Stuart/Tungsten 24 Gram Product models.

Project work is organized in one or more time-based intervals, called *versions*, which contain all of a modeling project's information for the defined time interval. Version project information includes project documents and resources, candidate and champion models, model performance reports, life-cycle configuration data, and scoring tasks.

The SAS Model Manager Life Cycle is a process template that guides SAS Model Manager project users through a sequence of modeling project life-cycle milestones. Life-cycle templates track, at a project version level, model progress through the milestones, as authorized users indicate that milestone component tasks have been started, completed, or approved. SAS Model Manager logs the

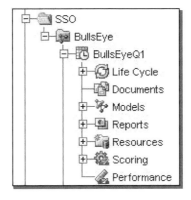

**Figure 1.9    SAS Model Manager project folder.**

dates, times, and individuals who are associated with individual life-cycle task and milestone status changes.

The SAS Model Manager life cycle that OSG chooses for the models in a version establishes a procedural time-phased roadmap. OSG has configured target milestone completion dates, and SAS Model Manager documents actual date- and time-stamp information for version life-cycle milestones and milestone tasks.

The simplest life-cycle template uses the model milestones of *develop, test, move to production*, and *retire*. Those milestones guide project users through the sequence of tasks to develop and select a champion model from candidate models, assess a new champion model's performance before deployment, deploy the champion model, and retire the champion model when time requirements or a better-performing model drives the status change.

## 1.5.4.2   Model Recalibration and Evaluation

Section 1.4.4 described why it is important to periodically check model performance to ensure that models are up-to-date and predictive for current data periods. The product-specific models that were built for adding product-based propensity scores to the CSV have now been registered in SAS Model Manager. SAS Model Manager creates reports that provide information about how current and relevant a model is as time passes. Figure 1.10 shows a characteristic report for the Bulls Eye Stuart/Tungsten 24 Gram Product models. Note that for the original models that were built in the third quarter of 2001, forward tracking indicates that the deviation indices are mild for each input except the DAYS_FIRST_PURCHASE variable, which reaches a significant level in the second quarter of 2002 (2002Q2).

The stability report for the Bulls Eye Stuart/Tungsten 24 Gram Product models is shown in Figure 1.11. Note that the deviation index is mild for the four quarters

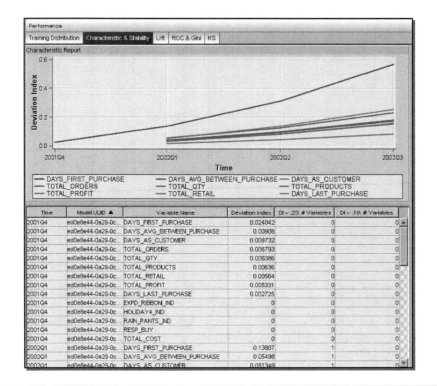

Figure 1.10    Characteristic report.

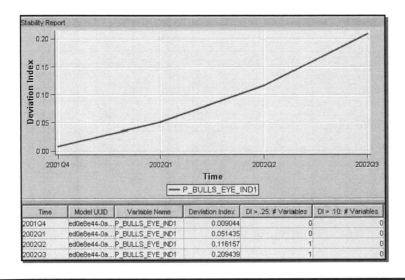

Figure 1.11    Stability report.

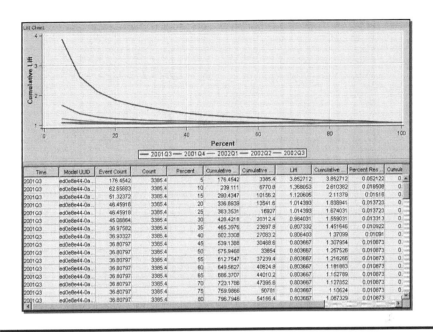

**Figure 1.12  SAS Model Manager time-based lift report.**

following the model build. However, because the deviation index is increasing, model recalibration is recommended in this case.

SAS Model Manager also reports classic model assessment charts and makes comparisons over time. The lift chart for the Bulls Eye Stuart/Tungsten 24 Gram Product models is shown in Figure 1.12 and indicates that time plays a major role when assessing lift for this model.

SAS Model Manager also manages the ROC and K-S assessment charts (Figure 1.13) and enables OSG to see the effect of time. These classic assessment charts also help determine appropriate times for model recalibration.

### 1.5.4.3 Model Executables

Multiple channels are typically created at each SAS Model Manager customer site. For example, one channel is for real-time scoring, another channel is for marketing campaigns, and a third channel can be used for testing before live production. For the OSG project, there were requirements to allow scoring execution within the test and production environments, as well as through a published channel to facilitate on-demand scoring through the SAS Real-Time Decision Manager.

Figure 1.14 provides an overview of the end-to-end functionality of SAS Model Manager for OSG.

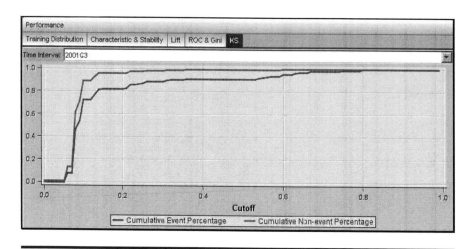

**Figure 1.13   KS report.**

## 1.5.5   *Business Rules Deployment*

### 1.5.5.1   *Case Study*

It is springtime and Sam is getting ready for the golf season. A couple of months ago he bought some winter golf gear: rain gloves, and an insulated wind-shirt from the local OSG retail store. He likes the OSG service and the quality and style of OSG apparel. Sam remembers the OSG mailer he threw away several few weeks

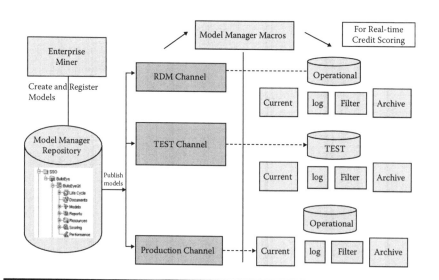

**Figure 1.14   SAS Model Manager publish channels.**

ago informing him that purchases made this month would count double toward OSG Gold status. Today he is in the market for a new set of clubs; double points would make him eligible for Gold status.

Sam logs on to the Internet and goes to www.osg.com. At the site, Sam's eye is caught by a sharp-looking golf outfit. He browses a little but does not make a purchase decision. He then heads to the golf club section of the Web site and drills down several pages to get to a page that contains a listing, by vendor, of their latest product offerings. Sam quickly finds the golf club set he is interested in, examines the price, and reads the reviews posted by several recent purchasers. Satisfied that this set is what he wants, Sam adds the clubs to his shopping cart and proceeds to the checkout page. On the checkout page, Sam enters his name, address, and credit card number, and then clicks OK. Sam has recently moved and he uses his new address on this transaction.

In the background, in real-time, the OSG Web site has been tracking the pages that Sam visits. After Sam adds the golf clubs to his shopping cart and makes his identity known, the set of pages that Sam has visited and the content of his shopping cart are sent from the Web Application Server to the SAS Real-Time Decision Manager. SAS Real-Time Decision Manager quickly accesses Sam's customer record from the OSG CSV to find pertinent information about Sam's demographic profile and previous retail, catalog, and online store purchases. The software's business rules can analyze this information. The software can also call SAS Model Manager to determine what other customers that fit Sam's profile purchase when they buy golf clubs. SAS Real-Time Decision Manager builds a list of value offerings for Sam that will be presented within the flow of his purchase transaction. The software realizes the following:

1. Sam is immediately eligible for double Gold status points.
2. Sam is eligible for free ground shipping because his purchase exceeds $100.
3. Sam now lives relatively close to an OSG retail store, so he could pick up the clubs at the retail store (because they are in stock), potentially saving Sam time and saving OSG the cost of ground shipment.
4. Customers that fit Sam's profile most often purchase golf bags and golf balls when purchasing golf clubs.
5. Sam was sent a 10 percent discount coupon that applies to most OSG products (but not golf clubs).
6. Sam was browsing the golf apparel section in this visit and his golf club vendor also has a line of apparel.
7. A number of vendors offer OSG rebates on closeout items.
8. Sam's new address is within 20 miles of a golf course with a special green fee offer being promoted by OSG.

In less than a second, the software accesses SAS Model Manager to score and retrieve a set of purchase propensities that match Sam's profile and to run the business rules that generate the offering list for Sam. The offer list is returned to the OSG Web Application Server and the list is sent in an easy-to-use format within the checkout transaction.

Sam quickly learns that he will immediately achieve Gold status in this purchase and that all items will be covered under that benefit. He decides to pick up the clubs at his local retailer, where the inventory will be set aside and made ready for his pick-up. He does a little more shopping and buys some closeout golf balls and uses his additional 10 percent discount to purchase a golf bag and several golf shirts that were suggested by SAS Model Manager. Sam also prints off the discount green fee coupon being offered by the local golf course.

The record of Sam's purchasing decisions is added to his record in the OSG CSVs in the next nightly batch processing cycle. The CSV will be used to target selected customers in an upcoming mail campaign that promotes tee times at local courses to selected OSG customers.

## 1.5.5.2 Components

### 1.5.5.2.1 Batch Execution

The CSV referenced in Section 1.5.1.1 is built in a scheduled batch process. As discussed previously, the CSV can serve many analytic purposes. There is one row in the CSV per customer and month. The propensity to buy selected classes of sporting goods products is determined for all customers. Sam's highest propensities are related to golf apparel, equipment, and such consumables as golf balls, tees, and gloves.

### 1.5.5.2.2 Real-Time Execution and Business Rule Integration

The business rules that drive the offer list and the scoring models for Sam's propensities were run in the middle of his transaction to provide revised propensity scores. The inputs to the business rules and scoring models reflect the updated demographic information, such as Sam's new address and his golf club purchase, which was not in the CSV when it was produced in the batch cycle. Thus, the CSV was updated and the scoring models were run with updated information during the transaction cycle. The information flow that is described in this scenario might be depicted as shown in Figure 1.15.

## 1.5.5.3 Scalability and Deployment across the Enterprise

As OSG grows in size, the SAS Real-Time Decision Manager and SAS Model Manager components of the IT infrastructure can grow along with the company. Both SAS Real-Time Decision Manager and SAS Model Manager can be configured to run in a server farm environment on different hardware platforms and operating systems. The system can be configured with fault tolerance and other features to enable true 24/7 operation. The number of servers can be increased or current servers can be replaced with faster models to meet the needs of a growing business.

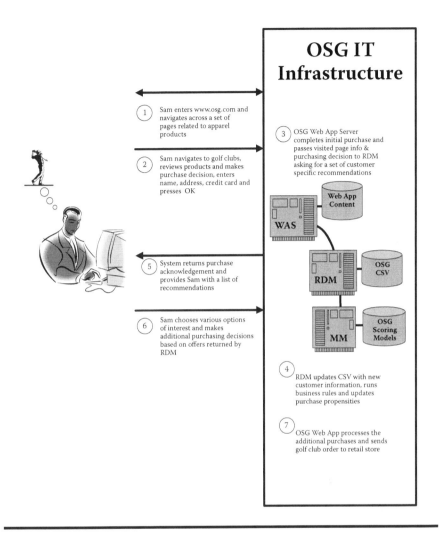

**Figure 1.15   OSG deployment infrastructure.**

## Table of Abbreviations

| Abbreviation | Meaning |
|---|---|
| ARIMA | AutoRegressive Integrated Moving-Average |
| ASP | Application service provider |
| AUC | Area under curve |
| CSV | Customer state vector |
| ESV | Entity state vector |
| GIGO | Garbage in, garbage out |

| Table of Abbreviations (Continued) | |
|---|---|
| *Abbreviation* | *Meaning* |
| IT | Information technology |
| LTV | Lifetime value |
| OSG | Orion Sporting Goods (case study) |
| POC | Proof of concept |
| POV | Proof of value |
| ROC | Receiver operating characteristic |
| ROI | Return on investment |
| SEMMA | Predictive modeling approach supported by SAS® Enterprise Miner( (Sample, Explore, Modify, Model, and Assess) |
| SOM | Self-organizing map |
| SPD server | SAS® Scalable Performance Data Server® |

## Copyright and Trademark Information

# References

Allison, Paul D., 1995. *Survival Analysis Using SAS: A Practical Guide*. Cary, NC: SAS Institute Inc.

Berry, Michael J.A. and Gordon S. Linoff, 2004. *Data Mining Techniques, second edition*. New York: John Wiley & Sons, Inc.

Brocklebank, John C. and David A. Dickey, 2003. *SAS® for Forecasting Time Series, second edition*. Cary, NC: SAS Institute Inc.

Han, Jiawei and Micheline Kamber, 2000. *Data Mining: Concepts and Techniques*. San Francisco, CA: Morgan Kaufmann.

Lu, Junxiang, 2003. Modeling Customer Lifetime Value Using Survival Analysis — An Application in the Telecommunications Industry, in *Proceedings of SAS Users Group International 28 Conference*, March 30–April 20, 2003, Seattle, WA.

SAS Institute Inc. SAS Enterprise Miner Documentation. Cary, NC: SAS Institute Inc. Available from http://support.sas.com/documentation/onlinedoc/miner/.

SAS Institute Inc. Functions and Call Routines, *SAS Language Reference: Dictionary*. Cary, NC: SAS Institute Inc. Available from http://support.sas.com/.

SAS Institute Inc. The LIFEREG Procedure, The PHREG Procedure. SAS/STAT User's Guide. Cary, NC: SAS Institute Inc. Available from http://support.sas.com/.

Wang, John, 2003. *Data Mining: Opportunities and Challenges*. Hershey, PA: Idea Group, Inc.

# Chapter 2

# Ensemble Strategies for Neural Network Classifiers

Paul Mangiameli and David West

## Contents

## 2.1 Introduction

Neural networks are becoming effective analysis tools in many application domains and particularly in business and health care. Many organizations are deploying neural network models for problems that have traditionally fallen under the responsibility of operations research [19, 22]. Smith and Gupta [19] surveyed the application of neural networks in a diverse range of business problems, including target marketing, demand and financial forecasting, and creditworthiness, to name a few. Neural network models are also proving effective in medical diagnostic decision support systems to identify the presence or absence of disease [11]. Lisboa [9] provides evidence of the health benefit from neural networks in medical intervention in oncology, critical care, and cardiovascular medicine.

There is increasing interest in forming ensembles (or committees) of neural network models. The lower generalization error of the ensemble produces better business decisions or more accurate diagnosis of disease. There are three major strategies for forming neural network ensembles that we investigate. The simplest is the cross-validation neural network (CVNN) ensemble where all ensemble members are trained with the same data [15]. The second and third strategies create perturbed versions of the training set, so that all ensemble members are trained with different variants of the original data. Bagging ensembles create a unique training set for each ensemble member by sampling with replacement over a uniform probability distribution on the original data [1]. This creates training sets where some observations are replicated and others may be missing. Boosting is also a re-sampling strategy, with a probability distribution that depends on the misclassification rate for each observation. After each boosting iteration, the probability of the misclassified observations increases while the corresponding probability of correctly classified observations decreases. As boosting progresses, the composition of the training sets becomes increasingly dominated by hard-to-classify examples [3].

More research is needed to understand the relative performance of these three ensemble strategies. The purpose of this chapter is to conduct a controlled experiment capable of producing statistically significant conclusions about the relative performance of the three ensemble strategies and the strategy of reliance on a single model. The focus is on two-group classification problems where the spatial data structure is characterized by two naturally occurring clusters. Simulated data is used to form controlled levels of the experimental variables, and for the construction of large test sets to increase statistical power. It is also important to quantify the impact of several design and exogenous variables on ensemble performance. To further these purposes, we pose the following specific research questions.

1. Can a neural network ensemble be expected to universally produce a more accurate decision than the strategy of relying on a single model for a decision, or are there some conditions where a single model is preferred?
2. Are the ensemble strategies that perturb the training set more accurate than the simple CVNN ensemble?
3. Does the complexity of the classification problem influence the relative performance of the neural network ensemble strategy?
4. Does the training sample size affect the relative performance of the neural network ensemble strategy? Training examples are scarce in many business and health-care applications; there is never too much data. In this research we study training set sizes ranging from a few hundred to a thousand observations.

5. Does missing information affect the relative performance of neural network ensemble strategy? Missing information may result from the physical inability to collect certain information or from not appreciating the significance of some information sources. Suboptimal feature selection methods may also result in the elimination of relevant variables from the ensemble.

6. Does the inclusion of irrelevant information affect the relative performance of a neural network ensemble strategy? Suboptimal feature selection may result in the inclusion of irrelevant variables in the ensemble model.

7. Do incorrectly labeled learning examples affect the relative performance of neural network ensemble strategies? In some applications (e.g., medical diagnosis), a gold standard is used to determine labels for the learning data. For example, a tumor biopsy might be used to determine a precise label for the presence or absence of breast cancer. In applications such as credit scoring, the label may be less precise because it is usually the subjective assessment of a human expert.

Section 2.2 reviews recent applications of neural network ensembles. Section 2.3 discusses the research methodology for constructing simulated datasets with controlled levels of the experimental variables. That section also defines algorithms for creating boosting and bagging ensembles. Section 2.4 provides a comparison of generalization errors for the neural network ensemble strategies. The chapter concludes with guidelines for implementing neural network ensembles.

## 2.2 Neural Network Ensemble Applications and Issues

For this research, an ensemble is considered a collection of a finite number of neural networks that are individually trained and whose individual member predictions are combined when classifying novel instances [14, 18]. Hansen and Salamon [4] provide some of the first research results to demonstrate that the generalization error of a neural network can be significantly reduced by ensembles of similar networks. They employ a technique where all ensemble members are trained on the same dataset, a CVNN ensemble. Differences among the ensemble members in a CVNN ensemble are largely derived from differences in the initialization of neural network weights. An explanation offered by Hansen and Salamon for the performance advantage of the ensemble is that the multitude of local minima encountered in the training of individual neural networks results in errors occurring in different regions of input space. The collective decision of the ensemble is therefore less likely to be in error than the decision made by any of the individual networks [4]. Krogh and Vedelsby [8] derive an expression for the ensemble generalization error, the difference between the weighted average of the generalization errors of the individual ensemble members and an ensemble ambiguity term. The ambiguity is defined as the variation of the output of ensemble members averaged over unlabeled data. Ambiguity essentially quantifies the disagreement among ensemble members.

The objective of ensemble methods that perturbs the training set in some manner (i.e., bagging and boosting) is to decrease the generalization error by increasing the ensemble ambiguity without a commensurate increase in the weighted error of ensemble members.

One of the most popular ensemble strategies is bootstrap aggregation, or bagging predictors, advanced by Breiman [1] using decision trees as a base classifier. Bagging uses multiple instances of a learning algorithm $(C_1(x) \ldots C_b(x))$ trained on bootstrap replicates of the learning set $(TB_1 \ldots TB_B)$. Plurality vote produces an aggregate decision from the models' individual decisions. If the classification algorithm is unstable in the sense that perturbed versions of the training set produce significant changes in the predictor, then bagging predictors can increase the decision accuracy by increasing the ensemble ambiguity. AdaBoost or "adaptive boosting" is another perturbation method for improving the performance of a learning algorithm [16]. AdaBoost constructs an ensemble by sequentially training an ensemble member with training sets that increase the prominence of certain hard-to-learn training examples that have been misclassified by earlier ensemble members. AdaBoost maintains a probability distribution, $D_t(t)$, over the original data available for training. In each round, a classifier (t) is trained by sampling with replacement from this distribution. After each round, the probability of incorrectly classified training examples increases and the probability of correctly classified examples decreases. The ensemble decision is obtained by a weighted vote [16]. Schwenk and Bengio [17] apply AdaBoost methods to neural network ensembles and report that boosting can significantly improve neural network classifiers. The authors conclude that boosting is always superior to bagging, although the differences are not always significant.

There is increasing interest in using ensemble methods, including bagging and boosting, in real-world classification applications. Hu and Tsoukalas [7] report that ensembles of multilayer perceptron (MLP) neural networks reduce the error in predicting the relative importance of situational and demographic factors on consumer choice. Sohn and Lee [20] employ ensembles of neural networks to improve the classification accuracy of road traffic accident severity. They test both bagging and boosting ensembles, and report a reduction in generalization error for the bagging neural network ensemble of 6.3 percent relative to the single neural network model [20]. Hayashi and Setiono [5] report increased accuracy diagnosing hepatobiliary disorders from ensembles of 30 MLP neural networks. They employ CVNN ensembles (without the data perturbation methods of bagging or boosting) with a relatively small training set size of 373 examples [5]. Zhou et al. [25] use ensembles of neural networks to identify lung cancer cells from needle biopsies. The authors report high overall accuracy and a low rate of false negatives. Zhang [23] aggregates 30 MLP neural networks to estimate polymer reactor quality, while Cunningham et al. [2] report improved diagnostic prediction for MDSS systems that aggregate neural network models. Zhilkin and Somorjai [24] explore bagging ensembles using combinations of linear and quadratic discriminant analysis, logistic regression, and MLP neural networks to classify brain spectra by magnetic resonance measurement. They report that the bootstrap ensembles are more accurate in this application than any "single best" model.

There is a need for more systematic study of the properties of neural network ensembles and the relative performance of these ensembles in classification applications. The contribution of this chapter is to investigate the relative performance of three strategies for forming neural network ensembles: (1) CVNN, (2) bagging, and (3) boosting. The generalization error of these strategies is compared at controlled levels of design and exogenous variables that influence the classification problem. These variables include classification complexity, training set size, missing information, and data imperfections that include irrelevant information and mislabeled training examples.

## 2.3  Research Methodology

We investigate the relative performance of MLP ensembles used in classification applications where the data conditions can be characterized as two naturally occurring clusters. This is typical of many problems where neural network models have been used in business and health-care classification decisions [9, 11, 19, 22]. Simulated data is used because it (1) allows for the construction of datasets with controlled levels of the experimental factors, and (2) facilitates the construction of large test sets, which increase the precision of error estimates. We investigate the effect of the following experimental conditions on the neural network ensemble generalization errors: (1) data dispersion and the resulting cluster overlap that defines the complexity of the classification problem, (2) small and large-sized training sets, (3) missing information (accomplished by removing some of the variables), (4) data imperfections that include irrelevant variables (variables that provide no information about cluster membership), and (5) confounding learning cases (observations that have been assigned to the wrong cluster membership).

The research methodology is presented in two parts. The first part (Section 2.3.1) describes the generation of datasets examined in this study. The second part (Section 2.3.2) describes the experimental design employed to estimate the neural network ensemble generalization errors at controlled levels of the experimental variables.

### 2.3.1  Generation of Datasets

This research focuses on data that has the spatial characteristics of two naturally occurring clusters. The definition of a cluster structure is an important operational consideration in the generation of artificial datasets. We define cluster structure around the properties of external isolation and internal cohesion [13]. This definition requires that members of one cluster be separated from members of all other clusters by fairly empty areas of space. Internal cohesion requires that entities within the same cluster should be similar to each other.

Two levels of classification complexity are investigated: (1) a low level that has a minimal amount of cluster overlap and, therefore, a relatively high classification accuracy; and (2) a high level of complexity with more pronounced levels of cluster overlap and a lower classification accuracy. We follow a well-established methodology for constructing simulated data to represent naturally occurring clusters [6, 10, 12, 13]. Twenty different base datasets (ten for each of two levels of classification complexity) are created with 18 variables and 10,000 observations, 5000 belonging to each cluster. This is accomplished by fixing the cluster centroids and varying the dispersion of observation about the centroids as follows:

■ Randomly fix the cluster centroid. This centroid will remain fixed for both levels of cluster dispersion.
■ Use a multivariate normal random number generator to disperse observations about the fixed cluster centroids. Higher levels of relative dispersion are obtained using larger variances to generate the cluster members. This expands the distance of the members from the cluster centroid and creates cluster overlap.

For each cluster, a range value is randomly generated for each dimension of input space. This range value is a random variable uniformly distributed between ten and forty units. The centroid of each cluster is the midpoint of this range. The distances between clusters are constant, independent of the level of dispersion. The points within a cluster are normally distributed about the cluster centroid. Each observation is tagged with a cluster ID to facilitate the identification of cluster membership. Differences between the two levels of dispersion are created by changing the value used for the standard deviation in the normal distribution to generate the cluster points. At the low level of classification complexity, the standard deviation is equal to one third of the cluster range for that dimension. Note that the cluster ranges are random variables, and therefore the standard deviations within the cluster will be different for each dimension and will vary in proportion to the range. Datasets for the high level of classification complexity are generated with the same technique but use standard deviations that are 1/1.5 of the cluster length, respectively.

Four irrelevant variables are added to each base dataset to yield a total of 22 variables. These irrelevant variables are uniformly distributed across the input space and provide no relevant information about cluster membership. Each of the 20 base datasets is partitioned into training, validation, and testing sets. We randomly remove subsets of 200 and 1000 observations to serve as neural network training sets, $T_i$. The training set size is maintained at these relatively small sizes because these conditions are typical of real-world classification applications occurring in business and health care. From the remaining observations we randomly remove subsets of 4500 observations to serve as an independent validation set, $V_i$, and a second subset of 4500 observations to serve as an independent holdout test set, $E_i$. To reduce the variability in estimates of the generalization errors, both the validation and test sets are large. We know that the ensemble generalization error is a sample from a binomial distribution with

**Table 2.1   Dataset Design**

| Experimental Condition | Design Factors | Experimental Levels |
|---|---|---|
| Base data classification complexity | 2 clusters<br>18 relevant variable<br>4 irrelevant variables<br>low and high<br>complexity | 2 |
| Training set size | Low: 200<br>High: 1000 | 2 |
| Available information | Basic data minus<br>6, 12 relevant variables<br>33%, 67%, 100% | 3 |
| Irrelevant variables | Basic data minus<br>2, 4 irrelevant variables<br>low and high | 2 |
| Confounding cases | 10%, 20% Targets<br>flipped<br>low and high | 2 |

a standard deviation of $\sigma = \sqrt{\frac{\bar{p}(1-\bar{p})}{N}}$. For those experimental conditions that involve missing information, we randomly identify and remove six or twelve of the eighteen relevant variables to generate datasets having 67 percent and 33 percent of the relevant information, respectively. In a similar manner, we randomly identify and remove two or four of the irrelevant variables to generate cases with two irrelevant variables and the clean data case. The experimental cases that involve confounding learning examples are created by randomly identifying subsets of 10 percent and 20 percent of the training cases and flipping the {-1, 1} target values, effectively creating learning cases that are mislabeled. The basis for dataset construction is summarized in Table 2.1.

## 2.3.2   Experimental Design

In this research, all ensembles are constructed with 100 individual members. This decision is based on findings that accurate boosting ensembles require a large ensemble membership [14]. We focus exclusively on the popular multilayer perceptron (MLP) neural network trained with the backpropagation algorithm. All neural networks have a single hidden layer. The number of neurons in the hidden layer is determined at each experimental condition using a genetic algorithm to identify a network configuration that minimizes the error on the validation data. The resulting number of hidden neurons ranges from five to fourteen.

At each experimental condition, an estimate of the mean generalization error for a single model is determined by averaging the model outputs for 100 successive iterations on each of the ten datasets constructed. Each cycle involves training the neural network model with $T_i$ and measuring the generalization error on the independent test set $E_i$. The validation set $V_i$ is used during this process to implement early stopping and avoid model over-fitting. The mean generalization error for the single model is then an average across the ten different training sets.

A corresponding estimate of the generalization error for the CVNN ensemble is obtained using a majority vote function applied to the outputs of the 100 single models (i.e., vote the results of 100 single models instead of averaging the outputs). The mean generalization error for the CVNN ensemble is also an average across the ten different training sets.

A bagging ensemble is constructed from a perturbed version of the original training set created by sampling form $T_i$ with replacement. This implies that some of the training set observations will be missing in the bagging training set, while other observations may be replicated several times. The data partitions used to construct the training set and to test the bagging ensembles (i.e., $T_i$, $V_j$, $E_i$) are the same partitions created in the earlier section for estimating the single neural network model and the CVNN ensembles. The bagging ensemble algorithm differs from the cross-validation algorithm in that 100 different bootstrap training sets are formed by sampling with replacement from the training set $T_i$. We refer to these bootstrap training sets by the symbol $T_{BAGij}$ where $i$ refers to the 1, ..., 10 different datasets, and $j$ the bootstrap replicate. A total of $j = 1$, ..., 100 bootstrap samples are generated. The specific algorithm for creating bagging ensembles follows.

## Algorithm for Bagging Ensemble

Given: training set of size n and base classification algorithm $C_t(\mathbf{x})$.

> Step 1: Input sequence of training samples $(x_1, y_1)$, ..., $(x_n, y_n)$ with labels $y \in Y = (-1, 1)$
>
> Step 2: Initialize probability for each example in learning set, $D_1(i) = 1/n$ and set $t = 1$
>
> Step 3: Loop while $t < B = 100$ ensemble members
>
> > a. Form training set of size n by sampling with replacement from distribution $D_t$, $n = \{200, 1000\}$
> > b. Get hypothesis ht: $X \to Y$
> > c. Set $t = t + 1$
>
> > End of loop
>
> Step 4: Output the final ensemble hypothesis: $C^*(x_i) = h_{final}(x_i) = \arg\max \sum_{t=1}^{B} I(C_t(x) = y)$

A boosting ensemble is also constructed by perturbing the original training set. For boosting, the sampling process is controlled by a probability distribution, $D_t(t)$, maintained over the observations in $T_i$. For the construction of the first ensemble member, $D_t(t)$ is a uniform distribution. At each iteration, a training set is generated by sampling with replacement from $D_t(t)$ (Step 3a), the neural network is trained and tested (Step 3b), and a weighted error is calculated from the sum of the probabilities of misclassified observations (Step 3c). An inflation factor, $\beta_t$ is calculated in Step 3e from the weighted error. In Step 3f, the probability of all misclassified observations is increased by multiplying the probability of each misclassified observation by the inflation factor $\beta_t$ and then $D_t(t)$ is renormalized. If the weighted error is ever less than zero or greater than 0.5 the distribution $D_t(t)$ is reset to a uniform distribution (Step 3d). After 100 ensemble members have been constructed in this fashion, the ensemble decision is determined by weighting the decision of each ensemble member by $\log(\beta_t)$ (Step 4). The specific boosting algorithm used in this research follows.

## Algorithm for AdaBoost Ensemble

Given: training set of size $n$ and base classification algorithm $C_t(\mathbf{x})$.

Step 1: Input sequence of training samples $(x_1, y_1)$, ..., $(x_n, y_n)$ with labels $y \in Y = (-1, 1)$

Step 2: Initialize probability for each example in learning set, $D_1(i) = 1/n$ and set $t = 1$

Step 3: Loop while $t < 100$ ensemble members:

    a. Form training set of size $n$ by sampling with replacement from distribution $D_t$

    b. Get hypothesis ht: $X \rightarrow Y$

    c. Calculate the weighted error rate: $\varepsilon_t = \sum_{i:h_t(x_i) \neq y_i} D_t(i)$

    d. If $\varepsilon_t \leq 0$ or $\varepsilon_t \geq 0.5$, then reinitialize $D_t(i) = 1/n$ and GOTO Step 3a

    e. Calculate $\beta_t = (1 - \varepsilon_t)/\varepsilon_t$

    f. Update probability distribution: $D_{t+1}(i) = \dfrac{D_t(i)\beta_t^{I(h_t(x_i) \neq y_i)}}{Z_t}$ where $Z_t$ is a normalization constant

    g. Set $t = t + 1$

    End of loop

Step 4: Output the final ensemble hypothesis: $C^*(x_i) = h_{final}(x_i) \sum \log(\beta_t)$

# 2.4 Generalization Error Results of Ensemble Strategies

## 2.4.1 Single Neural Network Model versus CVNN Ensemble

We first focus on a comparative analysis of the generalization error of the single neural network model and the CVNN ensemble. Table 2.2 reports the absolute level of the generalization error for the single model, the CVNN ensemble, and the

**Table 2.2 Single versus CV Generalization Error**

| Number of Variables | Training Size | Low Complexity Data | | | | | |
|---|---|---|---|---|---|---|---|
| | | Single Model | | CVNN Ensemble | | Single-CVNN | |
| | | Mean | Standard Error | Mean | Standard Error | Mean | Standard Error |
| 6 | Small Training | 0.2168 | 0.00376 | 0.2135 | 0.00392 | 0.0033 | 0.000642 |
| | Large Training | 0.1731 | 0.00205 | 0.1677 | 0.00187 | 0.0054 | 0.000606 |
| | Overall | 0.1949 | 0.00377 | 0.1906 | 0.00391 | 0.0043 | 0.000462 |
| 12 | Small Training | 0.1406 | 0.00328 | 0.1395 | 0.00303 | 0.0011 | 0.000428 |
| | Large Training | 0.0944 | 0.00260 | 0.0867 | 0.00289 | 0.0076 | 0.000666 |
| | Overall | 0.1175 | 0.00390 | 0.1131 | 0.0043 | 0.0044 | 0.000611 |
| 18 | Small Training | 0.0807 | 0.00549 | 0.0795 | 0.00532 | 0.0012 | 0.000328 |
| | Large Training | 0.0489 | 0.00138 | 0.0489 | 0.0014 | 0.0000 | 0.000258 |
| | Overall | 0.0648 | 0.00361 | 0.0642 | 0.00349 | 0.0006 | 0.000225 |
| Total Low Complexity | Small Training | 0.1460 | 0.00692 | 0.1442 | 0.0068 | 0.0019 | 0.000299 |
| | Large Training | 0.1055 | 0.00608 | 0.1011 | 0.00589 | 0.0043 | 0.000483 |
| | Overall | 0.1257 | 0.00488 | 0.1226 | 0.00482 | 0.0031 | 0.000301 |

| Number of Variables | Training Size | High Complexity Data | | | | | |
|---|---|---|---|---|---|---|---|
| | | Single Model | | CVNN Ensemble | | Single-CVNN | |
| | | Mean | Standard Error | Mean | Standard Error | Mean | Standard Error |
| 6 | Small Training | 0.3110 | 0.00483 | 0.3038 | 0.00505 | 0.0072 | 0.001089 |
| | Large Training | 0.2484 | 0.00263 | 0.2410 | 0.00234 | 0.0074 | 0.000824 |
| | Overall | 0.2797 | 0.00523 | 0.2724 | 0.00526 | 0.0073 | 0.000676 |
| 12 | Small Training | 0.2468 | 0.00551 | 0.2342 | 0.00618 | 0.0126 | 0.00137 |
| | Large Training | 0.1606 | 0.00392 | 0.1433 | 0.00284 | 0.0173 | 0.001411 |
| | Overall | 0.2037 | 0.00700 | 0.1887 | 0.00731 | 0.0149 | 0.001029 |
| 18 | Small Training | 0.2144 | 0.00513 | 0.2046 | 0.006 | 0.0098 | 0.001577 |
| | Large Training | 0.1100 | 0.00562 | 0.0880 | 0.00427 | 0.0220 | 0.001612 |
| | Overall | 0.1622 | 0.00836 | 0.1463 | 0.00909 | 0.0159 | 0.001416 |
| Total High Complexity | Small Training | 0.2574 | 0.00551 | 0.2475 | 0.00584 | 0.0099 | 0.000816 |
| | Large Training | 0.1730 | 0.00707 | 0.1574 | 0.00759 | 0.0156 | 0.001037 |
| | Overall | 0.2152 | 0.00565 | 0.2025 | 0.00603 | 0.0127 | 0.000697 |

| | | Single Model | | CVNN Ensemble | | Single-CVNN | |
|---|---|---|---|---|---|---|---|
| | | Mean | Standard Error | Mean | Standard Error | Mean | Standard Error |
| Grand Total | Small Training | 0.2017 | 0.0062 | 0.1959 | 0.0063 | 0.0059 | 0.0006 |
| | Large Training | 0.1393 | 0.0066 | 0.1293 | 0.0067 | 0.0100 | 0.0008 |
| | Overall | 0.1705 | 0.00454 | 0.1626 | 0.00449 | 0.0079 | 0.00047 |

paired difference CVNN–single model at each experimental condition. Standard errors are included to provide a perspective of the precision of the estimates. To avoid the dilemma of multiple t tests, an ANOVA model is used to determine if the differences in mean performance can be explained by the experimental conditions (classification complexity, training set size, missing variables, and data imperfections including irrelevant variables and confounding training cases). The ANOVA model is significant with an $F$ statistic of 43.6 and $p$ values less than 0.001 for all the main effects. This validates the experimental conditions used in this research to explain the levels of performance for the neural network ensemble strategies. The CVNN ensemble achieves a statistically significant lower generalization error across all the data conditions investigated. The "aggregate" generalization error of the single models is 0.1705, compared to 0.1626 for the CVNN ensemble. The mean difference in error is 0.0079, which is a 4.64 percent reduction in error by the CVNN ensemble. This difference is statistically significant, with a 95 percent confidence interval ranging from 0.0070 to 0.0088 (standard error of 0.00047).

Table 2.3 decomposes the aggregate mean difference in generalization error by classification complexity and training set size. The CVNN ensemble has a statistically significant reduction in error at both the low and high levels of classification complexity. The mean difference of 0.0031 at the low classification complexity represents a 2.47 percent reduction in the generalization error of a single model. The relative improvement by the CVNN ensemble is greater at the higher classification complexity level, with a magnitude of 0.1272, a 5.91 percent reduction. The size of the training set also influences the relative error of the CVNN ensemble. At the smaller training size (200 examples), the CVNN ensemble decreases the generalization error by 0.0059, a 2.93 percent reduction. At the larger training size (1000 examples), the improvement increases to 0.0100, or a 7.15 percent reduction. Table 2.3 suggests that the relative improvement in generalization error from the use of CVNN ensembles (instead of single neural network models) increases with the complexity of the classification problem and the training set size. This is

**Table 2.3  Single Model–CV Ensemble Generalization Error Effects of Classification Complexity and Training Size**

| | Mean Difference | Percent Reduction (%) | 95% Confidence Interval | |
| --- | --- | --- | --- | --- |
| | | | Lower | Upper |
| Low complexity | 0.003107 | 2.47 | 0.002512 | 0.003701 |
| High complexity | 0.012720 | 5.91 | 0.011342 | 0.014098 |
| Low training size | 0.005873 | 2.93 | 0.004800 | 0.006947 |
| High training size | 0.009953 | 7.15 | 0.008507 | 0.011400 |
| Aggregate error | 0.007913 | 4.64 | 0.006988 | 0.008839 |

**Table 2.4   Single Model–CV Ensemble Generalization Error Effects of Missing Information**

|  | Mean Difference | Percent Reduction (%) | 95% Confidence Interval | |
|---|---|---|---|---|
|  |  |  | Lower | Upper |
| 33% | 0.0058 | 2.44 | 0.004946 | 0.006654 |
| 66% | 0.0097 | 6.04 | 0.008128 | 0.011272 |
| 100% | 0.0083 | 7.31 | 0.006233 | 0.010367 |
| Aggregate error | 0.007913 | 4.64 | 0.006988 | 0.008839 |

consistent with results reported by Parmanto et al. [15] for cross-validation and boosting neural network ensembles formed with simulated and medical diagnosis datasets. Parmanto et al. [15] concluded that ensembles are most effective in situations that involve high noise (complexity).

Table 2.4 summarizes the effect of missing information on the relative advantage of the CVNN ensemble (versus a single neural network model). It is evident from this table that this relative advantage increases as the information content increases (i.e., the number of missing variables decreases). At the lowest level, six of the original eighteen variables are present in the training set (33 percent of the information content is available), and the mean reduction in error of the CVNN ensemble is 0.0058, a 2.44 percent reduction. At the intermediate level, the magnitude of the reduction increases to 0.0097 (6.04 percent). At the third level, where all eighteen variables are present, the relative reduction in generalization error increases to 0.0083 (7.31 percent). The lower and upper 95 percent confidence intervals (Table 2.4) indicate that all of the differences are statistically significant.

Table 2.5 defines the relative advantage of CVNN ensembles at several levels of data imperfections. For the clean data case, the reduction in generalization error for

**Table 2.5   Single Model–CV Ensemble Generalization Error Effects of Data Imperfections**

|  | Mean Difference | Percent Reduction (%) | 95% Confidence Interval | |
|---|---|---|---|---|
|  |  |  | Lower | Upper |
| Clean | 0.006433 | 4.27 | 0.004700 | 0.008167 |
| 2 Irrelevant | 0.007100 | 4.10 | 0.005347 | 0.008853 |
| 4 Irrelevant | 0.007100 | 4.18 | 0.005206 | 0.008994 |
| 10% Confounding | 0.008633 | 5.06 | 0.006534 | 0.010733 |
| 20% Confounding | 0.010300 | 5.2 | 0.007527 | 0.013073 |
| Aggregate error | 0.007913 | 4.64 | 0.006988 | 0.008839 |

the CVNN ensemble is 0.0064 (4.27 percent). When there are two or four irrelevant variables (i.e., variables that contain no relevant information for the classification decision) in the data, the reduction in error is 0.0071 in magnitude for both cases. This corresponds to a percentage reduction of 4.10 percent and 4.18 percent, respectively. The relative advantage of CVNN ensembles is slightly greater when there are confounding cases in the training set. For a level of 10 percent confounding cases, the reduction in error is 0.00863 (5.06 percent), and for the 20 percent level it is .0103 (5.2 percent). Table 2.5 suggests that CVNN ensembles achieve statistically significant lower levels of generalization error (relative to a single neural network model) at all levels of data imperfections investigated. There are no appreciable differences in the relative performance of the CVNN ensemble among the different levels of data imperfections. This implies that the relative advantage of CVNN ensembles is reasonably constant and independent of the presence of extraneous variables and confounding cases.The results summarized in Tables 2.3, 2.4, and 2.5 suggest that the relative advantage of CVNN ensembles (compared to a single neural network model) is greatest for conditions of high classification complexity, large training sets, and the inclusion of all relevant variables. At these specific experimental conditions, the relative reduction in generalization error for the CVNN ensemble ranges from 15 to 22 percent with a mean reduction in generalization error of 19.73 percent.

## 2.4.2 Ensembles Formed from Perturbed Training Sets

Section 2.4.1 established that the CVNN ensemble is more accurate than the single neural network model at every experimental condition investigated. We next compare the relative performance of ensembles produced by perturbing the training set (i.e., bagging and boosting) to the CVNN ensemble. Table 2.6 summarizes the absolute level of the generalization error for the bagging ensemble, the CVNN ensemble, and the paired difference CVNN — bagging at each experimental condition. The overall mean reduction in generalization error across all experimental conditions for the bagging ensemble (relative to the CVNN) is −0.0039. This represents an increase in the "aggregate" error of 2.4 percent, which is statistically significant with a 95 percent confidence interval ranging from −0.0050 to −0.0028. This implies that the CVNN ensemble is more accurate than the bagging ensemble for the data conditions investigated in this research.

Table 2.7 defines the relative differences between the CVNN and bagging ensemble across the experimental conditions of classification complexity and training set size. These results show that the bagging ensemble is statistically equivalent to CVNN ensembles for the low data complexity level because the 95 percent confidence intervals include zero. At the higher complexity level, the generalization error of the bagging ensembles is slightly larger than the CVNN with a reduction of −0.0073, a 3.6 percent increase in error. The relative error of the bagging ensemble is also slightly higher at both training set sizes with percentage changes of −2.45 percent and −2.47 percent.

**Table 2.6 CVNN versus Bagging Ensemble**

| Number of Variables | Training Size | Low Complexity Data | | | | | |
|---|---|---|---|---|---|---|---|
| | | CVNN Ensemble | | Bagging Ensemble | | CVNN-Bagging | |
| | | Mean | Standard Error | Mean | Standard Error | Mean | Standard Error |
| 6 | Small Training | 0.2135 | 0.00392 | 0.2136 | 0.00354 | -0.0002 | 0.00139 |
| | Large Training | 0.1677 | 0.00187 | 0.1672 | 0.00189 | 0.0005 | 0.00097 |
| | Overall | 0.1906 | 0.00391 | 0.1904 | 0.00387 | 0.0002 | 0.00084 |
| 12 | Small Training | 0.1395 | 0.00303 | 0.1363 | 0.00268 | 0.0032 | 0.00069 |
| | Large Training | 0.0867 | 0.00289 | 0.0956 | 0.00265 | -0.0089 | 0.00147 |
| | Overall | 0.1131 | 0.0043 | 0.1159 | 0.00345 | -0.0028 | 0.00118 |
| 18 | Small Training | 0.0795 | 0.00532 | 0.0771 | 0.00522 | 0.0024 | 0.00056 |
| | Large Training | 0.0489 | 0.0014 | 0.0494 | 0.0013 | -0.0005 | 0.00049 |
| | Overall | 0.0642 | 0.00349 | 0.0632 | 0.00332 | 0.001 | 0.00042 |
| Total Low Complexity | Small Training | 0.1442 | 0.0068 | 0.1423 | 0.00688 | 0.0018 | 0.00057 |
| | Large Training | 0.1011 | 0.00589 | 0.1041 | 0.00575 | -0.0029 | 0.00078 |
| | Overall | 0.1226 | 0.00482 | 0.1232 | 0.00474 | -0.0006 | 0.00052 |

| Number of Variables | Training Size | High Complexity Data | | | | | |
|---|---|---|---|---|---|---|---|
| | | CVNN Ensemble | | Bagging Ensemble | | CVNN-Bagging | |
| | | Mean | Standard Error | Mean | Standard Error | Mean | Standard Error |
| 6 | Small Training | 0.3038 | 0.00505 | 0.3155 | 0.00555 | -0.0117 | 0.00275 |
| | Large Training | 0.2410 | 0.00234 | 0.2406 | 0.00235 | 0.0005 | 0.00148 |
| | Overall | 0.2724 | 0.00526 | 0.278 | 0.00613 | -0.0056 | 0.00178 |
| 12 | Small Training | 0.2342 | 0.00618 | 0.2479 | 0.00512 | -0.0138 | 0.00283 |
| | Large Training | 0.1433 | 0.00284 | 0.1488 | 0.00289 | -0.0055 | 0.00138 |
| | Overall | 0.1887 | 0.00731 | 0.1984 | 0.00765 | -0.0096 | 0.00167 |
| 18 | Small Training | 0.2046 | 0.006 | 0.213 | 0.00436 | -0.0084 | 0.00211 |
| | Large Training | 0.0880 | 0.00427 | 0.093 | 0.00422 | -0.0051 | 0.00128 |
| | Overall | 0.1463 | 0.00909 | 0.153 | 0.00908 | -0.0067 | 0.00125 |
| Total High Complexity | Small Training | 0.2475 | 0.00584 | 0.2588 | 0.00572 | -0.0113 | 0.00150 |
| | Large Training | 0.1574 | 0.00759 | 0.1608 | 0.00731 | -0.0034 | 0.00085 |
| | Overall | 0.2025 | 0.00603 | 0.2098 | 0.00612 | -0.0073 | 0.00092 |

| | Training Size | CVNN Ensemble | | Bagging Ensemble | | CVNN-Bagging | |
|---|---|---|---|---|---|---|---|
| | | Mean | Standard Error | Mean | Standard Error | Mean | Standard Error |
| Grand Total | Small Training | 0.1959 | 0.0063 | 0.2006 | 0.0063 | -0.0048 | 0.0010 |
| | Large Training | 0.1293 | 0.0067 | 0.1325 | 0.0065 | -0.0032 | 0.0008 |
| | Overall | 0.1626 | 0.00449 | 0.1665 | 0.0046 | -0.0039 | 0.00056 |

The effect of missing information on the relative generalization error of the bagging ensemble is presented in Table 2.8. At all three experimental levels, the bagging ensemble exhibits a slightly higher generalization error. At the 33 percent level, the bagging ensemble generalization error is 1.16% greater than the CVNN.

**Table 2.7 CVNN–Bagging Ensemble Generalization Error Effects of Classification Complexity and Training Size**

| | Mean Difference | Percent Reduction (%) | 95% Confidence Interval | |
| --- | --- | --- | --- | --- |
| | | | Lower | Upper |
| Low complexity | −0.0006 | −0.49% | −0.0016 | 0.0042 |
| High complexity | −0.0073 | −3.60% | −0.0091 | −0.0055 |
| Low training size | −0.0048 | −2.45% | −0.0068 | −0.0028 |
| High training size | −0.0032 | −2.47% | −0.0048 | −0.0016 |
| Aggregate error | −0.0039 | −2.40% | −0.0050 | −0.0028 |

This increases to 4.10 percent at 66 percent and 2.76 percent when all variables are present. Table 2.9 summarizes the generalization error of the bagging ensemble (relative to the CVNN ensemble) for experimental conditions that involve data imperfections. Table 2.9 shows the bagging ensemble has an error that is equivalent to the CVNN ensemble for data imperfections involving confounding learning examples. For clean datasets, the bagging ensemble error is greater than the CVNN ensemble by 0.0044 (3.08 percent). The bagging ensemble error is also higher when irrelevant variables are present. The relative increase in error is 4.63 percent and 4.66 percent for two and four irrelevant variables, respectively. For the conditions investigated in this research, we conclude that a bagging neural network ensemble has an error equivalent to the CVNN ensemble for low classification complexity and for data imperfections involving confounding cases. The bagging ensemble achieves an error reduction of 0.0024 (1.67 percent) at the data condition of low complexity and high level of confounding variables. For all other experimental conditions, the neural network bagging ensembles have slightly higher errors ranging from 1.16 percent to 4.66 percent.

Table 2.10 contrasts the generalization error of a boosting ensemble to the CVNN ensemble. The boosting ensemble, like the bagging ensemble, has a slightly

**Table 2.8 CVNN–Bagging Ensemble Generalization Error Effects of Missing Information**

| | Mean Difference | Percent Reduction (%) | 95% Confidence Interval | |
| --- | --- | --- | --- | --- |
| | | | Lower | Upper |
| 33% | −0.0027 | −1.16 | −0.00471 | −0.00069 |
| 66% | −0.0062 | −4.10 | −0.00831 | −0.00409 |
| 100% | −0.0029 | −2.76 | −0.0044 | −0.0014 |
| Aggregate error | −0.0039 | −2.4 | −0.005 | −0.0028 |

**Table 2.9   CVNN–Bagging Ensemble Generalization Error Effects of Data Imperfections**

|  | Mean Difference | Percent Reduction (%) | 95% Confidence Interval | |
|---|---|---|---|---|
|  |  |  | Lower | Upper |
| Clean | −0.00443 | −3.08 | −0.00847 | −0.00040 |
| 2 Irrelevant | −0.00717 | −4.63 | −0.01147 | −0.00286 |
| 4 Irrelevant | −0.00773 | −4.66 | −0.01215 | −0.00332 |
| 10% Confounding | −0.0015 | −0.93 | −0.00506 | 0.00206 |
| 20% Confounding | 0.001167 | 0.62 | −0.00170 | 0.00403 |
| Aggregate error | −0.0039 | −2.4 | −0.00500 | −0.00280 |

higher "aggregate" generalization error across all data conditions investigated. The magnitude of this increase is 0.0042 (2.58 percent). Table 2.11 decomposes this "aggregate" difference in error by classification complexity and training set size. The results in Table 2.11 show that classification complexity does not materially impact the relative error of the boosting ensemble, with the difference in error ranging from −2.52 percent to −2.77 percent. At the low training set size, the boosting generalization error is statistically equivalent to the CVNN ensemble. At the higher training set size, the boosting error is significantly higher, a 7.47 percent increase relative to the CVNN ensemble.

The effect of missing information on the error of the boosting ensemble relative to the CVNN ensemble is given in Table 2.12. The boosting ensemble has a statistically significant lower error than the CVNN at the 33 percent level of information. This corresponds to conditions where much of the information relevant to the classification decision is missing. As more information becomes available, the relative error of the boosting ensemble increases by 0.006 (3.98 percent) at the 66 percent level and by 0.0093 (8.84 percent) when all information is available. Table 2.13 decomposes the "aggregate" difference in generalization error by several data imperfection conditions. The boosting ensemble is statistically equivalent to the CVNN ensemble for the clean data condition (the absence of any data imperfections). The boosting ensemble is also statistically equivalent to the CVNN ensemble at both levels of irrelevant variables. Confounding learning examples cause a pronounced degradation of the boosting ensemble error relative to the CVNN error. At the 10 percent level of confounding variables, the relative error increases by 0.0079 (4.9 percent). At the 20 percent level, the relative error increases by 0.0086, a 4.62 percent increase. This is most likely due to the tendency to overweight these confounding cases as they are frequently misclassified and consequently misplacing the classification boundary. Opitz and Maclin [14] also reported a deterioration of neural network boosting ensembles as noise levels in the data increase. Tables 2.11, 2.12, and 2.13 suggest that the boosting ensemble is most appropriate in situations that include small training sizes, clean data or data with irrelevant variables, and

Table 2.10  CVNN versus Boosting Generalization Error

| Number of Variables | Training Size | Low Complexity Data | | | | | |
|---|---|---|---|---|---|---|---|
| | | CVNN Ensemble | | Boost Ensemble | | CVNN-Boost | |
| | | Mean | Standard Error | Mean | Standard Error | Mean | Standard Error |
| 6 | Small Training | 0.2135 | 0.00392 | 0.2102 | 0.00422 | 0.0032 | 0.00170 |
| | Large Training | 0.1677 | 0.00187 | 0.17 | 0.00221 | -0.0022 | 0.00150 |
| | Overall | 0.1906 | 0.00391 | 0.1901 | 0.00372 | 0.0005 | 0.00119 |
| 12 | Small Training | 0.1395 | 0.00303 | 0.1386 | 0.00406 | 0.0009 | 0.00224 |
| | Large Training | 0.0867 | 0.00289 | 0.0929 | 0.00303 | -0.0062 | 0.00160 |
| | Overall | 0.1131 | 0.0043 | 0.1157 | 0.00412 | -0.0026 | 0.00145 |
| 18 | Small Training | 0.0795 | 0.00532 | 0.0933 | 0.00718 | -0.0138 | 0.00270 |
| | Large Training | 0.0489 | 0.0014 | 0.051 | 0.00339 | -0.0021 | 0.00242 |
| | Overall | 0.0642 | 0.00349 | 0.0721 | 0.00496 | -0.008 | 0.00198 |
| Total Low Complexity | Small Training | 0.1442 | 0.0068 | 0.1474 | 0.00637 | -0.0032 | 0.00155 |
| | Large Training | 0.1011 | 0.00589 | 0.1046 | 0.00597 | -0.0035 | 0.00110 |
| | Overall | 0.1226 | 0.00482 | 0.126 | 0.00469 | -0.0034 | 0.00095 |

| Number of Variables | Training Size | High Complexity Data | | | | | |
|---|---|---|---|---|---|---|---|
| | | CVNN Ensemble | | Boost Ensemble | | CVNN-Boost | |
| | | Mean | Standard Error | Mean | Standard Error | Mean | Standard Error |
| 6 | Small Training | 0.3038 | 0.00505 | 0.2943 | 0.00466 | 0.0095 | 0.00212 |
| | Large Training | 0.2410 | 0.00234 | 0.2409 | 0.00246 | 0.0001 | 0.00170 |
| | Overall | 0.2724 | 0.00526 | 0.2676 | 0.00462 | 0.0048 | 0.00150 |
| 12 | Small Training | 0.2342 | 0.00618 | 0.2318 | 0.00507 | 0.0024 | 0.00224 |
| | Large Training | 0.1433 | 0.00284 | 0.1645 | 0.00377 | -0.0212 | 0.00213 |
| | Overall | 0.1887 | 0.00731 | 0.1982 | 0.00573 | -0.0094 | 0.00228 |
| 18 | Small Training | 0.2046 | 0.006 | 0.1996 | 0.00575 | 0.005 | 0.00276 |
| | Large Training | 0.0880 | 0.00427 | 0.1144 | 0.0077 | -0.0264 | 0.00434 |
| | Overall | 0.1463 | 0.00909 | 0.157 | 0.00772 | -0.0107 | 0.00340 |
| Total High Complexity | Small Training | 0.2475 | 0.00584 | 0.2419 | 0.00544 | 0.0056 | 0.00140 |
| | Large Training | 0.1574 | 0.00759 | 0.1733 | 0.00672 | -0.0158 | 0.00215 |
| | Overall | 0.2025 | 0.00603 | 0.2076 | 0.00515 | -0.0051 | 0.00155 |

| | | CVNN Ensemble | | Boost Ensemble | | CVNN-Boost | |
|---|---|---|---|---|---|---|---|
| | | Mean | Standard Error | Mean | Standard Error | Mean | Standard Error |
| Grand Total | Small Training | 0.1959 | 0.0063 | 0.1947 | 0.0059 | 0.0012 | 0.00148 |
| | Large Training | 0.1293 | 0.0067 | 0.1390 | 0.0063 | -0.0097 | 0.00162 |
| | Overall | 0.1626 | 0.00449 | 0.1668 | 0.0042 | -0.0042 | 0.00091 |

**Table 2.11 CVNN–Boosting Ensemble Generalization Error Effects of Classification Complexity and Training Size**

| | Mean Difference | Percent Reduction (%) | 95% Confidence Interval | |
| --- | --- | --- | --- | --- |
| | | | Lower | Upper |
| Low complexity | −0.0034 | −2.77 | −0.00527 | −0.00153 |
| High complexity | −0.0051 | −2.52 | −0.00816 | −0.00204 |
| Low training size | 0.0012 | 0.61 | −0.00172 | 0.004116 |
| High training size | −0.0097 | −7.47 | −0.01284 | −0.00646 |
| Aggregate error | −0.0042 | −2.58 | −0.00599 | −0.00241 |

**Table 2.12 CVNN–Boosting Ensemble Generalization Error Effects of Data Imperfections**

| | Mean Difference | Percent Reduction (%) | 95% Confidence Interval | |
| --- | --- | --- | --- | --- |
| | | | Lower | Upper |
| Clean | 0.001567 | 1.09 | −0.00334 | 0.006474 |
| 2 Irrelevant | −0.0015 | −0.97 | −0.00626 | 0.003262 |
| 4 Irrelevant | −0.00477 | −2.87 | −0.01074 | 0.001207 |
| 10% Confounding | −0.0079 | −4.90 | −0.01439 | −0.00141 |
| 20% Confounding | −0.00863 | −4.62 | −0.01533 | −0.00193 |
| Aggregate error | −0.0042 | −2.58 | −0.00599 | −0.00241 |

**Table 2.13 CVNN–Boosting Ensemble Generalization Error Effects of Data Imperfections**

| | Mean Difference | Percent Reduction (%) | 95% Confidence Interval | |
| --- | --- | --- | --- | --- |
| | | | Lower | Upper |
| Clean | 0.001567 | 1.09 | −0.00334 | 0.006474 |
| 2 Irrelevant | −0.0015 | −0.97 | −0.00626 | 0.003262 |
| 4 Irrelevant | −0.00477 | −2.87 | −0.01074 | 0.001207 |
| 10% Confounding | −0.0079 | −4.90 | −0.01439 | −0.00141 |
| 20% Confounding | −0.00863 | −4.62 | −0.01533 | −0.00193 |
| Aggregate error | −0.0042 | −2.58 | −0.00599 | −0.00241 |

a high percentage of missing information. For these experimental conditions, the boosting ensemble achieves a lower generalization error than the CVNN ensemble by magnitudes that range from 2.23 percent to 4.99 percent.

The findings in this research are consistent with conclusions reached by Opitz and Maclin [14] for neural network ensembles tested on real-world datasets. They reported that bagging ensembles are generally more accurate than a single model, that boosting ensembles produce more varied results with occasional dramatic reductions and sometimes an increase in error, and that the CVNN ensemble is surprisingly effective. In this research, the accuracy of the bagging ensemble (error of 0.1665) and the boosting ensemble (error of 0.1668) are remarkably similar. Both are statistically significant reductions from the single model error of 0.1705. Each has different areas of relative strength. Bagging is most appropriate at low complexity levels and high levels of confounding variables. Boosting is most accurate in classification applications that involve small training sizes, a high percentage of missing information, and clean data or data with irrelevant variables. In aggregate, neither bagging nor boosting is as accurate as the CVNN ensemble with an error of 0.1626.

## 2.5  Guidelines for Ensemble Formation

The results of this research provide convincing evidence that a neural network ensemble strategy produces universally more accurate decisions than a strategy of relying on a single model. There is no evidence to contradict this claim; the CVNN ensemble produces a lower generalization error than the single model at each and every experimental condition investigated. Depending on the experimental condition, the CVNN ensemble reduces the error of a single neural network model by a range of 3 percent to 25 percent. The superiority of an ensemble strategy is not an original finding; the advantage of ensembles is well documented in the research literature. Our contribution to this issue is to quantify this result for neural network ensembles with statistically significant results.

The CVNN is frequently a better strategy than bagging or boosting methods that perturb the training set. The perturbation strategies, however, have promise for some specific experimental conditions. We find that bagging is most appropriate for problems with low classification complexity, and for situations where the labeling of training examples is imprecise. Boosting is recommended for situations that involve a small training set (i.e., 200), a significant amount of missing information, and where the training labels can be precisely identified.

The complexity of the classification problem does influence the relative performance of the neural network ensemble strategy. The motivation to use an ensemble strategy increases as the complexity of the classification problem increases. This motivation is strongest for the CVNN and boosting strategy. The training set size has different effects on the three ensemble strategies. The relative reduction in generalization error of both the CVNN and the bagging ensembles increases at the higher training set size of 1000 observations. The boosting strategy shows a marked decline in relative error reduction as the training set size increases. As the amount of missing information increases, the incentive to use any of the three ensemble strategies decreases. The boosting strategy is least impacted by missing information, and is the strategy of choice for situations where as much as 66 percent of the relevant information is missing. The inclusion of irrelevant information also has different impacts on the three neural network ensemble strategies. The relative error of the CVNN and bagging ensembles is relatively immune (i.e., the relative error is unchanged) to the inclusion of irrelevant variables while the boosting ensemble demonstrates a pronounced decrease in relative error. A similar pattern is observed for conditions of incorrectly labeled learning examples. The CVNN and bagging ensemble is immune to increasing levels of mislabeled examples. Mislabeled examples, however, are particularly detrimental to the relative error of the boosting strategy.

Can these findings generalize to real-world datasets? West et al. [21] have investigated ensemble strategies in financial decision applications. The bankruptcy prediction problem is characterized by a small dataset with 329 observations, with reasonably low complexity as evidenced by generalization errors less than 15 percent, and with an imprecise ability to label the learning examples; that is, bankruptcy is not a precise state. According to these conditions, the findings of this study would favor bagging ensembles and one would expect boosting to be competitive because of the small training set. The authors report that bagging is the most accurate ensemble in this application, with a generalization error of 0.126; the boosting error is 0.128 and the CV error is 0.129. The Australian credit data investigated by these authors is similar to the bankruptcy data in complexity and difficulty in labeling examples precisely but is a larger dataset with 690 examples. We would therefore expect the performance of boosting to degrade and the performance of CV ensembles to improve. This is exactly what the authors report. The boosting ensemble achieves an error of 0.128, followed by CV at 0.131 and boosting at 0.148. The third dataset investigated in [21] is the German credit data characterized by a moderately large number of observations (1000) and high complexity; the generalization error is about 0.25. The findings of this research would suggest that CV ensembles would be preferred. The authors report that the CV ensemble error is 0.242, followed by bagging at 0.251 and boosting at 0.255. There is much recent research directed at disease classification from gene expressions in DNA microarrays. This problem environment is characterized by a very small number of observations (100 or less), the potential for a significant level of redundant information (as feature sets are formed from tens of thousands of genes), low complexity with generalization errors frequently below 5 percent, and precise labeling of outcomes. This is an environment where we would expect boosting ensembles to perform well based on our research findings.

The reader is cautioned that the findings of this research are limited to data with spatial characteristics of two naturally occurring clusters. More research is needed to verify whether these results will generalize to other conditions with more than two clusters, or to data that is structured in other spatial patterns.

# References

1. L. Breiman, Bagging predictors, *Machine Learning*, 24, 123–140, 1996.
2. P. Cunningham, J. Carney, and S. Jacob, Stability problems with artificial neural networks and the ensemble solution, *Artificial Intelligence in Medicine*, 20, 217–225, 2000.
3. H. Drucker, C. Cortes, L.D. Jackel, Y. LeCun, and V. Vapnik, Boosting and other ensemble methods, *Neural Computation*, 6, 1289–1301, 1994.
4. L.K. Hansen and P. Salamon, Neural network ensembles, *IEEE Transactions on Pattern Analysis and Machine Intelligence*, 12, 993–1001, 1990.
5. Y. Hayashi and R. Setiono, Combining neural network predictions for medical diagnosis, *Computers in Biology and Medicine*, 32, 237–246, 2002.
6. K. Helsen and P.A. Green, Computational study of replicated clustering with an application to market segmentation, *Decision Sciences*, 22, 1124–1141, 1991.
7. M.Y. Hu and C. Tsoukalas, Explaining consumer choice through neural networks: the stacked generalization approach, *European Journal of Operational Research*, 146, 650–660, 2003.
8. A. Krogh and J. Vedelsby, Neural network ensembles, crossvalidation, and active learning, In *Advances in Neural Information Processing Systems*, 7, 231–238, 1995. MIT Press, Cambridge, MA.
9. P.J.G. Lisboa, A review of evidence of health benefit from artificial neural networks in medical intervention, *Neural Networks*, 15, 11–39, 2002.
10. P. Mangiameli, S. Chen, and D. West, A comparison of SOM neural networks and hierarchical clustering methods, *European Journal of Operational Research*, 93, 443–460, 1996.
11. R.A. Miller, Medical diagnosis decision support systems-past, present, and future: a threaded bibliography and brief commentary, *Journal of the American Medical Informatics Association*, 1, 8–27, 1994.
12. G.W. Milligan, An examination of the effect of six types of error perturbation on fifteen clustering algorithms, *Psychometrika*, 43, 325–342, 1980.
13. G.W. Milligan, An algorithm for generating artificial test clusters, *Psychometrika*, 50, 123–127, 1985.
14. D. Opitz and R. Maclin, Popular ensemble methods: an empirical study, *Journal of Artificial Intelligence Research*, 11, 169–198, 1999.
15. B. Parmanto, P.W. Munro, and H.R. Doyle, Reducing variance of committee prediction with resampling techniques, *Connection Science,* 8, 405–425, 1996.
16. R.E. Schapire, The strength of weak learnability, *Machine Learning*, 5, 197–227, 1990.
17. H. Schwenk and Y. Bengio, Boosting neural networks, *Neural Computation*, 12, 1869–1887, 2000.
18. A.J.C. Sharkey, On combining artificial neural nets, *Connection Science*, 8, 299–313, 1996.
19. K.A. Smith and J.N.D. Gupta, Neural networks in business: techniques and applications for the operations researcher, *Computers & Operations Research*, 27, 1023–1044, 2000.
20. S.Y. Sohn and S.H. Lee, Data fusion, ensemble and clustering to improve the classification accuracy for the severity of road traffic accidents in Korea, *Safety Science,* 41 1–14, 2003.

21. D. West, S. Dellana, and J. Quian Neural network ensemble strategies for financial decision applications, *Computers & Operations Research*, to be published.

22. B.K. Wong, V.S. Lai, and J. Lam, A bibliography of neural network business applications research: 1994–1998, *Computers & Operations Research*, 27, 1045–1076, 2000.

23. J. Zhang, Developing robust non-linear models through bootstrap aggregated neural networks, *Neurocomputing*, 25, 93–113, 1999.

24. P.A. Whilkin and R.L. Somorjai, Application of several methods of classification fusion to magnetic resonance spectra, *Connection Science*, 8, 427–442, 1996.

25. Z.H. Zhou, Y. Jiang, Y.B. Yang, and S.F. Chen, Lung cancer cell identification based on artificial neural network ensembles, *Artificial Intelligence in Medicine*, 24, 25–36, 2002.

*Chapter 3*

# Neural Network Classification with Uneven Misclassification Costs and Imbalanced Group Sizes

Jyhshyan Lan, Michael Y. Hu, Eddy Patuwo, and G. Peter Zhang

## Contents

## 3.1 Introduction

*Classification* is one of the most important areas in data mining. Classification arises when one tries to separate a number of objects into several classes or to determine whether or not an object belongs to a particular class. Many real-world decision problems are classification based. For example, in business settings, bankruptcy prediction, performance evaluation, target marketing, bond rating, credit scoring, and manufacturing process control are essentially classification problems. In scientific and medical fields, one sees common classification problems such as medical diagnosis, fingerprint detection, and speech and handwriting recognition.

There are many approaches to classification. Most of the scientific methods are based on statistical principles. Common statistical classification techniques include linear and nonlinear discriminant analysis, logistic regression, and k-nearest neighbor. The limitation of these techniques lies in the fact that to effectively apply them, the data structure and the underlying probability distribution must satisfy some restrictive assumptions [1, 2]. Therefore, their usefulness and effectiveness may be limited if the data does not conform to the requirement of the essential statistical assumptions.

*Artificial neural networks* (ANNs) are one of the alternatives to statistical classification methods. ANNs are data-driven methods and can theoretically approximate any fundamental relationship with arbitrary accuracy without prior assumptions on the underlying data and probabilistic structure. Thus, they are suitable for problems where observations are easy to obtain but the data structure or underlying relationship is unknown. Other important features of ANNs that make them attractive for classification problems include (1) their close relationship to the Bayes decision theory in terms of posterior probability estimation [3] and (2) their link to traditional statistical classifiers such as discriminant analysis, logistic regression, classification tree, and nearest neighbor methods [4].

ANNs have been successfully applied to a variety of classification problems in diverse fields. However, few applications in the literature take asymmetric misclassification costs into consideration. In many cases, researchers simply make the assumption of equal misclassification costs without considering the effect of uneven misclassification costs on classification results. Under this assumption, the objective of classification is to minimize the total number of misclassification cases, not the total misclassification cost, which is a more appropriate measure of classification performance. Although the equal cost assumption can simplify the model development, it may not be appropriate for many real situations where misclassification costs have severe, unequal consequences for different groups. Depending on the situation and the perspective of the decision maker, the misclassification cost differences can be quite large, significantly affecting the classification or decision-making consequence. For example, in bankruptcy prediction, a misclassification that resulted from classifying a well-managed bank as a failing one may have less severe consequence than misclassification derived from failure to detect a troubling bank for government regulators. A classification model based on an equal cost assumption cannot provide enough opportunity for early identification of potential financial decline to closely monitor those problem institutions and to take immediate corrective action. Therefore, a classification model with higher capability to detect insolvent institutions will be more appropriate for those information users, given the magnitude of the banking crisis and the enormous costs of resolution. Medical diagnosis is another common example of asymmetric misclassification cases. It is unlikely that misclassifying a benign tumor as a malignant one entails equal costs to misclassifying a malignant tumor as a benign one. As a result, medical examiners typically assign a relatively high cost associated with misclassifying a malignant tumor as a benign one to save patient's life or avoid legal issues. It is clear that in these situations, ignoring the unequal consequences of misclassification will generate bias and result in a classifier with little practical value.

Another issue associated with many classification problems is the imbalanced group size that occurs when there are many more observations in one group than in others. This imbalance causes many classifiers to be biased toward the large group. That is, they tend to classify most — if not all — observations to the largest group and still achieve a high classification rate. For example, in a two-group classification problem, if 95 percent of the observations are in one group, then by classifying all observations to this group, a classifier can achieve 95 percent of the overall correct classification result.

This chapter aims to explore the effects of asymmetric misclassification costs and imbalanced group sizes on ANN performance in practice. We use a medical diagnosis problem (thyroid disease diagnosis) for illustration. In thyroid diagnosis, the goal is to determine whether a patient has a normally functioning thyroid, an under-functioning thyroid (hypothyroid), or an overactive thyroid (hyperthyroid) with a number of attributes representing information on patients such as age, gender, health condition, and the results of various medical tests [5]. The thyroid diagnosis problem represents a difficult yet interesting classification problem because this is a three-group classification problem with extremely imbalanced group memberships. Among 7200 cases in the dataset, the largest group has about 92.6 percent observations and the smallest group has 2.3 percent. Because of the large sample size, one can use also a cross-validation approach to study the effect of sample size.

## 3.2 Literature Review

### 3.2.1 Neural Network Applications

Although the use of equal cost assumption may not be appropriate when the costs of classification errors actually differ, most researchers do not consider the consequences of the uneven misclassification cost. Limited previous research provides some evidence that the asymmetric misclassification cost can significantly influence a classifier's performance as well as the optimal decision making. In neural network research, Kohers et al. [6, 7] utilized different penalty cost functions in the context of overestimating and underestimating the actual future values to examine the effectiveness of ANN as forecasting composite models. Salchenberger et al. [8] evaluated the ability of ANNs to predict thrift institution failures by considering the effect of different cutoff points on Type I and Type II errors. Philipoom et al. [9] used a cost-based assignment scheme that suggests that the cost of early completion may differ in form or degree from the cost of tardiness. They found that implicitly ignoring unequal consequences in the due date assignment could be costly and ANN could be more appropriate for problems with unequal costs for earliness and tardiness than linear and linear programming approaches. They also suggested that ANN can be used for a wide range of cost functions, whereas the other methodologies are significantly more restricted.

Berardi and Zhang [10] investigated the effect of unequal misclassification costs on neural network classification performance. They found that when the misclassification cost for a particular group is high, the classifier seeks to increase the correct classification rate for that group. The price to pay for this increase in the correct identification of a specific group is a decrease in the correct identification of other groups. Their results suggest that different cost considerations have significant effects on the neural network classification performance, particularly for smaller groups, and that appropriate use of cost information could aid in optimal decision making in a situation in which correct identification of some groups is of utmost importance.

Pendharkar and Nanda [11] proposed an evolutionary neural network approach to incorporate uneven misclassification costs. They used both real-world and simulated data to show the effectiveness of their generic algorithm-based method in cost minimization compared with traditional statistical and machine learning methods.

In practical applications, the level of imbalance can be drastic, with the ratio of the smallest group size to largest group size as 1 to 100, 1 to 1000, 1 to 10,000, or higher [12–14]. Although it is difficult for ANNs to learn from imbalanced datasets, a large number of studies in the literature ignore the issue and proceed as though the data is balanced [15, 16]. However, some previous researchers in areas such as fraud detection, telecommunications management, oil spill detection, and text classification provide evidence that the imbalanced dataset can significantly influence ANN performance and optimal decision making [16–18].

The ability of feedforward ANNs to perform static pattern discrimination stems from their potential to create a specific nonlinear transformation into a space spanned by the outputs of the hidden units in which class separation is easier [15, 19]. This transformation is constrained to maximize a feature extraction criterion, which may be viewed as nonlinear, multidimensional generalization of Fisher's linear discriminant function. Because this criterion involves the weighted between-class covariance matrix, adaptive networks trained on a multi-group classifier problem exhibit a strong bias in favor of those classes that have the largest membership in the training data. The bias toward the large group is also an undesirable feature of networks in situations where information on one particular class may be more difficult or expensive to obtain than other classes.

## 3.2.2 Thyroid Disease Diagnosis

The main issue addressed here focuses on the effects of unequal misclassification costs and imbalanced group size on the classification performance of neural networks. To explore this issue, we use a thyroid disease diagnosis dataset for the analysis. Here is some basic information about the thyroid diseases and their diagnoses.

The thyroid gland is one of the most important organs in the body because thyroid hormones control metabolism and affect the functions of many other organs. A thyroid disorder results when something goes wrong in the process of generating hormones. The most common disorder is an underactive thyroid, known as hypothyroidism, in which not enough hormone is produced. Less frequent, the thyroid produces too much hormone, which is known as hyperthyroidism. Groups most commonly affected by thyroid dysfunctions include women and the elderly, where as many as 5 to 10 percent of people in these groups may be affected.

Thyroid disorders are often difficult to diagnose [20, 21]. One reason is the nonspecific nature of many thyroid symptoms. This is especially true for hypothyroidism because symptoms such as lethargy, confusion, weight gain, high cholesterol, and poor memory are easily confused with other psychiatric and medical conditions. The problem is often exacerbated in older patients whose symptoms are often masked by other medical problems [22].

Physicians rely heavily on blood tests to make diagnoses. Although lab tests are useful in diagnosing thyroid abnormalities, the positive predictive rate can be as low as 15 to –26 percent [23]. The high error rates occur because test results characteristic of hypo- and hyperthyroidism are not consistent across patients and are influenced by a variety of factors such as pregnancy, drug interactions, nonthyroidal illnesses, and psychiatric problems [24, 25].

Correct identification of thyroid disorders is important because a significant number of cases lead to death due to thyroid storm in acute hyperthyroidism and myxedema coma in hypothyroidism [26]. Although not as common in infants, it is critical to detect congenital hypothyroidism early because mental retardation and a variety of neurological disorders may result if the condition is not properly identified and treated.

Errors made in classifying thyroid conditions have a variety of potentially harmful effects. Patients misclassified as hyperthyroid may improperly receive drug or radioactive iodine treatment, or even have their thyroid surgically removed. Patients misdiagnosed as suffering from hypothyroidism may be placed on a lifelong hormone supplement regimen. Those classified as normal when actually suffering from a thyroid dysfunction, meanwhile, may experience long-term organ damage, be treated for other misdiagnosed conditions, or be forced to endure their thyroid-induced symptoms.

Therefore, the problem of diagnosing thyroid disorders entails unequal misclassification costs. The classification procedure based on maximum posterior probability simply to achieve maximum overall classification performance is not appropriate. In this problem setting, proper identification of hyper- or hypothy-roidal patients will be of much greater importance. The problem of diagnosing thyroid disorders also entails an imbalanced group size issue because approximately six million (7 percent) Americans suffer from hypothyroidism or hyperthyroidism while the remaining (93 percent) of Americans are normal [27]. The traditional classification techniques may not be effective in this case.

## 3.3 Misclassification Costs and Unbalanced Group Sizes

This section illustrates the effect of misclassification costs and group size on the classification procedures. To provide analytical results, we restrict our models to simple ones with two-group classification problems or linear output functions in neural networks.

### 3.3.1 Bayes Decision Rule

In constructing a procedure of classification, one wants to minimize the overall risk in making decisions for the expected cost of misclassification. We use a two-group classification problem for illustration. In this simple case, one can think of an observation with $p$ independent variables as a point in a $p$-dimensional space that is divided into two regions $R_1$ and $R_2$. If the observation falls in region $R_1$, we classify it as coming from group $w_1$, and if it falls in region $R_2$, we classify it as coming from group $w_2$. Following this classification procedure, we may make two types of errors in classification. The first error occurs when we classify the object into group $w_2$ while it is actually from group $w_1$. The second type of error occurs when the individual is from group $w_2$, but the classifier classifies it into group $w_1$.

To estimate the expected risk of misclassification, let the cost of classifying an individual from $w_1$ as one from $w_2$ be $C(2|1)$ and that of classifying an individual from $w_2$ as from $w_1$ be $C(1|2)$. Also assume that the prior probability that an observation comes from group $w_1$ is $P(w_1)$ and from group $w_2$ is $P(w_2)$. Let the density function of group $w_1$ be $P(x|w_1)$ and that of $w_2$ be $P(x|w_2)$. Let $R_1$ and $R_2$ be the region of classification as from $w_1$ and $w_2$, respectively, and the probability of correctly classifying an observation that actually is drawn from group $w_1$ is:

$$P(1|1,R_1) = \int R_1 \, P(x|w_1)dx \tag{3.1}$$

The probability of misclassification of an observation from $w_1$ is:

$$P(2|1,R_1) = \int R_2 \, P(x|w_1)dx \tag{3.2}$$

Similarly, the probability of correctly classifying an observation from $w_2$ is:

$$P(2|2,R_2) = \int R_2 \, P(x| \, w_2)dx \qquad (3.3)$$

And the probability of misclassifying such an observation is:

$$P(1|2,R_2) = \int R_1 \, P(x| \, w_2)dx \qquad (3.4)$$

Because the probability of drawing an observation from $w_1$ is $P(w_1)$, the probability of drawing an observation from $w_1$ and misclassifying it as from $w_2$ can be calculated as $P(w_1)P(2|1,R_2)$. Similarly, the probability of drawing an observation from $w_2$ and misclassifying it as from $w_1$ can be calculated as $P(w_2)P(1|2,R_1)$. Therefore, the expected cost of misclassification is the sum of the cost of each misclassification multiplied by the probability of its occurrence:

$$C(2|1) \, P(2|1,R_2) \, P(w_1) + C(1|2) \, P(1|2,R_1) \, P(w_2) \qquad (3.5)$$

The Bayes decision rule aims to find the decision region ($R_i$) such that Equation (3.5) is minimized.

### 3.3.2 Error Minimization and Imbalanced Dataset Bias

To minimize the error at the output of a network with linear output units is to minimize the following squared error function:

$$\Theta = \frac{1}{P} \| T - O \|^2 = \frac{1}{P} \|[T - (\lambda_0 + \Lambda H)]D\|^2 \qquad (3.6)$$

where $T$ is the $c \times P$ matrix of target patterns, $O$ is the $c \times P$ matrix of network output vectors, $\lambda_0$ is the $c \times 1$ vector of output biases, $\Lambda$ is the $c \times n_0$ matrix of weights between the $n_0$ hidden nodes and the $c$ output nodes, $H$ is the $n_0 \times P$ matrix of output patterns at the hidden layer, and $D$ is the $P \times P$ diagonal matrix of error weightings [15]. Minimizing the sum of the squared error function with respect to the bias vector produces the optimum solution for the bias as the following equation:

$$\lambda_0 = \bar{t} - \Lambda m^H \qquad (3.7)$$

where $\bar{t} \triangleq \frac{TD^2 1}{\sum_{P=1}^{P} d_P}$ is the weighted target mean and $m^H \triangleq \frac{HD^2 1}{\sum_{P=1}^{P} d_P}$ is the weighted mean pattern evaluated on the training set at the outputs of the hidden nodes. Let $\hat{T} = T - \bar{t} 1^*$ be the mean shifted target matrix and $\hat{H} = H - m^H 1^*$ be the matrix of mean-shifted hidden unit output patterns. The squared error function can be rewritten as the following equation:

$$\Theta = \frac{1}{P} \|[T - \Lambda \hat{H}]D\|^2 \qquad (3.8)$$

Minimizing this error function with respect to the weight matrix, we find that:

$$\Lambda = \widehat{T}D(\widehat{H}D)^{+} \tag{3.9}$$

After the operation of Moore-Penrose pseudo-inverse matrix, the sum of the squared error function can be expressed in the following form:

$$\Theta = \frac{1}{P} Tr\{\widehat{T}D^2\widehat{T}^{*} - \widehat{T}D^2\widehat{H}^{*}(\widehat{H}D^2\widehat{H}^{*})\widehat{H}D^2\widehat{T}^{*}\} \tag{3.10}$$

From Equation (3.10), to minimize the sum of the squared error function is to maximize the following equation:

$$J = Tr\{S_B S_T^{+}\} \tag{3.11}$$

where $S_T \triangleq \frac{1}{p}\widehat{H}D^2\widehat{H}^{*}$ can be interpreted as a weighted total covariance matrix, and

$$S_B \triangleq \left(\frac{1}{P}\right)^2 \widehat{H}D^2\widehat{T}^{*}\widehat{T}D^2\widehat{H}^{*} \tag{3.12}$$

can be interpreted as a between-class covariance matrix of the nonlinearly transformed input patterns.

Because the error minimization procedure involves the weighted between-class covariance matrix (where the weighting is determined by the square of the number of patterns in each class), adaptive networks trained on a multi-class problem exhibit a strong bias in favor of those classes that have the largest membership in the training data.

## 3.4 Research Methodology

### 3.4.1 *Data*

The dataset used in this study is selected from the well-known UCI (University of California – Irvine) data repository, which has been used as a benchmark for various machine learning techniques. There are 7200 cases in this thyroid disease dataset, which classifies a patient as having a normally functioning thyroid, an under-functioning thyroid (hypothyroid), or an overactive thyroid (hyperthyroid). The hyperthyroid class represents 2.3 percent (166 cases) of the data points, the hypothyroid class accounts for 5.1 percent (367 cases) of the observations, while the normal group makes up the remaining 92.6 percent (6667 cases). The classification of thyroid level is a challenging task because the dataset is highly imbalanced. For each of the 7200 cases, there are 21 attributes with 15 binary and 6 continuous variables used to determine in which of the three classes the patient belongs. These attributes represent information on patients such as age, gender, health condition, and the results of various medical tests [5]. The original dataset is further divided into two parts: the test set is composed of 3700 observations while the rest of the dataset is used for training purposes.

## 3.4.2 Research Design

To systematically investigate the effect of unequal cost, uneven group size, and sample size on neural network classifiers, a three-way factorial designed experiment is conducted. The first factor in this investigation is the misclassification cost. We consider six different levels of misclassification cost for each group, representing the relative degree of the seriousness of a misclassification between the normal and two disorder cases. These six levels are represented by a misclassification cost ratio (CR) among the three groups — (1:1:1), (3:1.5:1), (4.5:2.25:1), (7:3.5:1), (12:6:1), and (27:13.5:1) — where the ratio denotes the relative magnitude of one group misclassification cost over others. For example, (1:1:1) means that all misclassification costs are equal, while (3:1.5:1) indicates that the misclassification cost for group 1 (hyperthyroid) is twice as severe as that for group 2 (hypothyroid) and is three times as much as that for group 3 (normal thyroid). Although many other alternative cost values can be selected based on the specific situation and consideration, these selected levels reflect a reasonable range of possible values in this study as they have a significant impact on the subsequent classification decision (as discussed in the next section). In addition, we choose these ratios to match the relative differences in group size levels, as discussed below.

The second experimental factor is the imbalanced group size. We consider five levels of the imbalanced group size as the ratios of the sample sizes in these groups: (1:2:27), (2:4:24), (3:6:21), (4:8:18), and (5:10:15). As in misclassification cost ratios, these group size ratios represent a relative scale of difference in the sizes of the three groups. For example, (1:2:27) means that the smallest group (hyperthyroid) is only half the size of the next smallest group (hypothyroid), while the largest group (normal) is 27 times larger than the smallest group. We keep the relative size of the two smaller groups constant (ratio 1:2) to represent that ratio in the original dataset. However, in a real application situation, because the size of the large group may vary, we consider different proportions of large group in the whole dataset to examine its effect. Note that the sum of the group ratio sizes in each of these levels is equal to 30. Note also that in the most imbalanced group situation (i.e., ratio = 1:2:27), the largest group has 90 percent (27/(1 + 2 + 27)) of the total observations while at the other extreme, the largest group contains only 50 percent (15/(5 + 10 + 15)) of the total observations, which is a more balanced group case as the large group size equals the sum of the two smaller group sizes. In cases of insufficient observations in the smaller groups, we use the bootstrapping method to augment the group members.

Finally, we consider sample size effect. Just as in most practical situations, we are limited to available data where increasing sample size may not be feasible. Training sample size is varied at four levels, with sample size N = 3500, N = 2500, N = 1500, and N = 500. In each case, we randomly select a training sample from the original training sample of 3500 observations.

Realizing that neural networks are sensitive to the training samples, we use a resampling scheme to draw multiple samples to examine the robustness of the neural classifiers. With this scheme, for each sample size, we randomly draw 30 replications of samples for training. Then, neural networks trained on each of these replications are tested with the untouched test sample of 3700 observations.

### 3.4.3 Neural Networks

We use a feedforward type of neural network in this study. All networks employ one hidden layer. Twenty-one input nodes corresponding to twenty-one input attributes are used. Three binary output nodes are employed, corresponding to the three classes of thyroid conditions. The target value for each node is either zero (0) or one (1), depending on the true output class. The logistic activation function is used for both hidden and output nodes.

The number of hidden nodes is not easy to determine *a priori*. There are many rules-of-thumb proposed for determining the number of hidden nodes, but none of them works well for all situations. After a pilot experiment conducted with a varying number of hidden nodes with the original training sample, a network with three hidden nodes is used for the main investigation.

Training methodology is another important factor in designing feedforward neural networks. As noted previously, the purpose of neural network training is to estimate the node connection weights to minimize an error measure such as sum of squared errors or cross entropy. We use a more efficient, faster converging training method called Rprop (for Resilient backpropagation) [28]. To have more robust results, cross entropy instead of the sum of the squared error function is used as the objective function in the neural network training process.

## 3.5  Results

The effects of various sample sizes, misclassification penalty ratios, and group size ratios on the classification performance of neural networks are examined. As outlined previously, we use 30 resamples from the original training sample for each experimental setting that consider three factors: training sample size, misclassification cost, and unbalanced group size. Results are summarized over the 30 training samples. Although detailed tables are available for all scenarios, graphical analyses are used to facilitate the presentation of findings and patterns.

Figure 3.1 plots the overall classification rates with different misclassification cost ratios and different sample sizes for the group size ratio of (1:2:27). As the misclassification cost becomes more unequal, the overall performance of neural

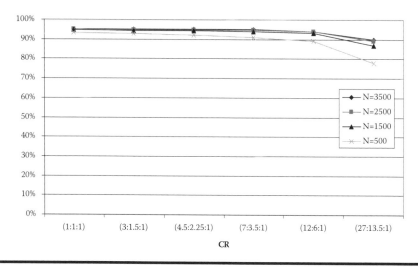

**Figure 3.1 The means of the overall classification rate for various misclassification cost ratios (CR) and training sample sizes (N) when the group size ratio is (1:2:27).**

networks deteriorates. However, the level of deterioration is uneven across the six levels of CR. It seems that from the CR = (1:1:1) to CR = (12:6:1), the effect of CR is not significant. At the most extreme case of CR = (27:13.5:1), the performance of neural classifier is significantly worse than that of other cost ratios. This non-linear decreasing pattern is consistent across all four sample sizes. It is also found that when the cost ratio is not high or the misclassification costs are not extremely uneven, the sample size effect is small. As the CR increases, the sample size effect becomes prominent. Figure 3.1 also suggests that when the sample size is equal to and greater than 1500, the overall difference in performance is quite small regardless of the cost ratio used.

The group size effect can be seen in Figures 3.2 through 3.5, which summarize the results of overall classification rates with different misclassification cost ratios and different sample sizes. Several observations can be made here. First, the patterns observed in Figure 3.1 remain true for other group size ratios. That is, as the CR increases, the classification rate decreases across all samples. In addition, larger sample sizes are relatively insensitive to the change of the cost ratio. But the smaller samples (especially with the sample size of 500) are quite sensitive to the change in CR. It is interesting to see that as the group size ratio becomes more balanced, the classification performance becomes worse for all sample sizes and for larger CR values. This suggests that when the groups are more balanced, unequal misclassification cost consequences can have a dramatic effect on the neural classifier, especially when the sample size is small.

Figures 3.6 through 3.10 plot the overall patterns of group classification performance at the five unbalanced group size levels from the extremely unbalanced case

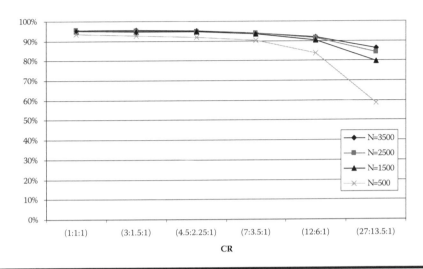

**Figure 3.2  The means of the overall classification rate for various misclassification cost ratios (CR) and training sample sizes (N) when the group size ratio is (2:4:24).**

with ratio (1:2:27) to the relatively balanced case with ratio (5:10:15). Several general observations are evident. First, assuming equal misclassification cost will have an uneven effect on group classification performance, especially when the group size is quite imbalanced. Specifically, these figures show that at CR equal to (1:1:1),

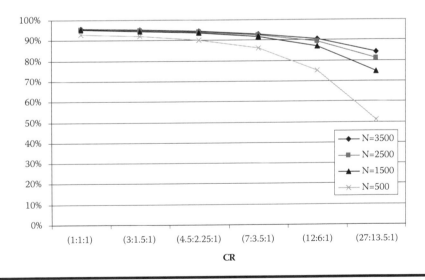

**Figure 3.3  The means of the overall classification rate for various misclassification cost ratios (CR) and training sample sizes (N) when the group size ratio is (3:6:21).**

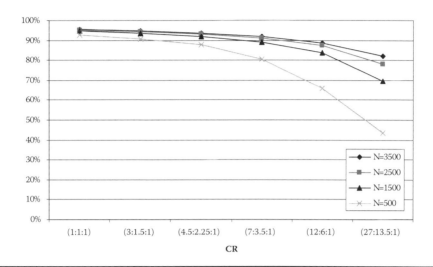

**Figure 3.4**   The means of the overall classification rate for various misclassification cost ratios (CR) and training sample sizes (N) when the group size ratio is (4:8:18).

classification performance for the smaller groups (groups 1 and 2) is poor while at the same time, the group classification rate for the largest group (group 3) is very good. Second, as the misclassification costs become more uneven from CR = (1:1:1) to CR = (27:13.5:1), the classification performance for the smaller groups — especially

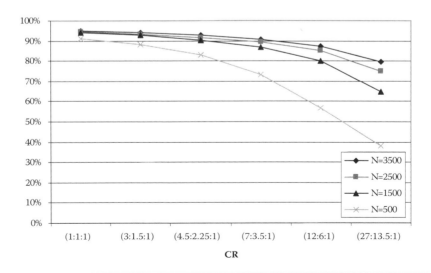

**Figure 3.5**   The means of the overall classification rate for various misclassification cost ratios (CR) and training sample sizes (N) when the group size ratio is (5:10:15).

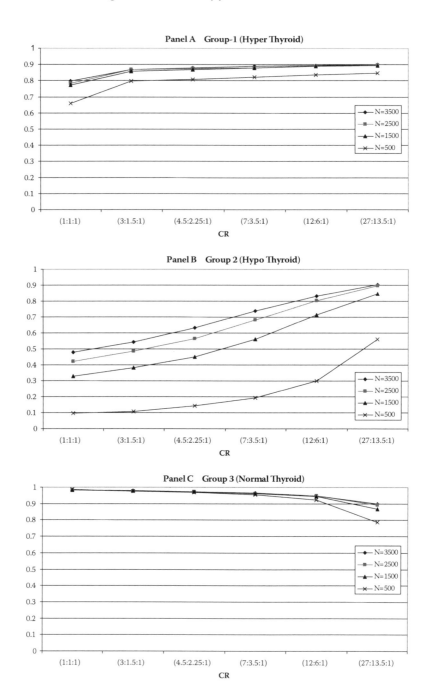

**Figure 3.6** The means of the group classification rate for various misclassification cost ratios (CR) and training sample sizes (N) when the group size ratio is (1:2:27).

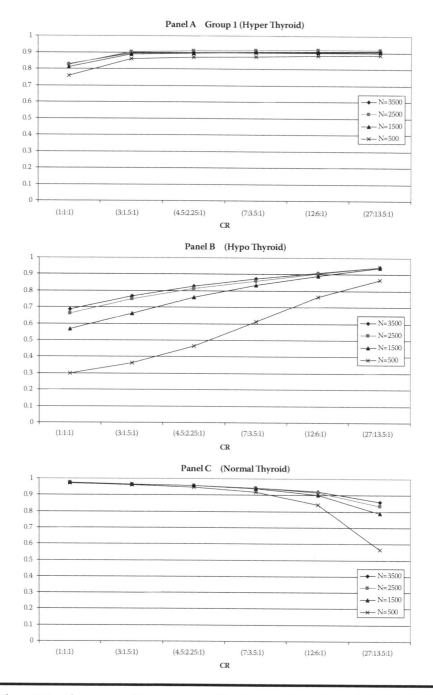

**Figure 3.7** The means of the group classification rate for various misclassification cost ratios (CR) and training sample sizes (N) when the group size ratio is (2:4:24).

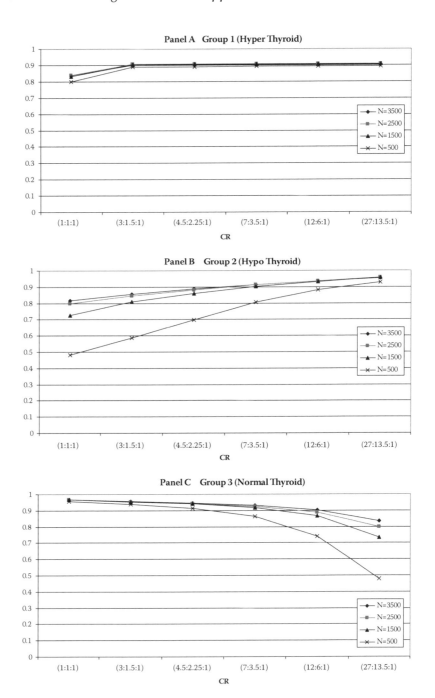

**Figure 3.8    The means of the group classification rate for various misclassification cost ratios (CR) and training sample sizes (N) when the group size ratio is (3:6:21).**

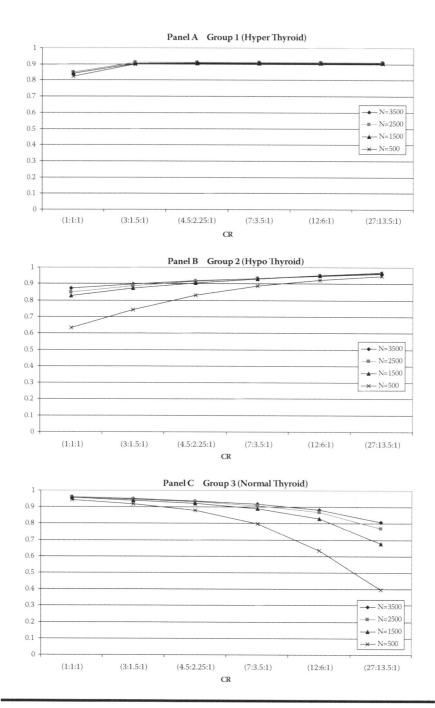

**Figure 3.9** **The means of the group classification rate for various misclassification cost ratios (CR) and training sample sizes (N) when the group size ratio is (4:8:18).**

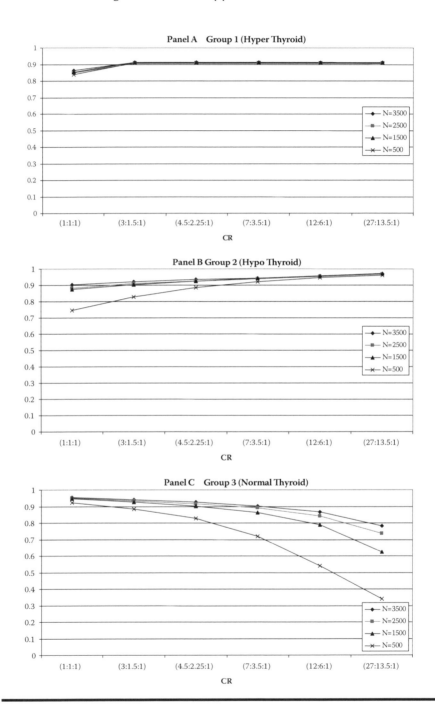

**Figure 3.10    The means of the group classification rate for various misclassification cost ratios (CR) and training sample sizes (N) when the group size ratio is (5:10:15).**

for group 2 — improves while it generally deteriorates for the large group (Group 3). This suggests that the misclassification cost information can be used to increase the group classification performance of the more important groups. Figures 3.6 through 3.10 also suggest that the use of misclassification cost information is particularly helpful for smaller yet more critical groups when the group sizes are very imbalanced. For example, in the extremely unbalanced group case (Figure 3.6), increasing the CR ratio from (1:1:1) to (27:13.5:1) greatly increases the group classification rate for Group 1 and Group 2 compared to the situation of relatively balanced group case (Figure 3.10) where CR ratio has relatively less effect on the classification rate for these groups. Finally, we observe that the group classification performance is affected by the sample size as in all cases (different combinations of the CR ratio and group size ratio with all three groups) the group classification performance is positively related to the sample size. That is, increasing the training sample size does help to improve the classification rate in each group. However, the sample size effect is uneven across all situations. It appears that the sample size does not play a significant role in the largest group (group 3) classification performance, especially when the misclassification cost ratio is equal or not significantly different and the group size is quite unbalanced (Figures 3.6 and 3.7). On the other hand, there is little sample size effect on smaller group classification performance when the misclassification cost is significantly unequal and the group size is relatively balanced (Figures 3.9 and 3.10). In other situations, however, sample size does have a significant impact on the classification performance for all groups.

## 3.6 Conclusions

Uneven misclassification and imbalanced class size are two important problems in neural network classification problems. However, most of these studies use the simplified assumption of equal consequence of a misclassification to ease model development and selection of classification decision points. With this assumption, the total or overall classification performance is the only objective to maximize. Although ANNs are often able to achieve high overall classification rates, it does not suggest that the result is useful for many practical decision-making problems where misclassification costs are unequal and group size is uneven. As demonstrated in this study, when a classification problem is dominated by one large group or the classification costs are extremely imbalanced, high classification rate does not indicate the usefulness of the ANN model to classify members in often more important and difficult smaller groups. Thus, in building a useful classification model, it is important to consider both misclassification cost consequence and the group imbalance issue to provide better decision-making capability to reduce overall risk.

This study revealed that both misclassification cost and group size have significant effects on ANN classification performance — not only for the overall situation, but also for the more important group classifications. Failing to consider these factors in designing a neural classifier will have a serious effect on the classification decision for many applications, including medical diagnosis. Through an application of thyroid disease diagnosis, we find that depending on different decision-makers' perspectives and situations, a significant improvement in classification performance for small but important groups can be achieved. With the cost adjustment, ANNs are more capable of achieving an optimal classification decision to reduce the risk of medical maltreatments. In addition, the sample size is found to be important in developing ANN classification models for imbalanced groups and unequal misclassification errors.

# References

1. Neter, J., Wasserman, W., and Whitmore, G.A., *Applied Statistics*, 4th ed., Irwin, Boston, MA, 1996.
2. Refenes, A-P., Ed., *Neural Networks in the Capital Market*, John Wiley & Sons, New York, 1995.
3. Richard, M.D. and Lippmann, R.P., Neural network classifiers estimate Bayesian posterior probabilities, *Neural Computation*, 3, 461, 1991.
4. Zhang, G.P., Neural networks for classification: a survey, *IEEE Transactions on Systems, Man, and Cybernetics*, 30, 451, 2000.
5. Quinlan, J., Simplifying decision trees, *International Journal of Man-Machine Studies*, 27, 221, 1987.
6. Kohers, G., Rakes, T.R., and Rees, L.P., The use of neural networks and combined forecasts in the prediction of portfolio returns with different penalty costs, in *Proceedings of the 1994 Annual Meeting of the Decision Sciences Institute,* Atlanta, GA, 1994, p. 1331.
7. Kohers, G., Rakes, T.R., and Rees, L.P., Predicting weekly portfolio returns with the use of composite models: a comparison of neural networks and traditional composite models, in *Proceedings of the 1996 Annual Meeting of the Decision Sciences Institute,* Atlanta, GA, 1996, p. 1332.
8. Salchenberger, L.M., Cinar, E.M., and Lash, N.A., Neural networks: a new tool for predicting thrift failures, *Decision Sciences*, 23, 899, 1992.
9. Philipoom, P.R., Wiegmann, L, and Rees, L.P., Cost-based due-date assignment with the use of classical and neural network approaches, *Naval Research Logistics,* 44, 825, 1997.
10. Berardi, V. and Zhang, G.P., The effect of misclassification costs on neural network classifiers, *Decision Sciences*, 30, 659, 1999.
11. Pendharkar, P. and Nanda, S., A misclassification cost-minimizing evolutionary-neural classification approach, *Naval Research Logistics*, 53, 432, 2006.
12. Pearson, R., Goney, G., and Shwaber, J., Imbalanced clustering for microarray time-series, in *Proceedings of the ICML '03 Workshop on Learning from Imbalanced Data Sets*, 2003.
13. Wu, G. and Chang, E.Y., Class-boundary alignment for imbalanced dataset learning, in *Proceedings of the ICML '03 Workshop on Learning from Imbalanced Data Sets*, 2003.

14. Provost, F. and Fawcett, T., Robust classification for imprecise environments, *Machine Learning*, 42, 203, 2001.

15. Lowe, D. and Webb, A.R., Exploiting prior knowledge in network optimization: an illustration from medical prognosis, *Network*, 1, 299, 1990.

16. Chawla, N., Bowver, L.H., and Kegelmeyer, W., SMOTE: synthetic minority over-sampling technique, *Journal of Artificial Intelligence Research*, 16, 321, 2002.

17. Fawcett, T. and Provost, F., Combining data mining and machine learning for effective user profile, in *Proceedings of the 2nd International Conference on Knowledge Discovery and Data Mining*, Evangelos Simoudis, Jiawei Han, and Usama Fayyad, Eds. AAAI Press, Menlo Park, CA, 1996, p. 8.

18. Kubat, M., Holte, R., and Matwin, S., Machine learning for the detection of oil spills in satellite radar images, *Machine Learning*, 30, 195, 1998.

19. Lowe, D. and Webb, A.R., Optimised feature extraction and the bayes decision in feed-forward classifier networks, *IEEE Transactions on Pattern Analysis and Machine Intelligence*, 13, 355, 1991.

20. Dos Remedios, L.V., Weber, P.M., Feldman, R., Schurr, D.A., and Tsoi, T.G., Detecting unsuspected thyroid dysfunction by the free thyroxin index, *Archives of Internal Medicine*, 140, 1045, 1980.

21. White, G.H. and Walmsley, R.N., Can the initial assessment of thyroid function be improved?, *Lancet*, 2, 933, 1978.

22. Bahemuka, M. and Hodkinson, H.M., Screening for hypothyroidism in elderly inpatients, *British Medical Journal*, 2, 601, 1975.

23. Fukazawa, H., Sakurada, T., and Yoshida, K., Free thyroxine estimation for the screening of hyper- and hypothyroidism in an adult population, *Tohoku Journal of Experimental Medicine*, 148, 411, 1986.

24. Gavin, L.A., The diagnostic dilemmas of hyperthyroxinemia and hypothyroxin-emia, *Advances in Internal Medicine*, 33, 185, 1988.

25. Wong, E.T. and Steffes, M.W., A fundamental approach to the diagnosis of diseases of the thyroid gland, *Clinical Laboratory Medicine*, 4, 655, 1984.

26. Nolan, J.P., Tarsa, N.J., and Dibenedetto, G., Case-finding for unsuspected thyroid disease: costs and health benefits, *American Journal of Clinical Pathology*, 83, 346, 1985.

27. Tunbridge, W.M., Brewis, M., and French, J.M., The spectrum of thyroid disease in a community: The Wickham Survey, *Clinical Endocrinology*, 7, 481, 1977.

28. Riedmiller, M. and Braun, H., A direct adaptive method for faster backpropagation learning: The Rprop algorithm, in *Proceedings of the International Conference on Neural Networks*, San Francisco, CA, 1993.

*Chapter 4*

# Data Cleansing with Independent Component Analysis

Guangyin Zeng and Mark J. Embrechts

## Contents

# 4.1  Introduction

An important problem in machine learning fields is to find a suitable representation of multivariate data. For example, in multivariate linear regression (MLR), the goal is to find some latent variables underlying the datasets. For reasons of computational and conceptual simplicity, the representation is often sought as a linear transformation of the original data. That is, each component of the representation is assumed to be a linear mixture of the original components. Well-known linear transformation methods include Multivariate Linear Regression (MLR) [1], Partial Least Squares (PLS) [2, 3], Principal Component Analysis (PCA) [1, 4], and factor analysis [5]. Independent Component Analysis (ICA) [6] is a recently developed method in which the goal is to find a linear or nonlinear representation of non-Gaussian data so that the components are statistically as independent as possible. ICA has gained wide attention since the mid-1990s and has been applied to many fields such as signal processing, image denoising, financial market data mining, telecommunication, etc.

This chapter first introduces some basic concepts and algorithms of ICA, and then focuses on the use of ICA for data cleansing, including data filtering and data preprocessing.

## 4.1.1  Blind Source Separation (BSS)

Now take a look at a signal processing problem. Assume that two people are speaking simultaneously in a room. There are two microphones located in two different locations. The two microphones record time signals denoted by $x_1(t)$ and $x_2(t)$, with $x_1$ and $x_2$ being the amplitudes and $t$ the time index. Each of these recorded signals is a weighted sum of the speech signals emitted by the two speakers, denoted by

$s_1(t)$ and $s_1(t)$. One can express this in Equation (4.1):

$$x_1(t) = a_{11}s_1(t) + a_{12}s_2(t)$$
$$x_2(t) = a_{21}s_1(t) + a_{22}s_2(t)$$

(4.1)

where $a_{11}$, $a_{12}$, $a_{21}$, $a_{22}$ are coefficients that depend on the distances of the microphones from the speakers.

The problem is to estimate the two original speech signals $s_1(t)$ and $s_2(t)$ using only the observed signals $x_1(t)$ and $x_2(t)$. This is called the cocktail-party problem, or Blind Source Separation (BSS) problem [7]. "Blind" means that one knows little or nothing about the source.

In general, one concentrates on the problem of modeling continuous-valued multivariate systems. Let us denote $X$ as the observed signal, which is an $n$-dimensional random vector variable; then the problem is to find the $m$-dimensional source $S$ defined by:

$$S = f(X)$$

(4.2)

The transform $f(:)$ will have some desirable properties, such as independence between sources $s_1(i = 1, 2, \ldots m)$, or minimizing the square errors. In most cases, the transform is assumed to be a linear transform. So the problem becomes to find a transform matrix $W$ that satisfies:

$$S = WX$$

(4.3)

where $S \in R^{m \times T}, W \in R^{m \times n}, X \in R^{n \times T}$. One assumes that there are $n$ observed signals and $m$ sources. Each row in the data matrix $X$ and $S$ is one signal. Each signal has $T$ data samples.

This problem is not easy because all one knows is only the observed signal $X$. One must estimate both the transform matrix $W$ and the source $S$.

Several methods have been developed to solve the above BSS problem. The most popular methods are second-order methods, such as Principle Component Analysis (PCA) and factor analysis. Second-order methods only use information contained in the covariance matrix of the data matrix $X$. The use of second order is based on the assumption that $X$ has a normal or Gaussian distribution. Then the distribution information is entirely captured by the second-order moment. But this is not usually true in practice. For example, recorded speech signals usually do not have Gaussian distributions. So second order methods such as PCA can only find uncorrelated components that are not independent components from mixtures.

Since the mid-1990s, a method for finding the linear transformation called Independent Component Analysis (ICA) has gained a lot of attention. ICA tries to find a transformation in which separated components are statistically as independent from each other as possible. ICA could be applied to blind source separation, noise filtering, feature extraction, and many other promising areas.

### 4.1.2 Independent Component Analysis

The goal of the BSS problem is to find a linear representation in which the components are independent. But second-order methods such as PCA can only find independent components up to the second order. In general, one cannot find really independent components. However, one can find components that are statistically as independent as possible. This leads to the following definition of ICA.

Assume that one has observed $n$ variables $x_1, x_2, \ldots x_n$, which are linear mixtures of $m$ independent sources $s_1, s_2, \ldots s_m$:

$$x_j = a_{j1}s_1 + a_{j2}s_2 + \cdots a_{jm}s_m, \quad \text{for } j = 1, 2, \ldots n \tag{4.4}$$

Here one assumes that the number of independent components is less than the number of observed mixtures, that is, $m \leq n$. Because one can always reduce the number of mixtures by a dimension reduction method such as Principle Component Analysis (PCA), one assumes that $m = n$ in the following analysis.

Using matrix notations, the above mixing model can be written as:

$$X = AS \tag{4.5}$$

where $S \in R^{m \times T}, A \in R^{n \times m}, X \in R^{n \times T}$ ($m \leq n$). Without loss of generality, one can assume that both the observations and the sources have zero mean. If this is not true, the observable variables $x_j$ can be centered by subtracting its mean. Sources will also be centered, as can be seen by taking expectations of both sides in Equation (4.5).

The statistical model in Equation (4.5) is called an Independent Component Analysis (ICA) model. The goal is to find the transform matrix $A$ and source $S$ based only on $X$ in which sources $s_i$'s are as independent as possible.

It is interesting that one can estimate the independent components from the mixtures based on no more assumptions but independence between sources. And independence is the only *priori* known about the source. Then the question becomes: How does one measure independence and use this to estimate the sources? In statistics, two random variables are independent if and only if any transform of the two random variables is uncorrelated. However, this is not a practical method to measure the independence, as one cannot enumerate all transformations. However, nongaussianity can be used to measure independence based on the Central Limit Theorem (explained later). So, by using nongaussianity, one can convert the BSS problem to an optimization problem. Optimization techniques such as the gradient descent method can be used to solve it. And thus one gets back the independent components.

### 4.1.3 History of ICA

The concept and technique of ICA was first introduced in the early 1980s by Hérault, Jutten, and Ans [8, 9]. They used nonlinear decorrelation to solve the blind source separation problem. ICA was mostly explored and used by French researchers at that time. In the first international workshop on higher-order spectral analysis in 1989, early papers on ICA were presented by Comon [11].

ICA gained wider attention after Bell and Sejnowski published their approach based on the infomax principle in the mid-1990s [12]. S. Amari and A. Cichocki proposed another algorithm by minimization of mutual information principle in 1996 [13]. After that, Hyvärinen and Oja presented the fast fixed point ICA algorithm [14–16], which is very efficient and can be applied to large-scale problems.

Since the mid-1990s, more and more researchers have joined in this field. The first international workshop on ICA was held in Aussois, France, in January 1999. The 6th International Conference on Independent Component Analysis and Blind Source Separation was held in Florida on March 2006. Interested readers can refer to http://www.cnel.ufl.edu/ica2006/ for details.

# 4.2 ICA Algorithms

This section discusses some basic concepts of ICA and the fast fixed point ICA algorithm. The discussion begins with how to measure independence, followed by presenting restrictions and ambiguities of ICA, preprocessing steps for ICA, and the fast fixed point ICA algorithm.

## 4.2.1 Criterion for Independence

The key to estimating independent components is nongaussianity. This is probably the main reason for the rather late emergence of the ICA algorithm. Most classical statistical theories assume random variables to have a Gaussian distribution, precluding any similar methods related to ICA. In practice, however, lots of variables do not have Gaussian distributions.

The Central Limit Theorem (CLT), a classical result in probability theory and statistics, states that if the sum of a number of independent random variables has a finite variance, then it will be approximately normally distributed. Thus, a sum of two independent random variables usually has a distribution that is closer to Gaussian than either of the two original random variables. This is shown in Figure 4.1. The two left figures are distributions of two independent random variables. The right figure is the distribution of the sum of the left two variables. It is clear that the distribution on the right is more like a Gaussian distribution than the two variables on the left.

Now go back to the ICA model in Equation (4.5). For simplicity, assume that all the independent components have identical distributions and the number of independent components is equal to the number of observed signals. Because sources are linear mixtures of observations $x_j$'s, consider a linear combination of $x_j$'s as one estimated independent component and denote it by:

$$\hat{s}_i = w_i^T X = w_i^T A S \tag{4.6}$$

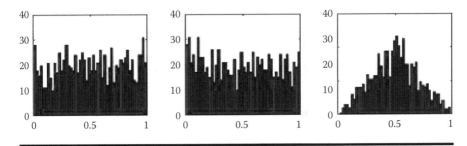

**Figure 4.1    CLT Demonstration: the two left figures are distributions of two random variables, and the right figure is the distribution of the sum of the left two random variables.**

where $w_i$ is a column vector to be determined. From Equation (4.6), one can see that if $w_i^T A$ has only one nonzero element, $\hat{s}_i$ will actually equal one of the independent components $s_i$. The question now becomes: How can one use the Central Limit Theorem to determine $w_i$ so that $w_i^T A$ becomes a base vector with only one nonzero element?

From Equation (4.6) one can see that $\hat{s}_i$ is a linear combination of $s_i$'s with weights given by $w_i^T A$. Because a sum of independent random variables is more Gaussian than any of the original variables, $\hat{s}_i$ is more Gaussian than any of the $s_i$'s and becomes least Gaussian when it in fact equals one of the $s_i$'s. In this case, only one element of the vector $w_i^T A$ is nonzero. Therefore, one could take $w_i$, a vector that maximizes the nongaussianity of $w_i^T A$. Such a vector would give a vector $w_i^T A$, which has only one nonzero component. And so one gets back to one of the independent components.

To estimate multiple independent components, one can do the same procedures several times. To avoid the algorithm to converge to the same optima, one can use deflation techniques, which are explained later.

## 4.2.2   Measures of Nongaussianity

As discussed above, one can obtain independent components by optimizing the nongaussianity of a sum of observations. Now the problem becomes how to measure quantitatively the nongaussianity of a random variable. Usually, one uses the fourth-order cumulant kurtosis or entropy metrics to measure the nongaussianity.

### 4.2.2.1   Kurtosis

The classical measure of nongaussianity is kurtosis, or the fourth-order moment. It is discussed in many books (e.g., [17]). The kurtosis of a random variable $y$ is defined by:

$$kurt(y) = E[y^4] - 3(E[y^2])^2 \qquad (4.7)$$

Here, one assumes that $y$ has a zero mean. The kurtosis of a Gaussian distributed random variable is 0. For most (but not all) nongaussian random variables, kurtosis is nonzero. Distributions having a negative kurtosis are said to be *subgaussian* (e.g., the uniform distribution). Distributions with a positive kurtosis are called *supergaussian* (e.g., the widely used *Laplacian* distribution or double exponential distribution).

One employs the absolute value of kurtosis to measure nongaussianity. The measure is zero for a Gaussian variable and greater than zero for most of nongaussian random variables. Kurtosis is widely used as a measure of nongaussianity because of its computational and theoretical simplicity. The drawback is that kurtosis is very sensitive to outliers. The value of kurtosis can depend on only a few observations in the tails of the distribution, which in most of cases are irrelevant observations. Next, one can introduce a more robust measure of nongaussianity, that of negentropy.

### 4.2.2.2  Negentropy

Negentropy [14] is based on the information theoretic quantity of differential entropy. Entropy is the basic concept of information theory. The entropy of a random variable can be interpreted as the degree of information that the observation of the variable gives. The more "random" — that is, unpredictable and unstructured — the variable is, the larger its entropy. For details on information theory, see [17–19].

The differential entropy of a random variable $y$ with probability density function $f(y)$ is defined as [20]:

$$H(y) = -\int f(y)\log(f(y))dy \qquad (4.8)$$

A fundamental theroem in information theory states that a Gaussian variable has the largest entropy among all random variables of equal variance defined in the range $[-\infty + \infty]$. So one could use entropy to measure the nongaussianity. One can define the negentropy of a random variable $y$ as:

$$J(y) = H(y_{gauss}) - H(y) \qquad (4.9)$$

where $y_{gauss}$ is a Gaussian random variable of the same mean and variance as $y$.

Because a Gaussian variable has the largest entropy among random variables having the same variance, negentropy is always non-negative. It is zero if and only if $y$ has a Gaussian distribution. Notice that kurtosis does not have this property; there are still some nongaussian random variables whose kurtosis is zero.

The reason for using negentropy or information theory to measure nongaussianity is that information theory measures information of a random variable directly and thus captures the fundamental structure of the variable. Negentropy is in some sense the optimal estimator for nongaussianity. The problem in using negentropy is that its computational cost is very high. Estimating negentropy using the definition would require an estimate (possibly nonparametric) of the probability density function (pdf), which requires numerous calculations. Therefore, simpler approximations of negentropy are very useful.

Hyvärinen [14] obtained an approximation of negentropy as shown in the following equation:

$$J(y) = \frac{1}{12}E(y^3)^2 + \frac{1}{48}kurt(y)^2 \tag{4.10}$$

In Equation (4.10), the first term on the right-hand side is zero if the distribution of the random variable is symmetric. Thus, the negentropy becomes equivalent to the square of the kurtosis. Thus algorithms based on this approximation will suffer from the same problem of nonrobustness with kurtosis. To resolve this problem, a more sophisticated and robust estimator has been made in Equation (4.11):

$$J(y) \propto [E\{G(y)\} - E\{G(v)\}]^2 \tag{4.11}$$

where $G(y)$ is a nonquadratic function and $V$ is a standard Gaussian variable. By choosing function $G$ wisely, one can obtain better approximations of negentropy. The following two functions have proved very useful:

$$G_1(y) = \frac{1}{a}\log(\cosh(ay)), G_2(y) = -\exp(-y^2/2) \tag{4.12}$$

where $a$ is a positive number within the range $1 < a < 2$. These approximations do not require estimates of pdf and thus are easier to calculate. For details of these approximations, refer to [21, 22].

### 4.2.3 Restrictions and Ambiguities of ICA

For the ICA model in Equation (4.5), it is easy to see that the following restrictions and ambiguities will hold:

1. There is, at most, one independent component that has a Gaussian distribution. This is because the sum of any two Gaussian distributed random variables still has a Gaussian distribution. So the optimization of nongaussianity makes no sense at all. This assumption holds in most of practical cases. For example, images data usually are sparse and have supergaussian distributions.

2. One cannot determine the amplitudes of the independent components. The reason is that both $S$ and $A$ are unknown; any scalar multiplier in one of the sources $s_i$ could always be cancelled by dividing the corresponding column of $A$ by the same number. As a consequence, one can assume that the weight vectors have unit 2-norm.
3. There is also a sign ambiguity for separated signals. One could multiply an independent component and the corresponding column vector of the mixing matrix $A$ by −1 without affecting the model. This ambiguity is, fortunately, insignificant in most applications.
4. One cannot determine the order of independent components. The reason is that both $S$ and $A$ are unknown, and the only assumption for the ICA model is the independence between components. One can freely change the order of the components, and call any of the independent components the first one.

## 4.2.4  Preprocessing Steps for ICA

For the ICA model in Equation (4.5), the goal is to search for $m$ weight vectors $w_i^T$ that give $m$ independent components by $s_i = w_i^T X$ (*for I* = 1, 2, …, *m*). Because one can always reduce the number of observations to the number of independent components, one can also assume that $n = m$ in the following analysis. The optimization of nongaussianity in $n$-dimensional space of vectors $w_i^T$ gives $2n$ local maxima corresponding to $s_i$ and $-s_i$, respectively. To find multiple independent components, one must find all these local maxima. This can be done by the gradient descent method. Independent components are estimated one by one to reduce computational costs and make the search algorithm simpler. To avoid the search converging to the same local maxima, one can constrain the search to an orthogonalized space that gives estimates uncorrelated with the previous ones. So before applying optimization techniques on the nongaussianity, one should run some preprocessing techniques, including centering and whitening.

### 4.2.4.1  Centering

From the beginning of this chapter, it is assumed that the observations have zero-mean. So the first and necessary preprocessing is to center the observations $x_j$'s, that is, subtract the mean $E\{x_j\}$ from $x_j$ (*for j* = 1, 2, …, *n*). This implies that $S$ is also centered, as can be seen by taking expectations on both sides of Equation (4.5).

### 4.2.4.2  Whitening

After centering, another useful preprocessing strategy called whitening is used to whiten the observed variables. The number of independent components is usually less than the number of observed signals, thus introducing redundancies in the original dataset. By whitening, one can transform the observed signals $X$, which is in $n$-dimensional space, into another $m$-dimensional space in which components are uncorrelated and have unit variances.

One popular method for whitening is to use the eigen-value decomposition (EVD) of the covariance matrix of data matrix $X$. One first calculates the eigen-values and discards those that are too small, as is often done in the statistical technique of Principal Component Analysis. $X$ is whitened by applying the transformation:

$$Y = VX \tag{4.13}$$

where $V$ is the whitening matrix, $X$ is the original signals, and $Y$ is the whitened signals. $V \in R^{m \times n}, X \in R^{n \times T}, Y \in R^{m \times T}$. The whitening matrix $V$ is given by:

$$V = D^{-1/2}E^{T} \tag{4.14}$$

where $D = diag(\lambda_1, \lambda_2, \dots \lambda_m) \in R^{m \times m}$, $E = [c_1, c_2, \dots c_m] \in R^{n \times m}$, with $\lambda_i$ the $i$-$th$-largest eigenvalue of the covariance matrix $C = E\{XX^{T}\} \in R^{n \times n}$, and $c_i$ the associated eigenvector corresponding to $\lambda_i$.

The above whitening often has the effect of reducing noise because the eigenvalues of noise components are usually smaller than those of normal signals, given that the signal-to-noise ratio is large enough.

Whitening is not necessary for all ICA algorithms. For example, there is no whitening in Haykin's ICA algorithm [23]. Haykin's ICA algorithm searches all the weight vectors at the same time and does not require orthogonalization of the weight vectors. However, in the popular fast fixed point ICA algorithm, whitening must be run to restrict the search of weight vector $W$ in an orthogonal space.

## 4.2.5 Fast Fixed Point ICA Algorithm

Several different ICA algorithms have been proposed using different measures and approximations of independence or nongaussianity; for example, Hyvärinen [14], Haykin [23], and Ham [24]. Most of these algorithms employ the gradient descent method for optimization. This section introduces a very efficient method called fast fixed point ICA, as proposed by Hyvärinen in 1997 [14].

### 4.2.5.1 Fast ICA for One Component

In the ICA model, the weight matrix $W \in R^{n \times n}$ has $n^2$ parameters. It would be very complicated to find all these parameters at the same time. To reduce the computational costs, one can try to find independent components one by one — that is, to find weight vector $w_i^T$ ($i = 1, 2, \dots n$), which only has $n$ parameters, one by one. This will greatly improve the algorithm efficiency and make ICA algorithms feasible to large-scale problems.

**Table 4.1   FastICA Algorithm for One Component**

1. Center the data;
2. Whiten the data;
3. Choose an initial (e.g., random) weight vector W;
4. Update weight: $\hat{W} = E(Xg(W'X)) - E(g'(W'X))W$
5. Normalize weight: $W = \hat{W}/\|\hat{W}\|$
6. If not converged, go back to Step 4,

where g() is a nonquadratic function, e.g., $g_1(x) = \tanh(a_1 x), g_2(x) = y\exp(-y^2/2)$.

By applying the gradient descent method on the negentropy approximated by Equation (4.11), the FastICA algorithm is derived as shown in Table 4.1. For details of the derivation of the FastICA algorithm, refer to [14–16, 21].

## 4.2.5.2   Estimating Several Independent Components

To estimate several independent components, one needs to run the one-unit Fast ICA algorithm several times. The key to extending the FastICA to estimate more than one independent component is based on the following property: The vectors $w_i$ corresponding to different independent components are orthogonal in the whitened space. Thus, one needs to orthogonalize the vectors $w_1, w_2, w_n$ after each iteration. And by this, one can prevent the weight vectors from converging to the same maxima.

A simple way of achieving orthogonalization is deflationary orthogonalization based on Gram-Schmidt decorrelation. This means that one estimates the independent components one by one. After estimating $p$ independent components, or $p$ vectors $w_1, w_2, w_p$, one runs the one-unit, fast fixed point ICA algorithm for $w_{p+1}$, and after every iteration step, subtract from $w_{p+1}$, the projections of the previously estimated $p$ vectors, as shown in Table 4.2.

The deflation steps can be inserted after step 5 in the FastICA algorithm in Table 4.1. Using the revised algorithm, one can estimate more independent components. A Matlab code of the FastICA is available online at http://www.cis.hut.fi/projects/ica/fastica/.

**Table 4.2   Deflation Steps for FastICA**

1. Let $W_{p+1} = W_{p+1} - \sum_{j=1}^{p} W_{p+1}{}^T W_j W_j$

2. Let $W_{p+1} = W_{p+1}/\|W_{p+1}\|$

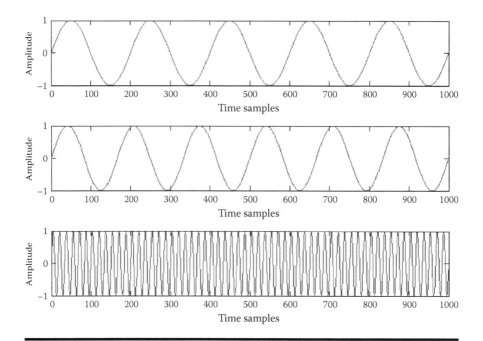

**Figure 4.2   Three original sinusoidal source signals.**

## 4.2.6   An Example

### 4.2.6.1   Example 1

Shown here is a simple example involving the separation of three sinusoidal signals with frequencies $f_1 = 500Hz$, $f_2 = 600Hz$, and $f_3 = 6000Hz$. They are sampled at $f_c = 100kHz$ with 1000 sample points. The original signals are shown in Figure 4.2.

In this example, we will use the same mixing coefficients in [24–25], but applying them to different sinusoidal signals. The mixing matrix is:

$$A = \begin{bmatrix} 0.0891 & 0.3906 & -0.3408 \\ -0.8909 & -0.6509 & 0.8519 \\ 0.4454 & 0.6509 & -0.3976 \end{bmatrix} \qquad (4.15)$$

Now one can apply ICA algorithms to separate the observed mixtures shown in Figure 4.3. First the signals are centered and whitened. In this example, no dimension reduction is needed; one assumes that the number of independent components is equal to the number of mixtures (i.e., 3). Now one can apply the fast

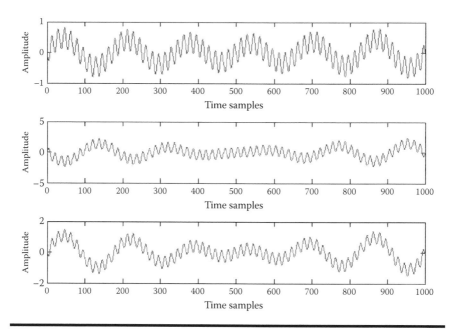

**Figure 4.3**  **Observed mixtures of the original three sinusoidal signals.**

fixed point ICA presented in the previous section and obtain an estimation of $A$ given by:

$$\hat{A} = \begin{bmatrix} 0.0891 & -0.3407 & -0.3905 \\ -0.8908 & 0.8518 & 0.6508 \\ 0.4453 & -0.3975 & -0.6508 \end{bmatrix} \qquad (4.16)$$

Looking at the results, one sees that the estimation of $A$ is nearly the same as $A$. The absolute error for each element in the matrix is only 0.0001. The estimated sources are nearly the same as the original sources. The estimated sources are shown in Figure 4.4.

Note that the order of the estimated source signals differs from that of the original signals (the third signal switch with the second signal), which corresponds to the change of the order of column vectors in A and $\hat{A}$. Also note that there is a sign change for the second signal. These are ambiguities associated with ICA.

## 4.3  Data Cleansing with ICA

Data cleansing is the act of detecting and correcting (or removing) corrupt or inaccurate records from a record set. Practical datasets are very complicated datasets and are usually corrupted by noise. It is very important to clean these datasets for

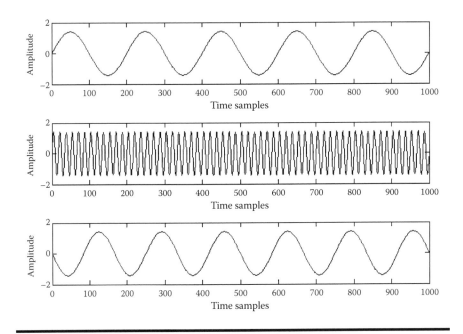

**Figure 4.4 Estimated sinusoidal signals using FastICA.**

later use. This section discusses the use of ICA for data cleansing in two different ways: (1) data filtering and (2) data preprocessing.

### 4.3.1 Data Filtering with ICA

In practice, many signals are mixtures of some independent components. One may need to filter out some of these underlying independent components, such as the noise component, and the high frequency component. Because one can estimate all these components, one can simply filter out any one of them, as discussed in the following.

Consider the ICA model in Equation (4.3) and Equation (4.5). Denote the weight matrix $W = [w_1, w_2, \ldots w_n]^T \in R^{n \times n}, w_i \in R^{1 \times n}$, and sources $\hat{S} = [\hat{s}_1, \hat{s}_2, \ldots \hat{s}_n]^T \in R^{n \times T}, \hat{s}_i \in R^{1 \times T}$. Then recover the observed signal $X$ by taking a pseudo inverse:

$$\hat{X} = (W^T W)^{-1} W^T \hat{S} \tag{4.17}$$

Then one can filter out any component $\hat{s}_i$ out by setting the corresponding weight vector $w_i$ to 0 as seen by:

$$\hat{X} = (W^T W)^{-1} W^T \hat{S}$$

$$= (W^T W)^{-1} \left( w_1^T s_1 + w_1^T s_1 + \cdots w_n^T s_n \right) \tag{4.18}$$

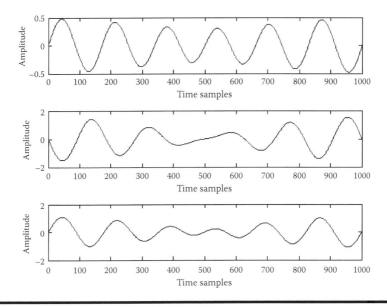

**Figure 4.5   Recovered mixtures with high frequency components filtered out.**

If $w_i$ is set to 0, then the effect of source $\hat{s}_i$ is eliminated in the recovered mixtures $\hat{X}$. And then one obtains the cleaned signals (e.g., signals with high frequency and noise components filtered out). It is also clear that one can filter out more than one component at the same time by setting several weight vectors to zero.

### 4.3.1.1   Example 2

Now return to Example 1 in the previous section. In looking at the separated components, one knows that the second component is a high-frequency component. Set the second row of the weight matrix to 0 and obtain the recovered signals as shown in Figure 4.5.

Compared with the original signals in Figure 4.3, it is clear that the high frequency components are successfully removed. Note that the second recovered signal looks different from the original mixture because of different scales.

Usually, noise components have high frequency. By looking at the graph, one can clearly identify the noise component and remove it from the signals.

## 4.3.2   Data Preprocessing with ICA

Another use of ICA for data cleansing is to use it as a preprocessing tool. In machine learning fields, PCA is widely used as a preprocessing tool. This sections shows that ICA is a better preprocessing method than PCA. In fact, ICA can be treated as a nonlinear PCA [26].

The ICA model is a statistical latent variables model as are many other models (such as PCA, PLS, MLR, etc.). The ICA model describes the essential structure of the datasets. It represents the dataset with a set of independent components. In contrast, PCA represents the dataset with a set of principal components. These principal components may be correlated and thus cannot give us a simple and discrete representation of the dataset.

Consider a regression problem. Assume that there are $n$ sample data points, and each data point has $m$ features and one response. The goal is to predict the response based on the features, which may be highly correlated.

One can always assume that each feature is a linear mixture of some underlying independent components. Before applying regression methods on the dataset directly, one can treat each feature as a random variable and apply ICA algorithms on them. After the ICA transform, one obtains $l$ "independent features" out of the $m$ original features ($l \leq m$). Then one applies regression methods on the transformed dataset and, in general, obtains better predictions.

### 4.3.2.1  Example 3

Now consider the Boston Housing problem. The Boston Housing dataset is available online at ftp://ftp.ics.uci.edu/pub/machine-learning-databases/housing/. The dataset was taken from the StatLib library, which is maintained at Carnegie Mellon University. It has 506 instances. Each instance has 13 numerical features and 1 response. These 13 features describe the situation of the house, such as the crime rate, tax rate, environment, etc. The response is the median value of the house.

We use Kernel Partial Least Squares (KPLS) as the regression method. The contrast experiment compares the results got by KPLS with and without ICA transform (called the ICA + KPLS method). We set the number of latent variables to five and use the Gaussian function with $\sigma = 5$ as the kernel function. The metrics used to assess the performance are q2, Q2, and RMSE as defined in the following:

$$q^2 = 1 - \left( \frac{\sum_{i=1}^{n}(\hat{y}_i - \bar{\hat{y}})(y_i - \bar{y})}{\sqrt{\sum_{i=1}^{n}(\hat{y}_i - \bar{\hat{y}})^2}\sqrt{\sum_{i=1}^{n}(y_i - \bar{y})^2}} \right)^2 \tag{4.19}$$

$$Q^2 = \frac{\sum_{i=1}^{n}(y_i - \hat{y}_i)^2}{\sum_{i=1}^{n}(y_i - \langle y \rangle)^2} \tag{4.20}$$

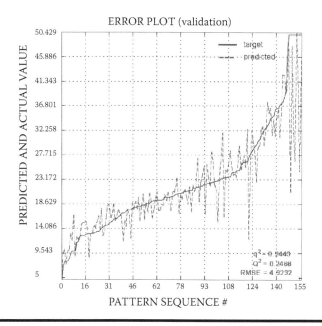

**Figure 4.6**   **Error plot for KPLS (# latent variables = 5, $\sigma = 5$).**

$$RMSE = \sqrt{\frac{1}{n} \sum_{i=1}^{n} (y_i - \hat{y}_i)^2} \qquad (4.21)$$

where $y_i$ is the actual response of the validation or training set, and $\hat{y}_i$ is the predicted response. It is clear that the smaller these metrics, the better the performance.

In the ICA + KPLS model, we set the number of independent components equal to the number of features (i.e., 13). The error plots for the KPLS model and the ICA + KPLS model are shown in Figure 4.6 and Figure 4.7, respectively.

These two methods perform similarly because they are both using KPLS with the same set of parameters. But the ICA + KPLS method performs better than the KPLS method with smaller q2, Q2, and RMSE as shown in the two figures. Note that in these two figures, data points have been sorted again with respect to the value of response to give a better view.

### 4.3.3   Some Practical Considerations

#### 4.3.3.1   How Many Independent Components Must Be Estimated?

One problem that often arises is to determine the number of ICs. Because dimension reduction or data compression by PCA is often needed, one must determine

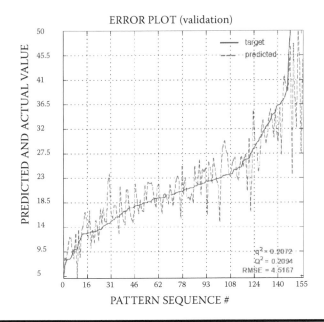

**Figure 4.7** **Error plot for ICA + KPLS model (# ICs = 13, # latent variables = 5, $\sigma = 5$).**

the number of principal components, which is the same as the number of ICs in the FastICA algorithm. By setting different numbers of ICs, one can achieve significantly different results [28]. The problem is usually solved by choosing the minimal number of principal components that explain the dataset well enough; for example, taking principal components such that the sum of selected eigenvalues account for 95 percent of the sum of all eigenvalues.

There are no general guidelines for choosing the number of principal components and the number of ICs. One method is to try different numbers of ICs from smaller to bigger and compare the results.

Another way to get the number of ICs is to use *priori* knowledge. For example, in the speech signals separation problem illustrated in Section 4.1, one knows that there are two people speaking and thus the number of ICs is set to 2. However, this is not true for most of cases.

Other methods such as use of information metrics and the Bayesian approach for determining the numbers of ICs are discussed in detail in [29, 30].

### 4.3.3.2 Which Component Must Be Filtered Out?

Another problem is to determine which component should be filtered out. Unlike PCA, no component is the first or last component in ICA. In most of cases, one aims at filtering out the noise component. If the components are time signals or images, one can figure out the noise component by looking at the plots of all the components. However, if the signals are not time signals or images and cannot be viewed directly, one needs some other metrics (e.g., entropy and mutual information). Note that noise has the maximal entropy among all random variables; one can filter out those components that have larger entropy compared to others. The drawback of using entropy is that it is not robust. Some structured signals, such as sinusoidal signals, have high entropy as well as noise.

There are no general guidelines for determining the components to filter out. Trial and error may be the only method applicable.

## 4.4  Conclusions

This chapter introduced the framework of Independent Component Analysis (ICA). ICA is a recently developed method for finding independent components underlying the dataset. It originated from the Blind Source Separation problem and has been widely applied to many fields.

Based on the optimization of nongaussianity, one can estimate independent components one by one. The data is often centered and whitened first. By whitening, one restricts the search of weight vector to an orthogonal space, which makes the estimation of ICs one by one possible and greatly simplifies the optimization problem.

Several ICA algorithms have been addressed in the literature. In addition to the fast fixed point ICA algorithm introduced in this chapter, Gaeta has proposed the use of maximum likelihood estimation for ICA [31]; Comon discussed the estimation of ICs by minimization of mutual information [32]; Bell and Sejnowski published their approach based on the infomax principle [12]; and Hérault, Jutten, and Ans addressed the use of nonlinear decorrelation criteria for ICA [8, 9]. These ICA methods are connected in essence. For details of the connection between these methods, refer to [31–36]; a good review appears in [37].

This chapter introduced the fast fixed point ICA algorithm and focused on the use of ICA for data cleansing, including data filtering and preprocessing. ICA proves very useful in this field. It can be used for high frequency and noise component filtering, and data preprocessing for machine learning.

ICA can be treated as a nonlinear PCA. It captures the essential structure of the dataset. In some sense, the ICA estimation is the optimal estimator for latent variables underlying the dataset.

The ICA model was a linear model when it was first introduced. The standard linear ICA model has been extended to the nonlinear case in [38–40]. Currently, a method called independent subspace analysis (ISA) has gained significant interest. In ISA, the components are divided into subspaces. Components in different subspaces are assumed independent, while components in the same subspace can be dependent. For details, refer to [41–43].

# References

1. T. Anderson. *An Introduction to Multivariate Statistical Analysis*. John Wiley & Sons, New York, 1958.
2. H. Wold. Path models with latent variables: the NIPALS approach. *Quantitative Sociology: International Perspectives on Mathematical and Statistical Model Building*. Academic Press, New York, 1975.
3. S. Wold, M. Sjöström, and L. Eriksson. PLS-regression: a basic tool of chemometrics, *Chemometrics and Intelligent Laboratory Systems*, 58:109–130, 2001.
4. Pearson, K. Principal components analysis, *The London, Edinburgh, and Dublin Philosophical Magazine and Journal of Science*, 6(2):559, 1901.
5. H. Harman. *Modern Factor Analysis, 2nd edition*. University of Chicago Press, 1967.
6. A. Hyvärinen and E. Oja. A fast fixed point algorithm for independent component analysis, *Neural Computation*, 9(7):1483–1492, 1997.
7. G. Burel. Blind separation of sources: a non-linear neural algorithm, *Neural Networks*, 5:937–947, 1992.
8. J. Hérault and B. Ans. Circuits neuronaux à synapses modifiables: décodage de messages composites par apprentissage non supervisé, *C.-R. de l'Académie des Sciences*, 299(III-13):525–528, 1984.
9. B. Ans, J. Hérault, and C. Jutten. Apdaptive neural architectures: detection of primitives. In *Proceedings of COGNITIVA '85*, Paris, France, 1985, pp. 593–597.
10. J.-F. Cardoso. Blind signals separation: statistical principles. In *Proceedings of the IEEE* 9:2009–2025, 1998.
11. P. Comon. Separation of stochastic processes. In *Proceedings of Workshop on Higher Order Spectral Analysis*, Vail, CO, 1989, pp. 174–179.
12. A. Bell and T. Sejnowski. An information-maximization approach to blind separation and blind deconvolution, *Neural Computation*, 7:1129–1159, 1995.
13. S.-I. Amari, S.C. Douglas, A. Cichocki, and H. Yang. A new learning algorithm for blind source separation. In *Advances in Neural Information Processing Systems 8*, MIT Press, 1996, pp. 757–763.
14. A. Hyvärinen and E. Oja. A fast fixed point algorithm for independent component analysis, *Neural Computation*, 9(7):1483–1492, 1997.
15. A. Hyvärinen. Fast and robust fixed-point algorithms for independent component analysis, *IEEE Transactions on Neural Networks*, 10(3):626–634, 1999.
16. A. Hyvärinen and E. Oja. Independent Component Analysis: algorithms and applications, *Neural Networks*, 13(4-5):411–430, 2000.
17. A. Papoulis. *Probability, Random Variables, and Stochastic Processes, 3rd edition*. McGraw-Hill, 1991.
18. T. Cover and J. Thomas. *Elements of Information Theory*. John Wiley & Sons, New York, 1991.
19. J.C. Principe and D. Xu. An introduction to information theoretic learning. In *Proceedings of IJCNN '99*, Washington, D.C., 1999, pp. 1783–1787.
20. C. Shannon and W. Weaver. *The Mathematical Theory of Communication*. University of Illinois Press, 1949.

21. A. Hyvärinen. *Independent Component Analysis*. John Wiley & Sons, New York, 2001.
22. A. Hyvärinen. New approximations of differential entropy for independent component analysis and projection pursuit. In *Advances in Neural Information Processing Systems*, Vol. 10, MIT Press, 1998, pp. 273–279.
23. S. Haykin. *Neural Networks — A Comprehensive Foundation, 2nd edition*. Prentice Hall, Englewood Cliffs, NJ, 1998.
24. F.M. Ham and I. Kostanic. *Principles of Neurocomputing for Science & Engineering*. McGraw-Hill, 2001.
25. J. Karhunen, E. Oja, L. Wang, et al. A class of neural networks for Independent Component Analysis, *IEEE Transactions on Neural Networks*, 8:486–504, 1997.
26. E. Oja. The nonlinear PCA learning rule in independent component analysis, *Neurocomputing*, 17:25–45, 1997.
27. K.E. Hild II, D. Erdogmus, and J. Principe, Blind source separation using Renyi's mutual information, *IEEE Signal Processing Letters*, 8(6):174–176, 2001.
28. A. Hyvärinen, J. Särelä, and R. Vigário. Spikes and bumps: artefacts generated by indepdendent component analysis with insufficient sample size. In *Proceedings of International Workshop on Independent Component Analysis and Signal Separation (ICA '99)*, Aussois, France, 1999, 425–429.
29. A. Cichocki, J. Karhunen, W. Kasprzak, and R. Vigário. Neural networks for blind separation with unknown number of sources, *Neurocomputing*, 24:55–93, 1999.
30. S. Roberts. Independent component analysis: source assessment and separation, a Bayesian approach, *IEEE Proceedings — Vision, Image & Signal Processing*, 145:149–154, 1998.
31. M. Gaeta and J. Lacoume. Source separation without prior knowledge: the maximum likelihood solution. In *Proceedings of EUSIPCO '90*, 1990, pp. 621–624.
32. P. Comon. Independent Component analysis — a new concept?. *Signal Processing*, 36:287–314, 1994.
33. M. Jones and R. Sibson. What is projection pursuit?, *Journal of the Royal Statistical Society*, Ser. A, 150:1–36, 1987.
34. B. Pearlmutter and L. Parra. Maximum likelihood blind source separation: a context-sensitive generalization of ICA. In *Advances in Neural Information Processing Systems*, 9:613–619, 1997.
35. J.-F. Cardoso. Informax and maximum likelihood for source separation, *IEEE Letters on Signal Processing*, 4:112–114, 1997.
36. J.-F. Cardoso. Entropic contrasts for source separation: geometry and stability. In S. Haykin, Ed., *Unsupervised Adaptive Filtering*, Vol. 1, John Wiley & Sons, New York, 2000, pp. 139–189.
37. A. Hyvärinen. Survey on independent component analysis, *Neural Computing Surveys*, 2:94–128, 1999.
38. G. Burel. Blind separation of sources: a nonlinear neural algorithm, *Neural Networks*, 5(6):937–947, 1996.
39. G. Deco and W. Brauer. Nonlinear higher-order statistical decorrelation by volume conserving neural architectures, *Neural Networks*, 8:525–535, 1995.

40. P. Pajunen, A. Hyvärinen, and J. Karhunen. Nonlinear blind source separation by self-organizing maps. In *Proceedings of Internation Conference on Neural Information Processing*, Hong Kong, 1996, pp. 1207–1210.
41. A. Hyvärinen and P. Hoyer. Independent subspace analysis shows emergence of phase and shift invariant features of natural images. In *Proceedings of International Joint Conference on Neural Networks*, Washington, D.C., 1999.
42. A. Hyvärinen and P. Hoyer. Emergence of phase and shift invariant features by decomposition of natural images into independent feature subspaces, *Neural Computation*, 12(7):1705–1720, 2000.
43. A. Hyvärinen and U. Köster. FastISA: a fast fixed-point algorithm for independent subspace analysis. In *Proceedings of European Symposium on Artificial Neural Networks*, Bruges, Belgium, 2006.

## Chapter 5

# A Multiple Criteria Approach to Creating Good Teams over Time

Ronald K. Klimberg, Kevin J. Boyle, and Ira Yermish

## Contents

## 5.1   Introduction

The ability of an employee to work well in a team or group is an important skill to many employers. Since the 1980s, studies have confirmed increasing reliance on workplace teams [2, 4]. In addition, an integral part of most undergraduate and graduate business programs includes team assignments. Consequently, it is vital that instructors at both the undergraduate and graduate levels develop teamwork skills in their students. One of the ways to accomplish this is by increasing student understanding of how teams are formed, how they work, and how the overall team performance can be improved by establishing discrete, objective, and quantifiable factors.

The objective of our model development is to improve the team selection process by reducing the level of dissatisfaction with team projects, and to improve each member's learning by balancing the appropriate knowledge and interpersonal skills that previous studies have shown to be important to team performance [7]. In many cases, the temporary nature of student teams is a detriment to team performance. Work teams tend to have members who know each other, have more permanence, and have a shared interest in the continued success of the organization. However, many similarities of team dynamics exist, and it is these attributes that are utilized in this model to improve student team performance and learning.

This chapter develops and applies a multiple-criteria, nonlinear integer programming model to improve the task of group identification and selection in an academic environment. The model is similar to the class of combinatorial assignment-type optimization problems that are NP-complete. We employed a commercial software package that uses state-of-the-art algorithms to solve the problem successfully over a three-semester period.

Section 5.2 provides a brief introduction to team formation approaches and to the team formation process used in our EMBA (Executive MBA) program. Sections 5.3 and 5.4 trace our sequential model development and application. Section 5.5 discusses our conclusions about the models and the process.

## 5.2  Background

### 5.2.1  Approaches to Team Formation

The use of teams, both in the workplace and academic settings, is a tool used with increasing emphasis and frequency. Nevertheless, negative attitudes by individuals toward team participation continue to exist, especially in the classroom setting. When probed, these student attitudes fall into the major categories of unclear goals for the team, lack of team leadership, internal conflict, "social loafing," and individual rather than group efforts [1]. Organizations serious about using teams do not hesitate to invest the time, money, and hours in training their workforce to improve team dynamics and team outcomes [5]. It is important that this emphasis is nurtured in the classroom to prepare students for this demand in their work environment. Faculty members need to appreciate that establishing student groups consists of more than just assigning a handful of students to a task and then expecting results. Rather, one of the goals of a team project should also be the development and enhancement of good team-working skills [1].

Using student groups in university business programs, especially graduate business programs, is a commonly employed pedagogy for enhancing learning as well as simulating "real world" or organizational workgroup relationships. The formation of student groups or teams, however, appears to be a more varied and haphazard process. The criteria most commonly used to assign students to teams vary from the instructor making the team assignments to the students being told to "choose up teams" [23]. Occasionally, the professor or program director may assign students according to some specific criterion or characteristic (for example, geographic proximity or major) [30]. In very few instances are these decisions based on either qualitative (categorical) or quantitative attributes of the students.

A significant body of research examines how teams deal with employee workgroup formation and performance [6]. Although many studies have been conducted on both the positive and negative aspects of group learning, the literature indicates that the preponderance of the measures of group efficacy focus on either results of group learning or the amount of or degree to which the instructor structures the group effort [3]. In contrast, the work in this chapter focuses on the beginning of the process, the procedures and methods by which groups are formed. It is our opinion that few, if any, quantitative or objective measures are used in this important and significant step in group learning. The primary issue is whether to let students form their own workgroups or to have the instructor make team assignments. Too often, students will form groups based on familiarity, friendship, or classroom "neighbors" [10, 24]. These personal proclivities may actually inhibit, rather than contribute to, enhanced learning because the groups tend to be more homogeneous than heterogeneous. Seldom, if ever, are considerations such as skills, knowledge, or contribution potential considered [7]. Rarely are teams formed with an optimal mix of knowledge, skills, abilities, personal characteristics, learning styles, and personality types.

The objective of team formation and team-centered learning is to enhance the creativity and problem-solving skills of these students. In addition to the traditional pedagogy of lecture, assignments, and research, a growing body of research suggests that an additional dimension of learning is fostered by team learning experiences [26]. However, simply increasing the number of group experiences for students will not necessarily result in an increase in learning or the development of team skills. In an attempt to improve all aspects of the group experience, the more structured, controlled, and balanced the team membership is, the more likely that both group efficiency and effectiveness will be improved [6].

## 5.2.2 EMBA Teams at Saint Joseph's University

This chapter concentrates on the team assignment problem in the EMBA program at Saint Joseph's University (SJU). Because teams are an important component of many lock-step, cohort-group EMBA programs, their formation is critical to program success. At SJU, the team compositions remained the same since program inception (circa 1990). Historically, teams were formed toward the end of the orientation phase of the program. Specifically, all the students were brought into a room and were instructed to form teams of between four and six members. Additionally, they were instructed that the entire class was not allowed to leave the room until all of the students were a member of a team. Teams were fixed (with minor occasional modifications) for the life of the 12- or 21-month life cohorts. Student and faculty concerns about team problems led to a review of this process and the development of a more objective procedure for team formation and rotation.

Factors that go into the composition of the team include technical expertise, geography, and personal chemistry. Because the teams will be facing a variety of challenges, it is important that each team exhibits a diversity of skills, a relative convenience to meet and work together, and an ability to pull together in times of adversity. Students were encouraged to take into consideration one another's various skills and Myers-Briggs type indicators. This process has its limitations as choices are generally made very quickly, without a great deal of thought and planning. Additionally, the process tends to be extremely stressful for introverted personality types. Students have commented that the experience can be compared to choosing teams in elementary school.

## 5.3  Initial Models

We first proposed to create teams objectively using the following team formation model [19]:

**Model I**

$$Max \sum_{k=1}^{P} \sum_{i=1}^{P} v_{ik} x_{ij} x_{kj} \tag{5.1}$$

*st.*

$$\sum_{j=1}^{J} x_{ij} = 1 \quad \forall\, i \tag{5.2}$$

$$\sum_{i=1}^{P} x_{ij} = S_j \quad \forall\, j$$

$$x_{ij} \in \{0,1\} \quad \forall i,\, j \tag{5.3}$$

$$x_{ij} = \begin{cases} 1 \text{ if student } i \text{ assign to group } j \\ 0 \text{ otherwise} \end{cases}$$

$$v_{ik} = \text{desirability of student } i \text{ to be with student } k$$

where:
  $i$: student $i$    $i = 1, \ldots, P$
  $j$: group $j$    $j = 1, \ldots, J$
  $P$: total number of students
  $J$: number of groups
  $S_j$: number of students in group $j$

The objective function (Equation 5.1) maximizes the total desirability of group assignments. The $v_{ik}$ desirability values are assigned by the students. This value would measure the desirability or undesirability of being in the same group as a fellow classmate. Two of the many possible approaches to assigning these weights are:

1. Each student assigns another student a number from 1 to P (where the larger the value, the more desirable it is to be in the same group).
2. There are a certain number of absolute points that can be assigned to students (e.g., 15, so that the sum of the absolute values of all the assignments must add up to 15); negative numbers as well as positive numbers can be assigned. Also, the assigned values can be only a couple of large values or many little values; in either case, the absolute sum of the values must equal the allotted amount.

Whichever approach is taken, each student's weight assignments must be kept confidential.

Constraint (5.2) ensures that each student is assigned to one and only one group. Finally, Constraint (5.3) makes sure that each group has the right number of students, $S_j$.

Model I is a member of the family of assignment problems and is similar to the quadratic assignment problem (QAP), the generalized quadratic assignment problem (GQAP), and the generalized assignment problem (GAP). The difference between Model I and the QAP and GQAP formulations lies in Constraint (5.3), where in QAP, the right-hand side values, $S_j$, all equal 1, while in GQAP, the constraint is a less than or equal to and each of the $x_{ij}$ values are weighted. GAP modifies Constraint (5.3) in the same manner as GQAP but the objective function is linear in GAP.

The QAP was first introduced by Koopmans and Beckmann in the context of a facility layout planning model [21]. Since that time, QAP as well as GAP and GQAP have been applied to many problem situations, including facility location [25], scheduling [14], and statistical data analysis [18]. However, QAP is known to be NP-complete [13], and GAP is NP-hard [27]. Even GAP with a linear objective function is known to be NP-hard [27]. Each remains a very difficult combinatorial optimization problem to solve. Only recently have optimal algorithms been developed to solve benchmark problems of size P = 36 for QAP [8]. In a typical class-team formation problem where 25 students and five groups are desired ( i.e., P = 25, $S_j$ = 5 $\forall j$), Model I would have 125 decision variables and 30 constraints.

A large number of heuristic methods, starting with the greedy algorithm [9] to recently developed meta-heuristic methods, have been employed to solve these problems. Meta-heuristic methods combine intelligent search procedures and increase computational speed to find optimal or near-optimal solutions to complex problems, nonlinear and integer. Two of the best-known meta-heuristic methods are genetic algorithms and tabu search. Genetic algorithm (GA) procedures were developed by Holland [17], while the principles and rules of tabu search (TS) were

**Table 5.1   Initial Optimal Solutions with the Three Packages**

| Software Package | Optimal Solution |
|---|---|
| Solver | 151 |
| Evolutionary Solver | Could not find a feasible solution |
| OptQuest | 153 |

created by Glover in the 1970s [15]. GA is an adaptive heuristic search algorithm based on the evolutionary ideas of natural selection and genetics such as inheritance, mutation, selection, and crossover. It is an intelligent exploitation of a random search within a defined search space to solve a problem. Tabu search uses a neighborhood search procedure to iteratively move from solution to solution until some stopping criterion has been satisfied. The solutions admitted to the new neighborhood are determined through the use of special memory structures. Genetic algorithms, tabu search, and their hybrids are effective heuristics to solve combinatorial problems, such as GAP-GA [22], TS [31], QAP-GA [28], hybrid GA [11], TS [29], hybrid TS/GA [31], and QAP-hybrid TS [8].

We used three mathematical programming software packages — Premium Solver in Excel (NLP option), Evolutionary Solver, and OptQuest — to solve Model I using a small set of hypothetical data (22 students into five groups generating 484 decision variables and 27 constraints). Evolutionary Solver in Premium Solver is a genetic algorithm package, while OptQuest (Version 2000) is part of Crystal Ball's Excel add-in package. OptQuest uses a methodology called scatter search, developed by Glover [16], which incorporates some of the genetic algorithm and tabu search features into one methodology. As shown in Table 5.1, the OptQuest package found the best optimal solution. However, it took a long time to search and solve each trial solution (in total, almost 0.5 hours on a Pentium M 780/2.26 GHz).

To decrease the model size, we reformulated Model I into the following nonlinear model [20]:

**Model II**

$$\text{Max} \sum_{k=1}^{N} \sum_{i=1}^{N} (v_{ik} + v_{ki}) d_{ik} \qquad (5.4)$$

st.

$$\sum_{j=1}^{J} x_{ij} = 1 \qquad \forall \, i \qquad (5.5)$$

$$\sum_{i=1}^{N} x_{ij} = S \qquad \forall \, j \qquad (5.6)$$

$$Max_{j} (x_{ij} + x_{kj} - 1) = d_{ik} \qquad \forall i, k$$

$$x_{ij}, d_{ik} \in \{0,1\} \qquad \forall i, j, k \tag{5.7}$$

$$d_{ik} = \begin{cases} 1 & \text{if student } i \text{ and student } k \text{ in the same group} \\ 0 & \text{otherwise.} \end{cases}$$

$$x_{ij} = \begin{cases} 1 & \text{if } i \text{ assigned to group } j \\ 0 & \text{otherwise.} \end{cases}$$

where:

$i$: student $i$    $i = 1, ..., N$
$k$: student $k$   $k = 1, ..., N$
$j$: group $j$      $j = 1, ..., J$
P: total number of students
J: number of groups
S: number of students in each group
S = Round(P/J + 0.5)
N = J * S

Given the designated number of groups, J, the actual number of students in the class, P, will not always be evenly divided by J. If it is not evenly divided, some groups may have one more member than another group. When this situation occurs, we create fictitious students; that is, we define S = Round(P/J + 0.5) and N = J * S. As a result, there are N − P fictitious students. In addition, the $v_{ik}$ value for all fictitious students would equal 0; that is, $v_{ik} = 0 \ \forall \ i, k > P$. For example, if the class size is 22, P = 22, and the designated number of groups is 5, J = 5. So, S = Round (22/5 + 0.5) = Round (4.4 + 0.5) = 5, and N = 5 * 5 = 25. As a result, three fictitious students are generated, N − P = 25 − 22, where each fictitious student $i$ would have $v_{ik} = 0 \ \forall \ k$. Finally, the solution to this particular example would have three groups with four students and two groups with five students.

Similar to Model I, the objective function in Model II (Equation (5.4) maximizes the total desirability of the group assignments and Constraints (5.5) and (5.6) are respectively similar to Constraints (5.2) and (5.3). Constraint (5.7) defines $d_{ik}$ as equaling 1 if student $i$ and student $k$ are in the same group (0 otherwise). In particular, given a pair of students $i$ and $k$, we have the possible combinations and corresponding $d_{ik}$ values listed in Table 5.2.

The definition of $d_{ik}$ requires us to generate only one P × P matrix instead of a J × P × P matrix. Reexamining the hypothetical example we looked at with Model I, with 25 students to be assigned to five groups, where we needed 3125 decision variables and 30 constraints, the corresponding problem formulated into Model II requires only 750 decision variables and 655 constraints. The number of

**Table 5.2  Possible Combinations and Corresponding Values of $d_{ik}$**

| $x_{ij}$ | $x_{kj}$ | $d_{ik}$ | Results (considering all groups $j$) |
|---|---|---|---|
| 0 | 0 | −1 | It cannot occur because each student must be assigned to a group (Constraint 5.5) and $d_{ik}$ cannot be negative |
| 1 | 0 | 0 | In this situation, student $i$ and student $k$ are in different groups |
| 0 | 1 | | |
| 1 | 1 | 1 | In this situation, student $i$ and student $k$ are in the same group |

decision variables is significantly less. However, Constraint (5.7) makes Model II nonlinear.

Furthermore, when examining the Solver and OptQuest solutions from Model I, we found some students had 0 (zero) satisfaction or no desirability achieved. To eliminate this possibility of students getting 0 satisfaction, we consider two new objectives:

$$\text{MaxiMin: } MAX\left\{MIN_i\left[\sum_{k=1}^{N} v_{ik}d_{ik}\right]\right\}$$

and

$$\text{MIN Standard Deviation: } MIN \ s\left[\sum_{i=1}^{N}\sum_{k=1}^{N} v_{ik}d_{ik}\right].$$

The MaxiMin objective maximizes the minimum student overall satisfied desirability achieved. The second new objective minimizes the standard deviation, s, of the individual student desirability attained.

Using OptQuest, we resolved our initial hypothetical example, using Model II, for each of our three objectives. Table 5.3 summarizes the results. Each row in Table III provides a summary measure of each solution:

- Sum: the sum of the total desirability of the group assignments.
- Min: the minimum desirability level achieved by an individual.
- Standard deviation: s, the standard deviation of the individual desirability attained.

**Table 5.3  Results of Model II**

| | | Objective | | |
|---|---|---|---|---|
| | | Sum | MaxiMin | Standard Deviation |
| | Sum | 342 | 306 | 291 |
| | Min | 5 | 10 | 7 |
| Measure | Standard Deviation | 5.23 | 2.30 | 2.26 |

When considering only the objective of maximizing overall satisfaction (Equation 5.4), the sum was 342, the minimum individual desirability achieved was 5, and the standard deviation of individual desirability attained was 5.23. Notice that the maximum value of the sum in Table 5.3 for each of the objectives is significantly larger than from Model I — approximately twice. The reason is that in Model II we double-counted the desirability values (i.e., above and below the diagonal). Furthermore, even with the doubling of values in Model II, we now found a better solution and also a solution with non-zero individual desirability achieved. When we solved the model using the MaxiMin objective, the overall desirability achieved decreased some, the minimum individual desirability attained doubled to 10, and the standard deviation was about half as large. So, this solution provides a little less overall satisfaction, but, a significantly better overall individual satisfaction with not as much variability. When solving for the last objective of minimizing the standard deviation, the last column in Table 5.3, the standard deviation was the lowest, only slightly less than the MaxiMin value and the overall Sum is the lowest out of the three and the minimum individual desirability achieved was in the middle.

We showed the Model II results summarized in Table 5.3 using the three objectives to the EMBA administration. Their initial reaction was very positive. However, after further examination and discussions, they felt strongly that such a model should also consider the skills of the students; that is, if possible, each group should have a strong accounting person, a strong finance person, etc. To address this added criterion, we developed the following constraint:

$$\sum_{i \in B_m} x_{ij} \geq g_m \quad \forall m, i \tag{5.8}$$

where:

$B_m$: set of students that have background/skill $m$

$g_m$: minimum number of students in a group with skill $m$

$$= Int\left(\frac{\text{\# of students with skill } m}{\text{\# of groups}}\right).$$

Constraint (5.8) would require each group to have at least the minimum number of people with each of the desired skills or background.

We randomly assigned "exceptional" skills to the students in our hypothetical example and reran Model II including Constraint (5.8) and for each of the three objectives. The results are summarized in Table 5.4.

The overall total satisfaction was the same for all three objectives but slightly less than the best solution in Table 5.3 where we did not consider balancing skills. The minimum individual desirability achieved was the same in all three cases and was equal to the best value in Table 5.3. The standard deviations were very close; and in comparison to the values in Table 5.3, they were in the middle range.

**Table 5.4   Results of Model II with Equation (5.8)**

|  |  | Objective | | |
|---|---|---|---|---|
|  |  | *Sum* | *MaxiMin* | *Standard Deviation* |
|  | Sum | 325 | 325 | 325 |
|  | Min | 10 | 10 | 10 |
| *Measure* | Standard Deviation | 3.3 | 3.2 | 3.2 |

The EMBA administration reaction to these new results was all the more positive. As a result, we developed the form shown in Table 5.5 to solicit student skills and competencies and applied the model during academic years 2004 and 2005 to our two EMBA programs. Student reactions were extremely positive. A typical response was that "this approach is more objective and not subjective like before." The administration was satisfied with this approach. However, students raised a number of concerns. First, students were reluctant to "rank" their classmates. Also, after several runs of the model, the administration felt that the desirability criteria should not be considered. "It's too much of a popularity contest." A second major issue was a significant shift in faculty and administration philosophy. They argued that keeping students in the same group throughout the entire program (three or five semesters) was more detrimental than the possible positive bonding that could occur. As a result, they wanted to see the groups change from semester to semester to provide students with the opportunity to interact with a wider variety of classmates.

**Table 5.5   Form to Input Student's Skills and Competencies**

| Functional Area (Please choose 2) | |
|---|---|
| Accounting |  |
| Finance |  |
| IT/MIS |  |
| General Management |  |
| Marketing |  |
| Major Skill Set (Please choose 2) | |
| Research |  |
| Data Analysis |  |
| Project Management |  |
| Team Management |  |
| Writing |  |
| Verbal Presentation |  |

## 5.4 Current Model

Given the above situation, our current model for developing teams is the following multiple-criteria, nonlinear, integer programming model:

**Model III**

$$\text{Min: } w_1 \sum_{i=1}^{P} v_i + w_2 \left[ \underset{j}{Max}\left( \sum_{m=1}^{M} f_{mj} \right) - \underset{j}{Min}\left( \sum_{m=1}^{M} f_{mj} \right) \right] + w_3 \sum_{m=1}^{M} \left[ \underset{m}{Max} \sum_{j=1}^{J} f_{mj} - g_m \right]$$

St. $\qquad\qquad\qquad\qquad\qquad\qquad\qquad$ (5.9)

$$\sum_{j=1}^{J} x_{ij} = 1 \qquad \forall\, i \tag{5.10}$$

$$\sum_{i=1}^{P} x_{ij} = S_j \qquad \forall\, j \tag{5.11}$$

$$\underset{j}{Max}\ (x_{ij} + x_{kj} - 1) = d_{ik} \qquad \forall\, i, k \tag{5.12}$$

$$v_i = \sum_{k=1}^{P} e^{(d_{ik} r_{ik})} - 1 \qquad \forall\, i \tag{5.13}$$

$$\begin{gathered}(5.14)\\ f_{mj} = \sum_{i=1}^{P} y_{im} x_{ij} \qquad \forall\, m, j \end{gathered}$$

$$x_{ij}, d_{ik} \in \{0,1\} \qquad \forall\, i, j, k$$

$$f_{mj} \geq 0 \qquad \forall\, j, m$$

where:

$i$: student $i$ $\qquad i = 1, \ldots, \text{P}$
$k$: student $k$ $\qquad k = 1, \ldots, \text{P}$
$j$: group $j$ $\qquad j = 1, \ldots, \text{J}$
$m$: skill $m$ $\qquad m = 1, \ldots, \text{M}$
D: desired group size
P: total number of students
J: number of groups = Int(P/D); where Int rounds off the number to an integer
N: total number of possible students where each group has the same number of students = D*J
M: total number of skills

$S_j$: total number of students to be assigned to group $j$

$$= \begin{cases} D & j=1,\ldots,N \\ D+1 & N+1,\ldots,P \end{cases}$$

$h_{ik}$ = number of times student $i$ and student $k$ have been in the same group

$r_{ik}$: a penalty for historically how many times student $i$ and student $k$ have been in the same group

$$= \begin{cases} 0 & \text{if } h_{ik} = 0 \\ 5^{(h_{ik}-1)} & \text{otherwise} \end{cases}$$

$$y_{im} = \begin{cases} 1 & \text{if student } i \text{ has skill } m \\ 0 & \text{otherwise} \end{cases}$$

$g_m$: minimum projected number of students with skill $m$ in a group

$$= Int \left( \frac{\sum_{i=1}^{P} y_{im}}{J} \right) \forall m$$

$$x_{ij} = \begin{cases} 1 & \text{if student } i \text{ assigned to group } j \\ 0 & \text{otherwise} \end{cases}$$

$$d_{ik} = \begin{cases} 1 & \text{if student } i \text{ and student } k \text{ are assigned to same group} \\ 0 & \text{otherwise} \end{cases}$$

$f_{mj}$ = sum of students with skill $m$ in group $j$

$v_i$ = weighted penalty for the number times student $i$ is assigned a group with students he/she has already been with

$w_1, w_2, w_3$ = weights assigned to objectives, such that $w_1 + w_2 + w_3 = 1$

The team formation model now has three objectives (Equation 5.9).

1. Minimize the number of times, more than once, that a student is in the same group with individuals he or she already has been in the same group.
2. Minimize the difference between the maximum and minimum of the sum of the skills in a group (i.e., minimize the range/difference of skills).

**Table 5.6  Some Typical Values of $h_{ik}$ and $r_{ik}$**

| Number of times in the same group, $h_{ik}$ | 0 | 1 | 2 | 3 |
|---|---|---|---|---|
| Penalty, $r_{ik}$ | 0 | 1 | 5 | 25 |

3. Minimize the sum of the differences for all skills between the maximum number of students with a particular skill in all the groups and the desired minimum number of students with that skill.

Constraints (5.10) and (5.11) are similar to previous models where Constraint (5.10) ensures that each student is assigned to one and only one group, and Constraint (11) makes sure each group $j$ is assigned $S_j$ students. Constraint (5.12) defines $d_{ik}$ as equaling 1 if student $i$ and student $k$ are in the same group; otherwise $d_{ik}$ is equal to 0, which similar to Constraint (5.7) in Model II. Constraint (5.13) defines the weighted penalty for each student $i$, $v_i$, for being more than once in the same group with other students. First, $r_{ik}$ is a penalty for being historically in the same group with another student. Table 5.6 lists some of the possible $r_{ik}$ penalty values. If two students are not in the same group, then $d_{ik}$ will equal 0, and hence, $d_{ik}r_{ik}$ will equal 0, regardless if they were previously in the same group. If two students are in the same group, then $d_{ik}$ will equal 1. If the two students were never in the same group prior to this model execution (or semester run), then $h_{ik} = r_{ik} = 0$ and therefore $d_{ik}r_{ik}$ will still equal 0. On the other hand, if two students are in the same group, $d_{ik} = 1$, and they were previously in the same group, perhaps one or more times, then $d_{ik}r_{ik}$ is weighted exponentially. For example, if it is the second time two students $i$ and $k$ are in the same group, then $d_{ik}r_{ik}$ will equal 1. As a result, in Constraint (5.13) $v_i$ is defined as an aggregate penalty for student $i$ being assigned to a group with one or more students that he or she has previously been in similar groups. The weighted sum of these $v_i$ values characterizes the first part of the objective function.

Constraint (5.14) defines $f_{mj}$ as the sum of students with skill $m$ in group $j$. This variable, $f_{mj}$, is used to depict the second and third parts of the objective function. The expression $\Sigma_{m=1}^{M} f_{mj}$ sums all skills in a group. The second part of the objective function takes the difference between the maximum sum of group skills and the minimum sum of group skills and attempts to minimize this difference, thus trying to balance the aggregate skills among the groups. The last part of the objective function attempts to balance the individual skills among the groups by minimizing the weighted sum of the difference between the maximum number of students with skill $m$ and the desired minimum, $g_m$, for each skill $m$.

Model III has now been successfully applied for the past three semesters for three different cohort groups. The model is executed before each semester. Parameters $h_{ik}$ and $r_{ik}$ are updated based on last semester's team assignments. Additionally, because some students leave the program, for personal or academic reasons, some other parameters must also be updated, that is, D, P, J, N, $S_j$, and $g_m$. Responses from students and administration to the team formation process, thus far, have been especially positive. Students find themselves getting to know more of their classmates. Moreover, students are more satisfied with team performance. The EMBA administration has noticed a significant decrease in personal and academic team related problems. Further, instead of one or two dominant teams, the faculty and administration have noticed more balance among the groups.

The above multiple-criteria, nonlinear, integer programming model has been solved in Excel using a newer version of Crystal Ball's add-in OptQuest (Version 7.2). The new OptQuest version now integrates algorithms based on tabu search, scatter search, a mixed integer programming solver, and a procedure to configure and train neural networks. Solution times are now less than seven minutes.

## 5.5 Conclusions

The process of developing teams, especially for lock-step, cohort programs such as an EMBA program may be critical to the class or program's success. We developed a multiple criteria nonlinear integer programming rotating team formation model to determine group compositions objectively. Using an Excel add-in, with state-of-the-art meta-heuristics, optimization, and data mining algorithms, we successfully solved this model. This model is currently being used to determine teams in the Saint Joseph's University EMBA program. In the future we will extend the model to consider possible other objectives, such as team "loafing." We will explore applying the model in other team-oriented programs and individual classes.

## References

1. Adams, S.G., Building Successful Student Teams in the Engineering Classroom, *Journal of STEM Education*, 4(3&4), 1–6, July–Dec. 2003.
2. Antonioni, D., How to Lead and Facilitate Teams, *Industrial Management*, 38(6), 22–25, 1996.
3. Bacon, D.R., The Effect of Group Projects on Content-Related Learning, *Journal of Management Education*, 29, 248–268, 2005.
4. Blanchard, K., Carew, D., and Parisi-Carew, E., How to Get Your Group to Perform Like a Team, *Training and Development*, 50(9), 34–38, 1996.
5. Buckenmyer, J.A., Using Teams for Class Activities: Making Course/Classroom Teams Work, *Journal of Education for Business*, November/December 2000, pp. 98–107.
6. Chapman, K.J., Meuter, M., Toy, D., and Wright, L., Can't We Pick Our Own Groups? The Influence of Group Selection Method on Group Dynamics and Outcomes, *Journal of Management Education*, 30(4), 557–569, 2006.

7. Connerly, M.L. and Mael, F.A., The Importance and Invasiveness of Student Team Selection Criteria, *Journal of Management Education*, 25, 471–494, 2001.
8. Cordeau J.F., Gaudioso M., Laporte G., and Moccia, L., A Memetic Heuristic for the Generalized Quadratic Assignment Problem, *INFORMS Journal on Computing*, 18(4), 433–443, 2006.
9. Cormen, T.H., Leiserson, C.E., Rivest, R.L., and Stein, C., *Introduction to Algorithms, 2nd edition,* McGraw-Hill, 2001.
10. Deibel, K., Team Formation Methods for Increasing Interaction during In-Class Group Work. *ITiCSE '05*, June 2005.
11. Drezner Z., A New Genetic Algorithm for the Quadratic Assignment Problem, *INFORMS Journal on Computing*, 15(3), 320–330, 2003.
12. Fleurent, C. and Ferland, J.A., Genetic Hybrids for the Quadratic Assignment Problem, *DIMACS Series in Discrete Mathematics and Theoretical Computer Science*, American Mathematical Society, 16, 190–206, 1994.
13. Garey, M.R. and Johnson, D.S., *Computers and Intractability: A Guide to the Theory of NP-Completeness*, W.H. Freeman and Co., San Francisco, 1979.
14. Geoffrion, A.M. and Graves, G.W., Scheduling Parallel Production Lines with Changeover Costs: Practical Applications of a Quadratic Assignment/LP Approach, *Operations Research*, 24, 595–610, 1976.
15. Glover, F., Heuristics for Integer Programming using Surrogate Constraints. *Decision Sciences*, 8:156–166, 1977.
16. Glover, F., Genetic algorithms and Scatter Search: Unsuspected Potentials. *Statistics and Computing*, 4:131–140, 1994.
17. Holland, J.H., *Adaptation in Natural and Artificial Systems*. University of Michigan Press, Ann Arbor, 1975.
18. Hubert, L.J., *Assignment Methods in Combinatorial Data Analysis*, Marcel Dekker, Inc., New York, 1987.
19. Klimberg, R.K., Lawrence, K., Rahmlow, H., and Sankar, S., A Comparison of Solution Techniques in a Spreadsheet Environment for a Multiple Criteria Approach to Creating Good Teams, *Decision Science Conference*, Washington, D.C., November 2003.
20. Klimberg, R.K., Rahmlow, H., and Panaseny, J.W., A Multiple Criteria Approach to Creating Good Teams, *Northeast Decision Sciences Institute Annual Meeting*, Pittsburgh, PA, March 2001.
21. Koopmans, T.C. and Beckmann, M., Assignment Problems and the Location of Economic Activities, *Econometrica*, 25, 53–76, 1957.
22. Lorena, L.A.N., Narciso, M.G., and Beasley, J.E., A Constructive Genetic Algorithm for the Generalized Assignment Problem, *Evolutionary Optimization*, 2002, pp. 1–19.
23. Millis, B.J. and Cottell Jr., P.G., *Cooperative Learning for Higher Education Faculty*. American Council on Education, Series on Higher Education, The Oryx Press, Phoenix, AZ, 1998.
24. Oakley, B., Felder, R.M., Brent, R., and Elhajj, I., Turning Student Groups into Effective Teams, *Journal of Student Centered Learning*, 2, 8–33, 2004.
25. Pardalos, P.M., Rendl, F., and Wolkowicz, H., *The Quadratic Assignment Problem: A Survey and Recent Developments*, DIMACS Series in Discrete Mathematics and Theoretical Computer Science, American Mathematical Society, 1994, pp. 1–42.

26. Rassuli, A. and Manzer, J.P., Teach Us to Learn: Multivariate Analysis of Perception of Success in Team Learning, *Journal of Education for Business*, 81, 21–28, 2005.
27. Sahni, S. and Gonzalez, T., P-Complete Approximation Problems, *Journal of the Association for Computing Machinery*, 23, 555–565, 1976.
28. Tate, D.M. and Smith, A.E., A Genetic Approach to the Quadratic Assignment Problem, *Computers & Operations Research*, 22(1), 73–83, 1995.
29. Taillard, E. D., Robust Tabu search for the quadratic assignment problem, *Parallel Computing*, 17, 443–455, 1991.
30. Website: http://members.tripod.com/MrGsPEpage/groups.htm
31. Yagiura, M., Ibaraki, T. and Glover, F., An Ejection Chain Approach for the Generalized Assignment Problem, *INFORMS Journal on Computing*, 16(2), 133–151, Spring 2004.

# APPLICATIONS OF DATA MINING

# Chapter 6

# Data Mining Applications in Higher Education

Cali M. Davis, J. Michael Hardin,
Tom Bohannon, and Jerry Oglesby

## Contents

# 6.1 Introduction

The goal of college student recruitment has always been to recruit, retain, and graduate the best qualified class of students. The best qualified class of students is measured by a college or university's institutional profile. An institutional profile is an indication of success in attaining students with the best grades, the best test scores, students who will persist, students who will graduate, and students who will be stewards giving of time and money to their alma mater. Higher education researchers from across the country have used data mining techniques to develop models to predict enrollment, retention, and donor giving. The development of enrollment prediction models has been an integral part of the field of institutional research for many years. The models have traditionally been used to predict the size of an incoming freshmen class. More recently, the enrollment prediction models have been used by admissions offices to target specific individuals who have a high probability of enrolling. The enrollment prediction models provide admissions counselors with valuable information to use during the recruitment process. Predictive modeling allows for the display of a personalized recruitment message in electronic and print media. Other benefits include improving the caliber of the freshmen class and better utilization of university resources.

Getting students to enroll at a particular college or university is important, but keeping them there is even more important. University presidents, provosts, and enrollment management officials would agree that student enrollment and retention go hand-in-hand. When students who are at-risk of leaving their university are identified, academic and social interventions can take place to help the student feel more connected to campus life. This, in turn, increases a student's likelihood to persist and therefore graduate.

Once a student graduates from a college or university, he becomes an alumnus of that institution. Colleges and universities depend exceedingly on the monetary and intangible contributions of their graduates. This makes donor giving another area in higher education where data mining can be useful. Potential major donors can be identified. Also, the amount of a donor gift can be predicted based on giving history as well as demographic and biological factors.

This chapter discusses three applications of data mining in higher education: (1) enrollment, (2) retention, and (3) donor giving. A general discussion of each application and its relevant background and importance are presented, followed by real-world case studies using the SAS Enterprise Miner™ software.

SAS Enterprise Miner™ is a powerful tool used in the development of predictive models. Section 6.2 outlines the philosophy of using the logistic regression model. Section 6.3 discusses data mining in student retention. Section 6.4 discusses how enrollment prediction models are developed and used in higher education. Finally, Section 6.5 outlines the donor giving model and its uses. From this point forward, the terms "university" and "college" can be used interchangeably.

## 6.1.1 Data Needs, Challenges, and Definitions

Most of the data used for predictive modeling in higher education is obtained from student records, standardized tests such as the ACT and SAT, admissions applications, financial aid data, and scholarship applications. Other data can be obtained from local surveys administered to students at summer orientation or at other points during the academic year. One national survey that provides valuable information on incoming freshmen is the Cooperative Institutional Research Program (CIRP) Freshmen Survey administered by the Higher Education Research Institute (HERI) at the University of California, Los Angeles. The CIRP Freshmen Survey helps institutions assess trends in the characteristics, attitudes, values, and aspirations of their entering freshmen. The survey form has reserved space for participating universities to ask optional questions to measure issues of interest to the campus itself.

As in most applications of data mining, the issue of timing of available data becomes critical. When does a records office have semester grade data? When does an admissions office get the final high school grade point average (GPA) for a student? How long before the financial aid office will have offers of loans and grants ready for distribution? All of these data elements could be essential in determining if a student will enroll or if a student will return for his second year. It certainly helps for the data miners to have good relationship with a variety of offices across the campus. Student affairs, financial aid, admissions, enrollment management, institutional research, records, and the registrar's office all play a fundamental role in helping the data miner understand, collect, and clean up the data file. If interventions will be administered, it also helps to have clear lines of communication with the academic colleges, residential life, academic support centers, the career center, the cultural and diversity center, and the counseling center. In addition to on-campus resources, standardized testing services such as the American College Testing Program (ACT) and the College Board are organizations that oftentimes provide data mining services for a reduced cost for affiliate institutions. Independent consulting firms also offer predictive modeling services on a contractual basis.

## 6.1.2 Enrollment Management Stages

It is helpful at this point to define some terminology to use throughout the rest of this chapter. A student can be defined as being a part of an enrollment management

**Table 6.1  Enrollment Management Stages and Definitions**

| Enrollment Management Stage | Definition of the Stage |
|---|---|
| Suspect student | A student who the university is interested in, but the student has not expressed interest (yet) |
| Prospective student/inquiry | A student who has expressed interest by contacting the institution, visiting the campus, or attending a campus-sponsored event |
| Applied | A student who has applied for admission to the institution |
| Admitted/accepted | A student who has been admitted/accepted at the institution |
| Deposit[a] | A student who has paid a monetary deposit expressing his or her intent to enroll at the institution |
| Enrolled | A student who is enrolled at the institution |
| Retained/continuing student | A student who stays enrolled at the institution |
| Graduate/alumnus | A student who graduates from the institution |
| Donor | A person (not necessarily a graduate) who donates money or time to the institution |

[a] Not required by all institutions.

stage at any point in time. Table 6.1 is a list of the enrollment management stages and short definitions of each stage.

A student can enter at any point prior to the "Applied" stage and exit at any point. These stages are progressive, and optimally a student moves from one stage to the next, although the time spent at any one stage is finite.

## 6.1.3  *Predictive Models and Model Assessment*

The SAS process for data mining is known as SEMMA. The SEMMA acronym is described in Table 6.2.

During the sampling phase, the data miner identifies the data to use. The dataset is partitioned into training, validation, and test datasets. The exploration phase enables the data miner to obtain descriptive statistics, identify important variables, and perform association analyses. The modification phase allows the data miner to

**Table 6.2    SEMMA Methodology of SAS**

| S | Sample | Identify input datasets |
|---|--------|------------------------|
| E | Explore | Explore datasets statistically and graphically |
| M | Modify | Prepare data for analysis |
| M | Model | Fit a predictive model |
| A | Assess | Compare predictive models |

transform variables, impute missing values, and create additional variables. In the modeling phase, the data miner fits a predictive model using a regression model, neural network, decision tree, or a combination of two or more of the models, called an ensemble model. Finally, the assessment phase allows for comparison of competing predictive models using such tools as lift charts and profit charts (SAS Institute Inc., 2005).

## 6.1.4    Enterprise Miner™

Enterprise Miner™ (EM) is the software developed by SAS that employs the SEMMA methodology. "EM software is an integrated product that provides an end-to-end business solution to data mining" (SAS Institute Inc., 2005). Analyses are performed by constructing process flow diagrams that follow the steps prescribed by SEMMA. EM will be the data mining software of choice used throughout the remainder of this chapter.

EM is point-and-click software that allows the researcher to direct the flow of analysis. Figure 6.1 provides an illustration of the types of nodes available within

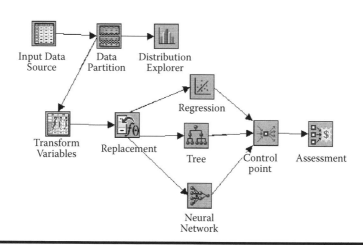

**Figure 6.1  Example Enterprise Miner™ process flow diagram.**

**Table 6.3    Explanation of Enterprise Miner Process Flow Diagram**

| Category | Node | Explanation |
|---|---|---|
| Sample | Input data source | Identify the data sources and define variable attributes |
| | Data partition | Partition datasets into training, test, and validation datasets |
| Explore | Distribution explorer | View distributions and generate summary statistics |
| Modify | Transform variables | Transform variables if necessary |
| | Replacement | Impute values for missing observations |
| Model | Regression, tree, neural network | Fit the specified type of model |
| Assess | Assessment | Compare models and predictions |

Enterprise Miner version 5.2, and Table 6.3 explains the nodes in Figure 6.1. Each of these nodes falls within one of the SEMMA categories.

Enterprise Miner enjoys several advantages over the use of PROC LOGISTIC in SAS. One example is its ease of use. In PROC LOGISTIC, one must write the code to perform the analysis. EM, however, generates the code automatically, based on parameters set by the user. Another advantage deals with missing values. If an observation has a missing value, PROC LOGISTIC discards that observation when generating a model. To "fill in the blanks," the user must write more code to perform all the necessary calculations. The "replacement" node in EM, however, allows the user to specify how to impute missing values automatically (such as the mean, median, or mode if the variable is numeric).

EM allows the data miner to generate many different models and assess them to find the best one. Finally, EM partitions the data automatically, as dictated by the user. If a researcher is using PROC LOGISTIC, he would have to partition the data himself before performing the analysis. As shown in the previous scenarios, Enterprise Miner is extremely user friendly, and knowledge of the SAS language is not required.

## 6.2  Logistic Regression

The goal in any regression analysis is to describe the relationship between a response variable and one or more predictor variables. Ordinary least squares (OLS) linear regression is the most well-known and widely used form of regression. When the response variable is binary, however, linear regression is not the appropriate method. Logistic regression should be used when there is a binary response variable.

### 6.2.1 Assumptions of the Linear Regression Model

To illustrate the need to use logistic regression with binary response variables, one needs to examine the assumptions of linear regression. Suppose $y$ is a response variable and $x$ is the predictor variable (not binary). The major assumptions of the linear regression model are as follows:

(1) $y_i = \alpha + \beta x_i + \varepsilon_i$

(2) $E(\varepsilon_i) = 0$

(3) $\text{var}(\varepsilon_i) = \sigma^2$              (homoscedasticity)

(4) $\text{cov}(\varepsilon_i, \varepsilon_j) = 0$

(5) $\varepsilon_i \sim$ Normal

### 6.2.2 Assumptions Violations with a Binary Response Variable

Now suppose the response variable ($y$) is binary with possible of values of 0 or 1. One can assert that assumptions (1), (2), and (4) still hold. However, if assumptions (1) and (2) hold for a binary $y$, then assumptions (3) and (5) necessarily fail. Using a binary response variable with possible values of 0 or 1, it can be shown that $\text{var}(\varepsilon_i) = (\alpha + \beta x_i)(1 - \alpha - \beta x_i)$. Therefore, $\text{var}(\varepsilon_i)$ is a function of $x$, and the assumption of homoscedasticity (assumption 3) is violated. If $y_i = 1$, assumption (1) implies that $\varepsilon_i = 1 - \alpha - \beta x_i$. If $y_i = 0$, however, $\varepsilon_i = -\alpha - \beta x_i$. Therefore, $\varepsilon_i$ has only two possible values. A normal distribution, however, has a continuum of values with no upper or lower bounds. Hence, the assumption of normally distributed errors (assumption 5) is violated.

### 6.2.3 More Problems with the Linear Model

By definition,

$$E(y_i) = 1 \cdot \Pr(y_i = 1) + 0 \cdot \Pr(y_i = 0) \tag{6.1}$$

If we define $p_i = \Pr(y_i = 1)$, then $E(y_i) = p_i$. Taking the expected value of both sides of the equation in assumption (1) yields $p_i = \alpha + \beta x_i$. This expression is often referred to as the linear probability model. Because $p_i$ is thought of as a probability, its values lie in the interval (0, 1). "If $x$ has no upper or lower bound, then for any value of $\beta$ there are values of $x$ for which $p_i$ is either greater than 1 or less than 0" (Allison, 1999). As a result of the aforementioned problems in using linear regression with a binary response variable, statisticians developed alternative methods of analysis that adhere to statistical properties.

## 6.2.4 The Logistic Regression Model

The odds of an event are defined as the ratio of the probability the event will occur to the probability the event will not occur. If one denotes the odds of an event as $O$ and the probability an event will occur as $p_i$, then:

$$O = \frac{p_i}{1 - p_i} \tag{6.2}$$

The problem with the linear probability model discussed in Section 6.2.2 is that the probability is bounded between 0 and 1, but linear functions are inherently unbounded. To solve this problem, transform the probability to an odds ratio, which will remove the upper bound. Next, take the natural logarithm of the odds, which will remove the lower bound. These transformations yield the following:

$$g(x) = \log\left[\frac{p_i}{1 - p_i}\right] = \alpha + \beta_1 x_{1i} + \beta_2 x_{2i} + \cdots \tag{6.3}$$

The function $g(x)$ is often called the logit. Solving the logit for $p_i$ yields:

$$p_i = \frac{\exp(\alpha + \beta_1 x_{1i} + \beta_2 x_{2i} + \cdots)}{1 + \exp(\alpha + \beta_1 x_{1i} + \beta_2 x_{2i} + \cdots)} \tag{6.4}$$

"This equation has the desired property that no matter what values one substitutes for the $\beta$'s and the $x$'s, the $p_i$ will always be a number between 0 and 1" (Allison, 1999). The errors of the logistic model follow the binomial, not normal, distribution.

## 6.2.5 Differences between a Logistic Regression Model and a Linear Regression Model

The interpretation of parameters is different between a linear regression model and a logistic regression model. In a linear regression analysis, a coefficient represents the rate of change in $y$ for each unit change in $x$. In a logistic regression analysis, however, a coefficient represents the rate of change in the *logit* for each unit change in $x$. Finally, the exponent of a coefficient in a logistic regression analysis can be defined as the odds of success for the predictor variable. For example, suppose a university would like to predict student enrollment based on whether or not a student visited the campus. The outcome variable is "enrollment." The predictor variable is "VISIT." Set the variable "VISIT" to 1 if a student visited the campus

**Table 6.4    Analysis of Maximum Likelihood Estimates**

| Variable | DF | Parameter Estimate | Standard Error | Wald Chi-Square | Pr > Chi-Square | Standardized Estimate | Odds Ratio |
|---|---|---|---|---|---|---|---|
| Intercept | 1 | −0.6040 | 0.0272 | 493.7053 | 0.0001 | | |
| Visit | 1 | 0.7077 | 0.0569 | 154.5133 | 0.0001 | 0.159755 | 2.029 |

and 0 if the student did not visit the campus. Refer to the SAS output from PROC LOGISTIC in Table 6.4.

The coefficient for VISIT is 0.7077, and the exponent of this coefficient is 2.029, which is the odds ratio as reported in the far-right column of Table 6.4. These results show that students who visit the campus are approximately two times more likely to enroll than those who do not visit the campus.

Although the linear regression and logistic regression models differ in assumptions, the goal of using either model is the same. The goal is "to find the best fitting and most parsimonious, yet a reasonable model to describe the relationship between an outcome (dependent or response variable) and a set of independent (predictor or explanatory) variables" (Hosmer and Lemeshow, 2000). Therefore, once a decision has been made to use logistic regression, one uses the same techniques employed in linear regression (i.e., tests of significance for coefficients, diagnostics, etc.).

When building a predictive model for higher-education research, the data miner must keep a few basic principles in mind. The predictive model must be attractive in structure. Avoid models with too many predictor variables. The model must be well-timed with available data. ACT and SAT scores are received throughout the year, so these resources provide large amounts of readily available student-level data. Finally, the predictive model creation and intervention plan should be feasible in cost with respect to the appropriate budget.

# 6.3  Student Retention

When using data mining to predict student retention, the target value is retaining a student for some amount of time. The significant predictor variables for identifying students who are more likely to return depend on the type of institution as well as student preferences.

## 6.3.1  Background on Student Retention

Higher-education literature suggests that, in general, socioeconomic level, distance to hometown, living on campus, and social connections made during the first six weeks of the term are vital in predicting whether or not a student will be retained. However, the social connections are difficult to assess. Club or organization participation is usually recorded within an organization's records and not in the university's Student Information System (SIS). This makes collecting the data tedious or even impossible in some cases.

Finally, it must be noted that most student information systems were not designed by statisticians or even by data miners. Limitations in these environments sometimes prevent the extraction of specific pieces of data. Data miners must constantly be creative in the construction of new variables from existing variables.

### 6.3.2  The Student as a Customer

In this chapter, retention (the target value) is defined as a student returning to campus for a second, or the sophomore, year. Those reading this chapter from corporate environments will be interested to know that the idea of calling a student a "customer" is greatly debated in the field of higher education. Some argue that it cheapens the relationship that universities have with their students. However, corporate officials value their customers and would disagree that the relationship is not as important. The bottom line is that students come to a university expecting a service and in most cases they are paying for that service. Therefore, calling a student a "customer" is not an inferior label.

### 6.3.3  Student Retention Case Study

The University of Alabama (UA) is a public, four-year research university located in Tuscaloosa, Alabama, that was founded in 1831 as Alabama's "flagship institution." Total annual enrollment at UA is approximately 24,000 students. In the early to mid-1990s, UA had a steady 81 to 84 percent retention rate of students from the freshmen to sophomore year, but the university's registrar wanted an analysis of why students were leaving UA. Around the same time, UA and SAS developed a partnership whereby students who complete a sequence of four graduate-level courses could receive a joint Data Mining Certificate from UA and SAS. During one of the first semesters that the course "Introduction to Data Mining" was taught, a representative from the UA registrar's office worked with the professor teaching the course to develop a class project for the students. The class was given a data file of enrolled freshmen from 1999, 2000, and 2001 and asked to develop a model to identify students who were at risk to leave UA. All student identifying information, such as the campus-wide ID number and social security number, was removed. The "assignment" was presented to the class as a business problem, and the students were asked to provide a solution using a real-world interpretation with supporting statistical evidence. The class was divided into five student groups; and at the end of the term, each group presented their results to their fellow students, the professor, and a group of representatives from the registrar's office. The student results were used as a starting point for retention modeling. A team of professors and graduate students worked to refine the model.

During the refining of the model (assessment step of SEMMA), some data issues became apparent. First, most freshmen at UA take English or math during their first semester. Specifically, most freshmen take English 101 or (English Composition). Also, it appeared that math courses had more levels to differentiate students, such as Intermediate Algebra, Finite Mathematics, Pre-Calculus, Trigonometry, and Calculus. Although age was not included in the original data file, it was computed by subtracting the date of data extraction from the student's date of birth. Age was thought to be important to be able to see potential differences in traditional freshmen who are 17 or 18 years old, as opposed to a nontraditional freshmen (adult learner, military personnel, etc.). Financial aid data was coded as a binary variable where 0 = No Financial Aid and 1 = Financial Aid. The data miners (or refiners of the model) knew that historically where a freshman lives is important in determining his or her attrition rates; a dorm variable was coded as 0 = Off-campus and 1 = On-campus. Another data adaptation was made for ACT and SAT test scores. Roughly 86 percent of UA-enrolled freshmen take the ACT; therefore, SAT total scores were converted to ACT composite scores using a standard conversion scale. The maximum of the true ACT composite and the ACT-converted SAT total was used as the score on a standardized test called ACT_High. To calculate a student's "distance from home" variable, the home county seat of each student was used to compute distance to Tuscaloosa, Alabama. For example, Huntsville is the county seat of Madison County. The distance from Huntsville to Tuscaloosa is 156 miles, so the variable value for distance to home was recorded as 156 miles for a student from Huntsville. Household income data for the students in the retention study was not available.

It was mentioned previously that the CIRP Freshmen Survey is a useful instrument for assessing a freshmen class. However, when students complete the survey, they have the option of providing their social security numbers to the institution. By not including a social security number, all identifying information is removed and the CIRP Freshmen Survey results cannot be matched with student record information. This is a hazard for data mining the survey results. At UA, the number of freshmen respondents to the CIRP Freshmen Survey during the 1999 to 2001 time period of interest was only 55 percent. The CIRP Freshmen Survey data was not used to build the student retention model.

When the retention model was complete, the logistic regression model gave the lowest misclassification rate and the best ROC curve. Table 6.5 gives the retention model's significant variables.

After finalizing the retention model, the problem was to select a cut-off (or threshold) value. The team of professors and UA's registrar discussed the cost of correctly identifying students who will not return versus the cost of misidentifying others. The "screening" model of Hand (1987, 1997) was consulted. Ultimately, a cut-off value of 0.60 was selected.

Each year at UA, approximately 150 to 200 freshmen are identified by the retention model as being "at risk" to leave before the start of their second year. The at-risk student's name, major, and other profile information is sent to the student's

**Table 6.5   UA Retention Model Variables**

| |
|---|
| UA cumulative GPA |
| English course |
| English course grade |
| Distance from UA to home |
| Race |
| Math course grade |
| Total earned hours |
| ACT_High |

advisor for intervention early in the spring semester of the freshmen year. Although the interventions of the advisors have not been evaluated due to inconsistencies in the interventions, the follow-up research suggests that the model has approximately an 85 percent correct classification rate.

The retention model was UA's first attempt at using data mining to help answer a higher-education question. The partnership between enrollment management staff and the data mining course proved a great success. The data mining students are still a valuable resource for helping enrollment management staff build retention models at UA.

## 6.4   Student Enrollment

Enrollment prediction models can be built for students at any stage of the enrollment management process. This section discusses two enrollment prediction models. One model uses the pool of inquiries to a university. The second model predicts enrollment from students who have been admitted to a university. Both models were built to provide the admissions office with powerful information to use in the recruitment process.

### 6.4.1   Background on Student Enrollment

Students enroll at an institution for a variety of reasons. Personal preferences (Yan, 2002; Hovland, 2004; Enger, 2005), family traditions, programs of study, scholarship offers, financial security (McPherson, 1991; Leslie and Brinkman, 1988), and distance from home are just a few of the factors that might come into play as to where a student enrolls in the fall. All are valid reasons and important to the student at some point or another during the recruitment process. Institutions, testing services, and independent consulting firms have made it their business to build models to predict which factors are important in determining enrollment behaviors. ACT, the College Board, and Noel-Levitz are just a few of the companies that build predictive models for institutions across the nation.

The university administration drives the need for enrollment predictions to estimate faculty resources, classroom space limitations, and budgetary conditions. Campus master plans usually derive from these predictions of how many students and where will they live, eat, and park. It is of utmost concern for university presidents to know what the enrollment predictions are for a few years ahead so that they can set goals and have project plans supported by the Board of Trustees of the institution.

Early ventures in data mining in higher education usually involve a team of admissions officials, usually at the counselor or recruiter level, looking at historical data of inquiries, applications, and enrolled students. Mapping software such as Microsoft MapPoint is helpful to have a visual display of where the students are coming from and if any trends are developing. It is also important to review academic indicators of successful enrollment such as ACT or SAT test scores and high school GPAs. Profile information is collected on a wide range of demographic variables when students complete the ACT and SAT. The profile sections of the ACT and SAT also give some indication about a student's intent to enroll at a particular institution. Students are asked about college choice ranking, preference as to the size of the institution, and preference as to the type (public or private) of institution when taking these standardized tests. In addition, the admissions application provides valuable information about a student's residence, intended major, and whether or not any relatives are graduates of the institution to which the student is applying. Admissions officials can review this data in a spreadsheet, with a graph, or on a map. These raw attempts at data mining are vital to have a grasp on the data available and its anecdotal importance for enrollment.

One important aspect of the job of a college admissions counselor is the visit to a high school. The admissions counselor, however, has only a limited amount of time for individual visits with prospective students. The enrollment prediction model scores play a critical role in planning a high school visit. The admissions counselor has the ability to obtain a list of prospective students from an individual high school. The list can be sorted by model score, and the admissions counselor can target those individuals who have a high probability of enrollment. Those students with low probabilities of enrollment can be approached with a "How can University X serve you better?" attitude. The model scores allow the admissions counselors to be efficient with their time and at the same time play an important role in data mining student data for a high school visit.

## 6.4.2 Students Applying to More Colleges

Today, students are applying to even more colleges than ever before. This, in turn, makes the recruitment process last until the day that fall enrollment is counted. This "census" is usually conducted the day after the university's deadline for dropping or adding a class. The increase in applications is also affecting attendance at summer orientation programs. In 2005, the University of Alabama reported that approximately 9.3 percent of new freshmen and transfers (223 students) at summer orientation attended at least two university orientation sessions before deciding where to enroll (Davis et al., 2005). The percentage remained the same for 2006 new freshmen and transfers at the University of Alabama.

## 6.4.3 Student Enrollment Case Study: Baylor University

Baylor University is a private, four-year research university located in Waco, Texas, that was chartered in 1845 by the Republic of Texas. Baylor is the largest Baptist university in the world and has a total student enrollment of approximately 14,000 students. Beginning in Fall 1998, Baylor instituted sweeping changes to the recruitment and financial aid process. Therefore, only one year's worth of historical data was used to build the model. Two models were to be developed: Texas inquiries and non-Texas inquiries. The Texas input dataset consisted of approximately 46,000 records, and the non-Texas dataset had approximately 30,000 records. Some of the input variables are given in Table 6.6. The "Mail Qualifying Score" and "Telecounselor Score" are numerical measures of an inquiry's interest in Baylor.

For the past two years, Baylor has operated a telecounseling center manned by current undergraduate students. The center collects information to build relationships with prospective students. The information collected or verified includes addresses, e-mail addresses, academic interests, and extracurricular interests. The main goal of the telecounselors, however, is to score the prospect based on the prospect's interest in Baylor. The scores are based on the following scale: 1 = Likely to Enroll, 2 = Likely to Apply, 3 = Needs More Information, and 4 = No Longer Interested. The information obtained by the telecounselors is uploaded to the university student database as the model variable "Telecounselor Score." The telecounselors then institute calling projects designed by admissions office staff.

**Table 6.6   Example of Variables in the Inquiry Model**

| Demographic | Visits | Contacts | Others |
|---|---|---|---|
| Gender | Campus visit | No. total contacts | Mail qualifying score |
| Ethnicity | Attended premiere | No. self-initiated contacts | Telecounselor score |
| Religion | | No. travel-initiated contacts | Territory |
| High school | | No. solicited contacts | Extracurricular interests |
| SAT score | | No. referral contacts | |

The pool of inquiries for Fall 1999 was used to predict enrollment for Fall 2000 inquiries. The recruitment process for the Fall 2000 freshman class began in the summer of 1999. Therefore, a model was needed before Fall 1999 enrollment was finalized. Historically, Baylor has experienced a high deposit-to-enrollment yield. As a result, "deposit" was used as an "intent to enroll" surrogate. Plans were made to revisit the model building process after Fall 1999 enrollment was complete.

The dataset was read by Enterprise Miner, and "deposit" was designated the target variable. Missing observations for numeric variables were imputed using mean imputation. For example, if an inquiry had a missing SAT score, the mean SAT score of all observed scores was used for that observation. Several stepwise logistic regressions were performed with an increasing number of variables in each regression. The best model was chosen as that which accounted for a large portion of the variance and misclassifications, yet was easily explained. Models with more than eight variables did not have significant improvements in explaining the variance in enrollment. Additionally, the misclassification rate stabilized at an eight-variable model. Therefore, the model containing eight variables was chosen for both Texas and non-Texas. Table 6.7 contains the eight variables that were found to be significant in the Texas and non-Texas model.

Intuitively, many of these variables make sense for a model built based on a pool of inquiries to Baylor. Therefore, the amount and type of contact that an inquiry would have with Baylor provides valuable information on the inquiry's probability of enrollment. The "Mail Qualifying Score" and "Telecounselor Score" provide good measures of a prospective student's likelihood to enroll. Baylor will, in the future, build a query to find all prospects with a minimum model score who have not been contacted by the telecounselors.

The enrollment prediction model is used in a variety of ways by the Office of Admission Services (AS) at Baylor University. Once a week, the inquiries to the university are scored using the model equation, and these scores are loaded into the university's student database. The AS then has the ability to access and make queries on the scores.

**Table 6.7  Baylor Inquiry Enrollment Model Variables**

| Texas Model | Non-Texas Model |
|---|---|
| Attended a premiere | Attended a premiere |
| Campus visit | Campus visit |
| Extracurricular interest | Extracurricular Interest |
| High school | High school |
| Mail qualifying score | Mail qualifying score |
| SAT score | No. self-initiated contacts |
| No. self-initiated contacts | No. solicited contacts |
| Telecounselor score | Telecounselor score |

Every summer, AS conducts a mass mailing of viewbooks to prospective Baylor students. These viewbooks are both expensive to produce and to mail. Using the model scores, AS has the capability of targeting those students who are most likely to enroll. As a result, AS sends viewbooks to the top 75 percent scoring inquiries. The other inquiries receive a stand-alone application and a reply card that enables the student to request more information, such as a viewbook. By segmenting the pool in this manner, AS is able to save substantial printing and postage costs. As this process is perfected and Baylor has more confidence in the models, AS officials at Baylor hope to eliminate all paper mailings to the lower scoring students.

### 6.4.4  Student Enrollment Case Study: University of Alabama

In 2003, the University of Alabama (UA) hired a new president who set a goal to increase total student enrollment to 28,000 by the year 2013. Student enrollment in 2003 was just above 20,000, so 28,000 in ten years seemed a rather lofty goal. Admissions officials knew that the number of incoming new freshmen would directly affect the increase in total enrollment. In addition to increasing the quantity of the freshmen class, the president also gave the admissions office the task of increasing the quality of the freshmen class. To accomplish this, UA had to become more targeted with recruitment efforts. Data from the Western Interstate Commission for Higher Education (2003) suggested that the high school graduation rate for the state of Alabama would remain relatively flat over the next 15 years. Therefore, UA would have to recruit out of state to meet the president's goals. Various initiatives were constructed and deployed, many of which were successful. UA hired regional recruiters to work for UA, but live in target markets for student recruitment. Also, the methods for purchasing names of prospective students became more strategic by looking at ACT and SAT scores of senders and applicants and where these students were located. However, no research had been done to identify what makes a student enroll at UA.

In May 2005, discussion began at UA to create a model to predict freshmen enrollment. The model would be used to give a numerical estimate of the size of the freshmen class and also assign each admitted student a probability of enrollment. The data sources were the admissions application, the ACT profile data section, scholarship data, and financial aid records. The model variables did not include whether or not a student lived on campus because UA freshmen were going to be required to live on campus beginning in fall 2006. Also, the CIRP Freshmen Survey and summer orientation evaluation data were not used because UA students complete these surveys after they are already on campus for summer orientation. Being at summer orientation is considered being one step closer to enrollment at UA than just being admitted.

Admitted freshmen from 2002, 2003, and 2004 were used to build and validate the predictive model. There were 22,932 admitted freshmen from 2002 to 2004. The freshmen class from 2005 had not been finalized when the model-building began; therefore, 2005 data was not used to build the model. No international students were included in the data because international students have different

**Table 6.8   New Categories for ACT Profile Section**

| New Category | Definition |
| --- | --- |
| "No Response" | The student had an ACT Composite score, but the profile question was left blank. |
| "No ACT" | The student did not have an ACT Composite score, indicating that he did not take the ACT. |

reasons for enrollment than domestic students. Outliers were removed from the data and missing data values for the ACT Composite, SAT Total, and high school GPA were imputed with the mean value. Inevitably, missing data occurred when a student refused to answer questions or was unable to express a preference in the profile section of the ACT. Therefore, two new categories were created. These categories are listed in Table 6.8.

There were 49 variables, both quantitative and qualitative, tested in the model for significance. The dataset was read by Enterprise Miner, and enroll (a binary variable) was named the target variable. Stepwise logistic regressions were performed and the best model was chosen based on the lowest misclassification rate and keeping the number of significant variables practical. The best model contained 14 variables. Table 6.9 contains the variables that were found significant.

"Financial Aid Total Aid" and "Financial Aid Budget" were used in the model upon the recommendation of the UA Financial Aid Office. They are all

**Table 6.9   UA Enrollment Model Variables**

| |
| --- |
| Financial Aid Total Aid |
| College Choice Number [a] |
| Financial Aid Budget |
| Race |
| College at UA |
| Level Parents Income [a] |
| High School Cumulative GPA |
| Expect to Apply Aid [a] |
| ACT_High |
| Residency |
| Varsity Athletics College [a] |
| College Size Preference [a] |
| Want Honors Courses [a] |
| Need Help Writing [a] |

[a] *ACT profile variable.*

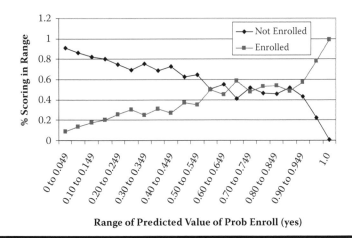

**Figure 6.2   Yield of 2005 UA freshman for each predicted probability range.**

encompassing of grants, loans, and scholarships. "Financial Aid Total Aid" is the total of all federal aid, scholarships, and outside resource aid. If "Financial Aid Total Aid" is 0, assume the student has funding for school. "Financial Aid Budget" is the cost for the student to attend UA as determined based on the Free Application for Federal Student Aid (FAFSA). If "Financial Aid Budget" is populated (that is, has a number), the student completed the FAFSA; if 0, no FAFSA was completed. "College Choice Number" has been shown by Hovland (2004) in previous ACT research to be important in predicting enrollment. Of the 14 significant variables, half are variables obtained from the profile section of the ACT.

The 2005 freshmen were scored in the model, and the results of the logistic regression showed a low misclassification rate of 25.7 percent when using a 0.5 probability cut-off value. Figure 6.2 shows the yield of 2005 freshmen for each predicted probability range, displayed in quintiles.

The model was used to estimate the 2006 freshmen class size at UA, and to help admissions counselors prioritize their contacts based on those with a higher probability of enrollment. The next step in using predictive modeling in enrollment at UA is to build state-specific models for states where UA regional recruiters are located. Additionally, UA is interested in targeting specific ranges of ACT and SAT scoring students. Research done through data mining will reveal what makes higher standardized test scorers more likely to enroll at the University of Alabama than a lower scorer.

## 6.5   Donor Giving

As a student reaches the end of the enrollment management process, universities hope that each alumnus (alumnae) will become a donor of his (her) money and time to help support the institution. The primary business question when modeling donor giving is how data mining is used to sustain maximally the fundraising efforts of a university.

## 6.5.1  *Donor Giving Background*

Universities across the nation rely heavily on the gifts provided by graduates and supporters of their institutions. Therefore, university presidents spend a lot of time networking with groups of high-profile alumni and personalities asking for monetary gifts as well as gifts of time through speaking engagements and volunteer events sponsored by the university. Alumni offices and associations collect vast amounts of demographic, biological, and professional data on graduates. This data, along with similar information on university supporters, facilitates the identification of established donor behavior. The donor behavior can also be linked to identifiable characteristics that can be used to find non-donors who possess donor characteristics.

Donors can be classified into one of five groups for donor management, as depicted in Table 6.10.

"Annual gift donors" are those who join alumni associations or scholarship clubs and make regular contributions on a yearly basis. "Major donors" are those who give the university a high dollar-amount gift. Indications of "high dollar" will vary by institution and year of donation. "Planned gift donors" are those who have willed estate or trust funds to a university. "Retention/upgrade donors" are those who increase their yearly regular contribution or move up to a higher dollar donation group. Finally, the "new donor" group is an important group that has potential to donate for the first time.

There has been a good base of research on donor giving. Elliot (2006), Clotfelter (2003), Wolverton (2003), Mercer (1996), Harrison (1995), McMillen (1988), and Keller (1982) discuss donor giving at various levels and to different types of institutions, both public and private. African-American donor giving research has been done by Cohen (2006). Special groups such as athletes and graduate students have been researched by Baade (1996) and Okunade (1996). However, with the exception of Gunsalus (2005) and Baade et al. (1993), not much research has been done to predict potential donors and their gifts. This section identifies important variables in using data mining tools to predict possible donors, repeat donors, and the amount of the donor's monetary gift.

**Table 6.10   Types of Donor Groups**

| |
|---|
| Annual Gift Donor |
| Major Donor |
| Planned Gift Donor |
| Retention/Upgrade Donor |
| New Donor |

## 6.5.2 Data Needs with Donors

The process of working through the variables and developing models for donor giving is a process similar to that of retention and enrollment modeling. It requires a team approach, including personnel from University Development, Institutional Research, the Alumni Association, and the President's Office. In each instance, the development of the donor profile requires identification of important variables. Data should be collected on graduation year, college of attendance within the university, academic major, and other variables such as date of birth, marital status, number of children, occupation, and gift history if it exists. Any major fundraising efforts should be noted before obtaining historical data. Data used in the model-building dataset that occurred during a time of a targeted campaign of giving will be affected and should be used with caution.

## 6.5.3 Donor Giving Case Study: Baylor University

In 2004, Baylor University was interested in how data mining could be used for fundraising efforts. Questions such as the following were considered:

1. How can we identify potential major donors?
2. How can we predict the propensity of a donor to make an annual gift?
3. How can we identify potential planned giving donors?
4. How can we identify current donors who could possibly move to the next level of giving?
5. How can we identify non-donors who have the characteristics of becoming a donor?
6. How can we predict the expected value of a donor's gift?

Baylor University used the five donor groups outlined in Table 6.10 to establish data mining for donor giving procedures. Each group serves a distinctive purpose to the Baylor University Development Office from the perspective of verification of ability to give, application to give, and the subsequent careful working of the application to the appropriate gift generation group. By tackling the questions sequentially, Baylor wanted to establish a process, a procedure, and a set of results that would serve the university to help facilitate the successful closure of the "Campaign for Greatness" in a timely manner. The "Campaign for Greatness" is Baylor's most recent endowment campaign. Baylor also wanted to provide a running start for the campaign that would culminate with the successful conclusion of the goals of "Baylor 2012." "Baylor 2012" is a ten-year vision statement developed to set goals for Baylor University to become a top-tier institution of higher education by the establishment of 12 imperatives. This section presents the results for the first modeling objectives — namely, the development of a general donor predictive model.

**Table 6.11    Variable Categories for the General Donor Giving Model**

| |
|---|
| Bio/demo data |
| Contact information |
| Degree data |
| Activities (alumni and collegiate) |
| Gift information |
| External rating information |
| Research data |

Datasets were constructed that consisted of variables from the previous ten years (1994 to 2004) to predict who would make a gift in the year 2005. The data sources were University Development, Institutional Research, the Alumni Association, and the President's Office. There were a total of 96 possible variables included in the modeling dataset. All variables can be placed into the categories shown in Table 6.11.

The data was read by Enterprise Miner™. The target variable modeled in this dataset was making a contribution in 2004. A profit theory matrix was established for the target variable to ensure classification cut-offs. The key issue in establishing the cut-off value is the extent to which misclassifications occur; that is, the classification of an individual/family who will not donate as a donor, or the classification of an individual or family who will donate as a non-donor. It seems inappropriate to treat these two types of classification mistakes with equal importance. Missing observations for numeric variables were imputed using mean values. Missing values for categorical variables were imputed using the mode, or most frequently occurring value of the variable.

Models were evaluated using the assessment node in the Enterprise Miner. In general, all the models examined were able to discriminate between donors and non-donors to approximately the same degree. For example, the models were all compared using the receiver operating characteristic (ROC) curve. Figure 6.3 shows the ROC graph for the donor giving model.

The area under the ROC curve is a common measure of the ability of a predictive model to distinguish between the two values of a binary target. The Lorentz curve (Figure 6.4) and the lift chart (Figure 6.5) note that all models appear to perform in a similar manner.

The Lorentz curve provides helpful insight into how a model might be applied. For example, if the decision-tree model was selected for implementation, the Lorentz curve shows that if a campaign was targeted at the top 30 percent of the prospects in the database to which the model is applied, then this group of individuals or families would contain approximately 86 percent of all prospects who are likely to donate.

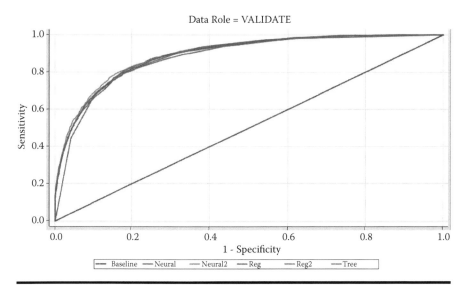

**Figure 6.3   ROC graph for donor giving methods.**

From a review of the model comparisons and evaluations, no one model appears superior to the others in its ability to distinguish between donors and non-donors. Thus, to select a model for implementation, a criterion of ease of interpretation is appropriate. Table 6.12 contains the variables that were found to be significant.

Baylor is constantly testing this model to assess its ability to predict donors with new data. Baylor is also adjusting and refining the model to achieve better results.

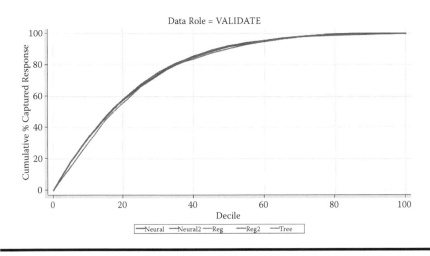

**Figure 6.4   Lorentz curve for donor giving models.**

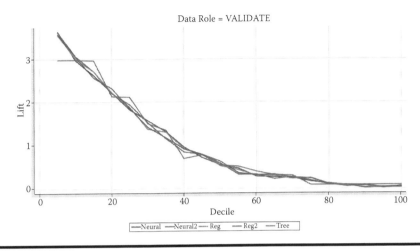

**Figure 6.5    Lift chart for donor giving models.**

**Table 6.12    Baylor Donor Giving Model Variables**

| |
|---|
| Gift five-year percentage |
| Model score |
| Logarithm of gift amount back one year |
| Rating claritas |
| Logarithm of mean gift amount for a five-year period |
| Gender |
| Contact asked a telemarketer |
| Alumni association activity |
| Marital status |
| State split |
| Age last year |
| Echelon rating |
| Gift ten-year percentage |
| Baylor Chamber membership |
| Contact asked a non-telemarketer |
| Alumni development activity |
| Church affiliation |
| College of Baccalaureate degree |
| Job group |
| Baccalaureate degree from Baylor |

## 6.6 Conclusion and Future Directions

Enrollment, retention, and donor giving predictions are concepts in higher education that benefit from the field of data mining. Predictive modeling allows colleges and universities to save time and money recruiting students and construct intervention plans to keep them enrolled at the institution. The cost to recruit a 2005 freshmen according to Noel-Levitz (2005) was approximately $454 per student. The attrition of students results in lost tuition dollars and other revenue generated by the institution and surrounding campus area. Donor giving predictions help colleges and universities create new programs, fund scholarships for students, and build academic and residential structures that supplement recruitment and retention initiatives.

With the increasing availability of data in higher education, recruitment, retention, and donor giving prediction models can be adjusted to reflect the time of year. Enrollment predictions will vary based on application and scholarship priority dates, as well as summer orientation registration and residential living deadlines. For the retention model, the use of mid-term grading by many institutions may change the point at which an at-risk student is identified or even contacted. Finally, donors who have a higher propensity to give around special holidays or times of institutional welfare can be approached with special marketing campaigns that encourage donation.

Customer relationship management (CRM) software will help build better models within the field of higher education as more specific data is collected on constituents. Many businesses already use CRM when contacting their customers. Admissions officials can monitor how many times an enrolled student was contacted as opposed to a non-enrolled student. Students can be classified not just by a probability model score, but also with a profile of enrollment (or retention). For example, a student with a high probability of enrollment may need only minimal contact with a few black-and-white mailers, while a student with a lower probability of enrollment may need a personal phone call and the colorful, impressive view book.

As with any organization, data miners in higher education must be aware and document any changes in standard practices. Admissions standards such as the GPA or ACT/SAT minimum score requirements may change to remain competitive with the academic market. Records offices might adopt a new grading scale that includes pluses and minuses (A+, A, A–, B+, ...). Alumni affairs offices might institute a new donation structure to allow for lifetime membership in the alumni association. All of these changes affect the data used to make decisions at institutions of higher education.

As students evolve from suspects to donors, data mining allows those in higher education to contact and assess engagement and satisfaction at all stages of enrollment management. It is a concept that may have begun in the business world; however, college and university administrators are well aware of the importance of data mining in higher education. It provides a new perspective on the student as a customer. Hopefully, data mining will continue to permeate all the hallowed halls of the colleges and universities of higher education in our country and beyond.

# References

Allison, P. D. (1999), *Logistic Regression Using the SAS System: Theory and Application,* Cary, NC: SAS Institute Inc.

Baade, R. A. and Sundberg, J. O. (1996), "Fourth Down and Gold to Go? Assessing the Link between Athletics and Alumni Giving," *Social Science Quarterly,* 77(4), 789–803.

Baade, R. A. and Sundberg, J. O. (1996), "What Determines Alumni Generosity?" *Economics of Education Review,* 15(1), 75–81.

"Baylor 2012" (2001), http://www.baylor.edu/vision/index.php?id=9690, Baylor University, Waco, TX.

"Campaign for Greatness" (2001), http://www.baylor.edu/Lariat/news.php?action=story&story=17083, Baylor University, Waco, TX.

Clotfelter, C. (2003), "Alumni Giving to Private Colleges and Universities," *Economics of Education Review,* 22(2), 109–120.

*Cost of Recruiting Report: Summary of Findings for Two-Year and Four-Year Institutions* (2005), Noel-Levitz, Iowa City, IA.

Davis, C. M., Johnson, D. B., Land, H. A., Mann, B. S., McGhee, M., and Radford, H. (2005), *Bama Bound 2005 New Student Orientation Report,* University of Alabama, Tuscaloosa, AL.

Enger, K. (2005), "New Students' College Choice Characteristics," *Trends,* 6(2), 1–2.

Grant, A. S. C. and Wolverton, M. (2003), "Gaps in Stewardship Quality at Three Institutions," *International Journal of Educational Advancement,* 4(1), 45–64.

Gunsalus, R. (2005), "The Relationship of Institutional Characteristics and Giving Participation Rates of Alumni," *International Journal of Educational Advancement,* 5(2), 162–170.

Hand D. J. (1987), "Screening versus Prevalence Estimation," *Applied Statistics,* 36(1), 1–7.

Hand D. J. (1997), *Construction and Assessment of Classification Rules,* New York, NY: John Wiley & Sons, Inc.

Harrison, W. B. (1995), "College Relations and Fund-Raising Expenditures: Influencing the Probability of Alumni Giving to Higher Education," *Economics of Education Review,* 14(1), 73–84.

Hosmer, D. W. and Lemeshow, S. (2000), *Applied Logistic Regression, 2nd Edition.* New York, NY: John Wiley & Sons, Inc.

Hovland, M. (2004), "Unraveling the Mysteries of Student College Selection," Paper presented at the 2004 ACT Enrollment Planner's Conference, Chicago, IL.

Introduction to SEMMA (2005), *Help Files of Enterprise Miner Software,* Cary, NC: SAS Institute Inc.

*Knocking at the College Door: Projections of High School Graduates by State, Income, and Race/Ethnicity,* Boulder, CO: WICHE.

Leslie, L. L. and Brinkman, P. T. (1988), *The Economic Value of Higher Education,* Washington, D.C: American Council on Education.

McPherson, M.S. (1991), "Does Student Aid Affect College Enrollment? New Evidence on a Persistent Controversy," *The American Economic Review,* 81(1), 309–318.

Okunade, A. A. (1996), "Graduate School Alumni Donations to Academic Funds: Microdata Evidence," *American Journal of Economics and Sociology,* 55(2), 213–229.

Yan, W. (2002), *Postsecondary Enrollment and Persistence of Students from Rural Pennsylvania,* Harrisburg, PA: Center for Rural Pennsylvania.

*Chapter 7*

# Data Mining for Market Segmentation with Market Share Data: A Case Study Approach

Illya Mowerman and Scott J. Lloyd

## Contents

## 7.1 Introduction

This is a chapter on data mining an existing prescription drug market that treats respiratory tract infections (RTIs) and comprises six competitors. One of the six competitors of the RTI market is the employer of one of the authors of this chapter; the company is referred to as Pharma.

Pharma understood the RTI market to have two niches: (1) strong antibiotics and (2) weak antibiotics. Pharma had one of the strong antibiotics. Pharma's antibiotic, referred to as S1, had been on the market for four years with a market share that had reached its plateau at 5.5 percent. This market share was far below Pharma's expectations, thus translating into lower than expected sales for the product, and lower than expected sales per salesperson, which is the main channel for promoting this drug. Lower sales per salesperson results in lower revenue per sales call than what was expected and budgeted, rendering a lower ratio of sales divided by sales calls, indicating to Pharma that the cost of sales was over-budget.

Given the low sales of S1 and its high costs per call, the company's sales targeting was called into question. The current marketing plan created ten groups of physicians, also called deciles, based on the amount of scripts (prescriptions) within the RTI market they had written (prescribed) in the past 12 months. The sales force would then call on the physicians of the higher deciles — and with a greater frequency, the higher the decile. Perhaps a different grouping of physicians would be more effective.

This chapter focuses on data mining, specifically cluster analysis techniques using the raw market share data of each drug in the RTI market at the physician (prescriber) level. The objective is to find better groupings of physicians, rather than deciles, to improve the sales and marketing efforts, thus lowering the cost per call made by the sales representatives.

In this chapter the authors use a large selection of clustering techniques used in data mining to compare and contrast the relative usefulness and interpretability of the clusters. Now that the objective of the analysis had been determined, the next step in this analysis was to limit the clustering techniques to those that more likely to form useful market niches for the specific data in this case study. Afterward, a brief background of the case is given. Then, the dataset is described. Next, the implementation of each of the selected techniques on the dataset is reported. Then a comparison of the results is presented, followed by the conclusions.

## 7.2 Overview

### 7.2.1 Clustering Techniques Implemented

The selected techniques include non-parametric hierarchical clustering, parametric non-hierarchical clustering, classification and regression trees, and neural networks.

The algorithms selected for hierarchical clustering include k-nearest-neighbor (KNN) (Wong et al. 1983) and the clustering methods proposed by Gitman (1973) and Huizinga (1978). The KNN algorithm uses the k-nearest-neighbor density function to compute dissimilarity measures, where the distance $r$ is measured from observation $x$ to the $k$th-nearest observation. The density of the KNN is computed by dividing the number of observations within the sphere $s$ of radius $r$ and center $x$ by the volume of $s$. The bias of KNN is that it tends to find clusters with very similar numbers of observations within each cluster.

The clustering algorithms proposed by Gitman in 1973 and Huizinga in 1978, similar in nature, use a density estimate similar to that of k-nearest-neighbor, calculated by dividing the number of observations within a neighborhood by the product of the volume of the neighborhood and the total sample size. The algorithm includes neighbors so as to increase the density of the neighborhood. The algorithm halts when no more neighborhoods can be joined while increasing the density of the newly formed neighborhood. The size of neighborhoods compared to greater neighborhoods is determined by the value of k, which like the KNN algorithm is determined by the researcher. The clustering algorithms proposed by Gitman in 1973 and Huizinga in 1978 have very little bias as far as the shape of the resulting clusters and the number of observations within each cluster.

The K-means algorithm (Hartigan 1975) is a non-hierarchical clustering technique, specifically a divisive or partitive technique that uses the Euclidean distance measure to partition a dataset into k clusters by grouping the observations so as to ensure that no movement of any observation from one cluster to another would further reduce the sum of squares of each cluster. The researcher is required to input the value of k (the number of clusters), which is most likely an iterative process, requiring the researcher to have a domain of understanding of the dataset that the researcher is seeking to cluster.

The K-means algorithm initiates by assigning seeds as the centroids of the clusters in a random fashion. The seeds are then allowed to move with each iteration of the algorithm to try to minimize the sum of squares within the cluster. The K-means procedure is very sensitive to outliers, and thus is prone to produce unique clusters with outliers. In addition, another bias of the K-means algorithm is that it has the tendency to produce spherical clusters (Milligan, 1980; Vesanto et al., 2000).

Classification and regression trees (CART) (Breiman et al., 1984) is a tree model that consists of a hierarchy of univariate binary decisions. A dataset is introduced into the algorithm specifying a dependent variable and independent variables. The data is then partitioned into two groups on the variable that best differentiates the dataset, at a determined value of that variable where the two resulting groups are as different as possible. Each group then descends through the tree as the model repeats this procedure of partitioning the data on the variable that best differentiates the descending data. The main difference between using a CART algorithm to obtain groups within a dataset and using the above-mentioned clustering techniques is that with CART, the researcher must define a dependent variable, and the splitting decisions are made on one variable at a time instead of using a combination of all variables in the dataset.

Since the introduction of CART, there has been extensive research on this algorithm. Bruntine (1992) and Chipman et al. (1998) discuss Bayesian extension to CART. Gehrke et al. (1999) studied the scalability of the CART algorithm for very large datasets.

The self-organizing map (SOM) introduced by Kohonen (1995) can be described as a nonlinear, ordered, smooth mapping of high-dimensional input data manifolds onto the elements of a regular, low-dimensional array. SOMs use a form of vector quantization to display in its simplest form, on a rectangle, a map of the input data where frontiers differentiate homogenous groups of data. This algorithm, being part of the domain of neural networks, differentiates itself from most neural networks with the feature that the SOM outputs the underlying characteristics of the different groups.

The SOM algorithm has been studied extensively; more than 4000 academic papers have been published in relation to it (Kohonen, 2001). The implementation of the SOM algorithm is quite extensive in the business world, including its implementation in finance (Serrano-Cinca, 1996), market segmentation (Rushmeier et al., 1997), as well as in many other areas of business.

Table 7.1 summarizes some of the outstanding characteristics of the techniques to be used.

## 7.2.2 Clustering Techniques Not Implemented

Other common parametric hierarchical clustering techniques will not be employed in this research, including average linkage (Sokal and Micheneer, 1958), complete linkage (Sorensen, 1948), single linkage (Florek et al., 1951a, b), Ward's minimum-variance (Ward, 1963), and centroid (Sokal and Micheneer, 1958).

The average linkage technique uses the average Euclidean distance between two observations each in different clusters; this method tends to join clusters with small variances, and there is bias in forming clusters of similar variance. The complete

**Table 7.1  Summary of Characteristics of Techniques Used**

| Algorithm | Forms clusters of equal size | Forms clusters of equal variance | Forms spherical clusters | Sensitive to outliers | Ability to form clusters of small size | Predeter-mined number of | Predefined Values (i.e. K) |
|---|---|---|---|---|---|---|---|
| KNN | No | No | No | Moderate | No | Yes | Yes |
| Modeclus | No | No | No | No | Yes | No | Yes |
| K-Means | No | No | Yes | Yes | Yes | Yes | No |
| SOM | No | No | No | No | Yes | No | No |
| CART | No | No | No | No | Yes | No | No |

linkage clustering technique uses the maximum Euclidean distance between two observations, each from different clusters; this method is strongly biased to produce clusters of similar diameters, and it is severely affected by moderate outliers (Milligan, 1980). Single linkage clustering uses the Euclidean distance of the two closest observations, each in different clusters. Single linkage has many theoretical virtues (Jardine and Sibson, 1971; Hartigan, 1981); nonetheless, this technique presents a poor performance in Monte Carlo studies (Milligan, 1980). In addition, single linkage fails to detect compact clusters. Ward's minimum-variance uses the distance between two clusters, the ANOVA sum of squares between the two clusters added up over all the variables. Ward's method is biased in creating clusters of roughly the same number of observations, and is very sensitive to outliers (Milligan, 1980). The centroid method compares the distance between clusters as the squared Euclidean distance between the centroids of the clusters; this method is more robust to outliers than most other hierarchical methods, but in other aspects does not perform as well as Ward's or average linkage (Milligan, 1980).

In reviewing the above-mentioned clustering techniques, the underlying definition of data mining was in conflict with these techniques. In data mining, the researcher is not to make any assumptions about the data In this case where clusters are to form, the assumption that the clusters should be of equal size, variance, or that there should be no compact clusters would go against the definition of data mining.

## 7.2.3  Case Background

The background of this study was initiated at a pharmaceutical company that promoted an antibiotic, which is designated throughout this chapter as S1, an antibiotic that treats respiratory tract infections. S1 had been in the U.S. RTI marketplace for more than four years at the time of this study. The market as defined by the marketing team of S1 was composed of six competitors, including three antibiotics of a lesser potency and three of a stronger potency; S1 was one of the stronger antibiotics. It should be noted that the RTI market was experiencing close to no growth, and this in conjunction with a stagnant market share was not sitting well with upper management's demands of higher profits — the bottom line.

The marketing department had used consultants in the past for obtaining previous market segmentations, while experiencing lower than expected market share, which was slightly over 5 percent at the time of the study. In an attempt to obtain a more insightful market segmentation, the marketing team turned to the sales operations department, specifically to one of the authors of this chapter, for a new segmentation.

The research question as defined by the marketing team was to obtain a market segmentation for promotional purposes that would enable higher market share and lower promotional costs. The process of obtaining the research question was not trivial; rather, it was an iterative process of questions and answers between the head of the marketing team for S1 and the sales operations analyst.

## 7.3 The Data

The dataset used was data on a specific* antibiotic market. The variables are all continuous. Each record describes the market volume measured in total number of prescriptions (also referred to as scripts) of a distinct prescriber (i.e., a physician); the market shares of each product for that specific prescriber within the specific antibiotic market, which will be referred to from here on as the market; samples of the drug given to the prescriber; and the number of sales visits made to the prescribers by sales representatives.

There are a total of six competitors within the market. The competitors can be divided into two distinct classes: (1) a stronger antibiotic and (2 a weaker antibiotic. The main difference between the two classes of antibiotics, as it refers to prescribing, is that some prescribers prefer to use a weak antibiotic as a first line of treatment, and if it has no positive results on the patient, then the prescriber will use the more potent antibiotics. Other prescribers tend to prescribe first a stronger antibiotic. The two types of antibiotics are not flagged in the data; rather, this is a point to be used in the analysis and is part of the domain knowledge of the data.

There are three weak antibiotics, which are referred to as antibiotics W1, W2, and W3. The strong antibiotics are referred to as S1, S2, and S3. The market volume variable is labeled M.

## 7.4 Implementations

The KNN procedure was implemented using SAS®. The KNN algorithm produced few clusters with many observations, accounting for approximately 90 percent of the population, and many clusters with very few observations each. The results reflect an extreme sensitivity to outliers, as well as a lack of capability to form different clusters within the bulk of the population.

An attempt was made to reduce the number of clusters by visualization, where clusters were graphed using a stacked bar chart (see Figure 7.1), but the clusters were too different to group together.

The implications of the sensitivity to outliers on the dataset used is that for practical modeling purposes, such as response models like regression, or logistic regression, the KNN algorithm was only able to produce two groups that were useful for modeling purposes. The other clusters produced were not useful for modeling purposes because they possess too few (less than 42) observations.

The K-means algorithm was implemented using SAS®. The number of clusters K was predetermined as 30. The algorithm presented sensitivity to outliers, which is expected to a certain degree, by forming clusters with very few observations. As

---

* Specific meaning that it pertains to a specific segment of the antibiotic market such as the urinary tract infection antibiotic market, or the respiratory tract infection market.

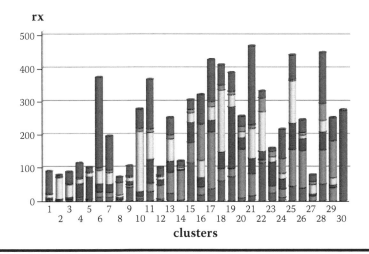

**rx**

**clusters**

**Figure 7.1    KNN algorithm: clusters graphed using a bar chart.**

previously discussed, these clusters with few observations are of little use for further modeling. Conversely, there were other clusters formed that possessed many observations. When the results from the K-means procedure were graphed as in Figure 7.1, the number of clusters was easily reduced, by combining similar clusters into eight clusters.

In the case of the technique developed by Gitman in 1973 and Huizinga in 1978, which was implemented using SAS® using the procedure called Modeclus with method = 1, there were 26 clusters formed, with cluster populations ranging from 65 to 3177. Most clusters were of acceptable size for further modeling. When the clusters were graphed on a stacked bar chart, it was observed that many clusters could be grouped together, forming seven groups. This method is designated Modeclus for simplicity.

After observing that the number of clusters could be reduced to a lower number, another attempt was made to form fewer clusters using the same algorithm but with a higher value for K. Although fewer clusters were obtained, the quality of uniqueness of the clusters suffered, concluding that the result that rendered a higher number of clusters, followed by a visual grouping of the clusters, rendered a better result.

The regression tree ran in MatLab® and then was pruned to an optimal level — "optimal" defined as the minimum value between cross-validation and re-substitution errors. To use the regression tree as a clustering technique, the researchers chose the product of interest (S1) as the dependent variable, and all other variables as independent variables. The optimal tree rendered 21 groups. The number of observations per group ranged from 22 to 4844, making the groups optimal for further modeling, although when graphed by the use of stacked bar charts, it appeared to the researchers that the number of groups formed could be reduced to 12. Figure 7.2 illustrates the resulting tree.

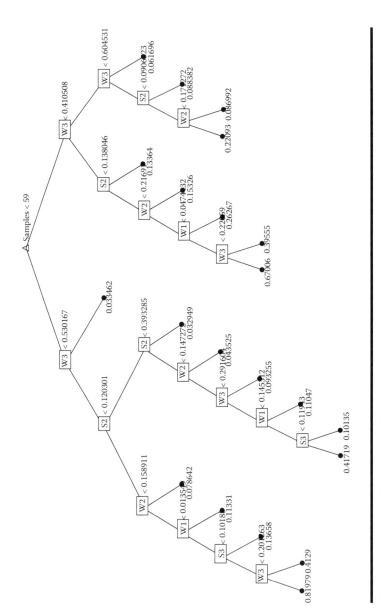

**Figure 7.2 Regression tree results.**

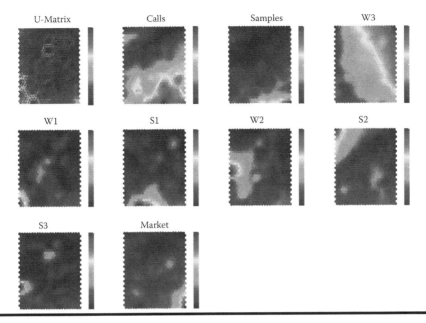

**Figure 7.3    SOM implemented with MatLab.**

The self-organizing map (SOM) implemented with MatLab® shown in Figure 7.3 partitioned the population in five distinguishable groups, but the use of these groups was limited. Nonetheless, the SOM was of great use for visualization purposes, enhancing the understanding of the characteristics of the population. SOMs are used in many cases as a visualization technique for high-dimensional data (Kohonen, 2001). The data was standardized using various techniques through SAS®, but the most interpretable SOM resulted using Z standardization.

A commonality was observed in all clustering techniques; variable W3 had a large presence in almost all clusters formed, which can be best explained by Figure 7.2, where W1 reflects a large presence in the market.

## 7.5    Comparison of Results

The task of evaluating the clustering technique can be subjective; nonetheless, this section addresses the quality of the clusters formed in an objective manner. The aspects evaluated included (1) the capabilities to form distinct clusters where each antibiotic has at least one cluster where that antibiotic has the highest market share; (2) the capacity to form clusters with mutually exclusive rules of belonging to each cluster formed; and (3) the simple statistics of the number of observations per cluster that illustrate if the algorithm is capable of forming clusters of unequal sizes.

**Table 7.2  Summary of Results: Capability to Form Distinct Clusters**

|      | Modeclus | K-Means | KNN | RT | SOM |
|------|----------|---------|-----|----|-----|
| w1   |          | x       | x   |    | x   |
| w2   | x        | x       | x   | x  |     |
| w3   | x        | x       | x   | x  |     |
| s1   |          | x       | x   | x  | x   |
| s2   | x        | x       | x   | x  |     |
| s3   |          | x       |     |    | x   |

The objective of forming at least one cluster for each antibiotic where that antibiotic has the highest market share is particular to the dataset at hand, as well as a business objective. It is of interest to a business to identify segments where the competitors are dominating in market share, enabling the firm's marketing team to develop a more focused promotional message. Another reason for identifying segments where the competitors are dominating is for ROI (return-on-investment) purposes after a promotional campaign, this done by identifying which targets have moved from clusters where the competitors dominated the market over to the cluster characterized by the dominance of the company's product; this is also referred to as market mobility.

Table 7.2 summarizes the results of the first objective. K-means was the only algorithm able to identify at least one cluster per antibiotic where that antibiotic dominates the market. Nonetheless, although the SOM did not form distinct clusters, the algorithm did produce a clear visualization where distinct clusters could be formed manually by the researcher.

The second characteristic evaluated was the mutual exclusivity of membership to each cluster. The evaluation was performed by the capability of developing rules for cluster membership. The SOM was able to form mutually exclusive groups, but of very low practical use. The K-means, KNN, and Modeclus algorithms formed mutually exclusive groups with greater practical use. The regression tree formed mutually exclusive groups with the characteristic of groups formed heavily at diverse levels of the dependent variable S1, which may be of great use if the focus of the research is more on the antibiotic S1 and not on the market (i.e., all the antibiotics).

The final aspect studied was the number of observations per cluster. The goal was not to discriminate better or worse, but rather to illustrate the tendencies of the algorithms. Table 7.3 lists the statistics of the number of observations per cluster for each algorithm.

Theory on KNN says that the algorithm has a tendency to form clusters of equal size (Wong and Lane, 1983); this was not observed here. The Modeclus algorithm was said to have little bias in forming clusters of equal size, but the results show that of all the algorithms, Modeclus created clusters with the most similar sizes. K-means follows the Modeclus algorithm in creating clusters of equal size, followed by the regression tree, and finally the SOM.

**Table 7.3 Statistics of the Number of Observations per Cluster for Each Algorithm**

|  | Modeclus | K-Means | KNN | RT |
|---|---|---|---|---|
| Mean | 796.58 | 666.13 | 666.13 | 685.57 |
| Standard Deviation | 777.90 | 1,173.01 | 1,694.73 | 1,267.70 |
| Skewness | 1.51 | 3.48 | 4.24 | 3.98 |
| Kurtosis | 2.00 | 13.53 | 20.00 | 15.24 |
| Max | 3,177 | 5,913 | 9,003 | 4,844 |
| Min | 65 | 6 | 1 | 22 |
| N Clusters | 26 | 30 | 30 | 21 |

## 7.6 Results Analysis

The most adequate technique for this particular market segmentation, and future modeling purposes, was the K-means algorithm. This algorithm produced clusters that were most unique among themselves, after visual grouping, making it easier to describe the unique characteristics of each cluster.

Although the K-means algorithm was found to be the best for this dataset, it is not to say that the other techniques were not of use. The SOM served as an excellent preliminary visualization tool, while the regression tree, Modeclus, and K-Nearest Neighbor served to confirm that the product labeled W3 is a product that has a large presence in most clusters, which has further implications.

Antibiotic W3 appears to be in a class by itself, and it may be interpreted that W3 is not a competitor, or that it possesses certain characteristics that make it a complement to the market rather than a competitor. That is, perhaps W3 is like the nails in the market of hammers, reflecting an association to the competing hammers rather than being a competitor itself.

With the unique behavior of W3 obtained through the clustering algorithms, the question arose among the marketing team as to if they had any knowledge of W3 being unique in any way from the other antibiotics in the RTI market, other than it not being one of the stronger antibiotics. The marketing team revealed that, through previous panel discussions and focus groups, W3 was considered, by a substantial group of prescribers, as a first and only line of therapy in certain cases of respiratory tract infections — this means that many physicians are able to correctly diagnose the severity of an infection when W3 will "do the trick." This then leaves no reason to prescribe another weaker antibiotic that may or may not cure the infection, or prescribe a stronger antibiotic that is unnecessary, and may create a future immunity to the stronger antibiotic. This confirms that, in a way, the prescriptions of W3 are the sales of nails in the hammer market. Interesting is that the marketing team already new this of W3 but had never thought of using this information in a market segmentation, nor did the marketing team ever perform further research with the sales data, as was done here, to verify the information obtained through the panels and focus groups.

The above situation reflects the need for researchers, those who are performing the data mining task, to go back to the initiator of the research for further understanding of the results [Hirji, 2001].

Because both the analysis of the sales data through cluster analysis and the research previously performed with the panels and focus groups demonstrated the uniqueness of W3 in that it is a form of competitor that cannot be overcome, at the moment of this study, W3, for the purposes of the marketing team of S1, was deemed no longer a competitor, and out of the market basket. The implications of the elimination of W3 from the RTI market basket, as defined by the marketing team, is that the number of financially beneficial prescribers for promotional purposes decreased from approximately 140,000 to approximately 40,000. Having a much smaller number of marketing targets now leaves the pharmaceutical company with alternatives, to include reducing the existing sales force, increasing the frequency of promotions calls to the now-reduced number of targets, or allocating the now freed-up capacity of the sales force to other drugs that the pharmaceutical company promoted. The implication for market segmentation is that the clustering process will need to be repeated after removing W3 from the dataset because it is no longer part of the RTI market as defined by the marketing team of S1.

## 7.7   Discussion

This chapter provided the results of implementing five clustering techniques on a dataset containing the market shares of six competitors in a market, the market volume, samples, and promotional sales calls of one of the competitors of the market. This situation can be observed in many situations across several industries, making the findings somewhat replicable and useful in similar situations. In addition, this chapter serves as a guide to researchers and practitioners who wish to segment a market for further modeling purposes, as well as giving directions for possible qualitative market research — or in the case of this chapter, to substantiate prior qualitative studies.

The need to use various clustering algorithms because there is no perfect one was illustrated, as well as that some overlap or similarity between the results of the diverse algorithms should be expected — as was observed with the behavior of W3 in each model. Finally, this chapter discussed the possible need to further reduce the number of clusters obtained by the algorithm used by means of visual reduction by graphing the cluster on a stacked bar chart.

The difference between a more traditional market segmentation and one labeled as being a data mining market segmentation is that when the data mining label is added, it is expected that unexpected information will surface, not to say that all new information will be as useful as was the case in this chapter, and without claiming that traditional market segmentations do not uncover unexpected information as well, but rather that it is expected in data mining.

# References

Breiman, L., Friedman, J.H., Olshen, R.A., and Stone, C.J. (1984), *Classification and Regression Trees*. Belmont, CA, Wadsworth.

Bruntine W.L. (1992), Bayesian Back-Propagation, *Complex Systems*, 5, 603–643.

Chipman, H., George, E., and McCulloch, R. (1998), Bayesian CART Model Search (with discussion), *Journal of the American Statistical Association*, 93, 935–960.

Everitt, B., Landau, S., and Leese, M. (2001), *Cluster Analysis, 4th edition*. Arnold Publishers.

Florek, K., Lucaszewicz, J., Perkal, J., and Zubrzycki, S. (1951a), Sur la Liaison et la Division des Points d'un Ensemble Fini, *Colloquium Mathematicae*, 2, 282–285.

Florek, K., Lucaszewicz, J., Perkal, J., and Zubrzycki, S. (1951b), Taksonomia Wroclawska, *Przeglad Antropol.*, 17, 193–211.

Gehrke, J., Ganti, V., Ramrakrishnan, R., and Loh, W.Y. (1999), Optimistic Decision Tree Construction, SIGMOD 1999. New York: ACM Press, pp. 169–180.

Gitman, I. (1973), An Algorithm for Nonsupervised Pattern Classification, *IEEE Transactions on Systems, Man, and Cybernetics*, SMC-3, 66–74.

Hand, D., Mannila, H., and Smyth, P. (2001), Principles of Data Mining. Bradford Books.

Hartigan, J.A. (1975), *Clustering Algorithms*, New York: John Wiley & Sons.

Hartigan, J.A. (1981), Consistency of Single Linkage for High-Density Clusters, *Journal of the American Statistical Association*, 76, 388–394.

Hirji, K.K. (2001), Exploring Data Mining Implementation, *Communications of the ACM*, 44(7), 87–93.

Huizinga, D.H. (1978), A Natural or Mode Seeking Cluster Analysis Algorithm, Technical Report 78-1, Behavioral Research Institute, 2305 Canyon Blvd., Boulder, CO.

Jardine, N. and Sibson, R. (1971), *Mathematical Taxonomy*, New York: John Wiley & Sons.

Kohonen, T. (2001), Self Organizing Maps, *Springer Series in Information Sciences*, Vol. 30, third edition.

Kohonen, T. (1995), Self Organizing Maps, *Springer Series in Information Sciences*, Vol. 30.

Milligan, G.W. (1980), An Examination of the Effect of Six Types of Error Perturbation on Fifteen Clustering Algorithms, *Psychometrika*, 50, 159–179.

Rushmeier, H., Lawrence, R.D., and Almasi, G.S. (1997), Visualizing Customer Segmentations Produced by Self Organizing Maps (Case Study), *IEEE Visualization*, 463–466.

Serrano-Cinca, C. (1996), Self Organizing Neural Networks for Financial Diagnosis, *Decision Support Systems*, 17, 227–238.

Sokal, R.R. and Micheneer, C.D. (1958), A Statistical Method for Evaluating Systematic Relationships, *University of Kansas Science Bulletin*, 38, 1409–1438.

Sorensen, T. (1948), A Method of Establishing Groups of Equal Amplitude in Plant Sociology Based on Similarity of Species Content and Its Application to Analysis of the Vegetation on Danish Commons, *Biologiske Skrifter*, 5, 1–34.

Vesanto, J. (2000), Using SOM in Data Mining, Master's Thesis, Helsinki University of Technology, Helsinki, Finland.

Ward, J.H. (1963), Hierarchical Grouping to Optimize an Objective Function, *Journal of the American Statistical Association*, 58, 236–244.

Wong, M.A. and Lane, T. (1983), A kth Nearest Neighbor Clustering Procedure, *Journal of the Royal Statistical Society, Series B*, 45, 362–368.

*Chapter 8*

# An Enhancement of the Pocket Algorithm with Ratchet for Use in Data Mining Applications

Louis W. Glorfeld and Doug White

## Contents

## 8.1  Introduction

The rapid development of database and data storage technology has led to the commonplace deployment of data warehousing and data mart systems in many businesses that store and allow easy retrieval of massive amounts of persistent historical data reflecting all aspects of a business' operations. The availability of such massive amounts of data has spurred the development of a complete process for the extraction, preprocessing, and analysis of huge datasets commonly called data mining (DM) to turn raw data into business intelligence to promote superior decision making that results in a competitive advantage. The emphasis in this chapter is on a very simple but common problem that is frequently encountered in the modeling step of the DM process. The simple, qualitative two-group classification problem is frequently encountered in such diverse areas as credit granting, customer relations management, and fraud detection. The classical approach to the two-group classification problem is to use linear discriminant analysis (LDA) or logistic regression analysis (LRA). A little-known alternative to both LDA and LRA is known as the pocket algorithm with ratchet (PAR) based on artificial intelligence (AI) neural network principles. Because of the PAR's simplicity, it scales well for DM applications. While the classification performance of the PAR has been demonstrated to actually exceed even that of LRA [5], the emphasis in DM does not always center on just classification accuracy. In some cases, the major thrust of a study would be on determining exactly which variables are major contributors to discriminating between the two groups under study.

## 8.2  The Inductive Decision Models

### 8.2.1  Linear Discriminant Analysis

Linear discriminant analysis (LDA) is the classical approach to two-group statistical classification. LDA relates a set of independent attribute variables to a dependent classification variable through a simple linear function whose parameters are estimated using ordinary least squares, resulting in:

$$Y_j = B_0 + B_1 x_{1j} + B_2 x_{2j} + \cdots + B_n x_{nj} + \varepsilon_j, \qquad (8.1)$$

where $Y_j$ is the classification variable, often coded 0 and 1, or –1 and 1; the $x_{ij}$ are the attribute variables; the $B_i$ are the parameter estimates; and $\varepsilon_j$ is the error term. The set of independent attribute variables is assumed to follow a multivariate normal distribution and the variance-covariance matrices for the two groups are assumed equal, although LDA can be quite robust to violations of these assumptions in some cases [6]. The primary problem with LDA is that it is very sensitive to the existence of extreme observations that can cause serious distortion of the classification boundary [7]. For the purposes of this study, LDA is primarily of interest as a benchmark for comparing the significance tests for determining the statistical significance of the attribute variables. Standard SAS [8] software was used to produce the LDA results.

## 8.2.2 Pocket Algorithm with Ratchet (PAR)

The perceptron was one of the earliest connectionist network models. It was developed specifically to solve completely linearly separable, two-group classification problems. The optimization process is a form of fixed step size stochastic gradient descent. Unfortunately, the perceptron model displays unstable oscillatory behavior when presented with a linearly nonseparable classification problem. To overcome this difficulty, Gallant [4] developed a modification of the perceptron training algorithm known as the pocket algorithm with ratchet (PAR) [3]. The objective of the PAR is to find a linear function of the training attributes that maximizes the rate of correct classification in the training sample. Gallant [3] provides a proof that the PAR will achieve this objective in a finite time period. Unlike the LDA model that optimizes a least squares objective function, the PAR directly optimizes the real criterion of interest, the rate of correct classification. The error function being minimized is simply the classification error rate. This fact explains both the simplicity and the robustness of the PAR. Extreme observations have no effect on the PAR classification boundary. The actual form of the output predicted value function has no effect on the PAR implementation. LDA or LRA functions both look the same to the PAR. The PAR gives a kind of maximum likelihood solution in the sense that it converges to a set of weights that correctly classifies a randomly chosen observation with maximum likelihood [3, p. 81].

The original version of the PAR as given by Gallant [3] was used in this study; it uses a linear function as given in Equation (8.1). Only a modification to the error weight adjustment was made based on a suggested improvement to perceptron learning given by Frean [2]. This correction penalizes errors with large weighted sums because this type of error tends to be overcorrected, which in turn will cause other errors. In addition, the magnitude of the error correction was made a function of the iteration number — (Total iterations – Actual iterations) / Total iterations — leading to the corrections getting smaller and smaller as the iterations proceeded to the final limit. It also should be noted that all variables have been range standardized, which will affect the actual size of the PAR coefficients.

The PAR algorithm is iterative and, for this study, the number of iterations was set to 1,000,000, which does not guarantee an optimal solution but will at least produce a close to optimal solution. One of the characteristics of the PAR is that the classification function is not unique, unlike LDA. Although the classification rate remains reasonably stable when the PAR is repeatedly applied to the same training dataset, the actual function coefficients can have considerable variation. Because the focus of this study is not on classification, but the actual function coefficients, the PAR was applied to the training data 1000 times and the resulting coefficients averaged. The resulting reference coefficients are those actually reported and the classification results are based on those coefficients. All programming for the PAR was implemented in the Java programming language.

## 8.3 Method

### 8.3.1 Sample

The sample for this study consists of a random sample of 750 mortgage loan applications from the Columbia, South Carolina SMSA: 500 accepted loan applications and 250 rejected loan applications. The sample was randomly split into two samples of 375 observations each using a stratified methodology. This process resulted in two equal-sized samples consisting of 125 rejected mortgage loans and 250 accepted mortgage loans. Given the data proportions, the best base classification rate would be 67 percent that could be achieved by assigning all observations to the loan acceptance group.

### 8.3.2 Variables

The sample consisted of 17 independent variables that described a number of personal characteristics of the loan applicants and characteristics of the property. In this study, the dependent variable is the status of the mortgage loan, categorized as either accepted or rejected. The coding scheme and some basic definitions of the variables used are given in Table 8.1.

Independent variable descriptive statistics for the entire sample are given in Table 8.2.

### 8.3.3 Training and Validation Process

It is well known that assessing a model's performance using the same data used to build the model will lead to optimistically biased results of the model's performance. To produce a less biased assessment of how a model's performance will generalize to new data not originally used to build the model, some form of model cross-validation is used. To facilitate the statistical comparison of model results and because a large sample of 750 was available, a traditional split sample cross-validation technique was used. In the traditional cross-validation technique, as

**Table 8.1   Coding for Mortgage Lending Data**

Applicant's Age (AA) – actual age of head of the household.

Applicant's Credit Rating (ACR) –
   0 = rating is considered to be neutral or favorable;
   1 = rating is considered to be a negative indicator.
Marital Status of the Applicant (AMS) –
   0 = reported as married on the application;
   1 = unmarried or separated as reported on the application.
Applicant's Occupation (AO) – percent of applicant's income (AI) derived from sales commissions earned by any of the applicants or co-applicants.
Accepted or Rejected (AOR) –
   –1 = rejected;
    1 = for accepted.
Lender's Yield (APR) – calculated using the requirements of Reg. Z.
Applicant's Race (AR) –
   0 = white;
   1 = non-Caucasian.
Applicant's Sex (AS) –
   0 = primary applicant was male;
   1 = primary applicant was female.
Applicant's Tenure in Occupation (ATO) – number of years in current employment.
Co-Applicant's Income (CI) – percent of applicant's total annual income made up of the co-applicant's annual income.
Co-Applicant's Tenure in Occupation (CTO) – number of years in current employment.
Dwelling Age (DA) – number of years that have elapsed since the dwelling was constructed.
Loan to Value Ratio (LVR) – loan principal requested in the application divided by the appraised value.
Neighborhood Age (NA) – mean age of the homes in the home's census tract.
Neighborhood Crime Rate (NCR) – per capita crime rate within the census tract of the home as reported by the Law Enforcement Assistance Administration.
Remaining Economic Life (REL) – number of years the home can be used without major rehabilitation as estimated by the appraiser.
Total Monthly Payments/Applications Income (TMPAIR) – total monthly payments monthly mortgage payment including principal, interest, tax escrow, and insurance plus the payments on other existing mortgage debts that existed at the time of the application.
Years to Maturity (YM) – time period of loan.

**Table 8.2 Mortgage Loan Predictor Variables and Summary Statistics**

| | | Grouping | | | |
|---|---|---|---|---|---|
| Code | Independent Variables | Accept (n = 500) Mean | $\delta$ | Reject (n = 250) Mean | $\delta$ |
| ATO | Applicant's Tenure in Occupation (years) | 7.0740 | 7.5519 | 4.6760 | 5.7298 |
| CTO | Co-Applicant's Tenure in Occupation (years) | 1.3160 | 3.1298 | .9560 | 2.2571 |
| AR | Applicant's Race | 0.0870 | 0.2653 | 0.1480 | 0.3558 |
| AS | Applicant's Sex | 0.0740 | 0.2620 | 0.0920 | 0.2896 |
| AMS | Applicant's Marital Status | 0.2380 | 0.3344 | 0.2080 | 0.4067 |
| APR | Annual Percentage Rate | 0.0958 | 0.0040 | 0.0923 | 0.0029 |
| YM | Years to Maturity | 29.2000 | 2.7523 | 28.4600 | 4.1591 |
| REL | Remaining Economic Life | 46.5780 | 8.0265 | 41.7840 | 10.6914 |
| DA | Dwelling Age | 10.9360 | 14.5788 | 14.1240 | 17.7097 |
| ACR | Applicant's Credit Rating | 0.0040 | 0.0532 | 0.2640 | 0.4417 |
| TMPAIR | Total Monthly Payments to Applicant's Income | 0.0198 | 0.0092 | 0.0273 | 0.0132 |
| LVR | Loan to Value Ratio | 0.7861 | 0.1468 | 0.9000 | 0.1240 |
| CI | Co-Applicant's Income | 0.0890 | 0.1855 | 0.0836 | 0.1648 |
| AO | Applicant's Occupation | 0.1597 | 0.3583 | 0.0912 | 0.2790 |
| AA | Applicant's Age | 36.6600 | 7.3198 | 34.3560 | 5.0738 |
| NCR | Neighborhood Crime Rate | 3.4080 | 5.9847 | 3.6280 | 5.6903 |
| NA | Neighborhood Age | 12.5465 | 6.8862 | 14.6568 | 6.9825 |

used in this study, the original sample is randomly split in half, and one half is used to build or train the model while the second half is used to validate the model's performance. Because the objective was primarily a comparison of the LDA and PAR model coefficients, the classification cut point was left at the usual value of .5, implying equal (or in this case unknown) costs of misclassification.

### 8.3.4 The Bootstrap Estimation of Standard Errors and Confidence Intervals

The purpose of the bootstrap methodology is to allow the development of basic statistical inference measures such as standard errors and confidence intervals for statistics where the mathematical development of such measures is intractable. This is exactly the situation for the PAR model. The basic bootstrap methodology is based on drawing repeated random samples of size n with replacement from the original sample of size n. The desired estimators are computed for each of the bootstrap samples drawn, and then the desired bootstrap statistics can be determined using the set of bootstrap estimators. For a detailed presentation, see Efron and Tibshirani [1].

For the PAR, both the nonparametric bootstrap standard error and the percentile confidence intervals were developed. Although the nonparametric standard error can be developed with a relatively small number of bootstrap samples, the percentile confidence interval requires a large number of bootstrap samples. Because a high degree of accuracy was desired for this study, 10,000 bootstrap samples were generated. A PAR model was developed for each bootstrap sample, and the coefficients for each of the independent variables were used to develop the nonparametric standard error and the 95 percentile confidence interval. One interesting twist to the normal bootstrap is the fact that the PAR coefficients are not unique, and this non-uniqueness will introduce additional variability beyond that of the normal bootstrap.

## 8.4 Results

### 8.4.1 Classification Analysis of the Mortgage Loan Data

The results of applying the two models to the training sample and validation sample of 375 mortgage loan applicants each are given in Tables 8.3 and 8.4; Table 8.3 presents the results of LDA and Table 8.4 presents the results of the PAR. The results of the training sample demonstrate the two models' ability to capture the loan-granting decision-making process. The LDA had an overall correct classification rate of 85.3 percent, while the PAR model had a rate of 87.2 percent. The slightly better performance of the PAR reflects the fact that it is designed to directly optimize the rate of correct classification.

The validation results are of primary interest. The results indicate that the PAR model also performed better than the LDA on the validation dataset. The PAR had an overall correct classification rate of 82.1 percent, compared to the 79.2 percent rate of the LRM. It is notable that the PAR performed better than the LDA on both the training *and* the validation data.

### 8.4.2 The Bootstrap Coefficients

Table 8.5 presents the results derived from the 10,000 bootstrap replications of the PAR. The bootstrap nonparametric standard errors of the coefficients along

**Table 8.3   LDA Training and Validation Classification Matrices for Mortgage Loan Data**

| | **Linear Discriminant Analysis: Training Data** | | | |
|---|---|---|---|---|
| | *Accept* | *Reject* | *Total* | *Classification Rate (%)* |
| Accept | 224 | 26 | 250 | 89.6 |
| Reject | 29 | 96 | 125 | 76.8 |
| Total | 253 | 122 | 375 | 85.3 |
| | **Linear Discriminant Analysis: Validation Data** | | | |
| | *Accept* | *Reject* | *Total* | *Classification Rate (%)* |
| Accept | 203 | 47 | 250 | 81.2 |
| Reject | 31 | 94 | 125 | 75.2 |
| Total | 234 | 141 | 375 | 79.2 |

with the pseudo t values obtained by dividing each coefficient by its corresponding standard error are displayed. While the standard error estimates are nonparametric, the t test itself is not. The reason the term "pseudo t" is used is that an investigation of the bootstrap distribution of the coefficients brought the use of a t test into

**Table 8.4   PAR Training and Validation Classification Matrices for Mortgage Loan Data**

| | **Pocket Algorithm with Ratchet: Training Data** | | | |
|---|---|---|---|---|
| | *Accept* | *Reject* | *Total* | *Classification Rate (%)* |
| Accept | 239 | 11 | 250 | 95.6 |
| Reject | 37 | 88 | 125 | 70.4 |
| Total | 276 | 99 | 375 | 87.2 |
| | **Pocket Algorithm with Ratchet: Validation Data** | | | |
| | *Accept* | *Reject* | *Total* | *Classification Rate (%)* |
| Accept | 220 | 30 | 250 | 88.0 |
| Reject | 37 | 88 | 125 | 70.4 |
| Total | 257 | 118 | 375 | 82.1 |

Table 8.5    Pocket Algorithm with Ratchet Parameter Estimates, Bootstrap Standard Errors, Pseudo t Values, and Bootstrap Percentile 95 Percent Confidence Intervals for the Training Sample

| Variable Identifier | Parameter Estimate | Standard Error | Pseudo t | 95% Confidence Lower | Interval Upper |
|---|---|---|---|---|---|
| Intercept | 0.2964 | 0.0520 | 5.70* | 0.0234 to | 0.6926* |
| ATO | 0.2105 | 0.0939 | 2.24* | −0.1447 to | 0.7160 |
| CTO | 0.0537 | 0.3748 | 1.43 | −0.1111 to | 0.2578 |
| AR | 0.0201 | 0.0213 | 0.95 | −0.0993 to | 0.1217 |
| AS | −0.0602 | 0.0355 | −1.70 | −0.1941 to | 0.0259 |
| AMS | 0.0087 | 0.0162 | 0.53 | −0.0400 to | 0.0973 |
| APR | −0.1456 | 0.0337 | −4.32* | −0.3581 to | −0.0120* |
| YM | 0.1226 | 0.0652 | 1.88 | −0.0075 to | 0.4199 |
| REL | 0.0981 | 0.0379 | 2.59* | −0.0393 to | 0.3340 |
| DA | 0.0937 | 0.0199 | 4.70* | −0.0008 to | 0.3011 |
| ACR | −0.2243 | 0.0512 | −4.38* | −0.6963 to | −0.0276* |
| TMPAIR | −0.3824 | 0.0747 | −5.12* | −0.8255 to | −0.0357* |
| LVR | −0.4647 | 0.0902 | −5.15* | −1.0409 to | −0.0496* |
| CI | 0.0132 | 0.0227 | 0.58 | −0.0760 to | 0.1265 |
| AO | 0.0490 | 0.0118 | 4.16* | −0.0249 to | 0.1343 |
| AA | −0.1006 | 0.1487 | −0.68 | −0.5833 to | 0.3481 |
| NCR | 0.0964 | 0.0577 | 1.67 | −0.0860 to | 0.3653 |
| NA | −0.1190 | 0.0443 | −2.69* | −0.3492 to | −0.0023* |

Note: An asterisk indicates variables found significant at the $p < .05$ level.

question. Figure 8.1 provides an example of a histogram of the bootstrap distribution of the last independent variable, NA.

As the histogram in Figure 8.1 demonstrates, the bootstrap distribution of NA is highly skewed left and would bring the actual validity of the t test into question. However, for comparison purposes, the pseudo t tests were computed and those with values greater than 1.96 were flagged as significant at the usual .05 level of significance.

The right-most column Table 8.5 presents the 95 percent bootstrap percentile confidence intervals (CIs). These confidence intervals can be considered nonparametric, and depend on no particular distributional assumptions. Because these CIs are based on the actual individual bootstrap coefficient values, they would be more affected by the non-uniqueness of the PAR coefficients than would the standard error estimates. Percentile confidence intervals that do not contain zero are identified by an asterisk.

The pseudo t tests identify the intercept and the variables ATO, APR, REL, DA, ACR, TMPAIR, LVR, AO, and NA as statistically significant. The CIs identify the intercept and APR, ACR, TMPAIR, LVR, and NA as statistically significant. In comparing the statistically significant pseudo t tests with the significant CIs, it is

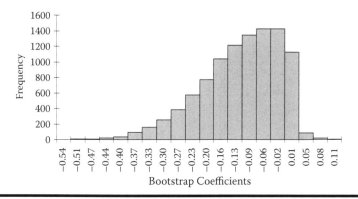

**Figure 8.1    Histogram of the distribution of bootstrap parameter estimates for 10,000 bootstrap samples of the neighborhood age variable.**

evident that the significant CIs are a subset of the significant pseudo t tests. The CIs are more conservative than the pseudo t tests.

### 8.4.3   Comparison of the LDA and PAR Significance Tests

Table 8.6 presents the results of running a classical LDA. The t tests and p values associated with the individual coefficients were used to identify variables statistically significant at the usual .05 level of significance. In addition to the intercept, APR, REL, DA, ACR, TMPAIR, LVR, AO, and NA are identified as statistically significant. The variables identified as statistically significant by the pseudo t tests and the CIs are also identified.

The classical t tests and the pseudo t tests correspond exactly, except for one variable. The pseudo t test identifies ATO as significantly significant while the classical t test does not. All variables indicated statistically significant by the CIs are also indicated as significant by the classical t tests. While there is only a rough correspondence between the size of the pseudo t tests and the size of the classical t tests, the correspondence between the CIs and classical t tests does show an interesting characteristic. The five variables indicated as statistically significant by the CIs correspond to the five variables indicated as statistically significant by the classical t tests with the smallest p values — all p values less than .0014.

## 8.5   Discussion

This study investigated the possibility of using the bootstrap to identify variables of statistical importance in the two-group classification model based on the PAR. Because the PAR is basically a computer algorithm, the analytical derivation of

**Table 8.6 Standard Linear Discriminant Analysis Parameter Estimates and Comparison of Variables Found Statistically Significant with Variables Found Significant by the Bootstrap Pseudo t Values and Bootstrap Confidence Intervals (CI)**

| Variable Identifier | Parameter Estimate | Standard Error | t Value | Pr > \|t\| | Sig. at Pseudo t | .05 CI |
|---|---|---|---|---|---|---|
| Intercept | 5.2268 | 1.0713 | 4.88 | <.0001* | * | * |
| ATO | 0.0204 | 0.0138 | 1.48 | 0.1391 | * | |
| CTO | 0.0026 | 0.0136 | 0.19 | 0.8492 | | |
| AR | 0.0122 | 0.1354 | 0.09 | 0.9283 | | |
| AS | −0.2794 | 0.1748 | −1.60 | 0.1110 | | |
| AMS | 0.0069 | 0.1340 | 0.05 | 0.9592 | | |
| APR | −0.0039 | 0.0010 | −3.73 | 0.0002* | * | * |
| YM | 0.0202 | 0.0131 | 1.55 | 0.1228 | | |
| REL | 0.0095 | 0.0046 | 2.04 | 0.0424* | * | |
| DA | 0.0056 | 0.0026 | 2.16 | 0.0314* | * | |
| ACR | −1.1394 | 0.1397 | −8.16 | <.0001* | * | * |
| TMPAIR | −21.6908 | 3.5333 | −6.14 | <.0001* | * | * |
| LVR | −1.6861 | 0.2628 | −6.42 | <.0001* | * | * |
| CI | 0.1297 | 0.2211 | 0.59 | 0.5579 | | |
| AO | 0.2168 | 0.1100 | 1.97 | 0.0494* | * | |
| AA | −0.0118 | 0.0144 | −0.82 | 0.4127 | | |
| NCR | 0.0157 | 0.0081 | 1.95 | 0.0519 | | |
| NA | −0.0215 | 0.0067 | −3.22 | 0.0014* | * | * |

*Note:* An asterisk indicates variables found significant at the p < .05 level.

such measures is mathematically intractable. While the PAR has been shown to have equal or better classification performance than typical statistical techniques such as LDA and LRA, the possibility of identifying discriminating variables of major importance in the PAR is often desirable. It was demonstrated that the development of standard errors and confidence intervals for the PAR model, based on the bootstrap principle, would be useful as a means for identifying variables of importance. A comparison of the coefficients identified as statistically significant in the linear PAR model were compared with those the classical LDA model identified as significant. The very close correspondence between the identified significant variables in the two models lends support to the validity of the bootstrap methodology in this application. Perhaps the major benefit of the use of the bootstrap percentile confidence intervals is the nonparametric nature of these confidence intervals. While such intervals appear conservative, this characteristic is also their strongest point.

From a practical point of view, identifying only the major variables that discriminate between two groups would seem a very useful goal. If identification of possible major and minor discriminating variables is desired, then the pseudo t tests could be used.

A limitation to the use of the bootstrap should be noted. While the PAR scales well for potential DM applications because of its simplicity, when bootstrapping is added, this desirable characteristic no longer holds. Use of the bootstrap with the PAR is very computationally intensive. The solution to this problem is to use sampling theory and base the bootstrap on a random sample of the potentially massive amount of available data. It is also the case that more computationally efficient methods for computing the bootstrap confidence intervals are available. Given some ingenuity in actual implementation, the bootstrap should be a useful tool to provide DM techniques such as the PAR with a means for statistical inference, where normally none exist.

# References

1. Efron, B. and Tibshirani, R.J., *An Introduction to the Bootstrap*, Chapman & Hall, New York, 1993.
2. Frean, M., Small Nets and Short Paths: Optimizing Neural Computations. Ph.D thesis, University of Edinburgh, Center for Cognitive Science, 1990.
3. Gallant, S.I., *Neural Network Learning and Expert Systems*, MIT Press, Cambridge, MA, 1993.
4. Gallant, S.I., Optimal linear discriminants. In *Proc. Eighth International Conference on Pattern Recognition*, Paris, 1986, pp. 849–852.
5. Glorfeld, L.W. and White, D., An alternative to logistic regression for use in data mining applications. In *Proc. Decision Sciences Institute 2004*, Boston, 2004, pp. 5261–5266.
6. Lachenbruch, P.A., *Discriminant Analysis*, Hafner Press, New York, 1975, pp. 40–50.
7. Ridgeway, G., Strategies and methods for prediction. In Ye, Nong (Ed.), *The Handbook of Data Mining*, Lawrence Erlbaum, Mahwah, NJ, 2003, pp. 159–191.
8. SAS Institute, *SAS Stat. Reference Manual*, SAS Institute Inc., Cary, 2001.

*Chapter 9*

# Identification and Prediction of Chronic Conditions for Health Plan Members Using Data Mining Techniques

Theodore L. Perry, Stephan Kudyba,
and Kenneth D. Lawrence

## Contents

## 9.1 Introduction

The world is moving into a new age of numbers where quantitative analytic techniques are bulling into new domains of business and imposing the efficiencies of math. Mathematical modeling techniques such as data mining are transforming the business of consulting, advertising, and media, to mention a few, and health care is no exception [1].

Data mining techniques have become an essential management tool in today's health care arena. Rising health care costs, the increasing prevalence rates of chronic conditions, and an aging population all add to the complexity and challenges facing our health care delivery systems as we move into the 21st century [2]. Health care spending in the United States was over $2.1 trillion dollars in 2006, and it is estimated that health care expenditures will represent nearly 20 percent of all U.S. spending by 2016 [3]. Major changes must occur over the next decade in the way we manage our health care resources to meet this need.

One of the biggest challenges facing health care today involves the management and analysis of massive and complicated claims datasets. This challenge also represents an opportunity to demonstrate the effectiveness of data mining methods as a resource allocation tool. To effectively manage large patient populations, it is essential to be as *proactive* as possible. Obviously, the best way to stop a patient from becoming a burden to the health care system (both clinically as well as financially) is to prevent the development of a condition or conditions that result in excessive utilization and cost [4]. Because it is not possible to personally attend to every patient in a large population, the best alternative resides in the application of analytic techniques that maximize the probability of delivering the appropriate medical resources to the right patients at the optimal time.

Predictive models based on total population categorization are usually optimized to identify moderate- to high-cost patients who will either migrate to high cost or remain high cost in subsequent years, within a defined medical condition category (e.g., Type II diabetes patients). Although this methodology is effective in categorizing a total population into high- and low-cost groups, it does not, however, focus on predicting those very low-cost patients who have yet to develop the condition of interest. It is these patients who represent the greatest opportunity cost and are seldom identified because in these types of cost/utilization predictive models, prior cost is usually the best predictor of future cost. That is, identification of disease onset is not the objective; it is the identification of future high-cost patients.

Although disease onset and future high cost are clearly not mutually exclusive, a fundamental challenge to predictive modelers is to create models that best predict those patients who will develop chronic conditions, hence migrating from very low cost to high cost. Congestive health failure (CHF) represents a significant opportunity to apply data mining techniques using health care claims information.

CHF is a classification of heart failure characterized by fluid build-up in the lungs and body, resulting from the inability of the heart to pump efficiently [5]. The purpose of this chapter is to illustrate predictive modeling techniques that optimize the prediction of patients who are at highest risk for development of CHF, thereby increasing the overall accuracy of the total population categorization.

## 9.2  Prediction of Congestive Health Failure (CHF)

Prevention of CHF represents a considerable savings opportunity for our health care system. According to the National Heart Lung and Blood Institute, more than 5 million people in the United States have heart failure, with nearly 600,000 new cases diagnosed each year [6]. Prevention of CHF involves lowering a person's risk factors, such as coronary artery disease, high blood pressure, high cholesterol, diabetes, and obesity. Although it is difficult to accurately determine the overall health care cost savings associated with the identification and subsequent prevention of CHF for patients, it is reasonable to suspect that these savings would be highly significant. Furthermore, even if the number of CHF cases averted was relatively small, it is well documented that early identification of heart failure leads to better clinical and financial outcomes [7].

Consequently, it was of interest to analyze health care claims data with the objective of predicting patients with CHF. Two major analytic methods were used to build these models: (1) logistic regression and (2) neural networks. These methods and results are discussed below.

## 9.3  Study Data

Data used for this study consisted of two complete years (i.e., 2004 and 2005) of Medicaid healthcare claims data from a large Medicaid program located in the southeastern United States. All protected health information (PHI) was removed from the data prior to these analyses, and CMS HCC identification algorithms [8] were used to create binary condition identification flags (e.g., 1 = has condition; 2 = does not have condition) across 70 health conditions for each patient. Two modeling datasets were created. A stratified random sample of 60,000 members was taken from both years. The stratification variable was CHF, which was proportionately allocated based on the overall prevalence rate of CHF in this population (i.e., 1.9 percent). The 2004 data was used to develop and train the models. Split-sample validation was used to ensure the reliability and validity of each model. The 2005 data was used to test and validate the results of the predictive models. Table 9.1 contains summary information for these datasets.

Table 9.1 Summary Information for Modeling Data

| Dataset Year | CHF(Total; %) | No CHF(Total; %) |
|---|---|---|
| 2004 | 1,141 (1.901%) | 58,859 (98.098%) |
| 2005 | 1,131 (1.885%) | 58,869 (98.115%) |

# 9.4 Analytic Methods and Procedures

The two analytic techniques used to analyze these study data were logistic regression and neural networks. These analyses were conducted using SAS® Version 9.1.3 and SAS® Enterprise Miner Release 4.2. A brief summary of each method follows.

## 9.4.1 Logistic Regression

Logistic regression is a statistical methodology used to analyze the relationship between categorical (i.e., binary, ordinal, or nominal values) variables and predictor variables [9]. Logistic regression is best used to predict discrete outcomes, such as the presence or absence of a disease condition. The objective of logistic regression is to predict the outcome category for individual cases. As with most predictive models, predictor variables (i.e., Predictors) are selected to accurately predict the response variable of interest (i.e., Target).

The logistic regression predictive modeling steps used in this study included:

Step 1: 2004 data import and stratified random sampling, proportionately allocated by CHF status.

Step 2: Segmentation into Training (60 percent) and Validation (40 percent) datasets.

Step 3: Definition and conduct of logistic regression, using stepwise variable selection, default optimization techniques, and a single binary CHF target.

Step 4: Assessment of outcomes using classification/misclassification rates, lift charts, receiver operating characteristics (ROC) curves, and C-statistics.

## 9.4.2 Neural Networks

Neural networks were first derived when scientists began developing ways to mimic the behaviors of neurons in the brain [10]. Neural networks have been used very successfully in predictive models, especially when dealing with many variables with various degrees of co-linearity and multiple data types. In its simplest configuration, a neural net consists of three layers: (1) inputs, (2) hidden nodes, and

(3) outputs. Inputs and outputs are somewhat analogous to predictors and targets in most general predictive models. The hidden nodes basically determine the complexity of the model or "classifier," and range from simple to extremely complex. Although it is commonly accepted that the explanatory value of neural networks is relatively weak (i.e., it is difficult if not impossible to fully explain the multiple nonlinear functions used by this type of model), these models, nevertheless, often provide the best approach to prediction problems.

The neural networks predictive modeling steps used in this study included:

Step 1: 2004 data import and stratified random sampling, proportionately allocated by CHF status.

Step 2: Segmentation into Training (60 percent) and Validation (40 percent) datasets.

Step 3: Definition and conduct of neural network, using misclassification rate model selection criteria, multilayer perceptron network architecture, and a single binary CHF target.

Step 4: Assessment of outcomes using classification/misclassification rates, lift charts, receiver operating characteristics (ROC) curves, and c+ statistics.

## 9.5 Modeling Results

The overall results of the CHF predictive model for both the logistic regression and neural network models are contained in Table 9.2. As shown in this table, both models performed well, demonstrating less than 2 percent misclassification of patients with CHF.

Another way to analyze these results is to display outcomes on a sensitivity curve (i.e., Lift Chart). A sensitivity curve compares the true positive capture rate (i.e., sensitivity) of a model at different screening thresholds. As illustrated in Figure 9.1, the sensitivity curve shows that both the logistic regression and neural network models perform nearly identically in identifying patients with CHF. At a screening

**Table 9.2 Results from Test and Validation Datasets for Study Models**

| Model Type | Misclassification Rate for Test Data | Misclassification Rate for Validation Data | Average Square Error Test Data | Average Square Error Validation Data |
|---|---|---|---|---|
| Logistic regression | 0.0187 | 0.0191 | 0.1261 | 0.1262 |
| Neural network | 0.0186 | 0.0186 | 0.1243 | 0.1245 |

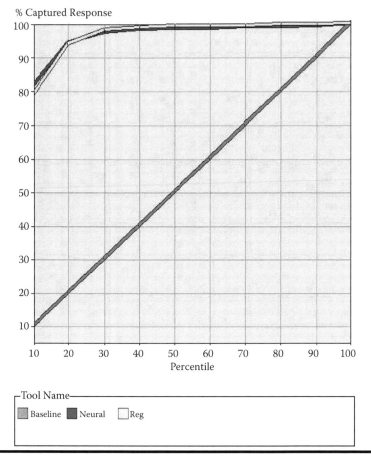

**Figure 9.1 Sensitivity curve comparison of logistic regression and neural network CHF classification model.**

threshold of 10 percent of the data, the logistic regression model accurately identifies 78.801 percent of patients with CHF and the neural network model accurately identifies 81.565 percent of patients with CHF. The baseline represents classification at chance (50/50) level.

To further illustrate the subtle differences in the performance between these two models, Table 9.3 provides a comparison of the true positive capture rates for the logistic regression and neural network models at all screening levels. As shown, the neural network model out-performs the logistic regression model at the smaller screening thresholds, while the logistic regression model begins to slightly out-perform the neural network model at the larger screen thresholds.

Table 9.3 Sensitivity Comparisons of Study Models
for CHF Identification

| Screening Threshold (%) | Logistic Regression Cumulative True Positive Capture Rate (%) | Neural Network Cumulative True Positive Capture Rate (%) | Improvement Using Neural Network Model for Identification |
|---|---|---|---|
| 10 | 78.801 | 81.565 | 3.507 |
| 20 | 93.879 | 94.211 | 0.353 |
| 30 | 98.036 | 97.368 | −0.681 |
| 40 | 98.772 | 98.340 | −0.437 |
| 50 | 99.298 | 98.596 | −0.706 |
| 60 | 99.298 | 98.596 | −0.706 |
| 70 | 99.298 | 98.905 | 0.395 |
| 80 | 99.545 | 98.947 | −0.600 |
| 90 | 99.649 | 99.123 | −0.527 |
| 100 | 100 | 100 | 0.0 |

## 9.6  Discussion and Conclusions

As the information age evolves and matures, organizations across industry sectors continue to capture and manage data resources that describe their operational activities. These information resources provide the underpinnings to better identifying and understanding trends, and cause-and-effect characteristics among operational variables. The combination of robust data resources along with complex analytic techniques enables decision makers to extract critical information that impacts their businesses and generates predictive models that produce expected process outcomes with greater accuracy.

This chapter illustrates the benefits of applying data mining techniques to analyze organizational data in one of the most critical industry sectors — health care. The results of the analysis conducted indicate that two data mining techniques — logistic regression and neural networks — produce accurate models that predict the likelihood of individuals to develop CHF, where the comparative accuracy between the two methodologies is marginal. With this information, health care providers can better allocate available resources to provide preventive care to those individuals in the high-risk category and therefore mitigate the future costs of extensive treatment of fully developed CHF. The results of mitigating the number of fully developed CHF cases are increased productivity for health care providers and, more importantly, a healthier patient population. As data resources continue to evolve along with analytic techniques, the potential benefits to the health care industry are far-reaching.

# References

1. Baker, Stephen. Math Will Rock Your World, *BusinessWeek Magazine*, January 2006 p. 54.
2. Crossing the Quality Chasm: A New Health System for the 21st Century. Committee on Quality of Health Care in America, Institute of Medicine, National Academy Press, Washington, D.C., 2001.
3. Poisal, J. *Health Affairs*, Feb. 21, 2007; online edition. News release, *Health Affairs*.
4. Chronic Disease Management Quality Improvement Efforts Yield Better Care Delivery. AHRQ Public Affairs, Harvard Medical School, March 1, 2007.
5. www.HeartFailure.org. Sponsored by the San Diego Cardiac Center and the Sharp Foundation for Cardiovascular Research and Education, 2006.
6. U.S. Department of Health and Human Services, National Institutes of Health, National Heart Lung and Blood Institute, March 2007.
7. Creating Healthy States: Promoting Healthy Living in the Medicaid Program. National Governors Association, 2007.
8. Centers for Medicare and Medicaid Services, Hierarchical Condition Categories Risk Adjustment Program.
9. Agresti, Alan. *An Introduction to Categorical Data Analysis.* John Wiley & Sons, Inc., 1996.
10. Data Mining: A Hands-On Approach for Business Professionals. Robert Groth, Prentice Hall PTR. 1998.

*Chapter 10*

# Monitoring and Managing Data and Process Quality Using Data Mining: Business Process Management for the Purchasing and Accounts Payable Processes

Daniel E. O'Leary

## Contents

# 10.1 Introduction

Recently, businesses have become more concerned about using transaction data to generate knowledge about the world in which they function, often referred to as so-called "business intelligence." This business intelligence typically is generated using tools such as data mining and knowledge discovery. Although much of that focus on business intelligence initially was generated about relationships with other firms, such as sales, increasingly there is a focus on internal processes. That focus of generating business intelligence about internal processes, to facilitate management and monitoring of those processes, is referred to as "business process management" (BPM). BPM can be used on any of a number of processes, such as sales analysis, accounts receivable analysis, inventory analysis, and other activities. However, this chapter focuses on purchasing and accounts payable processes so that particular metrics and approaches can be analyzed.

## 10.1.1 Purpose

BPM has received limited, if any, academic analysis to date but there has been substantial commercial development of BPM. Most commercial uses of BPM, particularly in accounts payable and purchasing, are aimed at a better understanding of payment activity and trends (Exhibit 10.1), and not at data quality or investigation of fraud. However, this chapter broadens that focus to examine data quality and consider how fraudulent activity might be spotted with BPM capabilities. Historically, when BPM and data quality are linked, it is a story that indicates how important data quality is to BPM. Unlike previous research, this chapter focuses more on how one can use BPM to monitor and ensure data quality.

Accordingly, the purpose of this chapter is to investigate how to assess and facilitate data quality, including spotting fraudulent activity. This is done using BPM as an organizing architecture for the data. The scope of this chapter is to investigate the processes of purchasing and accounts payable, within the context of business process management. As a result, this chapter focuses on the application of different approaches to facilitate data quality analysis of a process. Particular attention is given to data mining and its ability to ascertain when data seems appropriate or anomalous. There is also an effort to establish metrics that can be useful in facilitating the monitoring process.

## 10.1.2 This Chapter

This chapter proceeds as follows. While this section presents an introduction to the chapter and its purpose, Section 10.2 summarizes some of the ways that data quality controls are categorized to facilitate discussion. Section 10.3 briefly reviews the specific domain of purchasing accounts payable and some generic sources of data quality disruption in those areas. Section 10.4 reviews the notion of BPM, while Section 10.5 investigates metrics for purchasing and accounts payable that can be used to facilitate identification of data quality issues, such as fraud. Section 10.6 analyzes some approaches to determine how the data one sees matches up with what one would expect. Section 10.7 uses a data mining perspective to investigate the underlying data quality and how that data quality might be undermined by fraudulent data. Finally, Section 10.8 provides a brief summary of the chapter and its contributions.

## 10.2 Preventive and Detective Controls for Data Quality

The first step in ensuring data quality in virtually any setting is by using a strong set of preventive controls that prevent, to the extent possible, the entry of incorrect data or incomplete data. The second step is to build in additional controls that will facilitate detection of erroneous data or fraudulent data. In addition to characterizing controls as preventive or detective, controls also can be categorized as computer based or process based. This section investigates those control categories.

### 10.2.1 Preventive versus Detective Controls

Preventive controls are designed to limit errors or irregularities from being introduced into the data. A classic preventive control is a speed limit sign that indicates the upper bound on car speed. On the other hand, detective controls are designed to find errors or irregularities once they have been introduced to the data. A classic detective control is a radar gun that indicates how fast the car actually is going.

### 10.2.2 Computer-Based Controls

Computer-based controls use computer capabilities to provide control over the data quality. There are a number of computer-based controls that can facilitate data quality and control over a process, including the following.

#### 10.2.2.1 Individual Accounts

Perhaps the most important control is the ability to have individual accounts for each user. This makes each individual directly responsible for the activity in their account. In these settings, each individual has his own password to control access over the account and corresponding purchases. Individual accounts allow for "virtual signatures," to indicate which user accessed the information and made the purchases, etc.

### 10.2.2.2 Drop-Down Menus

To ensure that the data entered comes from a feasible set, drop-down menus can be used to limit choice to a feasible set of entries. As a result, drop-down menus facilitate the prevention of bad data.

### 10.2.2.3 Forcing Completion of Specific Fields

To ensure that all of the necessary data is entered, the transaction can be held until all necessary data items are completed. Forcing completion provides a preventive control to ensure that all appropriate fields are completed and a detective control to find out when appropriate fields are not completed.

### 10.2.2.4 Forcing a Particular Type of Data

To ensure data quality, some fields may require a particular type of data. For example, some fields may require numeric data, while other fields may require alphabetic data.

## 10.2.3 Process-Based Controls

Process-based controls also can facilitate data quality and control. Rather than using technology capabilities, instead process control is attained by taking a few key process steps, building control into the process using the process or activities within the process.

### 10.2.3.1 Responsibility

An important process-based control is to assign responsibility for individual and process-based activities. If responsibility is assigned, then that person can provide a control, either detective or preventive, to make sure the data is correct. If there is a problem, responsibility can indicate who to track down to resolve the problem.

### 10.2.3.2 Separation of Responsibilities

To minimize the potential for fraud and error, key responsibilities can be separated. For example, in the discussion later, the responsibilities of the purchasing agent and the accounts payable clerk are "separated." The purchasing agent decides from whom goods should be purchased and generates the purchase order, while the accounts payable clerk is responsible for matching all the appropriate documentation needed to generate payment to the vendor. A third person is responsible for actually signing the check for vendor payment. By separating these responsibilities, there is increased control, and inappropriate behavior can be limited, unless there is collusion among the employees. Further, because we separate responsibility, individuals can detect problems by seeing others work. As a result, there is increased control and inappropriate behavior can be limited, unless there is collusion among employees.

### 10.2.3.3 Authorization

Authorization is a control that requires some individual to take responsibility for allowing a particular event. For example, large purchases typically require authorization by some appropriate level of management, whether it is a manager, the CFO, the CEO, or the Board of Directors, typically through a review and signature, either actual or digital. Authorization can prevent some errors because review allows one person the ability to detect errors, while the fact that someone needs to authorize an activity can serve as a deterrent to prevent unauthorized activity.

## 10.3 Purchasing and Accounts Payable

Purchasing and accounts payable require quality data because much of an enterprise's performance is based on the goods that it purchases. There are at least three scenarios that provide the basis to generate detailed key performance indicators (KPIs) and approaches. The analysis presented here spans these three different approaches.

### 10.3.1 Scenario 1: Classic Purchasing and Accounts Payable

In this first scenario, information flows primarily using documents. Purchasing processes typically are initiated internally by a "requisition," where a need for a purchase is established. Requisitions also provide preventive controls because a manager generally must have responsibility for authorizing the purchase. After the requisition is received, a purchasing agent establishes a purchase order that typically lays out the contract with a particular vendor to purchase the goods. Purchasing agents ensure that the vendors chosen are legitimate vendors and that the products that they provide meet certain standards. Purchasing agreements are sent to the vendor, to receiving (so they know what to expect), and to accounts payable (responsible for payment); purchasing agreements are kept in purchasing for reference.

Generally, after the goods have been sent by the vendor, an invoice is issued by the vendor and sent to the purchasing firm. When the goods are received, people in the organization's receiving department create a receiving memorandum. Typically, accounts payable gets a copy of the purchase order, the invoice, and the receiving memorandum; matches them; and pays the bill. This process is summarized in Figure 10.1.

Information is periodically digitized as documents are processed if there is a computer-based system supporting the process. For example, purchase requisitions could be

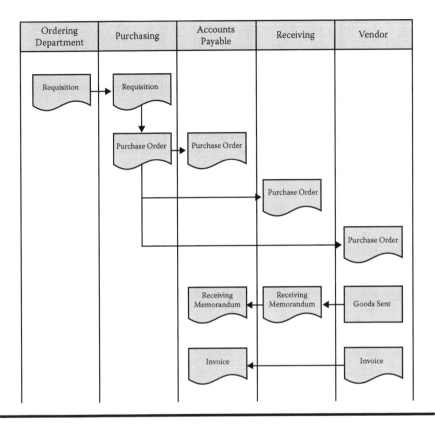

**Figure 10.1  Classic accounts payable and purchasing.**

created in digital format. Selected information from those forms could then be used to create a purchase order. It is likely that at least information about the vendor and the purchase are entered into the system so that, ultimately, the computer can be used to cut the check. Information could be exchanged digitally (e.g., using electronic data interchange). This would facilitate single rather than multiple entries of the same data. In this latter setting, data would need to be input a single time for each document. At the other extreme, data in each functional silo must be input digitally with each document. In the second case, as an example, purchase order information would be entered into four different systems (purchasing, accounts payable, receiving, and at the vendor).

There are a number of sources of data quality disruption in this classic setting, including potential errors and fraud. Errors can originate from many sources. For example, data entry can generate input errors (e.g., data entry errors). The more times a document is entered into a system, the higher the likelihood of error. Purchasing can generate purchase orders with errors, and vendors can generate invoices with errors. Further, controls may not work or may be overridden. Thus, this chapter later reviews approaches designed to detect anomalous data to facilitate quality data.

### 10.3.2 Scenario 2: E-Purchasing

With the advent of E-purchasing, a number of companies developed intranet-based systems designed to facilitate and control purchasing. In these so-called "E-purchasing systems," purchasing typically arranges with different suppliers to provide digital catalogs from which system users can make purchases. Users are typically provided different "roles" (preventive controls) that indicate what kinds of goods they are authorized to purchase (e.g., office supplies, computers, etc.). In addition, users may have individual budgets for their total and individual purchases. The system then limits the kinds of purchases that they can make and controls the expenses that they can incur. The system also guides them to a preselected set of products that meet organizational constraints.

This approach provides firms with ongoing and summary digital information about purchases and purchasers. Ultimately, managers have responsibility to review the data and authorize the purchases. Unfortunately, in some settings, roles and budgets are not fully implemented or monitored and authorized. In those settings, individuals may exceed their purchases and may make purchases that are later converted to cash for their personal use. Accordingly, the lack of preventive controls may suggest that detective controls be used to supplement the control environment.

### 10.3.3 Scenario 3: Emerging Purchasing and Accounts Payable

In another scenario, involving decentralized organizations (e.g., universities), organizations are adopting or have adopted processes and technology that require less direct involvement by purchasing specialists, as purchasing activities are transferred directly to employees. In this setting, many of the process controls are sacrificed because of cost-benefit relationships. For example, for low-cost items, the actual purchasers may be in a position of selecting vendors without an extensive selection process. Receipts are used to get reimbursement because it is cost beneficial. However, in those situations, that may mean that the corresponding vendors are not legitimate vendors, that corresponding products may not meet quality requirements, or that the resulting transactions may be partially or completely fictitious. Again, detective controls can be used to supplement the control environment.

## 10.4 Business Process Management: Monitoring Data Flows for Purchasing and Accounts Payable Data Quality

Monitoring data and data quality increasingly has fallen under the auspices of so-called "business process management." Business process management (BPM) has a number of definitions; however, we use the following:

BPM is the use of an integrated set of key performance indicators that are used to monitor an organizational process in real time. Business process management (BPM) is a management discipline that combines a process-centric and cross-functional approach to improving how organizations achieve their business goals. A BPM solution provides the tools that help make these processes explicit, as well as the functionality to help business managers control and change both manual and automated workflows.

**—Microsoft** [7]

Effectively, BPM uses "business intelligence" approaches as a means of monitoring data streams. Data is obtained in real-time from sources such as an enterprise resource planning (ERP) system. Key performance indicator (KPI) metrics are used to summarize the data. Those metrics are then analyzed and some of them are presented to the appropriate managers for review, often in the form of so-called dashboards, to facilitate monitoring. If the data is anomalous, then the manager can act on the data in real-time. Further, increasingly, KPIs are being forecast to see if they are likely to become anomalous in the future.

## 10.4.1  BPM Dashboards

BPM dashboards use real-time data feeds to provide users with easy-to-use and easy-to-read measurement devices. Typically, classic green, yellow, and red colors are used to cast a corresponding interpretation of under control, borderline, and out of control, respectively. In the following example, it is easy to see that it is an example of each setting, without any specific numeric values. In this way, status quo is maintained and problems are quickly isolated. As an example, a three-dial dashboard is presented in Figure 10.2. Each of the dials is monitoring a KPI. The KPIs that they represent are, left to right, in control (green), on the edge of being in control (yellow), and out of control (red). Typically, color-based dials are used to ease interpretation.

**Figure 10.2   Three-dial dashboard system.**

### 10.4.2 BPM Data Flows

In some cases, BPM data flows come from a single data source, such as an ERP system; however, in other cases they will come from disparate sources. In those settings, a consistent semantic mapping of the data will be necessary to ensure that the data and corresponding metrics are comparable. In some settings, this will prove one of the most important steps, and the BPM system will bring together disparate data flows under one system, sometimes for the first time. In some situations, a classic XML (eXtensible Mark-up Language) approach can be used to gather and label the data.

### 10.4.3 BPM Process Changes

However, in some situations, BPM is more than just capturing and managing KPIs on a particular process. In some cases, companies have changed the way they process invoices to facilitate BPM, particularly to meet the need for real-time data. Hasbro apparently developed a portal through which vendors could directly submit invoices [1]. After submission through the portal, invoices were routed to the appropriate vendor management teams for approval and from there for further processing. This approach increases the visibility of the approval and processing of the invoices, allowing them to better control the flow and understand bottlenecks, from time of submission to final payment.

### 10.4.4 Forecasts of KPIs

BPM systems may go beyond monitoring KPIs to actually monitoring forecasts of KPIs. Using real-time data, forecasts would be made and communicated to managers in a similar way as for real-time data. Forecast information would then be categorized as "in control," etc.

### 10.4.5 BPM Capabilities

What are key BPM capabilities? Historically, BPM takes data streams and puts them in a readable and accessible form so that managers can see critical data. As seen in Table 10.1, the focus has been on a range of important corporate issues. However, recently, BPM has been viewed as a potential tool for the analysis of fraud. For example, apparently the Louisiana Department of Social Services is now using BPM to facilitate identification of fraud [6]. This is one of the early applications aimed at using BPM to focus on issues other than productivity.

## 10.5 BPM Metrics: Purchasing and Accounts Payable

BPM metrics and systems can be used for different purposes. For example, BPM for accounts payable and purchasing can allow insight into cash outflows and facilitate cash planning. Historically, this means information about accounts payable

**Table 10.1    Cognos Performance Applications Accounts Payable**

Understanding Accounts Payable as Part of Financial and Supply Chain Analytics.

The pre-built reports and metrics of the Cognos Accounts Payable Analysis application give you a better understanding of your payment-related activity and trends. You can:

- Increase managerial productivity by reducing reporting and analysis time.
- See how much is due and when and the value of overdue accounts.
- Increase working capital by optimizing cash outflow strategies.
- Keep better control over cash outflow while maintaining strong vendor relationships.

Cognos Accounts Payable Analysis gives you more than 60 key performance indicators and more than 30 reports. These metrics and reports are grouped in four key areas of analysis, answering a variety of business questions:

- Accounts Payable Performance
  - What money is owed this period? What percentage is past due?
  - How quickly is the organization paying?
  - What percentage of accounts is not meeting terms? What is the value of overdue accounts?
- Accounts Payable Vendor Account
  - What is the current balance for a vendor account?
  - Which vendors are problematic? Why?
  - What is the cost to pay vendors, including errors, method of payment, and adjustments?
- Accounts Payable Cash Outflow
  - What is the expected cash outflow if no/all accounts take advantage of discounts?
  - What is the expected cash outflow based on the expected days to pay for each account based on payment patterns to date?
- Accounts Payable Organizational Effectiveness
  - How has account distribution across analysts changed as business has increased?
  - What was the total cost/savings for being in variance as related to payment terms?
  - What is the average/weighted average days past due?

*Source:* http://www.cognos.com/products/business_intelligence/applications/mod ules/payable.html.

that are outstanding, the accounts payable due to vendors, the extent of vendor discounts used, and the extent of overdue accounts. Table 10.1 provides summary of a BPM vendor's approach to purchasing and accounts payable, including goals and metrics.

However, historically, BPM has not focused much on ascertaining fraud and anomalous information. However, with the recent focus on the Sarbanes-Oxley Act, that focus could change. A number of metrics can be developed and monitored as part of a business process management system aimed at trying to find evidence of fraud or other data quality problems in purchasing and accounts payable. Some of those metrics include the following.

## 10.5.1 Number of Invoices Received from Suppliers

An important ongoing statistic is to capture the number of invoices received from each supplier on a monthly basis. Anomalous changes can indicate data quality problems. A steep increase or decrease in some vendor invoices may indicate that vendor numbers have erroneously been attributed to some invoices, for example, through data entry errors or a wrong vender number, whether purposefully or by accident. It may also indicate a fraudulent attempt by the vendor to obtain multiple payments.

## 10.5.2 Number of Transactions per System User

The system user varies based on the type of system in place, as discussed above. If one considers the number of transactions per accounts payable clerk, then the KPI provides a measure of productivity for the people involved in the accounts payable system. If one considers the number of transactions per worker using the system to buy goods, then the number of purchases can represent time spent away from their job, and also provide insight into how much productivity is spent on such issues.

Anomalous changes from month to month can indicate data input errors or fraud for at least two reasons. First, it may be that the wrong user is attributed to the transactions. An inappropriate user may be masquerading as another user. Second, if the user is replaced, then the replacement is likely a new user, and higher error rates are attributed to new users.

## 10.5.3 Percentage of Invoices Paid without a Purchase Order Reference

A classic fraud approach is to send goods and then invoice for them although the goods have not been ordered. This approach typically charges a premium price for substandard goods. As a result, firms often require a purchase order, as seen above in our three scenarios.

Further, although a preventive control is to require a valid purchase order number, in some systems without the proper controls there may no purchase order required to be associated with an invoice. The lack of a purchase order can indicate that the transaction is fraudulent or in error, but in any case anomalous.

### 10.5.4 Number of Invoices for a Purchase Order

Knowing that a purchase order number may be required, users in the process of doing a fraudulent transaction might use a legitimate purchase order number as part of the data input process, but one that is not appropriate for the particular invoice. In that situation, there are likely to be multiple invoices for a purchase order number. Thus, a list of the higher numbers of invoices per purchase order could be a KPI of interest.

### 10.5.5 Number of Users Using Each Vendor

In some cases, the number of users of a vendor can be indicative of a data quality problem such as fraud. For example, if a user and a vendor are working to defraud the company, it may be that the user would be the only one in the firm affiliated with that vendor.

### 10.5.6 Relative Size of an Invoice

There are a number of stories of organizations putting the decimal point in the wrong place on a payment, so that a $100 payment becomes a $10,000 or larger payment. Accordingly, a major concern is that the dollar amount of a payment not be excessive. There are a number of tests for ascertaining anomalies. One such test is the ratio of the largest payment to the second-largest payment (e.g., [8]). This can be generalized to the ratio of the j-*th* largest payment to the (j + 1)*st* largest payment. Whenever that ratio is substantial, it can indicate a problem with data quality and may be indicative of fraud. In the case where fraud was being purposefully committed and there was awareness of the existence of a test comparison between the first and second payment sizes, two large fraudulent transactions could be executed, thus mitigating the effectiveness of that test. As a result, comparison of more than the first two adjacent invoices would be appropriate.

## 10.6 Knowledge Discovery: Comparison to Expectations

Although preventive controls are critical to ensuring that data quality is high, an important approach to ensuring data quality is to compare data to "expectations" to see if the data meets those expectations. There are a number of bases of comparison, including Benford's law and other comparisons.

## 10.6.1 Benford's Law

One metric that can be traced and monitored to expectations is Benford's law [4, 10], which states that the first significant digit $d$ ($d \in \{1, ..., b - 1\}$) in base $b$ ($b \geq 2$) occurs with probability proportional to $\log_b (d + 1) - \log_b(d)$.

As a result, Benford's law establishes a set of expectations for the distribution of numbers. For many numeric generating processes, the first digit (or first and second, etc.) can be analyzed to see if it meets expectations. If it does not, then that can indicate an anomaly and that an investigation should be conducted to determine if there is some fundamental problem.

Numeric sequences could include a wide range of information; for example, in *State of Arizona v. Wayne James Nelson* (1993) [8], the accused was found guilty of attempting to defraud the state of roughly $2 million. A manager in the Arizona State Office of the Treasurer had diverted funds to a bogus vendor. The amounts of the 23 checks issued are shown in Table 10.2. The first digits are almost all 8 and 9,

**Table 10.2  Data from** *State of Arizona v. Wayne James Nelson* **(1993)**

| Date of Check | Amount ($) |
|---|---|
| October 9, 1992 | 1,927.48 |
| | 27,902.31 |
| October 14, 1992 | 86,241.90 |
| | 72,117.46 |
| | 81,321.75 |
| | 97,473.96 |
| October 19, 1992 | 93,249.11 |
| | 89,656.17 |
| | 87,776.89 |
| | 92,105.83 |
| | 79,949.16 |
| | 87,602.93 |
| October 19, 1992 | 96,897.27 |
| 1 | 91,806.47 |
| 1 | 84,991.67 |
| 1 | 90,831.83 |
| 1 | 93,766.67 |
| 1 | 88,336.72 |
| 1 | 94,639.49 |
| 1 | 83,709.28 |
| 1 | 96,412.21 |
| 1 | 88,432.86 |
| 1 | 71,552.16 |

the numbers that one would expect to see the least of. As a result, compared to Benford's law, the results are anomalous.

Not only can Benford's law be used to see if there is potential fraud, but it might also suggest that policies are not being followed or that particular policies are being avoided. For example, if there is a policy that expenses must be signed when they exceed a certain amount, an analysis of the data is likely to find an abnormal number of expenses filed just below the threshold. For example, if there is a cut-off of $500.00, where expenditures at $500.00 must be signed, there is likely an abnormally large number of expenditures around $400.00.

## 10.6.2 Accounts Payable Data Analysis

Given a database of accounts payable data, a number of comparisons between the data can be made to help establish the quality of the data. Three key data elements in accounts payable and purchasing are the invoice number, the amount of the invoice, and the vendor number.

### 10.6.2.1 "Same, Same, Same"

An important test of the quality of the accounts payable data is for duplicate payment of the same invoice to the same vendor (see, for example, [8]). In this situation, the data is investigated for the same invoice number, same amount, and same vendor. Such duplicate payments can occur if the vendor provides multiple copies at different times of the same invoice, whether as part of normal business practice or as part of a fraudulent approach. As part of the analysis, the accounts payable clerk ultimately responsible for the match must be determined so that it can be ascertained if there is a systematic problem.

### 10.6.2.2 "Same, Same, Different"

One test of the quality of accounts payable data is the "same, same, different" test (same invoice number, same amount, different vendor) (see, for example, [8]). The purpose of the test is to compare different accounts payable entries to determine if they are the same, and as a result, a bill has been paid more than once or if the wrong vendor has been paid. An invoice might be paid twice in the situation where the invoice was paid to the wrong vendor and then the correct vendor. The wrong vendor may have been paid, either purposely or by accident, such as an incorrect keying of the data. As part of the analysis, the accounts payable clerk ultimately responsible for the match must be determined so that it can be ascertained if there is a systematic problem.

### 10.6.2.3 "Same, Different, Different"

Another test of accounts payable data is the reuse of a purchase order number for other amounts or vendors. In a system that requires a purchase order number, a fraudulent entry could "reuse" a purchase order number to meet the need of providing a purchase order number with each entry. This test would allow detection of such reuse.

## 10.7 Data Quality-Based Data Mining

Purchasing and accounts payable systems depend on the underlying data in the system being "good data" to begin with. However, that assumption may not be true. One approach to analyzing data quality is to investigate the data using data mining, in order to determine if the basic data set contains any anomalies, indicating problems with the underlying data. For example, vendors may be fraudulent or goods may be bogus, in which case any transactions involving those vendors or goods would be suspect.

### 10.7.1 Determining "Inappropriate" Vendors

After the attacks on the World Trade Center, in New York City on September 11, airlines in the United States began comparing airline passenger lists to so-called "bad guy lists" for use in systems such as "NORA" (Non-Obvious Relationship Awareness). These systems were designed to find passengers who might be terrorists.

If the vendors that an organization does business with are not appropriate, then the data generated in interaction with those firms may be lacking quality, and the transactions may be fraudulent. As a result, similar to NORA, firms could compare their own employee, vendor, and customer lists to "bad guy lists" (BGLs) to facilitate determination as the "appropriateness" of employees, vendors, or suppliers. In some cases, a broader-based approach might be taken by including in that comparison incident and arrest systems. These comparisons are detective controls that may determine inappropriate vendors that were not prevented from being part of the system at the beginning.

### 10.7.2 Determining Fraudulent Vendors

Generally, vendors are third parties that operate at "arms length" from the particular organization. Data mining can be used to determine if there are any fraudulently created vendors. Vendor characteristics can be matched to characteristics of other agents associated with the organization. For example, vendors' characteristics can be compared against employees, because it would be rare that an employee would also be a vendor. If employees were vendors, then it would at least be of enough concern to enumerate and examine. Agent characteristics such as name, address, phone number, or even bank account numbers could be compared for similarity in the different databases.

### 10.7.3 Fraudulent Company Shipment Addresses

Products are "shipped to" particular addresses as part of purchase agreements. Generally, those "ship to" addresses are from a subset of organization addresses where the particular organization does business. As a result, if a "ship to" address does not come from that set, then it might indicate a fraudulent transaction and definitely would be anomalous. This likely would be even more indicative of a problem if the "ship to" address corresponds to an employee address. This is not to say that all such shipments would be suspect; for example, there may be a home office. However, such a correspondence between addresses could indicate fraudulently obtained goods.

### 10.7.4 Selected Issues in Comparison of Vendors

The analysis of shipment and vendor data could be done by people, but generally, using an intelligent system would be faster and possibly more effective, given the nature of the task. Such comparisons could take some intelligence to execute well. First, name information may be inconsistent. For example, "International Business Machines" may be in the database under that name or "IBM" or "I.B.M." or any of a number of other alternatives. Second, address conventions may be inconsistent. For example, at some point in addresses, "N." would need to be considered the same as "North" and "E." would need to be considered the same as "East." Similarly, other abbreviations, such as "St.", would need to be processed as "Street." Third, phone number information may be non-standard. For example, phone numbers could include dashes or not include that information. All of these issues would limit the ability of a system to correctly match vendors in different systems.

### 10.7.5 Bogus Goods

Left uncontrolled, users could conceivably order goods, have their company pay for them, and then resell the goods. For example, computer memory chips can be ordered by individuals in Scenario 3, likely from a vendor of their choice. It would be possible to contrive such purchases where the user was able to transfer the money from the company to himself, as long as each individual purchase and the purchases in aggregate did not exceed some amount. One approach to detect this kind of behavior is to keep track of different kinds of goods and how many of each kind each user orders.

To better control such purchases, additional preventive control information about goods could be specified. Goods could be characterized as "limited consumption goods." Whenever goods purchased exceed a certain amount, the purchases could kick out as anomalous. For example, computer memory chips could be characterized as a limited consumption good, where purchases for that type of good should not exceed some particular limit.

## 10.8 Summary and Contribution

This chapter investigated approaches to ensure and analyze data quality in a purchasing and accounts payable process, in the context of business process management. It summarized different types of controls, preventive and detective, and their use in computer systems and processes. Further, three different scenarios of how the purchasing and accounts payable processes would be generated were analyzed, as the particular implementation indicates what limitations are likely. Then the notion of business process management (BPM) was introduced. BPM provides a renaissance of managing processes, by integrating technology into that management process.

The primary contribution of this chapter is the development of an architecture for the use of business process management to analyze data within purchasing and accounts payable for data quality and potential fraud. Historically, BPM has not been aimed at those activities but has focused more on managing cash flows in the process. This was done by laying out some metrics to monitor process data, discussing how knowledge discovery could be used to determine if data is meeting expectations, and how data mining could be used to investigate the data quality of the underlying system information.

## References

1. Chen, A. "Hasbro Plays to Win with BPM," eWeek.com, August 2, 2004.
2. Cognos, "Cognos Financial Analytics," http://www.cognos.com/pdfs/whitepapers/wp_cognos_financial_analytics.pdf
3. Coderre, D. "Global Technology Audit Guide Continuous Auditing," The Institute of Internal Auditors, 2005.
4. Hill, T. "The first digit phenomenon," *American Scientist* 86 (July–August 1998), p. 358. http://www.americanscientist.org/template/ AssetDetail/assetid/ 15660; jsessionid= baa6gWCz81?fulltext=true
5. Lombardi Software, "Accounts Payable," http://www.lombardisoftware.com/bpm-accounts-payable.php#
6. Metastorm, "The Louisiana Department of Social Services," 2006, www.metastorm.com/customers/lodss/Louisiana%20DSS%20Success%20Story.pdf

7. Microsoft, "Business Process Management Overview," http://www.microsoft.com/biztalk/solutions/bpm/overview.mspx
8. Nigrini, M. "I've Got Your Number," *Journal of Accountancy*, May 1999. http://www.aicpa.org/pubs/jofa/may1999/nigrini.htm
9. Potla, L. "Detecting Accounts Payable Abuse through Continuous Auditing," *IT Audit*, The IIA, Altamonte, Springs, FL, Vol. 6, November 2003.
10. Wikipedia, Benford's Law, http://en.wikipedia.org/wiki/Benford's_law

*Chapter 11*

# Data Mining for Individual Consumer Models and Personalized Retail Promotions

Rayid Ghani, Chad Cumby, Andrew Fano, and Marko Krema

## Contents

# 11.1  Introduction

Retailers have been collecting large quantities of point-of-sale data in many different industries. Loyalty card programs at many grocery chains have resulted in the capture of millions of transactions and purchases directly associated with the customers making them. Despite this wealth of data, retailers have not been effective at providing individualized interactions and promotions to consumers. This is not to say that there has been no work attempted on retail transaction data. Research in mining association rules [2] has led to methods to optimize product assortments within a store by mining frequent itemsets from basket data [5]. Customer segmentation has been used with basket analysis in the direct marketing industry for many years to determine which customers to send mailers to. Additionally, a line of research based on marketing techniques developed by Ehrenberg [8] seeks to use a purchase incidence model with anonymous data in a collaborative filtering setting [9].

Traditionally, most of the data mining work using retail transaction data has focused on approaches that use clustering or segmentation strategies. This is usually done to overcome the data sparseness problem and results in systems that are able to overcome the variance in the shopping behaviors of individual customers, while losing precision on any one customer. The author believes that with access to the massive amounts of data being captured, and the relative high shopping frequency of a grocery store customer, one can develop individual consumer models that are based on only a single customer's historical data. This does not imply that previous approaches using clustering or association rules are inferior, but the goal in this chapter is to explore a new area that targets building individual models. Of course, in many situations, detailed historical data may not be available for every customer, in which case some form of generalization would be necessary and clustering approaches would be valuable.

A major reason that this area has not been more prominent in retail data mining research is that in the past there has been no individual channel to the customer for brick and mortar retailers. Direct mail is coarse grained and not very effective as it requires the attention of customers at times when they are not shopping and may not be actively thinking about what they need. Coupon-based initiatives given at checkout time are seen as irrelevant because they can only be delivered after the point of sale and often discarded by customers right away. However, with the advent of PDAs (personal digital assistants), in-store kiosks, and shopping cart-mounted displays such as the model shown in Figure. 11.1, retailers are in a position now to deliver personalized information to each customer as they navigate through the store.

Given the large amounts of data being captured by retailers and the emergence of personal devices that customers will have access to while shopping in retail stores, the challenge is to create applications and techniques that can learn patterns of behaviors for individual customers and then enable interactions that are highly personalized. This chapter describes work on predicting shopping lists for each customer as they enter a store. This shopping list predictor serves as an anchor on which to base further interactions. If one can predict what the customer is going to buy today, the next step is to predict customer behavior with respect to specific products and then use these predictions to "say" something about each product. We use customer purchase data from a retailer to create individual consumer models to detect and predict the behaviors of customers with respect to their shopping. Using list prediction as a base, these

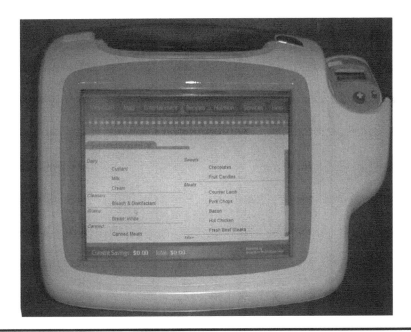

**Figure 11.1   Cart-mounted display device.**

consumer models enable the retailer to provide customers with individual and personalized interactions as they navigate through the retail store. The *Shopping Assistant* system is one aspect of the system that uses the predicted shopping list as a starting point for interacting with the customer. Instead of promoting random products, one uses the items on the predicted list to deliver personalized promotions. Each promotion and interaction with the customer is based on some attribute of the customer model that is learned for the customer. The major contributions of this work are as follows:

1. Shopping list prediction
2. Combining knowledge-based techniques with statistical and learning algorithms to build individual consumer models that capture different aspects of shopping behavior
3. Using these models to offer individual promotions to customers
4. Intelligent promotion planning: industrializing the use of the models by creating a set of tools that enable retailers to offer personalized promotions using visualization, interaction, simulation, and optimization techniques

The case study presented in this chapter deals with the retail industry and enabling personalized interactions within a store. In general, we believe that utilizing transaction data, learning individual behavioral models of customers (or entities in the data) using data mining techniques, and then optimizing higher-level objective functions based on these individual models is applicable in a variety of areas.

## 11.2  Related Work

There has been previous work on creating personal assistants for shopping. For example, the IBM Easi-Order system [4] and a system developed at Georgia Tech [12] use PDAs to display personalized grocery information to each shopper before and during their shopping trips. In the first system, a list is developed on the PDA, then sent to the store to be compiled and picked up. In the second, the PDA was used as an aid during the shopping trip to show locations and information on items in a list. The *1:1Pro* system described in [1] was designed to produce individual profiles of customer behavior in the form of sets of association rules for each customer, which could then be restricted by a human expert. Theoretically, these profiles could then be used to develop personalized promotions and predict certain purchases. However, there have been no significant efforts in the data mining community to create behavioral models for individual customers using real-world retail store data and then use those models to automatically create personalized promotions based on the higher-level business goals of the retailer and manufacturer.

## 11.3  Data

In our study, we use transactional data provided to us by a grocery store chain. The data spans a period of two years and contains purchase data for all customers in ten of their stores. This results in a dataset consisting of about 700,000 customers and 12.5 million transactions. Because the objective was to construct very detailed models, we decided to sample the dataset to get a smaller set of representative customers*.

From the overall set, 22,000 customers shopped between 20 and 300 times, which was judged to be the legitimate population for whom to predict lists. We use this entire dataset and create individual consumer models for each customer. For the shopping list prediction, we sampled this population to produce a dataset of 2200 customers with 146,000 associated transactions. Because the number of transactions for each customer follows a power law, uniform random sampling to select 10 percent of the customers would result in a sample skewed toward customers with a small number of transactions. To get a representative sample, we first split the population into deciles along three attributes: (1) total amount spent, (2) total number of transactions, and (3) $\frac{\#transactions}{amount\ spent}$. For each set of deciles, 10 percent of the data was selected with uniform probability from each decile. The 10 percent samples obtained for each attribute were found to be statistically similar to the other two (details omitted), and the final sample used was taken from total amount spent.

# 11.4  Individual Consumer Modeling

Our high-level goal is to create individual models for each consumer using only that consumer's own historical transaction data. These models are used to predict customer behavior and provide customers with individual and personalized interactions. The interactions we enable consist of a shopping list that is first presented to the customer as he enters the store and identifies himself. The second aspect of the interaction is providing promotions or offers for products on the shopping list as the customer navigates the store. This section first describes work on the creation of the shopping list predictor (classifier) and then describes the attributes that constitute the consumer model and are inferred for each customer. More details on predicting shopping lists can be found in [7].

## 11.4.1  Shopping List Prediction

We formally frame the shopping list prediction as a classification problem, describe the algorithms and methodology behind the system, and present results on the grocery dataset described in Section 11.3. Immediate advantages of the shopping list prediction task include a useful reminder for consumers of items they might otherwise have forgotten, which directly result in reclaimed revenues for the retailer.

Our results show that one can predict a shopper's shopping list with high levels of accuracy, precision, and recall. For retailers, the result is not only a practical

---

* We have conducted more experiments on a larger dataset and found similar results.

system that increases revenues by up to 11 percent, but also enhances customer experience and loyalty by giving retailers the tools to individually interact with customers and anticipate their needs, giving personalized promotions of the types we will introduce.

We define a set $C$ of customers, a set $T$ of transactions made by those customers, and a fixed set $P$ of product categories bought by these customers equivalent to those normally used on shopping lists. Within $T$ and $P$ we define for each $c \in C$ sets $T_c \subseteq T$ and $P_c \subseteq P$, consisting of the transactions of each customer $c$ and the product categories bought by customer $c$, respectively. For each transaction $t \in T_c$, our task then becomes to output a vector $y \in \{0, 1\}^{|P_c|}$ where $y_i = 1$ if for a given order of all categories in $P_c$, customer $c$ bought $p_i \in P_c$ in transaction $t$, and where $y_i = 0$ if customer $c$ did not buy $P_i$. We can then formulate the overall problem as $|P_c|$ binary classification problems for each customer and derive a separate classifier for each.

## 11.4.1.1  Machine Learning Methods

To approach the shopping list prediction task, we employ classification methods from machine learning. As discussed previously, the problem of predicting the overall assortment of categories purchased $y$ can be broken down into $|P_c|$ individual binary classifications. Each class can be thought of as a customer and product category pair. If the dataset consists of $|C|$ customers and an average of $q$ categories bought by each customer, one can construct $|C| \times q$ classes (and as many binary classifiers). For each of these classes $y_i$, a classifier is trained in the supervised learning paradigm to predict whether that category will be bought by that customer in that particular transaction. Here we present a series of examples of the form $(x, y_i)$, where $x$ is a vector in $\Re^n$ for some $n$, encoding features of a transaction $t$, with $y_i \in \{0,1\}$ representing the label for each example (i.e., whether or not the category corresponding to $y_i$ was bought).

We experimented with two kinds of machine learning methods to perform this task. First we trained decision trees (specifically using C4.5 [14]) to predict each class label. Next we tried several linear methods (Perceptron [15], Winnow [11], and Naive Bayes) to learn each class. These linear methods offer several advantages in a real-world setting, most notably the quick evaluation of generated hypotheses and their ability to be trained in an online fashion.

In each case, a feature extraction step preceded the learning phase. Information about each transaction $t$ is encoded as a vector in $\Re^n$. For each transaction, we include properties of the current visit to the store, as well as information about the local history before that date in terms of data about the previous four transactions. The assumption here is that examples and their labels are not independent, and that one can model this dependence implicitly by including information about the previous visits. This tactic is similar to methods in Natural Language Processing

(NLP) for tasks such as part-of-speech tagging, where tags of preceding words are used as features to predict the current tag [16].

The features included in example $(x^j, y_i^j)$ about transaction $t^j$ are:

1. Number of days at $t^j$ since product category was $p_i$ bought by that customer. We call this the *replenishment interval* at $t^j$.
2. Frequency of *interval* at $t^j$. For each category $p_i$ we build a frequency histogram per customer for the *interval* at purchase binned into several ranges (e.g., three to five days, seven to nine days). This histogram is normalized by the total number of times items in that category were purchased.
3. The interval range into which the current purchase falls. These are the same ranges as cited above.
4. Day of the week of the current trip.
5. Time of day for the current trip broken down into six four-hour blocks.
6. Month of the year for the current trip.
7. Quarter of the year for the current trip.

We also include all of the above attributes for the previous four transactions, $t^{j-1}, t^{j-2}, t^{j-3}, t^{j-4}$ in $(x^j, y_i^j)$. Additionally, we include four additional features with respect to each transaction in the local history:

1. Whether category $p_i$ was bought in this transaction
2. The total amount spent in this transaction
3. The total number of items bought in this transaction
4. The total discount received in this transaction

Note that the previous four features are only used for the local history of the current transaction and not for the current transaction itself. Because we are predicting the products bought for the current transaction when the customer enters the store, we obviously do not have access to these features.

In the case of decision tree learners, the above is the entire set of features used. For the set of linear classification methods utilized, it is often difficult to learn a linear separator function using a relatively low-dimensional feature space such as we have constructed. By combining basic features, effectively increasing the dimensionality of each example vector *x,* we increase the chance of learning a linear function that separates all the positive and negative examples presented. Once again, this tactic is similar to those used to learn classifiers in NLP contexts where combinations of words such as bi-grams and tri-grams are used as features in addition to the basic words.

Therefore for the linear methods, several combinations of the basic features listed above were added to each example to improve learnability. For each numbered feature type above, we combine it with those of the same type in the customer's previous four transactions (local history). For example, feature 4 ( day of the week for the current transaction) is combined with feature 4 of the previous transaction to produce a new feature. For the set-valued feature types above such as 4, Boolean features are instantiated for each value (e.g., one feature per day). The combinations of these features used are simple Boolean conjunctions. For the feature types corresponding to continuous valued attributes such as feature 2, we create a single real-valued feature. To create combinations of these features, we use a nonlinear transformation.

An additional set of methods explored in this experiment took the form of several *hybrid* methods. As discussed below, due to the large number of output classes we are trying to predict over all customers, we would like to evaluate the performance of our prediction strategies in aggregate with a single measure. However, as we treat each class as independent of each other for a given transaction (a simplifying, albeit untrue assumption), different classification methods can be used for different classes. This is our hybrid approach. In the experiments, we combined a baseline predictor with the various learned classifiers in the following fashion. If the category being predicted is within the top $n$ (for some $n$) categories by purchase frequency for a given customer, then we predict positive; otherwise we predict according to the output of a given learned predictor.

## 11.4.1.2 Evaluation

The problem of predicting grocery shopping lists is an interesting learning problem because of the sheer number of classes that must be predicted. Abstracting from the product level (around 60,000 products) to the level of relatively specific categories useful for grocery lists reduces this number to some degree. However, for real-world datasets such as the one we explore in Section 11.4.1.3, this number could be from 50 to 100 classes per customer, with tens of thousands of regular customers per store, resulting in millions of classification categories and classifiers.

In general, the metrics used to judge the performance of our list predictors per class are the standard *recall, precision, accuracy,* and *f-measure* quantities. For a set of test examples, *recall* is defined as the number of true positive predictions over the number of positive examples; *precision* is the number of true positive predictions over the total number of positive predictions; *accuracy* is the number of correct predictions over the total number of examples; and *f-measure* is the harmonic mean of *recall* and *precision*: $\frac{2 \cdot recall \cdot precision}{recall + precision}$.

In obtaining an overall measure of performance by which we measure our success in predicting shopping lists for large groups of customers, there are many considerations to take into account. Typically in a learning scenario with a large number of output classes, the above quantities can be aggregated in several ways. *Micro-averaged* results are obtained by aggregating the test examples from all classes together and evaluating each metric over the entire set. The alternative is to *macro-average* the results, in which case we evaluate each metric over each class separately, and then average the results over all classes. The first strategy tends to produce higher results than the second. When the number of classes is large and very unbalanced, the micro-averaged results are implicitly dominated by the classes with a large number of examples, while the macro-averaged results are dominated by the smaller classes. Macro-averaging is intuitively more attractive for our purposes as it gives an idea of how we are performing for the majority of customers rather than just those with a large number of transactions.

However, the transactional nature of the purchase datasource gives additional methods to aggregate our results. One option is to aggregate all examples associated with a single customer, obtain results for the above metrics for each set, and average them. This approach lets us know how we are performing for the *average customer*. Although these aggregate sets are still unbalanced, given that some customers shop more than others, the average results for this approach are generally between micro- and macro-averaging. We call this *customer averaging*. The final type of aggregating we can do is on the transaction level. Here we aggregate all the examples from each transaction, calculate each metric, and average the results over all transactions. We call this method *transaction averaging*. This averaging technique is perhaps most attractive of all in light of its ability to gauge how many categories per trip predicted are bought, and how many bought per trip are predicted. However, because it breaks up example sets within classes, it is difficult to compare this approach with the other aggregation techniques.

## 11.4.1.3   List Prediction Experiments

The transactional information present in the data includes the attributes described in the previous section and lists of products purchased in each transaction. Products are arranged in a hierarchy of categories. At a fairly specific level of this hierarchy, categories resemble grocery shopping list level items. Examples of these categories include cheddar cheese, dog food, sugar, laundry detergents, red wine, heavy cream, fat-free milk, tomatoes, etc. Some 551 categories are represented in the dataset forming the set $P$ as defined previously. Customers within our sample bought 156 distinct categories on average (with standard deviation of 59). Of these categories, we restrict the set $P_c$ for each customer to include only the categories bought on greater or equal to 10 percent of their trips. This brings the average size of $P_c$ for a given $c$ to 48 with a standard deviation of 27.59.

For each transaction for the customers in the sample, examples are constructed as detailed previously. The datasets for each class[*] ranged from 4 to 240 examples. For each class in the resulting dataset, the example sets are split into a training set composed of the first 80 percent of examples in temporal order, and a test set composed of the last 20 percent. We also show results for a *top-n* baseline predictor as discussed in Section 11.4.1.1, with a cutoff of ten categories. For the decision tree classifier, C4.5 was used with 25 percent pruning and default parametrization. For the linear

---

[*]   <customer, product category> pair.

**Table 11.1  Shopping List Classification Results**

|                    | Recall | Prec | F-Meas | Acc |
|--------------------|--------|------|--------|-----|
| Top-10             | .37    | .35  | .36    | .59 |
| Perceptron         | .38    | .26  | .31    | .65 |
| Winnow             | .17    | .36  | .23    | .79 |
| C4.5               | .22    | .34  | .24    | .77 |
| Hybrid-Perceptron  | .59    | .28  | .38    | .53 |
| Hybrid-Winnow      | .43    | .36  | .39    | .65 |
| Hybrid-C4.5        | .46    | .35  | .40    | .62 |

classification methods, the SNoW learning system was used [6]. SNoW is a general classification system incorporating several linear classifiers in a unified framework. In the experiments shown, classifiers were trained with two runs over each training set. Results averaged by transaction are shown in Table 11.1.

## 11.4.1.4  Fixing Noisy Labels

A major motivation for predicting shopping lists stems from the goal of reclaiming forgotten purchases. Of course, the data collected does not include information on the instances in which categories are forgotten. *A priori,* we would not like to make any assumptions about the instances in which forgetting has occurred. This artifact produces a dataset that has noisy labels; examples where a customer "should" have bought a particular product but forgot to do so show up as a negative example in our data. This not only creates noise in the training set (which can be overcome to some extent by robust learning algorithms), but also reduces the reported accuracy of the results. Examples where our system predicts an item is on the list are judged as incorrect if the customer did not buy that item (even if they forgot it). However, we would hope that the algorithms we examine should be somewhat robust to label noise as long as they are not overfitting the data. To estimate this robustness and determine the value of our suggestions via reclaiming forgotten purchases, we make some assumptions about the distribution of these instances and correct noisy label values in the test data. By training on the noisy data and then evaluating on the corrected test data, we hope to see the number of true positive predictions go up without a serious increase in false negatives.

The manner in which we estimate noisy labels in the test data to correct is described as follows. First, for each class $p \in P_c$ for a given customer, we find the mean $\mu$ and standard deviation $\sigma$ of the replenishment interval $i$.[*] Next, we identify examples for which $i \geq \mu + c \cdot \sigma$ for different constants $c$. For each of these examples that have negative labels, we determine whether any example within a

---

[*] Note that these moments exist without specifying a distribution over the replenishment interval.

**Table 11.2  Number of Forgotten Purchases Recaptured**

| - | Recaptured |
|---|---|
| Top-10 | 10,620 |
| Perceptron | 20,244 |
| Winnow | 5,251 |
| C4.5 | 9,134 |
| Hybrid-Perceptron | 23,489 |
| Hybrid-Winnow | 12,270 |
| Hybrid-C4.5 | 15,405 |

window of $k$ following transactions is positive. We estimate each of these examples to be an instance of forgetting, with noisy negative labels.

To evaluate the robustness of our predictors to this noise, we flip each noisy (forgotten purchase) negative label to be positive and reevaluate each classification method on the modified test data. This technique allowed us to evaluate whether our classification methods might be robust to this noise and correctly classify these instances of forgotten purchases. Table 11.2 shows how many examples, from the set of 47,916 examples that our heuristic tags as instances of forgetting, we "reclaim" as positive predictions. These reclaimed purchases result in increased sales for the retailer.

## 11.4.2 Identifying and Predicting Behaviors

Each consumer model consists of a variety of attributes that characterize that consumer. We discuss the attributes that make up our model and describe the methods used to calculate them. These attributes range from global attributes that apply to all aspects of a customer to product-specific attributes, calculated for every product the customer buys.

### 11.4.2.1 Basket-Size Variance

This attribute measures the variability in the total spend during a visit for a customer. It is a global measure because it spans the customer and is not calculated separately for specific products. If a person spends the same amount of money in every shopping trip, we call this person a fixed basket shopper, and this attribute will have a low value. If the customer has a lot of variance in spending from visit to visit, this attribute gets a high value. We use two variations of this score:

1. Calculate the distance of the basket-size distribution for each customer from a uniform distribution using KL-Divergence.
2. For a range of values of X and Y, we calculate the percentage of times X% of the customer's baskets (in terms of spending) were within $Y of each other.

### 11.4.2.2  Pantry-Loading or Hoarding Attribute

We calculate the score for Pantry-Loading or Hoarding behavior for each customer and product. This attribute is a measure of the individual consumer's response to a price-drop for a specific product. Specifically, we assess whether the consumer is a "negative hoarder" — taking advantage of the sale to satisfy future needs, while keeping overall consumption stable or even declining. The "positive hoarder," by contrast, takes advantage of the sale but his net consumption increases, as do net revenues for this customer on this product. This enables promotional strategies in which discounts are presented only to a specific type of hoarder.

We calculate the hoarding score by measuring the ratio of spending on a product before and after a sale, taking into account the replenishment rate for each customer.

One way to identify negative hoarders is by comparing the total revenue for the sale and the post-sale period with that of the pre-sale period. By identifying negative hoarders as those who spend less during the sum of the sale period and the post-period than they did during the pre-sale period, we calculate the amount of revenue lost for the store.

### 11.4.2.3  Brand Loyalty

Brand Loyalty scores are created in a variety of ways for every person, product category pair:

1. Brand Loyalty (Person, Product Category) = (Number of brands bought by person in this category) / (Total brands available in this category).
2. Similar to 1, except the score is changed so that brands that are popular get a lower score. Brands that are not very popular get a higher score.
3. We calculate the premium that is being paid by the customer for the brand that they are loyal to. If a person is loyal to the cheapest brand, reduce their loyalty score. If they are loyal to the most expensive brand, increase the score.

### 11.4.2.4  Individualized Product Substitutions

We calculate product substitution categories at multiple levels: store-level substitute groups and customer level. For example, Coke and Diet Coke may be substitutes at the store level but for a given customer, Coke and Diet Coke may NOT be substitutes.

For every customer and every pair of items in the store — say $i$ and $j$ — we calculate $P(i)$, $P(j)$, $P(i, j)$, where $P(X)$ is the probability that the customer will buy product $X$ and $P(X, Y)$ is the joint probability of buying both $X$ and $Y$. Let

$C(i, j) = 0$ if $i$ and $j$ are in different categories, 1 if they are in the same category. The substitution score for a customer and products $i$ and $j$ is high if $P(i, j) < P(i) * P(j)$ and $C(i, j) = 1$.

### 11.4.2.5  Behavioral Categories

We create several behavioral categories that each consist of a set of products that are bought by customers showing a very specific behavior. Examples of our behavioral categories include "TV dinner buyers," "vegetarians," "organic buyers," "smoking quitters," and "foodies." Due to limited space, we do not give an exhaustive list of categories that we construct.

Each of these categories consists of a set of products that fall into these categories. We calculate the Symmetric Ratio Spend Score (SRSS) for each customer C and each category T. $SRSS(C, T) = (C1/C2)^I$, where $I = 1$ if $C1 > C2$ or $-1$ otherwise, and $C1 = $ (Money spent on products from category T by customer C) / (Total spend of customer C), and $C2 = $ Average($C1$) for all customers who buy at least one product from category $T$.

We also calculate a Symmetric Ratio Quantity Score where, instead of using spending on a category, we use the number of products bought in that category.

The intuition behind using these scores is to capture how much more a particular person spends on a particular category compared to other customers who buy something from that category. A simple ratio score would be unbounded, ranging from 0 to infinity, and not be symmetric. The space from 0 to 1 is taken up by customers who spend less than the average, whereas 1 to infinity is taken by those who spend more than the average. By using the Symmetric Ratio Score, we use the sign to denote more or less than the average, and the actual number denotes the magnitude.

### 11.4.2.6  Price Sensitivity

We measure how sensitive shoppers are to prices for every product. When the data is sparse, we aggregate to the product category level. In addition, we enable comparisons across shoppers by calculating the percentile price they typically pay for a particular product. Knowledge of price sensitivity helps retailers target promotions to those who need the additional inducement to trigger a purchase.

The price sensitivities are calculated for each customer with respect to each product and using shrinkage-like techniques to smooth these estimates. Given customer C, product P, calculate pairs $(R_i, P(R_i))$ where $R$ is the set of all unique prices for product P during all of customer C visits, and $P(R_i) = $ Number of times customer C visited the store and bought product P at price $R_i$ / Number of times customer C visited the store and price of product P was $R_i$.

This gives us a price sensitivity distribution over all price points of a product for a particular customer. We also get a single score for the person, product pair by taking pairs $(R_i, P(R_i))$, and calculating a least squares fit to get a linear equation relating $R_i$ and $P(R_i)$. The slope of that line is the price sensitivity and $R^2$ is the confidence. These individual price sensitivities are aggregated and used to calculate price sensitivities at sub-category and category levels.

### 11.4.2.7 Price Efficiency

We calculate several measures of price efficiency for each customer. The idea behind these attributes is to capture how "savvy" the customer is in getting better prices than the rest of the population. The *opportunistic index* measures the average difference between the price the shopper paid and the most common price of a product (the mode of the daily price over two years). A person who shops on sales a lot will have a highly negative opportunistic index. However, his score would increase for getting a lower price than the mode price even if the product is not on sale. This will include permanent price drops, coupons, etc. The *coupon index* is more difficult to beat. It is the difference between the price the shopper paid and the price paid by most people that day (the mode of the day). This is a measure of how much of an individual price a shopper gets. It is not enough to shop on sales, the customer has to get a lower price than others are paying that day. This is useful for analyzing individual promotions such as coupons (unless they are very popular coupons that most people use during a day). The *sales ratio* is the ratio of number of products bought during sales to total number of products. It is useful for analyzing effects of advertised sales. We have a *sale sensitivity index* that is the percentage of change in quantity bought during the sale as opposed to normally. The index is computed for individual customers as well as individual products and product categories.

### 11.4.3 Consumer Interactions

A main part of our work following up on creating individualized consumer models has focused on how to interact with shoppers during their visits. One aspect worth discussing in this regard includes supporting varying degrees of privacy — from biometric check-in through anonymous shopping. Biometric or card-based identification allows us to make full use of individual models, while the anonymous shopping mode still allows us to create an incremental profile that enables a limited degree of personalization. This incremental profile could be created through clustering of anonymous shopper behaviors, or a nearest-neighbor technique with existing identified individual models.

In our system, as the shopper enters the store, we present a likely shopping list, followed by aisle-specific recommendations as shown in Figure 11.2. The aisle-specific recommendations presented for a given user are accompanied by specifically

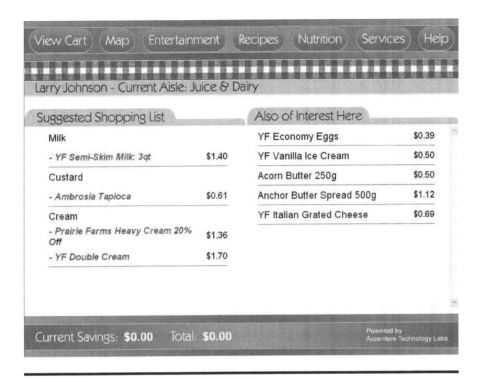

**Figure 11.2   Screen shot from shopping assistant.**

targeted personalized promotions. Section 11.5 describes a systematic method to create these promotions based on the goals of the retailer and manufacturer.

## 11.5  Intelligent Promotion Planning

Creating profiles of entities (customers, products, stores, etc.) has been tackled by many data mining studies. What has been traditionally missing from this research is a framework to manage these models at a high level, in a goal-directed manner. Creating individual models of customers that can predict consumer behavior is useful, but it also has enormous implications on how retailers do business and interact with manufacturers and customers. In addition to using newspapers, in-store displays, and end-caps to highlight their products and run promotions, retailers can influence individuals in a vastly different way using individual consumer models. These capabilities create the need for systems that can take high-level business goals and apply them at an individual customer level. As more and more corporations start using data mining in their everyday business, just predicting an event (or purchase) is not enough — what is also needed is a method to operationalize this capability.

Planning promotions based on individual models using the simulation and optimization techniques that follow allows retailers to evaluate the costs and benefits of such promotions with much greater efficiency. In addition, it allows manufacturers to pay for delivered business results in terms of new customers, enhanced loyalty, and incremental revenue and lift. Any retailer utilizing the system then has a distinct advantage in bidding for promotional dollars from a manufacturer. This section describes the process of planning promotions in an environment where individual consumer models are available.

As mentioned previously, creating consumer models is of value because it enables specific promotional strategies. These strategies include presenting a shopping list, including items likely to be forgotten, moving fixed basket size shoppers to higher-margin products, offering variable basket shoppers discounts on larger pack sizes, withholding discounts from "pantry loaders," extending the brand for the brand loyal by offering related branded products, etc. In each case, when a promotion is delivered to a particular customer based on some aspect of his individual model, there are a number of ways that it could have been generated.

One possible way would be to manually examine each customer's profile and predicted shopping list for the next trip, and create a set of promotions for each individually that serves the purposes of the store or product manufacturer. The obvious disadvantage of this approach is that it cannot scale well to thousands of customers across millions of transactions. An alternative is to manually create static rules defining if-then scenarios for giving particular promotions based on properties of an individual's behavioral model; for example, if customer $a$ is predicted to buy category $c$ and has brand loyalty $x$, then give an $n$% discount on product $p$. While this type of rule creation is arguably more scalable than a totally manual technique, promotions could be targeted much more dynamically to serve changing goals.

We propose that the task of creating personalized promotions based on individual models is no simpler than the creation of the individual models themselves. It requires facilities to view and reason about the goals, parameters, and results of a promotion for a single product, while simulating these promotions for each customer using their personal model. To this end, we have created an *Individualized Promotion Planning* system. This system allows a user to modify the purposes of each promotion using a set of high-level goals, which are mapped to the practical parameters of a sale to produce general rules of the type mentioned above. By simulating the effects of a promotion on each customer targeted with respect to specific retailer or manufacturer goals, this system allows a completely new type of pricing model for trade promotions, bringing the pay-for-performance philosophy to a domain that has traditionally been administered on a very crude basis.

The system also offers the advantage of building and simulating sets of rules collectively and evaluating their interactions rather than manually in isolation. Below we describe the operations of the Individual Promotion Planning system from goal selection, to optimization, simulation, and pricing. We believe that reasoning and optimizing trends on an aggregate level extrapolated from data in multitudes of complex individualized profiles can be done in many data mining domains dealing with transactional data.

## 11.5.1  Goal Selection

Promotions are presented to consumers for the retailer or product manufacturers to achieve certain goals. The scope of the goals available becomes much wider when individualized consumer models are present. For example, a manufacturer may care about many things beyond basic revenue levels, such as the brand loyalty of their consumers, or their market share. The four main goal areas we believe our individual consumer models may affect are:

1. *Brand goals.* These subgoals represent results reflecting the brand loyalty and number of consumers who buy a particular brand: *brand switches, brand extensions, new trials,* and *average loyalty level.*
2. *Revenue goals.* These subgoals represent revenue results for the product being promoted: *short-term revenue, long-term revenue, revenue trends.*
3. *Lift goals.* These subgoals represent results for relative volume increases over current levels: *short-term lift, long-term lift,* and *brand lift.*
4. *Market share goals.* These subgoals represent results for market share changes for a brand: *product market share.*

Our system allows the user to weight each of these high-level goal groups relative to each other and also assign weightings to each individual goal within a group. These weightings can be used in an optimization procedure to map goal weights to the appropriate promotion parameters that maximize the results for each goal.

## 11.5.2  Promotion Parameters

In a system designed to deliver promotions based on individual models of consumers, the parameters of these promotions include many more factors than the discount and duration of the sale. In principle, using information from individual models could allow us to assign personalized prices [3] and to show promotions to different consumers for different periods of time. However, in the initial system we have developed, we restrict the discount and duration of a promotion to a set amount across all consumers, in an effort to provide more compatibility with existing systems. The parameters available in the current system for the promotional rules are as follows:

1. *Discount*: the price reduction percentage applied to a product from its baseline price.
2. *Duration:* the period of time in days that a promotion will be shown to the target consumers.
3. *Minloy,maxloy:* the minimum and maximum loyalty scores for the consumers in the target group (between 0 and 100).
4. *Minhoard,maxhoard:* the minimum and maximum hoarding scores for the consumers in the target group (between −100 and 100).

5. *Minsensitiviy, maxsensitivity:* the minimum and maximum price sensitivity scores for the consumers (between 0 and 100).
6. *Mintrial,maxtrial*: the minimum and maximum new trial rate scores for the consumers (between 0 and 100) (Figure 11.3).

For a given customer $c$, the promotional rules will then have the following form: *if c has scores within ranges 3,4,5,6, then reduce price by discount for duration days.*

## 11.5.3 Simulation

The first main advantage of our system is its ability to show the user simulations of promotional results directly related to the goals of Section 11.5.1 by creating promotional rules based on the parameters described above and applying these rules iteratively to each customer. We then apply heuristic measures to gauge the results related to each goal defined above. Many other sets of heuristics or learned models could be created to explain the results. For each heuristic $h_i$ below, we sum $h_i$ over all customers to produce the final simulated result. Also, $sens(x)$ refers to the price sensitivity (Section 11.4.2) of the given customer for the given product at price $x$.

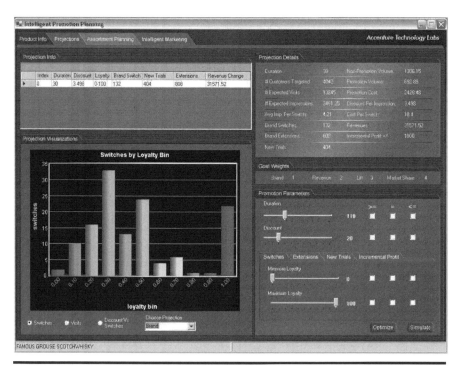

**Figure 11.3  Screen shot from the Promotion Planning prototype.**

*base* refers to the base price of the given product, while *discount* refers to the *discount* variable introduced in Section 11.5.2.

### 11.5.3.1 Brand Heuristics

$$h_{switch} = \begin{cases} result\_prob & \text{if } numvisits \geq loy_{other} \cdot conv\_rate \\ 0 & \text{else} \end{cases}$$

$$h_{extensions} = \begin{cases} result\_prob & \text{if } numvisits \geq \\ & (1 - loy_{this}) \cdot conv\_rate \\ 0 & \text{else} \end{cases}$$

$$h_{newtrials} = \begin{cases} result\_prob & \text{if } numvisits \geq \\ & (loy_{other} + newtrial) \cdot conv\_rate \\ 0 & \text{else} \end{cases}$$

$$h_{loyalty\_level} = sens(base - discount)$$
$$\cdot loyalty - change \cdot num\_visits$$

$$result\_prob = sens(base - discount)$$

In all of the above, we use the average replenishment rate per customer *repl_rate* (as detailed in [7]) to calculate the quantity *numvisits* as $\frac{duration}{repl\_rate}$. The conversion rate *conv_rate* is a constant estimated as an average of the number of visits by the customer required to obtain a positive result for each heuristic. The constant *loyalty_change* refers to the average loyalty level change estimated per promotion computed per customer or product.

### 11.5.3.2 Revenue Heuristics

The revenue heuristics encode the relative increase or decrease in revenues in the short term (promotion duration) and long term (four replenishment rates after promotion):

$$h_{short\_term} = (base - discount) \cdot sens(discount) \cdot num\_visits$$

$$h_{long\_term} = \begin{cases} hoarding\_score & \text{if } sens(base - discount) > .5 \\ 0 & \text{else} \end{cases}$$

The brand revenue heuristic is evaluated by summing either the short- or long-term revenue heuristics over all products in the brand.

### 11.5.3.3 Lift Heuristics

$$h_{short\_term} = (sens(base - discount) - sens(base)) \cdot num\_custs$$

$$h_{long\_term} = (sens(discount\_price) - sens(base)) \cdot \frac{hoarding\_score}{base}$$

The brand lift heuristic is evaluated by summing either the short- or long-term lift heuristics over all products in the brand.

### 11.5.3.4 Market Share Heuristics

$$h_{market\_share} = h_{switches} + \frac{h_{extensions}}{avg\_ext}$$

Here, *avg_ext* is the average number of extensions over all brands in the category. $h_{market\_share}$ is then the estimated increase/decrease in market share in terms of loyal customers over the next promotion period.

## 11.5.4 Optimization

In addition to simulation, our prototype offers the user a flexible optimization tool. In the optimization procedure, the user first enters relative weightings for each goal result defined in Section 11.5.1. The optimizer then attempts to set parameter values that optimize a closed-form approximation of each result heuristic described above in Section 11.5.3. Several types of constraints can be placed on each parameter variable within the framework.

More concretely, let $x_1 \dots x_n$ be the parameter variables described in Section 11.5.1. We define a hierarchical multi-objective optimization problem of the following form:

$$\operatorname*{argmax}_{x_1 \dots x_n} f(x_1 \dots n) = \operatorname*{argmax}_{x_1 \dots x_n} \begin{bmatrix} f_{brand}(x_1 \dots x_n) \\ f_{revenue} x_1 \dots x_n \\ f_{lift}(x_1 \dots x_n) \\ f_{mshare}(x_1 \dots x_n) \end{bmatrix}$$

$$wrt \ C = \{C_1 \dots c_k\}$$

where the set $C$ of constraints on $x_1 \ldots x_n$ is given by the user. We reformulate $f(x_1 \ldots x_n)$ as a weighted sum:

$$f(x_1 \ldots x_n) = g_1 \cdot f_{brand}(x_1 \ldots x_n) + g_2 \cdot f_{revenue}(x_1 \ldots x_n)$$
$$+ g_3 \cdot f_{lift}(x_1 \ldots x_n) + g_4 \cdot f_{mshare}(x_1 \ldots x_n)$$

Each term in this sum is itself expressed as a weighted sum, yielding a single objective function. The subobjectives are as follows:

$$f_{brand}(x_1 \ldots x_n) = b_1 \cdot switches(x_1 \ldots x_n) +$$
$$b_2 \cdot extensions(x_1 \ldots x_n) + b_3 \cdot newtrials(x_1 \ldots x_n)$$
$$b_4 \cdot loylevel(x_1 \ldots x_n)$$

$$f_{revenue}(x_1 \ldots x_n) = r_1 \cdot shortrev(x_1 \ldots x_n) +$$
$$r_2 \cdot longrev(x_1 \ldots x_n) + r_3 \cdot brandrev(x_1 \ldots x_n)$$

$$f_{lift}(x_1 \ldots x_n) = l_1 \cdot shortlift(x_1 \ldots x_n) +$$
$$l_2 \cdot longlift(x_1 \ldots x_n) + l_3 \cdot brandlift(x_1 \ldots x_n)$$
$$f_{mshare}(x_1 \ldots x_n) = m_1 \cdot prodshare(x_1 \ldots x_n)$$

Each term in the subobjectives is a closed-form approximation of the result of its associated heuristic, which in general may be nonlinear. For example, the *switches* term of $f_{brand}$ is defined as follows:

$$switches(x_1 \ldots x_n) =$$

$$\frac{\left(\frac{duration}{avg\_repl} - conv\_rate \cdot \frac{(minloy + maxloy)}{2}\right) \cdot custs(minloy, maxloy)}{duration^2}$$

where *avg_repl* is the average replenishment rate of customers who buy the target category, and *conv_rate* is the number of promotion instances needed to switch a customer with 100 percent loyalty to a competing brand (estimated from training transactions). We estimate the *custs* quantity by assuming the number of customers is distributed normally with respect to brand loyalty, and using the normal cumulative distribution function:

$$custs(minloy, maxloy) = \frac{1}{\sigma\sqrt{2\pi}} \int_{minloy/\sigma}^{maxloy/\sigma} e^{\frac{-(t-\mu)^2}{2\sigma^2}} dt$$

The set of constraints $C$ can contain equality/inequality constraints over any of the input variables $x_1 \ldots x_n$ to express rules such as *promotions on product p may never exceed 50 days in duration*.

To solve this nonlinear optimization task, we employed a sequential quadratic programming procedure. A line search is used to guide the SQP in a manner similar to [10, 13], with the solution implemented in Matlab.

## 11.6  Conclusion

This chapter described a real-world data mining project using customer purchase data from a retailer to create individual consumer models to detect and predict the shopping behaviors of customers. These consumer models enable the retailer to provide customers with individual and personalized interactions as they navigate through the retail store by making very fine, accurate predictions about a particular individual customer in a given shopping trip. The shopping list prediction system results in a direct increase of revenues by reminding customers of purchases they would otherwise forget. The shopping list also helps the system narrow down the list of products for which to give personalized promotions and discounts. We described a set of attributes that constitute the individual consumer model. These attributes are used to present personalized promotions to each customer based on their historical shopping data. We also described the Intelligent Promotion Planning system, which functions as a "mediator" between the high-level business goals of a retailer or product manufacturer and the individual promotions offered to customers. It not only offers an optimization capability, where optimal parameters of the promotion are chosen based on high-level goals set by the retailer, but also offers a simulation environment where many what-if scenarios can be considered and the results of potential promotions evaluated before implementation. We believe that utilizing transaction data, learning individual behavioral models of customers using data mining techniques, and then optimizing higher-level objective functions based on these individual models is applicable in a variety of areas.

We soon expect to implement the Individual Consumer Modeling system in a brick-and-mortar store, allowing us to evaluate the accuracy of the goal heuristics we have developed. At this point they can become the basis for a bootstrapped model that we can update continuously through active and online learning methods. Additionally, the setup of a larger-scale optimization problem representing each consumer's promotional variables (discount, duration, loyalty, etc.) directly such as in [3] should provide even greater efficiency in terms of maximizing goal results and correct pricing.

# References

1. G. Adomavicius and A. Tuzhilin. Using data mining methods to build customer profiles. *IEEE Computer*, 34(2):74–82, 2001.
2. R. Agrawal and R. Srikant. Fast algorithms for mining association rules. In *Proc. of VLDB-94*, Santiago, Chile, 1994.
3. C. Baydar. One-to-one modeling and simulation: a new approach in customer relationship management for grocery retail. In *SPIE Conference on Data Mining and Knowledge Discovery: Theory, Tools, and Technology IV*, 2002.
4. R. Bellamy, J. Brezin, W. Kellogg, and J. Richards. Designing an e-grocery application for a palm computer: Usability and interface issues. *IEEE Communications*, 8(4), 2001.
5. T. Brijs, G. Swinnen, K. Vanhoof, and G. Wets. Using association rules for product assortment decisions: a case study. In *Knowledge Discovery and Data Mining*, 1999, pp. 254–260.
6. A. Carlson, C. Cumby, J. Rosen, and D. Roth. The SNoW Learning Architecture. Technical Report UIUCDCS-R-99-2101, UIUC Computer Science Department, May 1999.
7. C. Cumby, A. Fano, R. Ghani, and M. Krema. Predicting customer shopping lists from point-of-sale purchase data. In *Proceedings of KDD-04*, ACM Press, 2004, pp. 402–409.
8. A. Ehrenberg. *Repeat-Buying: Facts, Theory, and Applications*. Charles Griffin & Company Limited, London, 1988.
9. A. Geyer-Schulz, M. Hahsler, and M. Jahn. A customer purchase incidence model applied to recommender systems. In *WebKDD2001 Workshop*, San Francisco, CA, August 2001.
10. S. Han. A globally convergent method for nonlinear programming. *Journal of Optimization Theory and Applications*, 22, 1977.
11. N. Littlestone. Learning quickly when irrelevant attributes abound: a new linear-threshold algorithm. *Machine Learning*, 2:285–318, 1988.
12. E. Newcomb, T. Pashley, and J. Stasko. Mobile computing in the retail arena. In *Proceedings of CHI2003*, ACM Press, 2003, pp. 337–344.
13. M. Powell. The convergence of variable metric methods for nonlinearly constrained optimization calculations. *Nonlinear Programming*, 3, 1978.
14. J. R. Quinlan. *C4.5: Programs for Machine Learning*. Morgan Kaufmann, 1992.
15. F. Rosenblatt. The perceptron: a probabilistic model for information storage and organization in the brain. *Psychological Review*, 65:386–407, 1958. (Reprinted in *Neurocomputing*, MIT Press, 1988.)
16. D. Roth. Learning in natural language. In *Proc. of the International Joint Conference on Artificial Intelligence*, 1999, pp. 898–904.

# OTHER AREAS OF DATA MINING

## Chapter 12

# Data Mining: Common Definitions, Applications, and Misunderstandings

Richard D. Pollack

## Contents

## 12.1  Introduction

Data mining is growing in usage and sophistication across numerous industries, government sectors, academic environments, political campaigns, and professional sports associations. The term has even entered the cultural lexicon, as evidenced by the popular Fox network show "24" in which characters are asked to "data mine" government databases to apprehend criminals. Data mining has become a new buzzword in virtually any environment that involves the manipulation or analysis of data. As such, the term also has become overused and misapplied. This chapter addresses what data mining is, common applications, and the improper use of the term and its applications. The foundation of this chapter is based on the author's actual experience across a variety of data mining engagements.

## 12.2  What Is Data Mining?

Data mining is the process of uncovering patterns and trends to identify opportunity in large databases for predictive purposes. The discovery tools involved in this process typically incorporate sophisticated statistical techniques that can be utilized through powerful software packages such as SPSS Clementine, SAS Enterprise Miner, and Spotfire (from Spotfire, Inc.). These tools are frequently applied to large data repositories, including data warehouses, data marts, and other large data stores.

Another defining characteristic of the data mining process, captured by the aforementioned tools, is the effective employment of visual analytics. Interactive, powerful, visual interfaces where data can be displayed, manipulated, and analyzed in a variety of forms is a hallmark of the modern data mining engagement. Currently, Spotfire is one of the best examples of this type of data mining tool (Figure 12.1).

"Training" is often a key part of the data mining process. Here, statistical models are "trained" on smaller random samples taken from a larger data set. Let us take a common financial example. Take a random subset of data, on a record-by-record basis, and code who is a credit risk and who is not by using those who have low credit scores (i.e., the risk group) and those who have higher credit scores (i.e., non-risk group). The model is trained on this credit-risk versus non-credit-risk subset, validated (and further adjusted where necessary) on similar samples from the larger dataset, and ultimately used to score new incoming data. Once developed, the model is periodically refined to maintain scoring accuracy.

In the example above, the data is mined for particular groups of individuals with certain behavioral characteristics. Knowing this information may help identify such people earlier in the future (e.g., to make better credit card offer decisions). In a similar vein, one also could identify a particular pattern or trend for mortgage defaults using data mining techniques to identify the behavioral profiles of risk and non-risk loan groups. Again, one could use such data — often referred to as historical data — to make better decisions, especially in the form of predictions.

In summary, using sophisticated software to train data to formulate algorithms to identify patterns and make behavioral predictions is key to the data mining process. One mines data to uncover opportunity in large datasets to enhance decision making. Following are more in-depth data mining examples as well as misapplications of the concept. Before that discussion, however, it is necessary to discuss how data is processed before initiating actual mining.

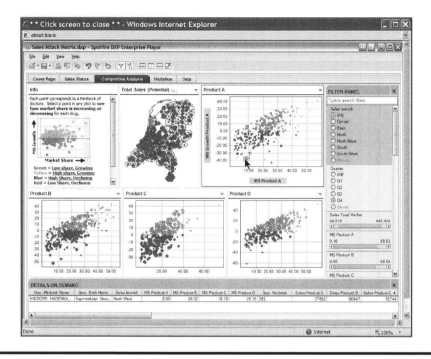

**Figure 12.1** The Spotfire data mining tool. (From ©2007 Spotfire. All rights reserved.)

## 12.3 Precursors to Data Mining

Data, of course, must be properly cleaned, merged (if applicable), and prepared in consistent and readable formats to be effectively analyzed. This applies to any analytic engagement, whether or not one is doing data mining. In data mining, cleaning and preparing the data can often be more challenging as a result of having:

1. Far more data
2. From multiple sources
3. Often in different formats
4. With greater amounts of historical data (older data often have more gaps and formatting issues)
5. Often with more data redundancy

Cleaning data under these conditions will take more time and require more sophisticated tools. Fortunately, the aforementioned data mining tools, especially the ones with greater interactive visual capabilities (Spotfire and Clementine), can facilitate this task. With advanced visual display techniques, particularly those that can produce graphics in multiple dimensions, it is far easier to spot outliers, patterns of missing data, data redundancies, and other aberrations in the data that could compromise analysis.

More time is usually spent on cleaning and preparing data for analysis than on the actual analysis itself. Although data mining tools are continually improving their capabilities to import, export, replace, visualize, and analyze data, there are almost always significant chunks of time spent on defining and recoding variables, reformatting, tracking down the reasons for aberrant data, and resolving reliability and validity issues (just to name a few). Data mining technology, at least at this point in time, seems to be evolving more quickly than the ability resolve data quality issues.

## 12.4  Data Mining Examples

As one can see in Table 12.1 (which is by no means exhaustive), data mining is common to many industries and sectors that affect our lives on a daily basis.

Following are three in-depth data mining examples, all from actual consulting engagements, that underscore core features of the data mining process.

### 12.4.1  Example 1: Telecommunications Industry

This example pertains to a large telecom company that used data mining to enhance the introduction of a new service to its customer base. Specifically, this company used data mining to identify patterns of consumers mostly likely to adopt a new service based on varying levels of monetary incentives. Consumer information included services they already had from the company, demographic and psychographic information, and views on competing brands.

The data covered tens of thousands of customers over a number of U.S. metropolitan areas with information on hundreds of variables, including the incentives that covered actual cash off a monthly bill and different levels of mail-in rebates. A decision tree algorithm called Exhaustive CHAID (Chi-squared Automatic Interaction Detector from SPSS' AnswerTree), which is ideal for finding opportunity in large data sets and is often used as a precursor for higher-order predictive models, was used to reduce the number of variables. Once a smaller set of variables was established, predictive models were formulated using logistic regression. The models scored every record in the data with uptake probabilities for the new service at every discount level.

The mining of the data revealed a key finding: a large incentive averse segment. Specifically, although on the surface counterintuitive, if the cash value of a discount in the form of a rebate was higher than the cash amount off a monthly bill, the probability of uptake was *lower*. Findings indicated that higher discounted rebates did not lead to higher uptake of the new service. This was a clear pattern in the data that was apparent across numerous geographies and income levels. Further investigation revealed that many consumers had been previously embittered by discount

**Table 12.1   Common Data Mining Examples**

| Industry/Sector | Data Mining Activity |
|---|---|
| Market research | Market segmentation, customer classification and grouping, patterns of loyalty and defection, and targeting, especially for retail industries |
| Government | Internal Revenue Service deploying algorithms to identify suspect tax returns; Department of Homeland Security programs that mine telephone and travel records for criminal and terrorist activity |
| Financial and insurance services | Credit scoring, fraud detection (big in Telecom too), and portfolio analysis/risk |
| Political campaigning | Build voter profiles from public databases (especially consumer and demographic) for message targeting (primarily via phone and direct mail); currently termed "microtargeting" |
| Internet commerce | Developing profiles of visitors and customers on large transactional Web sites; using such profiles to feed preference engines |
| College/university institutional research | Develop student profiles for prospects, applicants, and matriculants |
| Biotech/pharmaceutical/health care | Molecular simulation, patient profiles, risk assessment, outcomes research |
| Law enforcement | Mining a variety of databases for patterns of criminal behavior; profiling actual criminals |
| Professional sports | Using player statistics to predict the most effective match-ups based on copious amounts of player and team data |

schemes, especially rebates. Moreover, the study was conducted when large corporate scandals dominated the business news.

If the client did not have the foresight to mine the data, substantial resources would have been spent on marketing and advertising rebates that resulted in poor returns. The likelihood of purchasing the new service would have been severely compromised. The data mining results revealed a far more optimal strategy in which consumers would respond positively — drop the rebates and simply take cash off the consumers' monthly bills.

Following is another example of data being mined for the primary purpose of uncovering patterns of behavior to generate a practical solution to a business issue — this time, however, in the pharmaceutical industry.

## 12.4.2  Example 2: Pharmaceutical Industry

This engagement mined data to gain the greatest behavioral insight into physicians' prescription writing for an existing drug therapy (Drug X) that was experiencing flat market share. The client wanted to translate insights from the research into practical strategies that would enhance market position.

A list of Drug X prescription writers was obtained and contacted to conduct qualitative research. The purpose of this phase was to ascertain the current hot buttons and concerns about Drug X, especially in relation to its competitors. Findings from the qualitative research helped drive the formulation of questions for a quantitative survey. The quantitative survey also included psychographic items to assess physicians' attitudes, values, and lifestyles, all designed to enhance insight into their prescription writing behavior. The quantitative survey was fielded, based on a list of Drug X prescription writers. (To be included in the qualitative or quantitative phase of the study, the physician had to be writing at least moderate levels of Drug X in the recent past.)

Once the data was collected for the quantitative survey, physicians' writing behavior for Drug X (which came from an extremely large independent database) was linked to their survey data. (A physician's writing behavior is simply "what" happened. The survey was designed to uncover the "why" behind the "what" for Drug X.) The data was first segmented with decision tree algorithms and Principal Components Analysis. Two segments emerged from the bridged data:

> Segment 1: *Conservative traditionalists.* These were medium to high writing primary care physicians in the Drug X category, with a relatively stable Rx share of Drug X, who preferred "traditional" drug therapies and lacked innovative tendencies.
>
> Segment 2: *Active knowledge/information seekers.* These were high writing specialists in category, with a declining Drug X share, who kept current on clinical research in their field.

Clearly, promotional implementation approaches would be different for the above segments and this was easily addressed (more on this later). At this point in the study, however, a more complex quantitative challenge remained. Now that the data was bridged and mined for segments, the findings needed to be extended to the larger universe (of hundreds of thousands) of non-sampled doctors.

To predict the behavior of non-sampled doctors, a proprietary profile-based matching system was constructed to assess the psychographic dimensions associated with certain behavioral and demographic characteristics of sampled doctors. Once the psychographic dimensions associated with sampled doctors' behavior were ascertained, the behavioral characteristics of non-sampled doctors were extracted from extant physician databases and matched with the most likely psychographic dimensions. The resulting output from the predictive system:

1. Identified the best set and subsets of behavioral and psychographic variables that lead to prescribing Drug X
2. Provided a prescribing probability for any individual, or any segment of individuals, for Drug X

The predictive results that emerged from the model helped the client prepare segment-specific marketing materials and messages, which were then implemented by the sales force based on a given physician's profile.

This example captures core features of the data mining process: *using historical information* (i.e., Rx and primary research data) *to uncover meaningful predictive patterns of behavior* (i.e., physician segments) *to successfully address a practical business goal* (i.e., to enhance product uptake).

## 12.4.3 Example 3: Information Technology (IT) Industry

In this consulting engagement, the primary objective was to determine what drives the purchase of printers and multi-function devices in Europe, North America, and South America. Brand uptake by product in both consumer and corporate markets over the above geographic regions was known, as were consumer and corporate demographics. A large international phone survey was conducted, with both consumer and business sections, which contained demographic, psychographic, IT, and printer device questions.

Principal Components Analysis (PCA) was used to uncover patterns that formed psychographic dimensions, which laid the foundation for three purchasing segments: (1) those who like to inform themselves before a purchase, (2) those more influenced by sales people and advertisements, and (3) those who were primarily influenced by brand. These segments accounted for the majority of the survey respondents. A logit model was employed to generate printer device uptake probabilities across consumers and business segments over the geographic regions. Because irregular data patterns were detected in some of the variables used in the initial logistic regression analysis, a proprietary data mining algorithm translated these variables into categorical covariates before the final logits were run, resulting in greater predictive accuracy.

Once the printer-purchasing segments were formed on the primary market research data from the international survey, a critical question remained: How large are these segments in the actual geographic markets that were assessed? In short, what is the size of the market for printer devices? Another phone survey was conducted that simply asked consumers three to five questions, derived from the above analyses, to place them into purchasing segments. This also served the purpose of validating the findings from the primary research. Clearly, there would be a problem if the three to five questions could not accurately place consumers in the segments. Once the market was sized, sales and marketing plans appropriate to purchasing segments and regions were implemented. Sales for the printer devices increased overall, with some regions experiencing sharp increases in sales.

This final detailed example illustrates key aspects of a successful data mining engagement in the business realm: *uncovering meaningful behavioral patterns* (i.e., the three purchasing segments)*, allowing predictions to a larger universe of consumers to successfully implement and thus resolve a practical issue* — increasing sales. For readers interested in additional examples of employing data mining techniques to solve common business problems, see Berry and Linoff (2004).

## 12.5 Data Mining Techniques

Two useful data mining techniques — Exhaustive CHAID (which can be found in SPSS AnswerTree software) and Logistic regression — both referenced in the above examples, merit further discussion.

Decision tree algorithms are typically employed to segment groups of respondents that share similar characteristics. One of the most powerful of these algorithms is called Exhaustive CHAID (Chi-squared Automatic Interaction Detector), which is ideal for finding opportunity in large sets, and includes many desirable features:

1. Only uses variables that are statistically significant
2. Examines all combinations and permutations of variables
3. Combines categories of variables on-the-fly
4. Effectively analyzes categorical and continuous variables simultaneously
5. As a variable reduction tool, is often used as a precursor for higher-order predictive models (such as logit models, discussed below)
6. Is conservative — low probability of an effect being over-estimated
7. Is an effective data visualization tool
8. Corrects for chance findings, which translates into both more reliable and valid insights
9. Improved over original CHAID by providing optimal splits for variables
10. Determines key segmentation variables for accurate targeting
11. Can process and identify nonlinear relationships, unlike more traditional techniques such as cluster analysis

The ability to combine categories of variables on-the-fly (noted in above listing) is particularly important in terms of identifying key variables. For example, physician age may not be a significant variable when partitioned as (1) 28–39, (2) 40–49, (3) 50–59, (4) 60–69, (5) 70 and above. When repartitioned by E. CHAID (i.e., 28–49 and 50–69), the variable becomes significant. Exhaustive CHAID will automatically test all combinations and permutations of variables (thus the term "Exhaustive") to maximize power, often uncovering patterns not detected by other tools.

Logistic regression is a common and robust technique to score databases. Scoring typically refers to the probability of a particular event, such as the likelihood of purchasing a certain product. The scores (i.e., probabilities) generated by a logistic regression model range from 0 to 100 percent or can be used to develop a descriptive coding scheme. For example, individuals in a database with probabilities ranging above 65 percent might be labeled "Likely Buyers," as opposed to individuals with probability scores below 50 percent. Because it is common to score hundreds of thousands to millions of people in data mining applications, with every unique record receiving a score, logistic regression is a technique well-suited for such a situation.

Logit models have other advantages. For example, when compared to multiple regression models and discriminant analysis, logistic regression is far more robust to statistical violations including situations in which assumptions concerning various types of statistical normality are violated. Moreover, unlike multiple regression, logit models can process both linear and nonlinear data. Multiple regression only can deal with the former and would produce far less accurate results if there are nonlinearities in the data.

Logistic regression is often the key analysis that drives prediction for data mining applications across a number of different industries. It also is not unusual to see E. CHAID and Logistic regression applied in tandem, especially in cases where numerous variables must be reduced to a manageable set to be effectively processed by a logit model; E. CHAID is ideal for such a variable reduction task. To learn more about applied logistic regression, see Hosmer and Lemeshow's (2000) classic text.

## 12.6 Data Mining or Not?

Having discussed how data mining is defined and how it is commonly applied, let us examine some confusions and misunderstandings. Below are data mining FAQs and statements to which the author has been exposed over the years and that exemplify lack of clarity about the subject.

1. *Are we doing data mining when using Online Analytical Processing (OLAP) tools?* No. Although OLAP is a powerful way to view data from many vantage points in a multitude of forms, there is no predictive component and thus is missing a key component of the data mining process.
2. *Is Excel (2003) a data mining tool?* For the most part, no. First, by today's standards, it cannot handle large amounts of data due to column (256 max) and row (65,536 max) limitations.* Second, its statistical tools are limited, especially concerning predictive analytics.
3. *Is it true that there is really no process or criterion that separates data mining from statistical analysis techniques?* A relevant and logical question but the answer is essentially no. One of the major components that separates data

---

* Excel 2007 is reported to support 1,048,576 rows by 16,384 columns. As of the writing of this chapter, the software has not been commercially released by Microsoft.

mining from common statistical analysis is CRISP-DM (CRoss Industry Standard Process for Data Mining, 2000), a tool- and industry-neutral standard methodology for data mining with greater focus on the practical understanding and solving of business issues. Moreover, many statistical analytic techniques are not optimized to process large amounts of data.

4. *Data mining seems a bit esoteric and more germane to academic circles.* While academics have greatly contributed to the growth and development of data mining tools and techniques, and modern data mining does have roots in expert system approaches, the statement is essentially inaccurate. In data mining, there is greater emphasis on understanding the business issue, the data, and particularly generating practical and realistic solutions to a problem. Data mining engagements do not typically end with analysis but more often with successful deployment of strategies garnered from analytic insights. Both the previous table and detailed examples capture the practical and realistic nature of data mining engagements.

5. *Are SPSS' and SAS' long-established statistical programs data mining tools?* Yes, but they pale to the data mining capabilities of their bigger brothers. Both SPSS Clementine and SAS Enterprise Miner can process larger amounts of data more efficiently, have superior visual analytic capabilities (especially Clementine), as well as superior interactive capabilities, and can run multiple models simultaneously.

6. *Is data mining just another business fad?* No. Due to the:
   - Tremendous leaps in computer processing and storage power
   - Concomitant leaps in data collection capabilities, particularly transactional technologies in the consumer sector (both on- and offline)
   - Exponential growth of stored data and
   - Continual development of powerful analytic software, data mining will continue to grow in usage, applicability, and popularity.

# References

Berry, M.J.A. and Linoff, G. S. (2004). *Data Mining Techniques: For Marketing, Sales, and Customer Relationship Management, second edition.* John Wiley & Sons, Inc., New York.

Chapman, P. (NCR), Clinton, J. (SPSS), Kerber, R. (NCR), Khabaza, T. (SPSS), Reinartz, T. (DaimlerChrysler), Shearer, C. (SPSS), and Wirth, R. (DaimlerChrysler). (2000). CRISP-DM 1.0: Step-by-step Data Mining Guide. SPSS Inc., Chicago, IL.

Hosmer, D.W. and Lemeshow, S. (2000*). Applied Logistic Regression, Second Edition.* John Wiley & Sons, Inc., New York.

SAS® Enterprise Miner (2006). SAS Institute Inc., Cary, NC.

Spotfire® (2007). Spotfire, Inc., Somerville, MA.

SPSS AnswerTree® (2006), SPSS Inc., Chicago, IL.

SPSS Clementine® (2006), SPSS Inc., Chicago, IL.

*Chapter 13*

# Fuzzy Sets in Data Mining and Ordinal Classification

David L. Olson, Helen Moshkovich, and Alexander Mechitov

## Contents

## 13.1 Introduction

Data mining grew as an academic discipline in many fields, in a very short time. Growth in database technology led to explosive increases in the ability to gather and store information. An extreme instance is weather satellite data, providing a massive stream of detailed data with important clues as to what the weather would do. Governments, of course, have always faced the problem of making sense of masses of data in many fields. The medical field has dealt with important problems in diagnosing various diseases, leading to the specialized discipline of biometrics. While each discipline faces opportunities in dealing with masses of computerized data, each develops specialty tools to deal with their specific data circumstances.

In business, banks and retail organizations face similar problems. There are specialty problems fringing on engineering, such as how to deal with information available in the telephony industry. Many early business applications related to identifying association rules based on market basket data of various types. Primary business applications, however, tend to involve classification (Will loan applicants repay their loans? Will recipients of sales information provided at cost X respond by purchasing goods worth profit Y? Is insurance claim alpha likely to be fraudulent and thus merit investigation at cost Z).

At the same time, one can view a rather large number of classification tasks in business applications as tasks with classes reflecting the levels of the same property. Evaluating the creditworthiness of clients is often measured on an ordinal level as, for example, Excellent, Good, Acceptable, or Poor (Ben-David et al., 1989). Applicants for a job are divided into accepted and rejected, but sometimes there may be also a pool of applicants left for further analysis as they may be accepted in some circumstances (Ben-David, 1992; Slowinski, 1995). Different cars may be divided into groups such as Very Good, Good, Acceptable, or Unacceptable (Bohancec and Rajkovic, 1990). This type of task is called "ordinal classification" (Larichev and Moshkovich, 1994; Moshkovich et al., 2002). The peculiarity of the ordinal classification is that data items with "better" qualities (characteristics) logically are presented in "better" classes: the better the article in its characteristics, the closer it is to the class "Accepted." Moshkovich et al. (2002) showed that taking into account possible ordinal dependence between attribute values and final classes may lead to a smaller number of rules with the same accuracy and enable the system to extend obtained rules to instances not presented in the training dataset.

There are many data mining tools available to cluster data, to help analysts find patterns, and to find association rules. The majority of data mining approaches to classification tasks work with numerical and categorical information. Not many data mining techniques take into account ordinal data features.

Real-world application is full of vagueness and uncertainty. Several theories on managing uncertainty and imprecision have been advanced, to include fuzzy set theory (Zadeh, 1965), probability theory (Pearl, 1988), rough set theory (Pawlak, 1982), and set pair theory (Zhao, 1989, 2000). Fuzzy set theory is used more than the others are because of its simplicity and similarity to human reasoning. Although there are various different approaches within this field, many view the advantages of the fuzzy approach in data mining as an "interface between a numerical scale and a symbolic scale which is usually composed of linguistic terms" (Dubois et al., 2006).

Fuzzy association rules described in linguistic terms help increase the flexibility for supporting users in making decisions. Fuzzy set theory is being used more and more frequently in intelligent systems. A fuzzy set $A$ in universe $U$ is defined as $A = \{(x, \mu_A(x)) \mid x \in U, \mu_A(x) \in [0,1]\}$, where $\mu_A(x)$ is a membership function indicating the degree of membership of $x$ in $A$. The greater the value of $\mu_A(x)$, the more $x$ belongs to $A$. Fuzzy sets can also be thought of as an extension of the traditional crisp sets and categorical and ordinal scales, in which each element is either in the set or not in the set (a membership function of either 1 or 0).

Fuzzy set theory in its many manifestations (interval-valued fuzzy sets, vague sets, gray-related analysis, rough set theory, etc.) is highly appropriate for dealing with the masses of data available. This chapter reviews some of the general developments of fuzzy sets in data mining, with the intent of seeing some of the applications in which they have played a role in advancing the use of data mining in many fields. It will then review the use of fuzzy sets in two data mining software products, and demonstrate the use of data mining in an ordinal classification task. The results will be analyzed through comparison with the ordinal classification model. Possible adjustments of the model to take into account fuzzy thresholds in ordinal scales are discussed.

## 13.2 The Use of Fuzzy Sets in Data Mining

Research in data mining is widespread, involving a variety of applications. The discussion is organized by technique, beginning with neural network technology, pattern classification, cluster analysis, and genetic algorithms, and ending with association rules.

### 13.2.1 *Neural Networks*

Simpson (1992) presented a method to use neural networks to classify fuzzy data. A min-max function was used to determine the degree to which any observation was a member of a particular class. Neural networks provided the ability to better identify nonlinear and unexpected patterns. The fuzzy min-max neural network classifier performed at least as well as other neural network, fuzzy, and traditional classification methods for the three datasets tested. The fuzzy min-max neural network classifier was a generalization of the k-nearest-neighbor classifier. Zhang et al. (2000) presented a neural-network procedure capable of processing both numerical and linguistic data. Hu et al. (2004) proposed a two-phased method, first building a fuzzy knowledge base from transactional data and then finding weights of product attributes through a single-layer perceptron neural network. Linguistic input from customer evaluation of alternatives and attributes was fuzzy, and the approach enabled dealing with highly nonlinear preference input. The analysis was able to cluster data and to estimate attribute part-worths.

Neural networks can be applied to many data mining applications. They tend to work relatively better when nonlinear relationships are present. They are very suitable to deal with fuzzy inputs.

### 13.2.2 Pattern Classification

One application (Abe, 1995) generated fuzzy rules over variable fuzzy regions to pattern classification. The technique, using attribute hyperboxes, was tested on classification data and to the problem of license plate recognition. This research found that the number of rules obtained could be controlled through an expansion parameter (like minimum support and confidence). The more rules, the more accurate the classification. The method was compared with the fuzzy min-max neural network approach of Simpson (1992). The more complex the dataset relationships, the better the neural network methods did.

Liu et al. (1999) used a fuzzy matching technique to match discovered patterns against their expectations. This technique was intended to identify more interesting patterns. Fuzzy association rule generation resulted.

### 13.2.3 Cluster Analysis

Drobics et al. (2002) gave a three-stage approach to clustering. First, self-organizing maps were used to represent input data to allow visualization. Second, this cleaned data was used to identify and display fuzzy clusters of similarity using a modified fuzzy c-means clustering algorithm. Third, fuzzy rules were generated through inductive learning. The approach was tested on classification data, image segmentation data, and a complex classification dataset. The self-organizing map used in the first phase provided data reduction that made the approach suitable for dealing with large datasets.

Three articles addressed the clustering of Web data. De and Krishna (2002) dealt with user transactions with the intent of finding recommendations for new user transactions. The similarity of transactions was measured, and fuzzy proximity relations of these transactions were used to cluster. Le (2003) applied fuzzy logic to assess Web site popularity and satisfaction. Association rules were mined. Input fuzzy sets were attributes describing Web site characteristics. Output fuzzy sets were the set of attributes describing Web visitors as belonging to predefined classes of customer experience and business inclination. Lee and Liu (2004) provided a framework for information retrieval and filtering in Internet shopping. Agent technology was used to fuzzify data in Web mining. Once a shopper input product requirements, those requirements were converted into fuzzy variables based on membership functions stored in the knowledge base. When fuzzy requirements for a customer were collected, a Fuzzy Buyer agent entered the Web to locate products and negotiate price. A fuzzy neural network was used to select products. After completing product classification, the system would return products meeting customer specifications.

### 13.2.4  Genetic Algorithms

Bruha et al. (2000) proposed a method to process symbolic attributes. They used CN4 beam search technology to categorize numerical attributes. Fuzzification of data was applied, reflecting binary data into three categories: (1) clearly class 0, (2) uncertain, and (3) clearly class 1. A genetic learning algorithm was then used to process each observation into the best-fitting category. The approach was applied to credit screening data. The fuzzy approach was expected to be more accurate but no significant difference was detected. By exploring more hypotheses in parallel, significantly better results were obtained, although much greater computational support was required.

### 13.2.5  Association Rules

Association rules mining provides valuable information in assessing significant correlations that can be found in large databases. An association rule is an expression of $X \rightarrow Y$, where $X$ is a set of items and $Y$ is a single item. Support refers to the degree to which a relationship appears in the data. Confidence relates to the probability that if a precedent occurs, then a consequence will occur. For example, from the transactions kept in supermarkets, an association rule such as "Bread and Butter $\rightarrow$ Milk" could be identified through association mining. Many algorithms have been proposed to find association rules mining in large databases. Most, such as the APriori algorithm (Agrawal et al., 1993) and its improvement (Agrawal and Srikant, 1994), identify correlations among transactions consisting of categorical attributes using binary values. Some data mining approaches involve weighted association rules for binary values. Cai et al. (1998) proposed two algorithms of association rules mining with weighted items. Lu et al. (2001) assigned a weight not only for each time interval, but also for each item in his mixed weighted association rules mining.

Most of the previous studies focused on categorical attributes. Transaction data in real-world applications, however, usually consists of quantitative attributes, so some data mining algorithms for quantitative values also have been proposed (Srikant and Agrawal, 1996), wherein the algorithm finds association rules by partitioning the attribute domain, combining adjacent partitions, and then transforming the problem into a binary state.

A number of researchers (Kuok et al., 1998; Zhang, 1999; Hong et al., 2000; Bosc and Pivert, 2001; Shu et al., 2001; Ladner et al., 2003) have considered mining fuzzy association rules for quantitative values; most based their methods on the important APriori algorithm. Each of these researchers treated all attributes (or all the linguistic terms) as uniform. However, in real-world applications, the users perhaps have more interest in the rules that contain fashionable items. Decreasing the requirement for support value and for confidence level to get rules containing fashionable items is not considered a good decision because the efficiency of the algorithm will decrease and many uninteresting rules will be generated simultaneously (Lu et al., 1999.)

One possible approach to the problem is to partition data into categorical data and thus create fuzzy grids. Many approaches to discretization of data are data-driven or automated. One was based on a clustering technique (Fu et al., 1998). Use of a genetic algorithm for the same problem was proposed by Kaya and Alhajj (2005). The main disadvantage of purely data-driven algorithms is their possible inability to interpret the resulting fuzzy sets. This is avoided in some approaches with predefined fuzzy partitions (see, for example, Hu et al., 2002; Au and Chan, 2001.) These approaches allow discovered rules to be expressed in natural language. Such rules are more understandable to a human user.

### 13.2.6 Rough Sets

Peng et al. (2004) provided a recent use of rough set theory application of data mining involving fault diagnosis in the electrical industry. They included a review of 11 rough set applications generating decision tree rules in such diverse application areas as image filtering, software engineering, mechanical engineering, geography, automotive design, medical decision making, and business applications such as risk management, marketing, financial prediction, and company acquisition.

### 13.2.7 Linear Programming

In reality, in most cases, current approaches often fail to provide "perfect separation" of classes so that overlapping does exist. Linear Programming models, usually called linear discriminant models, are used to handle the overlapping problem.

The first Linear Programming model used was that of Freed and Glover's (1981, 1986) original formulation:

(Model 1) $$\text{Maximize } \sum_i k_i \beta_i$$

Subject to:

$$A_i X \geq b - \beta_i, A_i \in G1$$
$$A_i X \leq b + \beta_i, A_i \in G2$$

where $A_i$ is given, $X$ and $b$ are unrestricted, and $\beta_i \geq 0$. G1 and G2 represent the classified group number. To follow the diagnosing power of programming models based on linear programming, mixed integer models and multiple objective models are also developed for classification problem in data mining field.

A good alternative Linear Programming model is DEA (data envelopment analysis). In DEA issues, fuzzy sets theory has been well utilized to develop Fuzzy DEAZ models (e.g., Saowanee, 2003; Guo and Hideo, 2001).

Fuzzy sets approaches are widespread in data mining. We use some experimental settings to analyze the effectiveness of "fuzzification" of continuous scales in an ordinal classification task.

## 13.3 Fuzzy Set Experiments in See5

The authors had access to two very useful data mining software tools: (1) PolyAnalyst and (2) See5. PolyAnalyst uses fuzzy set theory within a number of algorithms to obtain more robust models in applications such as discriminant analysis. These operations are internal to the system. See5, which is decision tree software, allows users to select options to soften thresholds through selecting a fuzzy option. This option would insert a buffer at boundaries (which is how PolyAnalyst also works). The buffer is determined by the software based on analysis of sensitivity of classification to small changes in the threshold. The treatment from there is crisp, as opposed to fuzzy. Thus, in decision trees, fuzzy implementations seem to be crisp models with adjusted set boundaries.

See5 software was used on a real set of credit card data (Shi et al., 2005). This dataset had 6000 observations over 64 variables plus an outcome variable indicating bankruptcy or not (variables defined in Shi et al., 2005). Of the 64 independent variables, nine were binary and three were categorical. The problem can be considered an ordinal classification task as the two final classes are named as "GOOD" and "BAD" with respect to financial success. This means that majority of the numerical and categorical attributes (including binary ones) can be easily characterized by more preferable values with respect to "GOOD" financial success.

The dataset was balanced to a degree, so that it contained 960 bankrupt outcomes ("BAD") and 5040 not bankrupt ("GOOD") outcomes. Winnowing was used in See5, which reduced the number of variables used in models to about 20. Using 50 percent of the data for training, See5 selected 3000 observations at random as the training set, which was then tested on the remaining 3000 observations in the test set. Minimum support on See5 varied over the settings of 10, 20, and 30 cases. Pruning confidence factors were also varied, from 10 percent (greater pruning), to 20 percent, 30 percent, and 40 percent (less pruning). Data was locked within nominal data runs, so that each treatment of pruning and minimum case settings was applied to the same data within each repetition. Five repetitions were conducted. Rules obtained were identical across crisp and fuzzy models, except fuzzy models had adjusted rule limits. For example, in the first run, the following rules were obtained:

| CRISP MODEL: | RULE 1: | IF RevtoPayNov ≤ 11.441, | then GOOD |
| | RULE 2: | IF RevtoPayNov > 11.441 AND | |
| | | IF CoverBal3 = 1 | then GOOD |
| | RULE 3: | IF RevtoPayNov > 11.441 AND | |
| | | IF CoverBal3 = 0 AND | |
| | | IF OpentoBuyDec > 5.35129 | then GOOD |
| | RULE 4: | IF RevtoPayNov > 11.441 AND | |
| | | IF CoverBal3 = 0 AND | |
| | | IF OpentoBuyDec ≤ 5.35129 AND | |
| | | IF NumPurchDec ≤ 2.30259 | then BAD |
| | RULE 5: | ELSE | GOOD |

The fuzzy model for this dataset:

| FUZZY MODEL: | RULE 1: | IF RevtoPayNov ≤ 11.50565 | then GOOD |
| | RULE 2: | IF RevtoPayNov > 11.50565 AND | |
| | | IF CoverBal3 = 1 | then GOOD |
| | RULE 3: | IF RevtoPayNov > 11.50565 AND | |
| | | IF CoverBal3 = 0 AND | |
| | | IF OpentoBuyDec > 5.351905 then | GOOD |
| | RULE 4: | IF RevtoPayNov > 11.50565 AND | |
| | | IF CoverBal3 = 0 AND | |
| | | IF OpentoBuyDec ≤ 5.351905 AND | |
| | | IF NumPurchDec ≤ 2.64916 | then BAD |
| | RULE 5: | ELSE | GOOD |

Binary and categorical data are not affected by the fuzzy option in See5. They are considered already "fuzzified" with several possible values and corresponding membership function of 1 and 0.

Table 13.1 shows overall numbers of rules obtained and error rates for models run with all initial data (numeric and categorical scales).

The number of rules responded to changes in pruning rates and minimum case settings as expected (the tie between 20 percent and 30 percent pruning rates can be attributed to data sampling chance). There were no clear patterns in error rates by treatment. Fuzzy models were noticeably different from crisp models in that they had higher error rates for bad cases, with corresponding improvement in error in the good cases. The overall error was tested by $t$-test, and the only significant differences found were that the fuzzy models had significantly greater bad error than the crisp models, and significantly less cheap error. The fuzzy models had slightly less overall average error, but given the context of credit cards, bad error is much more important. For data fit, here the models were not significantly different. For application context, the crisp models would clearly be preferred.

**Table 13.1   See5 Decision Tree Results for Continuous and Categorical Data**

| Prune (%) | Minimum Cases | Crisp Rules | Crisp Bad Error | Crisp Cheap Error | Crisp Total Error | Fuzzy Bad Error | Fuzzy Cheap Error | Fuzzy Total Error |
|---|---|---|---|---|---|---|---|---|
| 10 | | 5.571 | 390.929 | 98.500 | 489.429 | 444.500 | 46.286 | 490.286 |
| 20 | | 10.143 | 390.000 | 98.571 | 488.571 | 431.714 | 54.286 | 486.000 |
| 30 | | 10.143 | 379.714 | 109.143 | 488.857 | 431.286 | 55.929 | 486.929 |
| 40 | | 12.000 | 388.286 | 99.929 | 488.214 | 430.143 | 55.429 | 485.571 |
| | | | | | | | | |
| | 10 | 15.000 | 379.550 | 107.700 | 487.250 | 424.300 | 59.800 | 483.750 |
| | 20 | 7.950 | 385.250 | 107.300 | 492.550 | 432.100 | 58.450 | 490.550 |
| | 30 | 5.350 | 394.250 | 92.300 | 486.550 | 440.750 | 46.100 | 486.650 |
| Overall | | 9.433 | 386.350 | 102.433 | 488.783 | 432.383 | 54.783 | 483.983 |

In this case, introducing fuzzy thresholds in the rules did not lead to any significant results. The usage of small fuzzy intervals instead of crispy thresholds did not significantly improve the accuracy of the model and did not provide better interpretation of the introduced "interval rules." On the other hand, crisp data was not significantly better than the fuzzy data.

The same tests were conducted with presenting relevant binary and categorical variables in an ordinal form. See5 allows stating that the categorical scale is "[ordered]" with the presented order of attribute values corresponding to the order of final classes. The order is not derived from the data but is introduced by the user as a preprocessing step in rules and tree formation.

See5 would not allow locking across datasets, and required a different setup for ordinal specification, so we could not control for dataset sampling across the tests. Some categorical or binary variables such as "Months late" were clearly ordinal and were marked as ordinal for this experiment. Categorical variables with no clear ordinal qualities such as "State" were left nominal. Test results are given in Table 13.2.

The number of rules clearly decreased. The expected response of a number of rules to pruning and minimum case settings behaved as expected, with the one anomaly at 20 percent pruning, again explainable by the small sample size. Total error rates within the ordinal model were similar to the nominal case given in Table 13.1, with fuzzy model total error rates showing up as slightly significant (0.086 error probability) in the ordinal models.

Comparing nominal and ordinal models, the number of rules was significantly lower for ordinal models (0.010 error probability.) There were no significances in errors across the two sets except for total error (ordinal models had slightly significantly lower total errors, with 0.087 error probability). This supports our previous finding that using ordinal scales where appropriate leads to a set of more interesting rules without any loss in accuracy (Moshkovich et al., 2002).

**Table 13.2  See5 Decision Tree Results with Appropriate Categorical and Binary Variables Marked as Ordinal**

| Prune (%) | Minimum Cases | Crisp Rules | Crisp Bad Error | Crisp Cheap Error | Crisp Total Error | Fuzzy Bad Error | Fuzzy Cheap Error | Fuzzy Total Error |
|---|---|---|---|---|---|---|---|---|
| 10 | | 5.857 | 400.214 | 85.929 | 486.143 | 425.643 | 56.571 | 482.214 |
| 20 | | 5.714 | 403.286 | 86.143 | 489.429 | 427.857 | 56.429 | 484.286 |
| 30 | | 7.929 | 382.786 | 104.143 | 486.929 | 675.071 | 66.143 | 484.071 |
| 40 | | 9.000 | 395.000 | 94.286 | 489.286 | 427.857 | 58.214 | 486.071 |
| | | | | | | | | |
| | 10 | 10.000 | 398.300 | 90.900 | 489.200 | 604.850 | 57.850 | 482.700 |
| | 20 | 6.500 | 377.100 | 112.550 | 489.650 | 414.600 | 67.550 | 482.150 |
| | 30 | 4.500 | 403.550 | 78.900 | 482.450 | 428.900 | 53.650 | 482.550 |
| Overall | | 7.000 | 392.983 | 94.117 | 487.100 | 482.783 | 59.683 | 482.467 |

# 13.4  Fuzzy Sets and Ordinal Classification Task

Previous experiments showed very modest improvements in the rule set derived from introducing fuzzy intervals instead of crisp thresholds for continuous scales using See5. Interpretation of the modified rules was not "more friendly" or "more logical." Using stable data intervals was, in general, slightly more robust than using crisp thresholds. Considering that, ordinal properties of some categorical/binary attributes led to a better rule set although this did not change the fuzzy intervals for the continuous scales. This supports our previous findings (Moshkovich et al., 2002.)

One of the more useful aspects of fuzzy logic may be the orientation on the partition of continuous scales into a pre-set number of "linguistic summaries" (Yager, 1991.) In Au and Chan (2001), this approach was used to form fuzzy rules in a classification task. The main idea of the method is to use a set of predefined linguistic terms for attributes with continuous scales (e.g., "Young," "Middle," "Old" for an attribute "Age" measured continuously). In this approach, the traditional triangular fuzzy number is calculated for each instance of age in the training dataset; for example, age 23 is presented in "Young" with a 0.85 membership function and in "Middle" with a 0.15 membership function (0 in "Old"). Thus, the rewritten dataset is used to mine interesting IF-THEN rules using linguistic terms.

The method was used for data mining several datasets. All continuous scales were divided into uniform linguistic terms (without corresponding expert/contextual input described in the method itself). The resulting accuracy of the models was compared with the results of three other techniques, including C4.5 (which is implemented in See5). It performed slightly better in accuracy (by about 5 percent) than See5 for two of the datasets, which could be characterized as a classification task with two ordered classes (loan application and diabetes presence). The accuracy of both approaches was similar for the last dataset in which the classification of SALARY assumed a continuous testing variable.

One of the advantages of the proposed approach stressed by the authors is the ability of the mining method to produce rules useful to the user. In Chan et al. (2002), the method was used to mine a database for the direct marketing campaign of a charitable organization. In this case, the domain expert defined appropriate uniform linguistic terms for quantitative attributes. For example, an attribute reflecting the average amount of donation (AVGEVER) was fuzzified into "Very low" (0 to $300), "Low" ($100 to $500), "Medium" ($300 to $700), "High" ($500 to $900), and "Very High" (over $700). The analogous scale for the frequency of donations (FREQEVER) was presented as follows: "Very low" (0 to 3), "Low" (1 to 5), "Medium" (3 to 7), "High" (5 to 9), and "Very High" (over 9). Triangular fuzzy numbers were derived from these settings for rule mining. The attribute to be predicted was called "Response to the direct mailing" and included two possible values, "Yes" and "No." The database included 93 attributes, 44 having continuous scales.

Although the application of the method produced a huge number of rules (31,865) with relatively low classification accuracy (approximately 64 percent), the authors argued that for a task of such complexity, the selection of several useful rules by the user of the results was enough to prove the usefulness of the process. The presented rules found useful by the user were presented as follows:

**Rule 1**: IF a donor was enrolled in any donor activity in the past (ENROLL= *YES*), THEN he or she will have RESPONSE = *YES*

**Rule 2**: IF a donor was enrolled in any donor activity in the past (ENROLL = *YES*) AND did not attend it (ATTENDED = *NO*), THEN he or she will have RESPONSE = *YES*

**Rule 3**: IF FREQEVER = *MEDIUM*, THEN RESPONSE = *YES*

**Rule 4**: IF FREQEVER = *HIGH*, THEN RESPONSE = *YES*

**Rule 5**: IF FREQEVER = *VERY HIGH*, THEN RESPONSE = *YES*

One can infer two conclusions based on these results. First, if obvious ordinal dependences between final classes of RESPONSE (YES/NO) and such attributes as ENROLL, ATTENDED, and FREQEVER were taken into account, the five rules could collapse into two without any loss of accuracy and with higher levels for measures of support and confidence: Rule 1 and a modified Rule 3 in the following format: "IF FREQEVER is at least MEDIUM, THEN RESPONSE = YES." Second, although presented rules are "user friendly" and easily understandable, they are not as easily applicable. Overlapping scales for FREQEVER makes it difficult for the user to apply the rules directly. It is necessary to carry out one more step: agree on the number where "MEDIUM" frequency starts (if we use initial database) or a level of a membership function to use in selecting "MEDIUM" frequency if we use the "rewritten" dataset. The assigned interval of 3 to 5 evidently includes "HIGH" frequency (which does not bother us) but also includes "LOW" frequency, which we possibly would not like to include in our mailing list. As a result, a convenient approach for expressing continuous scales with overlapping intervals at the preprocessing stage may be not so convenient in applying simple rules.

If assigning the linguistic terms was done in a crisp way initially, the problem would be a traditional classification problem with nominal scales. Ordered classes would suggest that the quality of the result can be improved if appropriate ordinal scales are used for some attributes.

The ordinal classification assumes that "cases with better characteristics should be placed in a better class." Formally, the ordinal classification problem can be presented as follows. Let $U$ (universe) present all possible objects in the task. $X \subseteq U$ is any subset of these objects (data items in a dataset). Objects from $X$ are distributed among k classes: $C_1, C_2, ..., C_k$, indicating the degree to which the object satisfies the overall output quality (from the lowest to the highest). This means that if $x, y \in X$, and $C(x) > C(y)$, object $x$ has a higher overall output quality than object $y$. Each object is described by a set of attributes $A = \{A_1, A_2, ..., A_p\}$. Each attribute $A_i$ has an ordinal scale $S_i$ (possible values are rank ordered from the lowest to the highest in quality against this attribute). $A_i(x) \in S_i, A_i(y) \in S_i$, and $A_i(x) > A_i(y)$ means that object $x$ has higher quality on attribute $A_i$ than object $y$.

In the loan application case, ordinal classification may tell us, for example, that a middle-aged applicant with low risk and high income has a better chance to pay the loan on time than a young applicant with low risk and high income. For the mail campaign, one can expect that more frequent donations in the past should lead to a better chance of positive response; or that if those who enroll in the donor events but do not come often have a positive response, it would be even more probable for those who enroll and attend donor events.

This presentation of the ordinal classification task allows use of this knowledge to make some additional conclusions about the quality of the training set of objects. Ordinal classification allows introduction of the notion of the consistency of the training set as well as completeness of the training set. In the case of the ordinal classification task, quality of consistency in a classification (the same quality objects should belong to the same class) can be essentially extended: all objects with higher quality among attributes should belong to a class at least as good as objects with lower quality. This condition can be easily expressed as follows: if $A_i(x) \geq A_i(y)$ for each $i = 1, 2, ..., p$, then $C(x) \geq C(y)$.

One can also try to evaluate representativeness of the training set by forming all possible objects in $U$ (one can do that because one has a finite number of attributes with a small finite number of values in their scales) and check on the proportion of them presented in the training set. It is evident that the smaller this proportion, the less discriminating power one will have for the new cases. We can also express the resulting rules in a more summarized form by lower and upper border instances for each class (Moshkovich et al., 2002).

Advantages of using ordinal scales in an ordinal classification task do not lessen the advantages of appropriate fuzzy set techniques. Fuzzy approaches allow for softening strict limitations of ordinal scales in some cases and provide a richer environment for data mining techniques. On the other hand, ordinal dependences represent essential domain knowledge that should be incorporated as much as possible into the mining process. In some cases, the overlapping areas of attribute scales can be resolved by introducing additional linguistic ordinal levels. For example, one can introduce an ordinal scale for age with the following levels: "Young" (less than 30), "Between young and medium" (30 to 40), "Medium" (40 to 50), "Between medium and old" (50 to 60), and "Old" (over 60). Although it will increase the dimensionality of the problem, it would provide crisp intervals for the resulting rules.

Ordinal scales and ordinal dependences are easily understood by humans and are attractive in rules and explanations. These qualities should be especially beneficial in fuzzy approaches to classification problems with ordered classes and "linguistic summaries" in the discretization process. The importance of ordinal scales for data mining is evidenced by the appearance of this option in many established mining techniques. See5 includes the variant of ordinal scales in the problem description (See5). The rough sets approach includes a special technique to deal with ordinal scales (Greco et al., 2002).

## 13.5 Conclusions

Fuzzy representation is a very suitable means for humans to express themselves. Many important business applications of data mining are appropriately dealt with by fuzzy representation of uncertainty. This chapter reviewed a number of ways in which fuzzy sets and related theories have been implemented in data mining. The ways in which these theories are applied to various data mining problems will continue to grow.

Ordinal data is stronger than nominal data. There is extra knowledge in knowing if a greater value is preferable to a lesser value (or vice versa). This extra information can be implemented in decision tree models, and our results provide preliminary support to the idea that they might strengthen the predictive power of data mining models.

Our contention is that fuzzy representations better represent what humans mean. Our brief experiment focused on how much accuracy was lost using fuzzy representation in one application — classification rules applied to credit applications. While we expected less accuracy, we found that the fuzzy models usually actually were more accurate. While this was only one case, we think that there is a logical explanation. While fuzzification will not be expected to yield a better fit to training data, the models obtained using fuzzification will likely be more robust, which is reflected in potentially equal if not better fit on test data. The results of these preliminary experiments indicate that implementing various forms of fuzzy analysis will not necessarily lead to a reduction in classification accuracy.

# References

Abe, S. and M.-S. Lan, A method for fuzzy rules extraction directly from numerical data and its application to pattern classification, *IEEE Transactions on Fuzzy Systems*, 3(1), 18–28, 1995.

Agrawal, R., T. Imielinski, and A. Swami, Mining association rules between sets of items in massive databases, *Proceedings of the ACM SIGMOD International Conference on Management of Data*, Washington, D.C., 1993, pp. 207–216.

Agrawal, R. and R. Srikant, Fast algorithms for mining association rules in large databases, *Proceedings of the 20th VLDB Conference*, 1994, pp. 487–499.

Au, Wai-H. and K.C.C. Chan, Classification with degree of membership: a fuzzy approach, *IEEE International Conference on Data Mining*, 2001, pp. 35–42.

Ben-David, A. Automated generation of symbolic multiattribute ordinal knowledge-based DSSs: methodology and applications, *Decision Sciences*, 23(6), 157–172, 1992.

Ben David, A., L.A. Sterling, and Y.H. Pao, Learning and classification of monotonic ordinal concepts, *Computational Intelligence*, 5(1), 45–49, 1989.

Bohanec, M. and V. Rajkovic, Expert system for decision making, *Sistemica*, 1(1), 145–157, 1990.

Bosc, P. and O. Pivert, On some fuzzy extensions of association rules, *Proceedings of IFSA-NAFIPS 2001*, Piscataway, NJ: IEEE Press 2001, pp. 1104–1109.

Bruha, I., P.K. Chan, and P. Berka, Genetic learner: discretization and fuzzification of numerical scales, *Intelligent Data Analysis*, 4, 445–460, 2000.

Cai, C.H., W.-C. Fu, C.H. Cheng, and W.W. Kwong. Mining association rules with weighted items, *Proceedings of 1998 International Database Engineering and Applications Symposium*, Cardiff, Wales, 1998, pp. 68–77.

Chan, K.C.C., W.-H. Au, and B. Choi, Mining fuzzy rules in a donor database for direct marketing by a charitable organization, *IEEE International Conference on Cognitive Informatics,*, 2002, pp. 239–246.

De, S.K. and P.R. Krishna, Mining Web data using clustering technique for Web personalization, *International Journal of Computational Intelligence and Applications*, 2(3), 255–265, 2002.

Drobics, M., U. Bodenhofer, and W. Winiwarter, Mining clusters and corresponding interpretable descriptions — a three-stage approach, *Expert Systems*, 19(4), 224–234, 2002.

Dubois, D., E. Hullermeier, and H. Prade, A systematic approach to the assessment of fuzzy association rules, *Data Mining and Knowledge Discovery*, 2006, pp. 1–26.

Freed N. and F. Glover F, A linear program ming approach to the discriminant problem, *Decision Sciences*, 12, 68–74, 1981.

Freed, N. and F. Glover, Evaluating alternative linear programming models to solve the two-group discriminant problem, *Decision Sciences*, 17, 151–162, 1986.

Fu, A., M.H. Wong, S.C. Sze, W.C. Wong, W.L. Wong, and W.K. Yu, Finding fuzzy sets for mining fuzzy association rules for numerical attributes, in IDEAL '98, *1st International Symposium on Intelligent Data Engineering and Learning*, Hong Kong, 1998, pp. 263–268.

Greco S., B. Matarazzo, and R. Slowinski, Rough approximation by dominance relations, *International Journal of Intelligent Systems*, 17, 153–171, 2002.

Guo, P., and H. Tanaka, Fuzzy DEA: a perceptual evaluation method, *Fuzzy Sets and Systems*, 119(1), 149–160, 2001.

Hong, T.-P., C.-S. Kuo, and S.-C. Chi, Trade-off between computation time and numbers of rules for fuzzy mining from quantitative data, *International Journal of Uncertainty, Fuzziness and Knowledge-Based Systems*, 9, 587–604, 2001.

Hu, Y.-C., Mining fuzzy association rules for classification problems, *Computers & Industrial Engineering*, 43(4), 735–750, 2002.

Hu, Y.-C., R.-S. Chen, and G.-H. Tzeng, Generating learning sequences for decision makers through data mining and competence set expansion, *IEEE Transactions on Systems, Man, and Cybernetics – Part B*, 32, 679–686, 2002.

Hu, Y.-C., J.-S. Hu, R.-S. Chen, and G.-H. Tzeng, Assessing weights of product attributes from fuzzy knowledge in a dynamic environment, *European Journal of Operational Research*, 154, 125-143, 2004.

Kaya, M. and R. Alhajj. Genetic algorithm based framework for mining fuzzy association rules, *Fuzzy Sets and Systems*, 152(3), 587–601, 2005.

Kuok, C., A. Fu, and H. Wong, Mining fuzzy association rules in databases, *ACM SIGMOD Record*, 27, 41–46, 1998.

Ladner, R., F.E. Petry, and M.A. Cobb, Fuzzy set approaches to spatial data mining of association rules, *Transactions in GIS*, 7, 123–138, 2003.

Larichev, O.I. and H.M. Moshkovich, An approach to ordinal classification problems, *International Transactions on Operations Research*, 82, 503–521, 1994.

Lee, R.S.T. and J.N.K. Liu, IJADE Web-miner: an intelligent agent framework for Internet shopping, *IEEE Transactions on Knowledge and Data Engineering*, 16, 461–473 2004.

Lee, W.-J. and S.-J. Lee, Discovery of fuzzy temporal association rules, *IEEE Transactions on Systems, Man, and Cybernetics – Part B*, 34, 2330–2342 2004.

Lertworosirikul, S., S-C. Fang, J.A. Joines, and H.L.W. Nuttle, Fuzzy data envelopment analysis (DEA): a possibility approach, *Fuzzy Sets and Systems*, 139(2), 379–394, 2003.

Li, X., Fuzzy logic in Web data mining for Website assessment, *International Journal of Computational Intelligence and Applications*, 3(1), 119–133, 2003.

Liu, B., W. Hsu, L.-F. Mun, and H.-Y. Lee, Finding interesting patterns using user expectations, *IEEE Transactions on Knowledge and Data Engineering*, 11(6) 817–832, 1999.

Lu, S.-F., H. Hu, and F. Li, Mining weighted association rules, *Intelligent Data Analysis*, 5, 211–225, 2001.

Moshkovich, H.M., A.I. Mechitov, and D. Olson, Rule induction in data mining: effect of ordinal scales, *Expert Systems with Applications Journal*, 22, 303–311, 2002.

Pawlak, Z., Rough set, *International Journal of Computer and Information Sciences*, 11, 341–356, 1982.

Pearl, J., Probabilistic reasoning in intelligent systems, *Networks of Plausible Inference*, San Mateo, CA: Morgan Kaufmann, 1988.

Peng, J.-T., C.F. Chien, and T.L.B. Tseng, Rough set theory for data mining for fault diagnosis on distribution feeder, *IEE Proceedings – Generation and Transmission Distribution*, 151, 689–697, 2004.

See5 - http://www.rulequest.com, no date.

Shi, Y., Y. Peng, G. Kou, and Z. Chen, Classifying credit card accounts for business intelligence and decision making: a multiple-criteria quadratic programming approach, *International Journal of Information Technology & Decision Making,* 4, 581–599, 2005.

Shu, J., E. Tsang, and D. Yeung, Query fuzzy association rules in relational databases, in *Proceedings of IFSA-NAFIPS 2001,* Piscataway, NJ, IEEE Press, 2001, pp. 2989–2993.

Simpson, P.K., Fuzzy min-max neural networks. I. Classification, *IEEE Transactions on Neural Networks,* 3, 776–786, 1992.

Slowinski, R. Rough set approach to decision analysis. *AI Expert,* 1995, pp. 19–25.

Srikant, R. and R. Agrawal, Mining quantitative association rules in large relational tables, *The 1996 ACM SIGMOD International Conference on Management of Data.* Montreal, Canada, June 1996, pp. 1–12.

Yager, R.R., On Linguistic Summaries of Data, in G. Piatetsky-Shapiro and W.J. Frawley (Eds.), *Knowledge Discovery in Databases,* Mento Park, CA: AAAI/MIT Press, 1991, pp. 347–363.

Zadeh, L.A., Fuzzy sets, *Information and Control,* 8, 338–356, 1965.

Zhao, K.-G., Set pair analysis — a new concept and new systematic approach, *Proceedings of National System Theory and Regional Analysis Conference,* Baotou (In Chinese), 1989.

Zhao, K.-G., *Set Pair Analysis and Its Preliminary Application,* Zhejiang Science and Technology Press (In Chinese), 2000.

Zhang, W., Mining fuzzy quantitative association rules, *Proceedings of IEEE International Conference on Tools with Artificial Intelligence 1999,* Piscataway, NJ: IEEE Press, 1999, pp. 99–102.

Zhang, Y.-Q., M.D. Fraser, R.A. Gagliano, and A. Kandel, Granular neural networks for numerical-linguistic data fusion and knowledge discovery, *IEEE Transactions on Neural Networks,* 11(3), 658–667, 2000.

# Chapter 14

# Developing an Associative Keyword Space of the Data Mining Literature through Latent Semantic Analysis

Adrian Gardiner

## Contents

# 14.1 Introduction

The term "data mining" (DM) is metaphoric reference to digging through (turning over) large amounts of earth ("data") for the purpose of extracting something of value*. While *value*, in this respect, may be transient and contextual, one can frame notions of *value* in terms of decision-maker utility. For example, utility should arise when new and interesting structures within datasets are identified (Fayyad and Uthurusamy, 2002), insights are gained, or useful reports produced (Kurgan and Musilek, 2006). One can also view DM as a collection of *tools* for the analysis of large databases and discovery of trends, patterns, regularities, and knowledge. Given its computational emphasis, some authors also consider DM as an area of computational intelligence that offers theories, techniques, and tools for processing and analyzing large datasets (Buddhakulsomsiri et al., 2006). Given that perhaps the most fundamental challenge of DM is pattern recognition, Pechenizkiy et al. (2006) reason it is

---

* Other metaphorical references to DM have included: knowledge extraction, information discovery, information harvesting, data archeology, and data pattern processing (Fayyad et al., 1996a).

therefore not surprising that much DM research focuses on tool development (e.g., developing new algorithms, or improving the speed or accuracy of existing ones).

Some authors also emphasize that DM is only one of the steps within a broader knowledge discovery (KD) process (see, for example, Cios and Kurgan, 2002; Fayyad et al., 2002). Notwithstanding this process view of DM, both Cios and Kurgan (2002) and Kurgan and Musilek (2006) assert that there is common confusion in understanding the terms of "data mining" (DM), "knowledge discovery" (KD), and "knowledge discovery in databases" (KDD). Kurgan and Musilek (2006) clarify the distinction between DM and KD by emphasizing that DM focuses on low-level technical methods, while KD is the process that seeks to gain knowledge about an application domain. Extending this definition, when the KD process is applied specifically to data repositories, one can refer to this process as KDD. It follows that a wider view of the definition of DM — which, in effect, equates to a systems view of DM — should therefore cover the process of applying DM methods, interpreting outcomes, measuring changes in utility, and an understanding of the application domain. The growing importance of the systems view to DM is reflected in the following words of Pechenizkiy et al. (2005b, p. 68): "We believe that the study of the DM development and DM use processes is becoming equally important now when many technological aspects within DM research have been solved at least in usable level."

## 14.1.1 Open Issues within the Data Mining Field

With the burgeoning of DM-related research and development, it comes as no surprise that the status and future of the field have come under increasing interest from researchers and practitioners. Central to this debate are meta-issues and fundamental questions, including identifying the theoretical foundations of DM; gauging the level of maturity of the DM field; investigating the identity, scope, nature, core, sub-areas, and boundaries of the DM field; determining the value arising from innovations and advances within the DM field, in relation to industry practice; and addressing whether the DM field deserves recognition as an independent scientific discipline (academic field) within the wider computer science and statistics communities. Clearly, these issues and questions are closely related. For example, elaboration of a theoretical foundation for DM may allow for a more definitive articulation of the scope, nature, and boundaries of the DM field. However, one must be cautious of this circular reasoning, as one could also easily insist that a prerequisite to a theoretical foundation of DM is an acceptable DM ontological framework.

## 14.1.2 Theoretical Foundations of Data Mining

Recently, Yang and Wu (2006) identified developing a unifying theory of DM as one of the most challenging problems facing the DM community. It is therefore of concern that Mannila (2000) considers the study of the foundations of DM as being in its infancy, and at this time, there are probably more questions than answers. The growing realization of the importance of a DM foundation is highlighted in Chen's (2002) call to focus more on the understanding of the nature of DM as field, instead of as a collection of algorithms. The promise of a foundational theory of DM is that it may provide a degree of ontological and epistemological clarity, thereby bringing about consensus within the DM community. For example, a formal model of DM could perhaps provide a common ground on which various DM methods could be studied and compared (Yao, 2001), and also provide a focus for future research endeavors.

There have been several recent attempts to forward the debate on the foundations of DM. Both Chen (2002) and Yao (2003) advocate that the theoretical foundations of DM can be studied along three primary dimensions: (1) philosophical, (2) technical, and (3) social. The philosophical dimension deals with the nature and scope of DM, and includes primitive notions of DM, such as what constitutes notions of knowledge, and interestingness. The technical dimension, on the other hand, covers DM methods and techniques while the social dimension concerns the social impact and consequences of DM.

Along the technical dimension, there has been work on identifying more primitive notions of DM, including attempts to formulate mathematically "well-defined" definitions of patterns. For example, Xie and Raghavan (2002) support the application of Bacchus' probability logic to more precisely define intuitive notions, such as "pattern," "previously unknown knowledge," and "potentially useful knowledge." In addition, a granular computing approach to DM theory also has been suggested (Yao, 2001; Lin, 2002; Tsumoto et al., 2002). The basic ingredients of granular computing include subsets, classes, and clusters of a universe (Yao, 2000). Accordingly, a *granulation* of the universe requires the decomposition (granulation) of the universe into parts (concepts), or the grouping of individual elements into classes, based on available information and knowledge (Yao, 2001). This approach also emphasizes that many methodologies and algorithms (e.g., rule-based mining) aim to produce rules that describe relationships between concepts. Some of the relationship types endorsed by Yao (2001) include closeness, dependency, association, indistinguishability, similarity, and functionality. In this approach, a *concept* consists of two parts: its *intension* and *extension*. The intension consists of all properties of a concept, while the extension represents the set of instances. Yao (2001) suggests that rules can be expressed in terms of the respective concept intensions, while rule interpretation (e.g., rule classification) requires consideration of their extensions.

The absence of a widely endorsed foundational theory of DM is perhaps reflected in the contrasting views on the level of maturity of the DM field. For example, Yao (2006) considers that DM is a relatively new field and has not yet formed its own theories, views, and culture. In contrast, Kurgan and Musilek (2006) characterize the area of KD and DM as a very dynamic research and development area that is reaching maturity. These contrasting views perhaps support Colet's (1999) assertion that, "depending on whom you speak with there are differing views on the maturity of data mining." Colet's (1999) own view is that "data mining is a young and rapidly maturing technology." Other researchers see the development of DM algorithms as maturing, while other areas are less so (Pechenizkiy et al., 2005a). Certainly, the issue of field maturity is not unique to the DM field (for example, see Ebert (1997) for a discussion of maturity of the software engineering discipline, and Rust (2006) for a discussion of the maturity of the marketing field).

### 14.1.3  Motivation and Focus

Perhaps the most fundamental issue, in terms of the philosophical dimension of DM foundations, is establishing the scope and nature of the DM field (Chen, 2002; Yao, 2003). It is unfortunate, therefore, that even in addressing this most elementary-level issue, there appears to be a significant degree of discord. For example, some authors have questioned whether statistics as a discipline should be concerned with DM, and whether DM should be considered part of the statistics discipline (see, for example, Friedman, 2001; Mannila, 2000).

In terms of establishing the scope and nature of the DM field, Yao (2003, p. 256) recently suggested that identifying a range of core topics within the DM field is an important step:

> "…one needs to examine the goal of data mining, the principal contributing disciplines to data mining, the architecture of data mining systems, and methods of data mining researches. It is necessary to identify a range of topics that help define the goal and scope of data mining and numerous dimensions along which the field can be explored."

In response to Yao's (2003) call, this chapter presents evidence with regard to which core topics (focal concepts) have attracted the most interest from within the DM academic community, as evidenced by the published literature. In this respect, we agree with Yao's (2003) view that identification of core DM concepts, and associations between them, may become a catalyst to enable a greater level of debate on the scope and definition of the DM field.

While one can subjectively undertake a discussion of the state and scope of the DM field, for example, through a discussion forum, given the nature of the topic, we chose to gather empirical evidence on these issues by applying a data-driven approach (namely, applying latent semantic analysis (LSA) to a large corpus of DM-related bibliographic data). Moreover, we present the results through the development of an AKS (associative keyword space), which is a form of *conceptual space* within which core concepts are identified, as well as important associative relationships. In addition, the development of the AKS provided an opportunity to identify co-occurrence relations (paths) between core concepts, retest the fundamental

DM problems, highlight interdisciplinary research, recognize possible boundaries of interest and scope within the DM field, and provide further evidence on the issue of whether the DM field is a fragmented or cohesive field of research. Overall, this work aims to add to the debate with respect to the scope, nature, and boundaries of the DM field.

The remainder of this chapter is laid out as follows. Section 14.2 introduces the idea of conceptual spaces and, in doing so, defines what is meant by an associative keyword space (AKS). Section 14.3 introduces LSA and specifically discusses its mathematical foundations. Section 14.4 outlines the method followed in this chapter and, in particular, provides details of the process followed in applying LSA to our corpus. Section 14.5 presents the AKS produced through LSA and discusses some of the suggested associations between keywords indicated by our model. Finally, Section 14.6 summarizes the conclusions and the weaknesses of this study.

## 14.2 Conceptual Spaces

Within knowledge engineering, information science, and cognitive science, the issue of how to represent and organize concepts and their relationships (i.e., knowledge organization structures) has attracted much attention. Unfortunately, there now exists a confusing array of approaches evident in the literature, including: associative concept space (van den Berg and Schuemie, 1999); associative concept network (French, 2000); concept indices (Voss, Nakata, and Juhnke, 1999); concept maps (Novak and Cañas, 2006); concept networks (see, for example, Ding, Chowdhury, and Foo, 2001); concept spaces (Houston et al., 2000); conceptual graphs (Sowa, 1999); conceptual networks (Koike and Takagi, 2007); conceptual spaces (Gärdenfors, 2004); co-word occurrence keyword space (Thakur et al., 2004); co-word spaces/co-word association maps (Mane and Börner, 2004*); lexi maps (Monarch, 2000); semantic maps (Coulter et al., 1998); semantic networks (Steyvers and Tenenbaum, 2005); terminology graphs (Aizawa and Kageura, 2003); ontologies; thesauri; and taxonomies. While acknowledging there are numerous subtle semantic differences between these modeling approaches, we use the term "conceptual spaces" (a term borrowed from Gütl and García-Barrios, 2005) to refer collectively to these representations.

Broadly speaking, there are two general classes of conceptual spaces: (1) similarity conceptual spaces and (2) associative or functional conceptual spaces. Similarity conceptual spaces attempt to organize concepts in terms of similarity in meaning, or alikeness (i.e., semantic (concept) similarity — see, for example, Budanitsky and Hirst, 2001), rather than whether they have a functional relationship or frequent association (such as for the concepts of pencil–paper). An example of a well-known similarity conceptual space is GO (gene ontology), which is an ontology of gene terms

---

* Mane and Börner (2004) also describe their model as a *topic word co-occurrence network*.

used widely within the bioinformatics community (The Gene Ontology Project). The GO consists of structural is-a/part-of hierarchical relationships, rather than free-form conceptual associations. Therefore, for many similarity conceptual spaces, there may be a natural ordering of concepts that is independent of any corpus (sample). In contrast, associative or functional conceptual spaces attempt to model concepts that are related in some way. Accordingly, these approaches seek to develop a knowledge structure in which objects of interest (i.e., concept instances) are positioned within a virtual space (sometimes a multidimensional virtual space) relative to each other in terms of their degree of relatedness. For models presented in spatial terms, proximity of position generally indicates the degree of relatedness (association) — with concepts in closer proximity being more related than concepts with lower proximity. In addition, models may feature edges or arcs connecting nodes. It therefore follows that a natural representation of associative (or functional) conceptual spaces is through a graph, where graph nodes denote concepts and edges denote association paths.

An example of an associative conceptual space is an associative concept space (ACS) (Van der Eijk et al., 2004). In contrast to fully term-based approaches, such as traditional applications of LSA (see, for example, Deerwester et al., 1990), to construct an ASC, a corpus is preprocessed using a thesaurus to identify concepts. The ACS algorithm (Van der Eijk et al., 2004) is then applied to the corpus to position concepts within a multidimensional Euclidean space. The final spatial position a concept takes is a result of the offset of two forces: (1) a learning rule (which moves concepts in closer proximity, and is based on a Hebbian-type learning algorithm applied to the co-occurrence data); and (2) a forgetting rule (which moves concepts further apart). The ACS algorithm is similar to LSA in that it can recognize higher-order relationships (indirect associations) within a dataset.

There are also other ways in which associative conceptual spaces types may differ. For example, some approaches attempt to capture concepts, while others focus more on topics, or terminology (see, for example, Mane and Börner, 2004; Ord et al., 2005). While topics and concepts, in many cases, will be adequate proxies for each other, some concepts may manifest in pluralistic terms. Different terminological manifestations are widely referred to as the synonym problem (Van Der Eijk et al., 2004). Other complexities include that certain terms may map to a concept, but at different levels of abstraction; or a particular term may be overloaded, in that it may have multiple meanings (i.e., is polysemous).

While many attempts to develop ontologies and taxonomies aim to be exhaustive and corpus independent, examples of the construction of other types of concept structures can be best characterized as proto-ontology, or a precursor of an ontology (a term we have taken from Voss et al., 1999), and identified concepts and inter-concept relationships may potentially be biased by the chosen corpus. In these cases, the absence of a concept (or an expected association) can sometimes be as informative as its inclusion.

While the most comprehensive ontologies, such as *Wordnet*, have resulted from primarily manual development by human experts, there have been numerous attempts to automate construction of some types of conceptual spaces. For example, Ord et al.'s (2005) visualization plots of topic area associations in animal behavior research were developed using automated text mining technologies. Another example along these lines is that of Van Der Eijk et al. (2004), who developed an ACS for literature-based discovery (LBD). Similarly, Mane and Börner's (2004) construction of a co-word space of networked topics also utilized text mining techniques, although the resulting visualizations were also examined and interpreted by domain experts.

This chapter introduces a type of associative conceptual space referred to as an associative keyword space (AKS). We define an AKS as a conceptual space in which keywords are represented as nodes, and edges between concepts represent significant associations. In this respect, association strength is determined by the degree of conceptual *relatedness* between keywords. Although a number of measures have been suggested in the literature for *relatedness*, we use the most common measure of relatedness, which is based on the notion of co-occurrence. The use of co-occurrence data to identify relationships between concepts has been applied in a number of areas of research, such as knowledge discovery (Swanson and Smalheiser, 1997), co-word analysis (Coulter et al., 1998), bibliometric analysis (Van Raan, 2003), to name just a few. A simple definition of co-occurrence (assuming the unit of analysis is individual words within a corpus) is the "co-occurrence of two or more words in one document or in different documents" (Diodato, 1994, p. 54, as cited in Onyancha and Ocholla, 2005). In this respect, a document can be a word window, sentence, or complete document (Mahn and Biemann, 2005).

Although we use the notion of co-occurrence, it is also important to appreciate that studies utilizing co-occurrence measures of relatedness can use different co-occurrence techniques, and as a result, differ in their level of measure sophistication. As summarized in Börner et al. (2003), measures of similarity between knowledge units can be placed broadly into scalar (e.g., co-word techniques, such as Jaccard indices), vector (e.g., LSA), and simple correlation (e.g., Pearson's $R$) categories. Of these three categories, vector measures of co-occurrence are the most complex. An advantage of some vector-based techniques (such as LSA) over simpler techniques is their ability to recognize higher-order relationships between concepts. Recently, Kontostathis and Pottenger (2002) demonstrated that LSA uses up to fifth-order term co-occurrence. A higher-order (second or higher) relationship exists within a dataset when an association is imputed between two directly noninteractive items (i.e., items that do not directly co-occur).

## 14.3 Latent Semantic Analysis

Latent semantic analysis (LSA) (originally known as latent semantic indexing) was originally proposed by Deerwester et al. (1990). LSA is a sophisticated statistical-based technique that can automatically extract and represent implicit higher-order structure in the association (similarity) of terms within documents. Consequently, the basic input into LSA is a large corpus of text. It should be appreciated that because LSA is typically applied as a fully term-based approach, it is therefore not an example of traditional natural language processing nor an artificial intelligence program, as it does not make use of word order, thesaurus, ontologies, knowledge bases, semantic networks, grammars, syntactic parsers, or morphologies (Landauer et al., 1998). Text similarity judgments obtained using LSA have been found to be consistent with human word sorting and category judgments (Landauer et al., 1998). Moreover, LSA has been applied within a number of domains, including information retrieval (Dumais, 1990), essay grading, text comparison (Foltz et al., 1999), just to name a few.

LSA is a technique based on co-occurrence — that is, the input into LSA is co-occurrence data within the target corpus. The underlying assumption in LSA is that related concepts co-occur more frequently in corpus entries than do nonrelated concepts (Van Der Eijk et al., 2004). Landauer et al. (1998, p. 6) suggest that another way to think of LSA is that it "represents the meaning of a word as a kind of average of the meaning of all the passages in which it appears, and the meaning of a passage as a kind of average of the meaning of all the words it contains." Essentially, LSA derives the semantic structure within a corpus (i.e., the "latent semantic structure," which is sometimes called hidden causes, or higher-order) by taking into consideration the contextual-usage meaning of words (Landauer and Dumais, 1997).

It is important to appreciate that a number of factors can impact the performance of LSA, including the choice of corpus and corpus-based representation, information theoretic weightings\*, and selection of the number of dimensions†. In addition, LSA shares the challenge of many DM techniques in that it must be able to reduce the number of dimensions within the data space (i.e., deal with the curse of dimensionality, where sample size requirements grow exponentially with the number of variables), deal with the empty space phenomenon (i.e., high-dimensional spaces are inherently sparse) (Carreira-Perpiñán, 1996), while at the same time reducing the noise within the dataset (Kontostathis and Pottenger, 2006).

Singular value decomposition (SVD) is widely viewed as an essential and core component of LSA (cf. Wiemer-Hastings, 1999), and is the primary mechanism that allows LSA to address the problem of high dimensionality within a dataset‡. The role of SVD within LSA is illustrated in the following description of the LSA process: this process typically starts with processing the corpus to produce a co-occurrence matrix

---

\* Information theoretic weightings are commonly applied to control for common words within the corpus that may add noise, and thereby inhibit semantic distillation (Wiemer-Hastings, 1999).

† These factors are further discussed below.

‡ It should be remembered that as each vector of word counts within a vector-space model can possibly represent a potential dimension instance, the number of dimensions in many text corpuses, therefore, can easily number in the thousands (Huang et al., 2003).

of terms-by-documents, in which each cell is the number of times that each respective term has occurred in that document. Next, an SVD algorithm (see, for example, Press et al. (1992, pp. 67–70) for an example SVD algorithm) is applied to this matrix dataset to decompose the matrix. SVD refers to a theorem of linear algebra whose proof supports that any $m \times n$ matrix ($\chi$) can be decomposed (factorization of the original matrix X) into three matrices: (1) a term-by-dimension matrix, T, (2) a singular value matrix, S, and (3) a document-by-dimension matrix, D, which represents a $k$-dimensional approximation of X. Both T and D have orthonormal columns, while S is a diagonal matrix containing scaling values such that when the three components are matrix-multiplied, the original matrix is reconstructed. The key to dimensionality reduction is S, which contains a set of ranked, linearly independent factors ("singular values") that are all positive and ordered in decreasing magnitude. Given the ranked order of factors, the first $k$ factors (dimensions) can be kept, and the other smaller ones set to zero. After dimension ($k$) selection, the original matrix can be reformulated; but given that some factors have been set to zero, the resulting reconstituted matrix ($\hat{X}$) will only be approximate (i.e., a reduced model). This reduced model has proved the closest in the least squares sense to X (Deerwester et al., 1990). Moreover, with the dropping of some minor dimensions, the model can be further simplified by deleting zero rows and columns of S, and the corresponding columns of T and D. Essentially, by choosing a subset of the original dimensions, the amount of co-occurrence information is compressed into a smaller space (Wiemer-Hastings, 1999). With regard to $\hat{X}$, comparing the similarity between two column vectors indicates the extent to which the two columns are similar (if a column represents a document, we are referring to the similarity of two documents). Deerwester et al. (1990) use the cosine measure to estimate the degree of vector similarity, where a cosine value near 1 means that the documents or terms have similar meaning. In contrast, the cosine of totally dissimilar vectors will be close to 0. Therefore, the similarity score in comparing, for example, two publication titles will be driven by the number and context of common words (Ord et al., 2005) and, logically, also documents in which a word does not occur (i.e., context). Put simply, Ord et al. (2005, p. 1402) state that "the analysis isolates each word in a title and searches for the same term in other document titles. When the program finds common vocabulary, it creates a link between the documents. The more links shared between records, the greater the assumed overlap in topic area." Furthermore, the SVD of a matrix has a nice geometric interpretation (Chatterjee, 2000). Accordingly, one can view the $m \times n$ matrix X as a list of the coordinates of $m$ points in an $n$-dimensional space.

## 14.4 Method

Many LSA studies provide only a brief description of how the LSA process was applied. For example, some studies fail to make clear the number of dimensions factored into the LSA process. Both Haley et al. (2005) and van Bruggen et al.

(2006) urge researchers to describe their analyses and data in more detail to promote comparison of findings and to aid understanding of the LSA technique. Accordingly, this section outlines in detail both the LSA process, and the steps and decisions taken in applying LSA.

### 14.4.1 The LSA Process

The LSA process typically features the following main steps: corpus selection, corpus pre-processing and data extraction, application of weighting schemes, choice of dimensionality and generation of the latent semantic space, and choice and application of similarity methods. However, for this study, a further final step was included: knowledge domain visualization.

### 14.4.2 Corpus Selection

As the focus of this chapter is DM-related literature, we chose to focus on published works of research (i.e., articles) that featured the term "data mining" either in the article's title, keyword list, or abstract. Given the exploratory nature of this study, we chose not to search on any "specific terms" that arguably some DM researchers or practitioners might consider related to DM, as we thought doing so could possibly bias article selection. Accordingly, to enact the search, we searched for the term "data mining" on the Institute for Scientific Information's (ISI) *Web of Knowledge*™ (which includes the *Science Citation Index, Social Science Citation Index,* and the *Arts and Humanities Citation Index*) citation database. Note that although the *Web of Knowledge* is arguably the premier citation service, Cameron (2005) specifically warns that ISI covers only a segment of the journals published in each discipline. Accordingly, the articles identified in our search and included in our corpus should be considered only a sample of all DM literature published within the respective publication window, rather than being a complete population of DM-related articles.

The respective publication window was restricted to articles listed in the (ISI) *Web of Knowledge* during the period from January 1, 2000, to December 31, 2005. Our ISI search returned 4194 entries*, and the full bibliographic details of these entries were downloaded in text form from the *Web of Knowledge* Web site to a local personal computer for further processing. While the number of entries in the corpus may appear to be large†, it is relatively small when compared with large corpuses featured in some other LSA studies, where the terms or documents within a corpus can number on the order of 10,000 (Wiemer-Hastings, 1999). In this

---

\* The number of entries within the corpus may differ, depending on the unit of analysis. Here, the unit of analysis is assumed to be the document.

† As explained below, a number of entries were subsequently deleted from the initial corpus.

respect, our corpus perhaps can be best characterized as a small-scale, domain-specific corpus (see Van Bruggen et al., 2006).

### 14.4.3 Data Extraction and Corpus Pre-Processing

The main unit of analysis in this study consists of the keywords that authors typically use to semantically tag their work to indicate the primary subjects of their articles. The inclusion of only author keywords within the corpus has a major advantage when compared to more open text corpuses, in that authors of the corpus entries presumably expend considerable effort in keyword choice. In addition, keywords present a succinct semantic representation, where there is minimal noise in comparison with using words appearing over a greater text range, such as within an abstract or an article's body. In effect, the use of keywords enables significant noise reduction, thus offsetting some of the possible limitations from having a relatively small corpus. On the other hand, using keywords as the main unit of analysis has problems, such as data sparseness, due to the fact that, at most, an individual article may be represented by only a few keywords.

Once bibliographic details were downloaded from the ISI database, we wrote a parser to go through the entries to extract only the keywords for each article. (Parsers are algorithms that identify and break data into smaller elements according to their structure or syntax within a data file.) Accordingly, entries in our initial corpus that had no keywords listed were excluded from further analysis. The culling of these entries reduced the number of entries in the corpus to 2220. Once all keywords were extracted, keyword instances were manually inspected in order to perform keyword term stemming. The stemming process, for example, looked for synonymous keywords (by way of example, the terms *association rule, association rules, association rule mining, association mining, association rule discovery, quantitative association rules, efficient association rule mining, simple association rules,* and *apriori algorithm* were all coded as *association rule*. In another example, the keywords *geographic information system, geographic information systems, geospatial data, geospatial decision support system, gis, large spatial databases, spatial analysis, spatial data analysis, spatial data mining, spatial information system,* and *spatial information systems* were stemmed to the term *spatial information systems*.)*.

As is common in many studies using co-word analyses, our analysis then focused on keywords with the highest frequencies. To determine keyword frequency, we loaded the keyword entries into an Oracle database, and wrote a script to return a frequency count of unique keyword instances. Our database query identified 5368 unique keywords within our corpus. To ensure there were a sufficient number of articles with that keyword instance included within the initial corpus,

---

\* A full list of keyword transformations (which numbered 553) is available from the author on request, and was made available to the reviewers of this chapter.

**Table 14.1    High-Frequency Keywords (within Classifications)**

| Main DM Problem Classes | Applications / Domains | Foundational Concepts |
|---|---|---|
| **Association** | bioinformatics | algorithm |
|    association rule |    cancer | data analysis |
|    frequent item set |    gene expression | feature extraction |
| **Classification** |    genetics | feature selection |
|    classification |    high-throughput screening | pattern recognition |
|    decision tree |    microarray | performance |
|    rule induction |    molecular | prediction |
| **Clustering** |    protein | visualization |
|    clustering | business intelligence | |
| **Sequence** | customer relationship management (CRM) | **Context Technologies** |
|    sequence | decision support | data warehouse |
| | electronic commerce | database |
| **Statistics** | information retrieval | internet |
|    statistics | intrusion detection | xml |
|    regression | knowledge discovery | |
| | knowledge management | **Soft Computing Methodologies** |
| **Artificial Intelligence** | personalization | fuzzy set |
|    artificial intelligence | recommender systems | genetic algorithm |
|    inductive logic programming | security | neural network |
|    machine learning | spatial information systems | rough set |
| | text mining | self organized map |
| **Data Mining Process** | time series | support vector machine |
|    knowledge discovery in database | web mining | |
|       exploratory data analysis | | **Issues** |
| | | privacy |

the frequency threshold was set at 15. This cutoff resulted in the selection of 56 keywords for further analysis. Collectively, we refer to these keywords as the keyword shortlist . Table 14.1 lists the entries within the keyword short-list. The keywords in Table 14.1 have also been classified according to suggested keyword groupings that arose from the LSA analysis, which is discussed in a later section.

After the members of the keyword short-list were established, entries in our corpus without at least one of the keyword short-list entries were dropped from further analysis. This step led to the corpus being decreased to 777 entries (with an average of 2.43 keywords per entry). Finally, to further reduce the level of "noise" within the corpus, keywords within the remaining entries that were not members of the keyword short-list were deleted from their respective entries.

## 14.4.4  *Weighting*

As discussed previously, it is common in LSA applications to apply information theoretic weightings to transform the values in the frequency text-document matrix X (Nakov et al., 2001). Term weighting is used to control for noise from commonly occurring words (e.g., "of" and "the") that may inhibit semantic distillation. A common weighting method is "log entropy," based on Information Theory, which multiplies values by their information gain (Wiemer-Hastings, 2004). However, the use of term weightings in the current study was judged inappropriate because

use of keyword stopping, as described above, ensured that noise from other terms within the bibliographic database were effectively isolated. Therefore, there was no justification to assign words unequal weights, as all keywords should presumably be meaningful. However, the keyword "data mining" was purposely omitted from the keyword short-list, as this term, while perhaps not a keyword in every entry in the corpus, was assumed to be a common factor across all corpus entries and therefore its inclusion within the LSA analysis was considered to have the potential to introduce "noise" into the analysis.

## 14.4.5 Latent Semantic Space Generation and Dimensionality Reduction

Entries in the bibliographic database that contained two or more keywords in the keyword short-list were then processed into a co-occurrence matrix (document-term frequency matrix), with each separate article mapping to a column vector. The co-occurrence matrix, therefore, featured 777 column vectors. Conversion of this matrix into a latent semantic vector space was performed using the *R* statistical software (The R Foundation) and specifically *R*'s *lsa* package (Wild, 2005). Use of the *lsa* package allowed us to apply the SVD algorithm and subsequently reduce the resulting matrices to effect dimension reduction.

Creating the LSA vector space required stipulating the number of singular values (dimensions). The decision as to how many singular values to use is a judgment as to which singular values are meaningful, and which compromise noise (Efron, 2005). Notwithstanding the importance of choosing the number of dimensions to use in SVD, there is no formal and universally accepted algorithm to provide guidance. While the use of 200 to 500 singular values is quite common (Wiemer-Hastings, 1999), Van Bruggen et al. (2006, p. 5) stress that "[t]he number of documents needed for the LSA is not dependent on the size of the domain (or text database), but on the dimensionality of the domain." Moreover, given that Deerwester et al. (1990) originally demonstrated the LSA technique using only two dimensions, there is no clear mathematical reason for LSA failing to accommodate a low number of dimensions. However, complications are more likely to arise from the properties of the corpus. For example, it would be very unlikely that the mining of open text would warrant using a low number of dimensions.

The problem of determining the number of factors, dimensions, and singular values to retain is a general problem within studies applying dimensionality reduction techniques (e.g., LSA, factor analysis, and principal component analysis). Accordingly, a number of approaches have been proffered to estimate the optimal number of singular values. Examples of these approaches include using a visual Scree test (Cattell, 1966); the eigenvalue-one criterion (Guttman, 1954); selecting the number of singular values that optimizes a performance criterion, such as the correlation with ratings by human raters (Wiemer-Hastings, 1999); parallel analysis (Velicer and Jackson, 1990); and amended parallel analysis (Efron, 2005). Recently, van Bruggen et al. (2006) introduced a novel approach specific to LSA for dimensionality determination, where a sensitivity analysis is performed across a range of singular values to identify the number of singular values that offer optimum discrimination between documents with overlapping content and documents that share little overlapping content. In their study, they identified 35 singular values as providing maximum discriminatory power (their term-document matrix consisted of 287 documents, 4376 unique words, and 311 average words per document). In addition, Van Bruggen et al. (2006) demonstrated that a relatively low number of dimensions (compared with the number of unique words) can account for a large proportion of the total variance in term-frequency matrix cell frequencies, with the first singular value accounting for much of the variance.

The variety of approaches to estimating the optimal number of singular values suggests that much empirical and theoretical work is still needed on this issue. It is therefore of little surprise that judgment is still an important factor in deciding the number of singular values. This view is supported by Wiemer-Hastings and Graesser (2000, p. 163), who provide the practical advice that "the best number of dimensions must be empirically determined with respect to a particular domain and task." However, we can accept that the optimal number of singular values will be affected by characteristics of the corpus, including its size, uniformity (e.g., number of different terms), level of abstraction, and dimensionality (Wiemer-Hastings and Graesser, 2000; Kontostathis, 2005).

Given that the current study limited attention to the 54 most frequently used keywords*, the theoretical maximum number of dimensions to consider was this number. However, on reviewing the final keyword list, we formed expectations that the number of underlying dimensions would be considerably less; for example, we expected that keywords within the keyword short-list referring to biological phenomena would be strongly associated, thus potentially forming a keyword cluster (i.e., a semantic dimension). However, to determine whether our analysis was sensitive to different values of $k$, we re-performed the analysis for different $k$ values (i.e., $k = 5, 10, 15, 20$). Results of this sensitivity analysis showed that the degree of association between certain keyword pairs was relatively stable across different $k$ values, while the association strength between other keyword pairs was more volatile. To control for the noted association strength volatility, we therefore adopted a strategy of excluding any keyword association that failed in the sensitivity analysis to return an association strength above the designated association threshold for at least two of the above four $k$ conditions.

---

* The original keyword short-list (as detailed in Table 14.1) actually has 56 entries. However, keywords for *internet* and *information retrieval* were subsequently dropped from further analysis, as an inspection of entries within the corpus that featured these keywords were judged to contain inconsistent use of these terms (different interpretations). For example, the keyword *information retrieval* sometimes occurred in corpus entries that focused on document retrieval, and sometimes in entries focusing on optimization of database queries.

## 14.4.6 Similarity

The cosine is a commonly used measure of vector similarity in LSA applications (Wiemer-Hastings, 2004). While Nakov (2000) reviews other possible similarity measures, such as Pearson's correlation, or the angle between vectors, we chose to use the cosine value as a measure of vector association. Calculation of the cosine matrix of the latent semantic space was calculated using $R$'s cosine function. The axes within the cosine matrix were then reversed so that each vector represented a unique term (as opposed to representing a document instance).

## 14.4.7 Knowledge Domain Visualization

Knowledge domain visualization (KDV) is a set of visualization technologies applied to facilitate knowledge domain understanding. KDV exploits powerful human vision and spatial cognition to help humans mentally organize and electronically access and manage large complex information spaces (Mane and Börner, 2004). Unlike scientific visualizations, KDVs are created from data that have no natural spatial reference, such as sets of publications, patents, or grants. The KDV technique used in this study was to create a network plot in which each node represents an instance in the keyword short-list, and edges (links) indicating associations between nodes. Connections (edges) between nodes in the plot therefore assert an association between the featured keywords (i.e., connected terms are more likely to appear together within the same context, compared with unconnected terms).

The first step in developing the KDV was to export the cosine matrix, which was calculated in $R$, in CSV (comma delimited) format. A *VBA* script was then run to initialize to zero any cosine values within the matrix that were equal to or less than 0.71. This transformation was performed to reduce clutter in plots caused by superfluous links between terms (as the cosine matrix contained similarity measures for every binary combination of terms), and to leave within the AKS only those associations of greatest strength — that is, this transformation effectively set a significant threshold of association (similarity) to a cosine value of 0.71, thus preserving in the final model only the most substantial links between keywords. While selecting an appropriate threshold level is primarily left to the judgment of the researcher, the cut-off we selected was not very different from that used by Ord et al. (2005), who used cut-offs of 0.70, 0.70, 0.74, and 0.755 in their study of trends in animal behavior research*.

---

* At this point, we excluded from the final AKS the following keywords as they had no associations with any other keywords above the association threshold: *knowledge discovery in databases, prediction,* and *feature selection.* This action resulted in the keyword list decreasing from 54 to 51 entries.

To draw the network plot, we used *Pajek* software visualization software (Batagelj and Mrvar, 1997, 2003). To convert the cosine matrix into the acceptable *Pajek* format, we ran a *perl* script to produce the necessary input file. Within *Pajek*, the actual network was drawn using the Kamada–Kawai (KK) algorithm (Kamada and Kawai, 1989) with a circular starting position. The KK algorithm is an example of a force-directed layout algorithm, which equates the LSA weights between terms as the respective forces.

## 14.5 Analysis

This section first presents the final AKS model, then discusses how to interpret the model, and finally investigates some of the suggested associations between keywords indicated within this model.

### 14.5.1 An AKS of the Data Mining Literature

The final AKS of the DM literature is presented in Figure 14.1.

### 14.5.2 Interpreting the AKS

Although the AKS featured in this chapter was produced through the application of a sophisticated analytical technique to a well-defined corpus of bibliographic information, we should acknowledge that the visual nature of the final model implies its analysis is open to interpretation (i.e., some degree of interpretive analysis is required). Given this concern, we now discuss some of the meta-structural properties of the AKS. In addition, the next section contains a discussion of the validity of the model assertions.

In our model, most nodes are directly or indirectly linked together*. Given that all the articles included in our corpus are related in some way to the DM domain, this outcome is perhaps not surprising. Nodes linked by an edge in the model assert that there exists within the corpus an association above the deemed threshold between the concepts that each node represents. Given that these relationships are confined by the attributes of the corpus, care should be exercised in terms of generalizing the proposed associations outside the corpus parameters. Furthermore, although each edge has a weight, it is customary not to include these weights within the final model. This convention is in contrast, for example, to some other types of association models, such as models claiming causal or temporal paths or relationships (e.g., structural equation

---

* There is no requirement that all nodes are linked, as the AKS is not a network. Accordingly, if concepts share no significant association, they should not be connected.

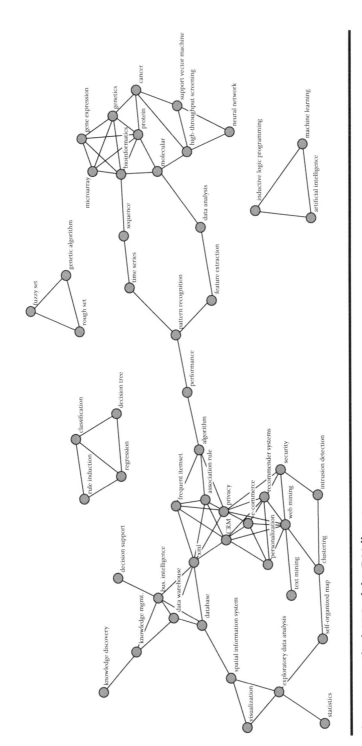

**Figure 14.1** Final AKS of the DM literature.

models [SEMs]). Such models typically show edges connecting explicit and latent variables, together with their estimated co-variation, and uncertainty measurements of this relationship (i.e., statistical significance). However, in these types of models, it should be appreciated that although the validity of the proposed relations has been validated through statistical sampling, the strength and direction of the relationships connecting concepts are estimates only. In contrast, our model is presented at a more abstract level — a relationship is drawn between concepts if it is considered significant, in terms that its similarity measure is above some threshold. In addition, the direction and nature of the relationship are not required, as the relationships in our model do not attempt to represent causal-type relationships between concepts, but rather represent co-occurrence relationships. Therefore, our model is structural in nature and does not claim to be informative in terms of causal or temporal relationships.

### 14.5.2.1 Keyword Clustering within the AKS

It should also be appreciated that the length of edges connecting nodes in the AKS do not necessarily represent a visual cue to the strength of the respective cosine values. As noted above, the algorithm used to draw the model in this study was the KK algorithm (Kamada and Kawai, 1989). The KK algorithm is an example of a forced-directed algorithm, and these types of algorithms seek to draw graphs in an aesthetically pleasing way. Accordingly, these types of algorithms generally try to position nodes in a graph so that all the edges are more-or-less of equal length, and there are as few crossing edges as possible (Wikipedia, 2006a). However, when a set of concepts (keywords) has many interconnections, a force-directed layout algorithm will tend to shorten the length of connecting edges, as there are many edges exerting force to form a center-of-force density. As a result, the nodes may appear to be visually clustered. For example, such a clumping of connections (nodes within close spatial proximity) is evident in our model with respect to the concepts in Table 14.1 that we classified as relating to the concept of *bioinformatics*. In addition, when analyzing the model, we should be aware that concept clustering can indicate the potential existence of a meta-latent concept at a higher level of abstraction.

### 14.5.3 Model Validation and Analysis

To confirm the validity of our model, we reviewed in detail the generated keyword association rankings for the following keywords: *association, classification, clustering, sequence,* and *bioinformatics.* (As outlined below, the first four terms represent the four basic classes of DM problems, as identified by Houston et al. (1999), while the keyword *bioinformatics* was included because the initial analysis of keyword frequencies produced a number of biological-related terms.) Our review sought to identify any potential anomalies in the rankings, when compared with rankings

**Table 14.2   High Cosine Rankings for Select Keywords** ($k = 10$, cosine $> = 0.71$)

| Keywords | Association Rule | | Classification | | Sequence | | Clustering | | Bioinformatics | |
|---|---|---|---|---|---|---|---|---|---|---|
| Cosine values | frequent itemset | 0.97 | rule induction | 0.85 | bioinformatics | 0.74 | intrusion detection | 0.73 | genetics | 0.98 |
| | customer relationship management | 0.91 | regression | 0.80 | microarray | 0.71 | web mining | 0.73 | protein | 0.97 |
| | privacy | 0.86 | decision tree | 0.78 | | | self organized map | 0.72 | microarray | 0.95 |
| | xml | 0.84 | | | | | | | gene expression | 0.94 |
| | algorithm | 0.81 | | | | | | | cancer | 0.81 |
| | | | | | | | | | sequence | 0.74 |
| | | | | | | | | | database | 0.71 |

made by two human experts*. The association strength rankings produced by the cosine analysis ($k = 10$) are listed in Table 14.2 for each respective keyword. The rankings in Table 14.2 were reviewed both by the researcher and two experts in the field of computing. Specifically, the reviewers were asked to identify any potential surprises within the high-cosine keyword rankings. (A surprise, for example, would be if a keyword was given a low rank where, *a priori*, a high rank was expected by the experts.) For the purposes of this analysis, high cosine values were defined as having a cosine value greater than or equal to a threshold of 0.71 (the same threshold for association strength). Several other comments made by the reviewers are discussed in the following subsections.

### 14.5.3.1   Bioinformatics Keyword Cluster

In reviewing the model, there is a clear cluster of life science-related keywords, which we refer to as the *bioinformatics cluster*. Bioinformatics is a multifaceted discipline, combining many scientific fields, including computational biology, mathematics, molecular biology, and genetics (Fenstermacher, 2005). We, therefore, chose to name this cluster *bioinformatics* for the principal reason that we felt the keywords within this cluster shared a common theme. In effect, we assert that *bioinformatics* is an example of a meta-latent variable.

In this study, keywords with a high cosine value with the keyword *bioinformatics* referred mainly to biological concepts or subdisciplines (i.e., *genetics, protein, microarray, gene expression, cancer,* and *molecular*). Two other keywords (*database, sequence*) also returned high cosine values in the $k = 10$ case†. Thereafter, there was a substantial gap in cosine value strength to the next keyword (high-throughput screening, 0.50). While it is no surprise that biological concepts returned high cosine

---

* We should highlight that a problem recognized by Mane and Börner (2004) in the evaluation and interpretation of a topic word co-occurrence network — which is similar to an AKS — is that there may not be many domain experts who are familiar enough with the diverse number of concepts presented in such a model.

† Because a high cosine value between *database* and *bioinformatics* was not identified across the other $k$ conditions, the link between these two keywords was omitted from our final model. However, for the purposes of model validation, we have included a discussion of the feasibility of a high cosine value between these keywords.

values with *bioinformatics*, it was initially less clear why the keywords *sequence* and *database*, which do not refer specifically to life science concepts, also received high cosine values with *bioinformatics*. In addition, one of the expert reviewers flagged the keyword *high-throughput screening*, which received a relatively low cosine value with *bioinformatics* in the analysis, as a potential surprise, as it appeared to be a concept related to biology.

In a closer examination of the *bioinformatics* literature, a high cosine value between *database* and *bioinformatics* is plausible. Many biological applications (e.g., whole-genome sequencing efforts, microarray technologies, and the mapping of single nucleotide polymorphisms [SNP], proteomics) require the storage and retrieval of enormous amounts of data (Fenstermacher, 2005), and involve complex object models and a wide range of different data types (Ostell, 2005). Moreover, in some cases, these databases (particularly sequence databases) are growing rapidly in terms of required storage capacity (Ostell, 2005). For example, Ostell (2005) reported that *GenBank* contains 74 billion base-pairs of gene sequence and has a doubling time of about 17 months. Given the data storage challenges facing biologists, it is therefore not surprising that data storage within the context of life sciences has attracted the attention of researchers. Consequently, work has addressed specific database-related issues within the context of biological applications, such as data warehousing, query performance, data integration, and metadata management (see, for example, Bassett et al., 1999; Mangalam et al., 2001; Mattes et al., 2004). In addition, database platforms, such as *GeneX*, have been developed specifically for biomedical data storage and analysis (Mangalam et al., 2001). Our corpus also included several examples of articles that focused on the issue of data storage within life science applications. For example, Mattes et al. (2004) discussed a number of database-related issues, such as standardization of data inputs, data quality, integration across data repositories, and data sharing, in the context of establishing a publicly accessible toxicogenomics database. Notwithstanding the clear importance of data management in life science DM endeavors, it appears that we failed to find sufficient evidence from our analysis to support the assertion that data management ranks as a central research theme for life science data miners, as this association failed our sensitivity analysis test, as outlined above. Accordingly, we omitted this association from our final model, as a high cosine value was not reported between the keywords *database* and *bioinformatics* for other values of $k$.

In contrast, the direct path association in our model between the keywords *sequence* and *bioinformatics* is not surprising. While sequence pattern identification and measures of sequence similarity have wide applications (for example, mining association rules and sequential patterns to discover customer purchasing behaviors from a transaction database (Yen and Lee, 2006) or temporal association rule mining to identify time-dependent correlations (Winarko and Roddick, 2005)), the importance of sequences within life science DM has been emphasized in many publications. As Bassett et al. (1999) stressed, in biology, the "mining" of sequence databases has now been going on for more than two decades. Searching for sequence similarity in vast datasets that may contain, for example, nucleotide and amino acid sequences, is critical to biologists in determining the chemical structure, biological function, and evolutionary history of organisms (Oracle, 2006).

As discussed above, one of our expert reviewers flagged the keyword *high-throughput screening* as a concept related to life sciences (and therefore life sciences DM). Consequently, this objection raised questions as to why the analysis failed to establish a significant cosine value between this keyword and the keyword *bioinformatics*. Wikipedia (2006b) described high-throughput screening (HTS) as a method for scientific experimentation, especially for drug discovery, and is relevant to the fields of biology and chemistry. This definition, therefore, implies that HTS is not necessarily a term restricted to biology. Such a view of HTS was confirmed in our analysis, as the corpus included several entries that featured the keyword *high-throughput screening* but did not focus on life science research (see, for example, Corma and Serra, 2005; and Farrusseng et al., 2005). Given the broader focus of HTS-related research, it is therefore understandable that this keyword has a relatively lower cosine value with the keyword *bioinformatics*. Notwithstanding this plausible explanation, we also reviewed the keyword rankings associated with *high-throughput screening* and the path distance in our model between the keywords *bioinformatics* and *high-throughput screening*. The highest ranked keywords with *high-throughput screening* ($k = 10$) were *neural network* (0.82), *support vector machine* (0.80), *molecular* (0.77), and *cancer* (0.74). Therefore, although *high-throughput screening* did not return a high cosine association value with *bioinformatics**, this keyword had a high cosine value with the keyword *molecular*, which, in turn, ranked highly with the keyword *bioinformatics*. As a consequence, the path distance between the keywords *high-throughput screening* and *bioinformatics* was only two segments. In short, although there was a low cosine value between these keywords, their close spatial proximity within the model suggests that a relationship does indeed exist between them. In the case where two keywords (concepts) are connected, but through an intermediate link†, this represents a second-order co-occurrence relationship (Kontostathis and Pottenger, 2006). That is, the suggested relationship between *high-throughput screening* and *bioinformatics* comes from the transitive relation: *high-throughput screening* co-occurs with *molecular* (three entries in the final corpus) and *molecular* co-occurs with *bioinformatics* (six entries in the final corpus).

With regard to the periphery of the bioinformatics cluster, one of our expert reviewers also questioned the proposed relation in the model between the keyword *high-throughput screening* and the keywords *neural network* and *support vector machine*. On closer analysis, after vetting corpus entries that failed to feature at

---

* In our corpus, there was only a single entry (i.e., Shen et al., 2005) that included both the normalized keywords *bioinformatics* and *high-throughput screening*.

† For example, *high-throughput screening–molecular,* and *molecular–bioinformatics.*

least two keywords on the keyword short-list, only nine entries remained. Of these entries, four contained a reference to the keyword *neural network*. Given the prominence of the keyword *neural network* within entries within the corpus with the keyword *high-throughput screening*, the high cosine value between these keywords is understandable. However, the small number of articles featuring the keyword *high-throughput screening* included in the analysis is clearly a weakness in this study.

In addition, one of the expert reviewers also questioned the positioning of the keyword *neural network* in the model — where it is associated with only two other keywords: *high-throughput screening* and *support vector machine*. On closer inspection, the high cosine value between the keywords *high-throughput screening* and *neural network* appears driven by the predominance of the *neural network* keyword within entries featuring the keyword *high-throughput screening*, and not the opposite case (i.e., out of 108 entries that featured the keyword *neural network*, only four contained the keyword *high-throughput screening*; moreover, there were 16 other keywords with first-order co-occurrences with higher frequencies ahead of the keyword *high-throughput screening*). A possible assertion from these observations is that the association weights between these two keywords are asymmetric (i.e., directional). Consequently, to confirm the directional nature of the association between these keywords, we systematically replaced each entry that featured both keywords *high-throughput screening* and *neural network* with the keywords *high-throughput screening* and *dummy_keyword*, and recalculated the cosine values. Results of these calculations are presented in Figure 14.2. It is clear from Figure 14.2 that the cosine

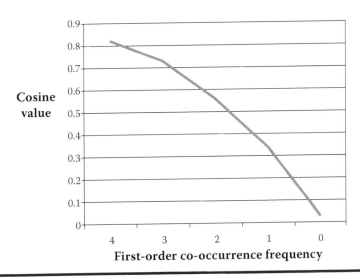

**Figure 14.2**  **Simulated association strength (cosine values) (for the association between keywords *neural network* and *high-throughput screening*).**

values between the keywords *high-throughput screening* and *neural network* are sensitive to the number of entries that feature these keywords together, thus raising the concern that cosine values may be volatile for small sample sizes, and some relationships suggested by the LSA may be directional.

Whereas constructions of models showing directional connections between nodes (e.g., directed acyclic graphs [DAGs]) may be common, for example, in Bayesian network modeling, we failed to find any academic publication that had utilized LSA for the purposes of DAG construction. In contrast, the assumption that appears to pervade much LSA work is that co-occurrence of terms translates to concept similarity — that is, if concept A and concept B tend to co-occur, concept A is *similar* to concept B. At the same time, if concept A is *similar* to concept B, then the opposite must also be true. However, when dealing with association, rather than purely similarity, concept co-occurrence may allude to the strength of an association between concepts (i.e., underlying functional relationships or frequent associations), rather than solely concept similarity. For example, two concepts may have a clear functional relationship (e.g., *pencil–paper*) but should not be regarded as being semantically equivalent (Budanitsky and Hirst, 2001).

## 14.5.3.2 Artificial Intelligence Keyword Cluster

The machine learning cluster consists of three associated keywords: *inductive logic programming* (11 entries), *machine learning* (90 entries), and *artificial intelligence* (10 entries). This cluster is inclusive in that it has no links to other keywords. Although this cluster appears isolated, given the relatively large sample of entries with the keyword *machine learning*, there were still first-order co-occurrences between this keyword and 35 other keywords in the keyword short-list. However, the LSA failed to identify any other keyword as having a high cosine value with keywords within this cluster. Furthermore, similar to the relationship between the keywords *high-throughput screening* and *neural network*, there was evidence that the cosine values between keywords within this cluster were affected by sample size, and reflected directional associations (of the eleven entries for *inductive logic programming*, five featured first-order co-occurrences with the keyword *machine learning*; and of the ten entries for *artificial intelligence*, five featured first-order co-occurrences with the keyword *machine learning*). Moreover, it was interesting that a direct association was made in the model between the keywords *inductive logic programming* and *artificial intelligence*. As no entries in the corpus featured these two keywords together (i.e., there was no first-order co-occurrence), this linking is another example of second-order co-occurrence. Keeping in mind the words of De Raedt (1996), who stated that "[i]nductive logic programming is a research area situated in machine learning and logic programming, two subfields of artificial intelligence," the association the LSA made between the keywords *inductive logic programming* and *artificial intelligence* appears supportable.

### 14.5.3.3 Classification Keyword Cluster

The structure of this cluster had similarities with the artificial intelligence cluster, in that the nodes are isolated. There are four associated keywords within this cluster: *classification* (128 entries), *decision tree* (63 entries), *rule induction* (12 entries)*, and *regression* (21 entries). Although this is an isolated cluster, given the relatively large sample of entries with the keyword *classification*, there were first-order co-occurrences with 35 other keywords in the keyword short-list. However, the LSA again failed to identify any other keyword as having a high cosine value with keywords within this cluster. The association between the keywords *classification*, *decision tree*, and *rule induction* is not surprising given that examples of supervised learning approaches to classification include tools such as decision trees and rule-based techniques (Houston et al., 1999). Moreover, it is also interesting that the keyword *regression* is associated with each other keyword within this cluster. As Fayyad et al. (1996b) considered both regression algorithms and case-based reasoning† as supervised learning approaches applied to data *classification* problems, this association is therefore not surprising.

### 14.5.3.4 Soft Computing Methodologies Keyword Cluster

Mitra (2002) identifies fuzzy sets, neural networks, genetic algorithms, and rough sets as soft computing methodologies. Other authors (e.g., Zhi-qiang et al., 2005) have also identified support vector machine — a term also featured in the keyword short-list — as a soft computing methodology. Zadeh (1965) differentiates soft computing from conventional (hard) computing, in the terms that soft computing approaches are tolerant of imprecision, uncertainty, partial truth, and approximation. Given our model features, a cluster with three out of four of these "core" soft methodologies — with the notable omission of *neural network* — we labeled this cluster soft computing methodologies.

To better understand the omission within this cluster of the keyword *neural network*, we first reviewed the first-order co-occurrence frequencies. Out of 108 entries that featured the keyword *neural network*, 17 contained the keyword *genetic algorithm* (which was the highest-ranked keyword in terms of first-order co-occurrence frequencies‡), 15 entries contained the keyword *fuzzy set* (which was the second-highest ranked keyword in terms of first-order co-occurrence frequencies), and 9 entries contained

---

* A careful reader may note that the frequency of this keyword appears to be below the initial frequency threshold set for determination of keyword short-list membership. The reason that this keyword was in the keyword short-list is that in our initial corpus its frequency was above the cut-off; however, further filtering steps applied to the initial corpus, as outlined above, led to some entries with this keyword being dropped from the final corpus used as a basis to generate our model.

† The keyword *case-based reasoning* was excluded from our analysis because it lacked sufficient support (i.e., its occurrence frequency was below the frequency threshold).

‡ In all, there were 36 keywords from the keyword short-list that had first-order co-occurrences with the keyword *neural network*.

the keyword *rough set* (which was the eighth-highest ranked keyword in terms of first-order co-occurrence frequencies). Moreover, the keyword *neural network*, in terms of first-order co-occurrence frequencies, for the keywords *genetic algorithm*, *rough set*, and *fuzzy set* was ranked first, fourth, and first, respectively. Therefore, in terms of first-order co-occurrence frequencies, the association between the keyword *neural network* and other soft computing methodology keywords appeared to be pronounced. Notwithstanding this analysis of first-order co-occurrences, we must remember that the cosine of an association in LSA is also determined by calculated higher-order associations. Accordingly, we must conclude that in our analysis, the pattern of higher-order co-occurrences influenced the cosine values between the keyword *neural network* and other keywords that represented other forms of soft computing.

### 14.5.3.5  Business Keyword Cluster

The largest cluster of keywords within the AKS (namely, association rule, customer relationship management (CRM), electronic commerce, frequent item set, recommender systems, personalization, web mining, XML, and privacy) appear to share a reference to business. For example, an application frequently associated with association rule mining is market basket analysis — that is, discovering customer purchasing patterns by extracting associations or co-occurrences from transactional databases (Chen et al., 2005). Moreover, we should note that the high cosine value between the keywords association rule and frequent item set is not surprising, given that the name of the most influential algorithm used to identify association rules — the Apriori algorithm — reflects the fact that it uses prior knowledge of frequent item set properties (Duru, 2005). Another clear example of a business-related concept is CRM, which is an application to support retaining long-term and profitable relationships with its customers (Cunningham et al., 2006). Other keywords within the business keyword cluster, namely, electronic commerce, recommender systems, personalization, web mining, and XML, also refer to aspects of doing business, but more specifically, doing business using Internet technologies. For example, recommender systems are now used by many E-commerce Web sites, such as Amazon.com, to generate product suggestions for customers (i.e., predict a user's preference for items). As these product recommendations are commonly tailored to each customer, they are also an example of how electronic commerce enables Web personalization. In addition, Web mining is used by some Web sites to understand users' Web behavior, thus providing insight into how to potentially adapt future interactions, with the ultimate goal of improved user satisfaction (Anand and Mobasher, 2005). Insights from Web mining, for example, can be used in recommender systems (Jun, 2005). Another keyword within this cluster — XML — is a semantic mark-up language designed principally to enable cross-platform messages between trading partners for the primary purpose of enabling E-commerce transactions. Recently, Cios and Kurgan (2002) emphasized that XML and XML-related technologies have great potential to benefit the

DM field. The remaining keyword within this cluster is privacy. Recently, the ability to mine data, such as click streams or prior transactions, has raised the issue of how to do so while preserving the privacy of individuals. Sensitivity to this issue has been heightened by the rapid increase in E-commerce transactions, where many Web sites routinely solicit their customers' personal information as part of the transaction.

Also positioned within the AKS in proximity to the business keyword cluster are a number of peripheral keywords, whose positioning also appears as one would expect. For example, the keyword *decision support* is associated with the keyword *business intelligence*. This association is not surprising, given that forms of business intelligence, such as On-Line Analytical Processing (OLAP), have arguably grown out of the decision support tradition. Also associated with the keyword *business intelligence* are the keywords *data warehouse, database, XML*, and *knowledge management*. Again, the indicated associations between these keywords are not surprising; for example, business intelligence applications such as OLAP are usually part of a wider data warehouse implementation. In turn, a data warehouse is clearly an example of a sophisticated type of database system. In part, knowledge management (KM) is a strategy to manage an organization's knowledge assets to support organizational decision making (Zyngier et al., 2004). Accordingly, because business intelligence and decision support can also be viewed as types of applications that seek to improve decision making and generate knowledge from organizational data assets, we can therefore view them as components of an organization's broader knowledge management infrastructure. Therefore, the association between these keywords, rather than being surprising, is expected.

Another peripheral keyword to the business keyword cluster is *security*. This keyword is linked to the keywords *privacy, recommender systems, web mining*, and *intrusion detection*. An example of an article in our corpus that features the keyword *security* is that of Zhan et al. (2005), who address the problem of collaboratively conducting association rule mining without disclosing privately held data to any other party. Their approach involves developing a secure protocol (using homomorphic encryption techniques) that each party can use to conduct the desired computation and exchange results. Because Zhan et al.'s (2005) work features the keywords *privacy, security*, and *association rule mining*, it is an example of an entry within our corpus that illustrates the possible connection between security and privacy.

### 14.5.3.6  Keyword Threads

The AKS also features a number of threads that link to the main keyword clusters. For example, one thread includes the keywords *data analysis, feature extraction, pattern recognition, performance*, and *algorithm*. Table 14.1 classified these keywords as *foundational concepts**. We regard these keywords as foundational to DM

---

\* Two keywords classified in Table 14.1 as foundational concepts — namely, *feature selection* and *prediction* — were excluded from the final AKS model because the LSA failed to make significant associations between these and other keywords.

theory because we consider them to refer to fundamental challenges common to most DM endeavors. For example, central to most DM endeavors is consideration of an appropriate algorithm — and a factor that may affect algorithm choice and design is clearly algorithm performance. In addition, all DM endeavors and algorithms arguably deal with some form of data analysis and pattern recognition. The final foundational concept keyword featured in the AKS — *feature extraction* — refers to a fundamental DM preprocessing step (Park, 2006). It also seems fitting that the foundational concepts keyword thread appears positioned centrally within our AKS model, and effectively stands between the two largest keyword clusters — namely, the business keyword cluster and the bioinformatics keyword cluster.

The final foundational keyword featured in the AKS — *visualization* — however, appears in the AKS remote from the other foundational concepts. This keyword, in contrast, is linked to the keywords *spatial information systems* and *exploratory data analysis*, with the third keyword also linked to the keyword *self-organized map*. Notwithstanding this seeming disconnect, we argue that the positioning of visualization within the AKS is understandable, as *spatial information systems*, *exploratory data analysis*, and *self-organized map* all deal with visualization in some form. For example, interfaces for *spatial information systems* typically support visualization of spatial data objects, and "looking at pictures" is a fundamental activity of *exploratory data analysis* (Tukey, 1977). Another method frequently used for exploratory data analysis is self-organized maps (SOMs) (Kaski, 1997), which use a neural network approach to analyze high-dimensional datasets. Traditionally, the SOM is presented as a topographic visualization (i.e., graphic map display). The *self-organized map* keyword is also associated with the keyword *clustering*, which again is understandable, given that SOMs can be used to visualize the clustering tendency of data within different regions of a data space (Kaski et al., 1998).

There are also several other associations suggested within the AKS that appear plausible. For example, the keyword *text mining* is associated with *web mining*. Wang (2000) lists "Web content mining" (i.e., automated text analysis of Web pages) as one of the three main foci of Web mining*. According to Wang (2000), "web content mining" focuses on the discovery or retrieval of useful information from the Web contents, data, or documents. Given this objective, it is therefore easy to appreciate the relevance of text mining to Web mining. Another association within the AKS is between the *security, intrusion detection*, and *clustering* keywords. Again, these associations appear plausible. For example, the detection of unauthorized access to computer systems is clearly a security issue. Furthermore, the suggested association between intrusion detection and clustering underlies that intrusion detection is a domain in which clustering approaches have been applied. Our corpus featured

---

* The other two main foci identified by Wang (2000) are Web structure mining and Web usage mining.

four examples of this pairing of keywords: Burbeck and Nadjm-Tehrani (2004); Li and Ye (2002); and Oh and Lee (2003, 2004).

## 14.6 Conclusions and Weaknesses

This chapter used LSA to analyze the article keywords of a corpus of DM articles published during a six-year window (January 1, 2000, through December 31, 2005) and listed in the ISI Web of Knowledge™ citations index database. It then presented the findings visually by developing an AKS, which included the most frequently featured DM-related keywords found in the preliminary analysis. Overall, we found that LSA allowed us to reduce the dimensionality of the DM research space to a point where a number of logical connections (associations) between concepts (as represented by their respective keywords) were highlighted within the final AKS model. In addition, the *process* of developing the AKS of the DM literature provided the opportunity to reflect on a number of issues, including the validity of the basic classes of DM problems, and the nature and scope of the DM field. Overall, while we found the DM field both interdisciplinary and domain rich, we also formed the view that the much of DM research is closely tied to the basic classes of DM problems (see below) and the exploration of what we refer to as the DM foundational concepts. This section concludes with insights obtained when applying LSA for the purposes of developing conceptual spaces, together with perceived weaknesses of this study.

### 14.6.1 *Validity of the Basic Classes of Data Mining Problems*

Agrawal et al. (1993) proposed three basic classes of DM problems, to which Houston et al. (1999) added *sequence* as a fourth class:

1. *Classification*: establishing rules and definitions of different groups to enable partitioning a given dataset into disjoint groups.
2. *Clustering*: an iterative approach to partitioning a dataset into homogeneous subpopulations (groupings) using actual data rather than classification rules imposed externally.
3. *Association*: finding rules for which a particular data attribute is either a consequence of or an antecedent to.
4. *Sequence*: deals with ordered data, such as temporal data related to stock market and point-of-sales data.

While neither Houston et al. (1999) nor Agrawal et al. (1993) present this list as a typology of DM problems, and other classifications of DM problems and tasks have been proposed (see, for example, Fayyad et al., 1996b; Shaw et al., 2001), 47.6 percent of the entries included in our final corpus featured at least one keyword that was considered synonyms for these four basic classes of DM problems.

In short, there is clear evidence that these basic classes of DM problems still domi-nate much of DM research.

In addition, the AKS generated for our study supports the assertion that each of these problem classes possesses a degree of concept distance, in that keywords representing each respective problem class are associated with different keywords. For example, in our study, the keyword *sequence* is associated with keywords *time series* and *bioinformatics*; the keyword *classification* is associated with the keywords *decision tree* and *rule induction*; the keyword *association rule* is part of the business keyword cluster; while the keyword *clustering* is associated with keywords *intrusion detection, self-organized map,* and *web mining.* Given these mappings, we therefore believe there is some support to consider each problem class as a distinct sub-field within the greater DM field, as each problem class appears to be associated with different domains and has been treated within the literature in relative isolation. However, we should acknowledge that this assertion is perhaps tempered by a con-cern that a potential weakness of the AKS generated for this study is that it fails to adequately express the breadth of the relationships between the basic DM problem classes and other concepts reflected in the AKS. Nevertheless, because this study is exploratory, we purposely focused on identifying only the "strongest" associations between keywords, and accordingly, the high cosine threshold used in this study may have excluded a number of other possible empirical associations.

## 14.6.2 The Nature and Scope of the Data Mining Field

This study provides insight into the scope, nature (fabric), and boundaries of the DM field. First, we identified in the corpus of DM bibliographic information the keywords with the highest frequencies. This simple analysis demonstrated that the field of DM is diverse, in not only the algorithmic techniques applied, but also in problem classes, applications, and foundational concepts studied. We then went further, by applying LSA to develop an AKS of the DM concept space, in an attempt to establish semantic relationships between these terms. The process of applying LSA and building the AKS allowed us to reflect upon the positioning of the concepts that these keywords represented within the overall DM field.

Second, we found that DM techniques have been applied within a diverse range of application domains (see Table 14.1), including bioinformatics, business, spatial information systems, etc. This finding supports the view of Fayyad and Uthurusamy (2002), who stressed that specific applications have always been an important aspect of DM practice. In this respect, we see this diverse range of DM applications as a possible indicator that the DM field is maturing, not only in terms of algorithm design, but also in its recognized value proposition (hence, leading to wider adop-tion). That is, we suggest that DM applications are no longer seen as "experimental" but rather are now viewed as an acceptable and mature technology for generating new knowledge, and hence are being recognized as having the potential to deliver real utility to decision makers. With a wide range of applications, and the sourcing of techniques from a number of related disciplines, including soft computing, statistics, and artificial intelligence, our findings also agree with Fayyad et al. (1996c), who see DM as being an inherently interdisciplinary field of research. Notwithstanding the interdisciplinary nature of DM, we still identified what we believe to be a number of foundational concepts within the DM field, which include algorithm design, algorithm performance, data analysis, feature extraction, feature selection, pattern recognition, prediction, and visualization.

### 14.6.3 The Rising Importance of Bioinformatics within the Data Mining Field

Perhaps the most striking observation from our analysis is that life sciences DM is now a prominent component within the DM landscape. Consequently, our corpus included numerous examples of life science DM applications. In addition, DM endeavors are being undertaken for a broad range of life science sub-fields, such as cancer, microarray, and genetics.

Of the four basic classes of DM problems (Houston et al., 1999), the DM problem class of *sequence* appears to have received the most attention within the bioinformatics field. As discussed above, the importance of this DM problem class to the field of bioinformatics is not surprising, given the importance of sequence databases to advances in this field. From our analysis, we believe that DM applications in bioinformatics will become an increasingly important and rich source of future innovations within the DM field.

### 14.6.4 The Use of Soft Computing Methodologies in Data Mining

To deal with potential limitations in traditional statistical approaches to tasks, such as prediction, our model highlights that soft computing technologies, such as neural networks, have now become an important component of the modern DM field. Other authors (see, for example, Liu et al., 1999) have noted also that soft computing technologies may be challenging pure statistics as the primary and traditional method for data analysis, in that soft computing methodologies offer a wealth of approaches that can contribute substantially to the effective analysis of larger datasets (Liu et al., 1999).

### 14.6.5 Insights into the Application of LSA

In this study, we believe we have demonstrated that LSA is a powerful association technique; and within the current context, LSA was able to produce associations that were largely understandable and meaningful to human reviewers, and with relatively few surprising omissions. However, our experience provided some important lessons, as well as highlighting a number of potential weaknesses in applying this technique. First, our experience with the development of AKS emphasized the importance of corpus pre-processing. For example, to reduce noise in keyword associations, we undertook an extensive stemming process; and in doing so, we encountered another challenge in that there appeared to be little standardization in the authors' choice of keywords, which made the stemming process complex and time consuming. In total, we implemented 553 stemming rules to bring more standardization to the keyword population, which understandably was a very time-consuming process. Second, as noted in our analysis of the relationship between the keywords *neural network* and *high-throughput screening*, LSA association strength can be affected by small sample size. Furthermore, we noted that in our study, LSA appeared to be unable to discern between associations that appear to be directional. Third, we found for certain keywords, such as those representing soft computing methodologies, that although they shared a relatively high frequency of first-order co-occurrences with some other keywords, our LSA had trouble identifying these associations.

## 14.6.6 Weaknesses of this Study

Our study contains a number of clear weaknesses. First, analysis of the final model is open to interpretation. Second, the corpus included in this study does not contain entries for all DM articles published during the study window. Some of the reasons why some DM articles may have been excluded from our analysis include that fact that many entries in the ISI database did not have keywords listed; the ISI database does not cover all journals, and some of these omitted journals may have featured DM-related articles; and the study was restricted to a narrow time window. These weaknesses may also lead to criticism of this study for having a sample size that some LSA practitioners might regard as inadequate for conducting a comprehensive LSA. However, to some extent, the sample size of this study was constrained by a number of factors, such as the number of DM-related publications within the analysis period. Another weakness in the study is that we chose to focus on keywords only. Analysis of full article texts or titles may have yielded different results. In addition, the AKS produced by the LSA appeared to exclude several associations we expected to find. For example, the relationships between soft computing methodologies and other keywords and concepts in the AKS arguably fail to illustrate that these methodologies have been applied within a number of application domains. Finally, although the AKS features many "understandable" associations, and thus provided a valuable overview of the DM field, interpretation of any high level (abstract) model makes drawing concrete conclusions difficult.

# References

Agrawal, R., T. Imielinski, and A. Swami (1993). Database mining: a performance perspective. *IEEE Transactions on Knowledge and Data Engineering,* 5(6): 914–925.

Aizawa, A., and K. Kageura (2003). Calculating association between technical terms based on co-occurrences in keyword lists of academic papers. *Systems and Computers in Japan,* 34(3): 85–95.

Anand, S. and S. Mobasher (2003). BI intelligent techniques for web personalization. *International Joint Conferences on Artificial Intelligence 2003 Workshop, Intelligent Techniques for Web Personalization,* Acapulco, Mexico.

Bassett, D.E., M.B. Eisen, and M.S. Boguski (1999). Gene expression informatics — it's all in your mine. *Nature Genetics,* 21: 51–55.

Batagelj, V. and A. Mrvar (1997). Pajek: Program Package for Large Network Analysis, University of Ljubljana, Slovenia. Retrieved May 24, 2006, from http://vlado.fmf.uni-lj.si/pub/networks/pajek/

Batagelj, V. and A. Mrvar (2003). Pajek — Analysis and visualization of large networks. In M. Jünger and P. Mutzel (Eds.), *Graph Drawing Software,* Springer, Berlin. pp. 77–103.

Börner, K., C. Chen, and K.W. Boyack (2003). Visualizing knowledge domains. *Annual Review Information Science,* 37: 179–255.

Budanitsky, A., and G. Hirst (2001). Semantic distance in WordNet: an experimental, application-oriented evaluation of five measures. *Workshop on WordNet and other Lexical Resources, Second Meeting of the North American Chapter of the Association for Computational Linguistics,* pp. 29–34.

Buddhakulsomsiri, J., Y. Siradeghyan, A. Zakarian, and X. Li (2006). Association rule-generation algorithm for mining automotive warranty data. *International Journal of Production Research,* 44: 2749–2770.

Burbeck, K. and S. Nadjm-Tehrani (2004). ADWICE — Anomaly detection with real-time incremental clustering. *Conference on Information Security and Cryptology 2004,* pp. 407–424.

Cameron, B.D. (2005). Trends in the usage of ISI bibliometric data: uses, abuses, and implications. *Portal-Libraries and the Academy,* 5: 105–125.

Cattell, R.B. (1966). The Scree Test for the number of factors. *Multivariate Behavioral Research,* 1: 245–276.

Carreira-Perpiñán, M.Á. (1996). A review of dimension reduction techniques. *Technical Report CS-96-09.* Dept. of Computer Science, University of Sheffield, U.K.

Chatterjee, A. (2000). An introduction to the proper orthogonal decomposition. *Current Science,* 78: 808–817.

Chen, Y.L., K. Tang, R.J. Shen, and Y.H. Hu (2005). Market basket analysis in a multiple store environment. *Decision Support Systems,* 40: 339–354.

Chen, Z. (2002). The three dimensions of data mining foundation. *Proceedings of IEEE ICDM '02 Workshop on Foundations of Data Mining and Knowledge Discovery,* pp. 119-124. Retrieved August 25, 2006, from http://imej.wfu.edu/articles/1999/2/04/index.asap.

Cios, K.J. and L. Kurgan. (2002). Trends in data mining and knowledge discovery. In N.R. Pal, L.C. Jain, and N. Teoderesku (Eds.), *Knowledge Discovery in Advanced Information Systems,* Springer.

Colet, E. (1999). The maturation of data mining. *The On-Line Executive Journal for Data-Intensive Decision Support,* April 6, Vol. 3.

Corma, A, and J.M. Serra (2005). Heterogeneous combinatorial catalysis applied to oil refining, petrochemistry and fine chemistry. *Catalysis Today,* 107: 3–11.

Coulter, N., I. Monarch, and S. Konda (1998). Software engineering as seen through its research literature: a study in co-word analysis. *Journal of the American Society for Information Science,* 49(13): 1206–1223.

Cunningham, C., I.Y. Song, and P.P. Chen (2004). Data warehouse design to support customer relationship management analyses. *ACM International Workshop on Data Warehousing and OLAP,* pp. 14–22.

Deerwester, S., S.T. Dumais, G.W. Furnas, T.K. Landauer, and R. Harshman. (1990). Indexing by Latent Semantic Analysis. *Journal of the American Society for Information Science,* 41(6): 391–407.

De Raedt, L. (Ed.) (1996). *Advances in Inductive Logic Programming*, IOS Press.

Ding, Y., G.G. Chowdhury, and S. Foo (2001). Bibliometric cartography of information retrieval research by using co-word analysis. *Information Processing Management,* 37: 817–842.

Diodato, V. (1994). *Dictionary of Bibliometrics.* Haworth, New York.

Dumais, S.T. (1990). Enhancing performance in latent semantic (LSI) indexing. *Behavior Research Methods, Instruments and Computers*, 23(2): 229–236.

Duru, N. (2005). An application of Apriori algorithm on a diabetic database. *Knowledge-Based Intelligent Information and Engineering Systems,* 1: 398–404.

Ebert, C., T. Matsubara, T. Webb, M. Pezzè, and O.W. Bertelsen (1997). The road to maturity: navigating between craft and science. *IEEE Software,* 14(6): 77–82.

Efron, M. (2005) Eigenvalue-based model selection during latent semantic indexing. *Journal of the American Society for Information Science and Technology,* 56(9): 969–988.

Fayyad, U., G. Grinstein, and A. Wierse, Eds. (2002). *Information Visualization in Data Mining.* Morgan Kaufmann Publishers, San Francisco.

Fayyad, U. and R. Uthurusamy (2002). Evolving data mining into solutions for insights. *Communications of the ACM,* 45(8): 28–31.

Fayyad, U., G. Piatetsky-Shapiro, and P. Smyth (1996a). The KDD process for extracting useful knowledge from volumes of data. *Communications of the ACM,* 39(11): 27–34.

Fayyad, U., G. Piatetsky-Shapiro, and P. Smyth (1996b).From data mining to knowledge discovery: an overview. In U. Fayyad, G. Piatetsky-Shapiro, P. Smyth, and R. Uthurusamy (Eds.), *Advances in Knowledge Discovery and Data Mining.* AAAI Press, pp. 1–34.

Fayyad, U., G. Piatetsky-Shapiro, and P. Smyth (1996c). From data mining to knowledge discovery in databases. *AI Magazine,* 17(3): 37–54.

Farrusseng, D., C. Klanner, L. Baumes, M. Lengliz, C. Mirodatos, and F. Schuth (2005). Design of discovery libraries for solids based on QSAR models. *Qsar and Combinatorial Science,* 24(1): 78–93.

Fenstermacher, D.A. (2005). Introduction to Bioinformatics. *Journal American Society Information Science and Technology,* 56: 440–446.

Foltz, P.W., D. Laham, and T.K. Landauer (1999). The intelligent essay assessor: applications to educational technology. *Interactive Multimedia Electronic Journal of Computer-Enhanced Learning,* 1(2).

French, R.M. (2000). Peeking behind the screen: the unsuspected power of the standard Turing Test. *Journal of Experimental and Theoretical Artificial Intelligence,* 12: 331–340.

Friedman, J.H. (2001). The role of statistics in the data revolution? *International Statistics Review,* 69: 5–10.

Gärdenfors, P. (2004). Conceptual spaces as a framework for knowledge representation. *Mind and Matter,* 2(2): 9–27.

Gütl, C. and V.M. García-Barrios (2005). The application of concepts for learning and teaching. In *Proceedings of 8th International Conference on Interactive Computer Aided Learning (ICL 2005),* Villach, Austria.

Guttman, A.R. (1954). Some necessary conditions for common factor analysis. *Psychometrika,* 19(2): 149–161.

Haley, D.T., P. Thomas, A. de Roeck, and M. Petre (2005). A Research Taxonomy for Latent Semantic Analysis-Based Educational Applications. Open University, Technical Report Number 2005/09. Retrieved August 12, 2006, from: http://computing-reports.open.ac.uk/index.php/content/download/187/1136/file/TR2005_09.pdf

Houston, A.L., H. Chen, S.M. Hubbard, B.R. Schatz, T.D. Ng, R.R. Sewell, and K.M. Tolle (1999). Medical data mining on the Internet: research on a cancer information system. *Artificial Intelligence Review,* 13: 437–466.

Houston, A.L., H. Chen, B.R. Schatz, S.M. Hubbard, R.R. Sewell, and T.D. Ng (2000). Exploring the use of concept space to improve medical information retrieval. *International Journal of Decision Support Systems,* 30: 171–186.

Huang, S., M.O. Ward, and E.A. Rundensteiner (2005). Exploration of dimensionality reduction for text visualization. *The Third International Conference on Coordinated and Multiple Views in Exploratory Visualization (CMV 2005).* pp. 63 –74.

Jun S.H. (2005). Web Usage Mining Using Support Vector Machine. *Lecture Notes in Computer Science,* 3512: 349–356.

Kamada, T. and S. Kawai (1989). An algorithm for drawing general undirected graphs. *Information Processing Letters,* 31: 7–15.

Kaski, S. (1997). Data exploration using self-organizing maps. *Acta Polytechnica Scandinavia. Mathematics, Computing and Management in Engineering Series No. 82.* D.Tech. thesis, Helsinki University of Technology, Espoo.

Kaski S., J. Nikkilä, and T. Kohonen (1998). Methods for interpreting a self-organized map in data analysis. In Verleysen, M., Ed., *Proceedings of ESANN'98, 6th European Symposium on Artificial Neural Networks.* D-Facto, Brussels, Belgium, pp. 185–190.

Koike, A. and T. Takagi (2007). Knowledge discovery based on an implicit and explicit conceptual network. *Journal of the American Society for Information Science and Technology,* 58(1): 51–65.

Kontostathis, A. and W.M. Pottenger (2002). A Mathematical View of Latent Semantic Indexing: Tracing Term Co-occurrences. Technical Report, LU-CSE-02-006, Department of Computer Science and Engineering, Lehigh University.

Kontostathis, A. and Pottenger, W.M. (2006). A framework for understanding LSI performance. *Information Processing and Management,* 42(1): 56–73.

Kontostathis, A., W.M. Pottenger, and B.D. Davison. (2005). Identification of critical values in latent semantic indexing (LSI). Identification of critical values in latent semantic indexing (LSI). In T.Y. Lin, S. Ohsuga, C. Liau, X. Hu, and S. Tsumoto (Eds.), *Foundations of Data Mining and Knowledge Discovery,* Springer-Verlag, pp. 333–346.

Kurgan, L.A. and P. Musilek (2006). A survey of knowledge discovery and data mining process models. *The Knowledge Engineering Review,* 21(1): 1–24.

Landauer, T.K., P.W. Foltz, and D. Laham (1998). Introduction to latent semantic analysis. *Discourse Processes*, 25: 259–284.

Landauer, T.K. and S.T. Dumais (1997). A solution to Plato's problem: the Latent Semantic Analysis theory of the acquisition, induction, and representation of knowledge. *Psychological Review*, 104: 211–240.

Li, X. and N. Ye. (2006). A supervised clustering and classification algorithm for mining data with mixed variables. *IEEE Transactions on Systems, Man, and Cybernetics — Part A*, 36(2): 396–406.

Lin, T.Y. (2002). Issues in modeling for data mining, *Proceedings of Computer Software and Applications Conference 2002*, pp. 1152–1157.

Liu, X., R. Johnson, G. Cheng, S. Swift, and A. Tucker (1999). Soft computing for intelligent data analysis. *Proceedings of the 18th International Conference of the North American Fuzzy Information Processing Society*. IEEE Press, New York, pp. 527–531.

Kurgan, L.A. and P. Musilek (2006). A survey of knowledge discovery and data mining process models. *The Knowledge Engineering Review*, 21(1): 1–24.

Mahn, M. and C. Biemann (2005). Tuning co-occurrences of higher orders for generating ontology extension candidates. *Proceedings of the ICML-2005 Workshop on Learning and Extending Lexical Ontologies Using Machine Learning Methods*, Bonn, Germany.

Mane, K. and K. Börner (2004). Mapping topics and topic bursts in PNAS. *Proceedings of the National Academy of Sciences*, 101(Supplement 1): 5287–5290.

Mangalam, H., J. Stewart, J. Zhou, K. Schlauch, M. Waugh, G. Chen, A.D. Farmer, G. Colello, and J.W. Weller (2001). GeneX: an Open Source gene expression database and integrated tool set. *IBM Systems Journal*, 40(2): 552–569.

Mannila, H. (2000). Theoretical frameworks for data mining, *Special Interest Group on Knowledge Discovery and Data Mining Explorations*, 1(2): 30–32.

Mattes, W.B., S.D. Pettit, S.A. Sansone, P.R. Bushel, and M.D. Waters (2004). Database development in toxicogenomics: issues and efforts — genomics and risk assessment: mini-monograph. *Environmental Health Perspectives*, 112(4): 495–505.

Mitra, S.P., S.K. Pal, and P. Mitra (2002). Data mining in a soft computing framework: a survey. *IEEE Transactions on Neural Networks*, 13(1): 3–14.

Monarch, I.A. (2000) Information science and information systems: converging or diverging? *Proceedings of the 28th Annual Conference of the Canadian Association for Information Science*. Retrieved August 14, 2006, from: http://www.slis.ualberta.ca/cais2000/monarch.htm

Novak, J.D. and A.J. Cañas (2006). The theory underlying concept maps and how to construct them. Technical Report IHMC CmapTools 2006–01, Florida Institute for Human and Machine Cognition. Retrieved October 12, 2006, from: http://cmap.ihmc.us/Publications/ResearchPapers/TheoryUnderlyingConceptMaps.pdf

Nakov, P. (2000). Getting better results with latent semantic indexing. In *Proceedings of the Students Presentations at European Summer School in Logic, Language and Information 2000*. Birmingham, U.K., pp. 156–166

Nakov, P., A. Popova, and P. Mateev (2001). Weight functions impact on LSA performance. In *Proceedings of Recent Advances in Natural Language Processing (RANLP 2001)*. Tzigov Chark, Bulgaria, September 5–7, 2001, pp. 187–193.

Oh, S.H. and W.S. Lee (2003). An anomaly intrusion detection method by clustering normal user behavior. *Computers and Security*, 22(7): 596–612.

Oh, S.H. and W.S. Lee (2004). A clustering-based anomaly intrusion detector for a host computer *IEICE Transactions on Information and Systems*, E87-D(8): 2086–2094.

Onyancha, O.B. and D.N. Ocholla (2005). An informetric investigation of the relatedness of opportunistic infections to HIV/AIDS. *Information Processing and Management*, 41: 1573–1588.

Oracle (2006).*Oracle Data Mining*, Last visited December 22, 2006: http://www.oracle.com/technology/products/bi/odm/DS_BI_Mining_OracleDataMining_10gR1_0104.pdf

Ord, T.J., E.P. Martins, S. Thakur, K.K. Mane, and K. Börner (2005). Trends in animal behaviour research (1968–2002): ethoinformatics and the mining of library databases. *Animal Behaviour*, 69: 1399–1413.

Ostell, J. (2005). Databases of discovery. *ACM Queue*, 3(3): 40–48.

Park, C.H. (2006). Similarity-based sparse feature extraction using local manifold learning. In the *Proceedings of Tenth PAKDD*, pp. 30–34.

Pechenizkiy, M., S. Puuronen S., and A. Tsymbal (2005a). Competitive advantage from data mining: lessons learnt in the information systems field. In: *Proceedings 1st International Workshop on Philosophies and Methodologies for Knowledge Discovery*, Denmark, IEEE CS Press, Copenhagen, pp. 733–737.

Pechenizkiy, M., S. Puuronen S., and A. Tsymbal (2005b). Why data mining research does not contribute to business? In C. Soares et al. (Eds.), *Proceedings of Data Mining for Business Workshop, DMBiz* (European Conference on Machine Learning and the European Conference on Principles and Practice of Knowledge Discovery in Databases 2005), Porto, Portugal, pp. 67–71.

Pechenizkiy, M., S. Puuronen S., and A. Tsymbal (2006). Does relevance matter to data mining research? Technical report TCD-CS-2006-23 The University of Dublin, Trinity College. Retrieved November 23, 2006, from: http://www.win.tue.nl/~mpechen/publications/FDM_chapter.pdf

Press, W.H., B.P. Flannery, S.A. Teukolsky, and W.T. Vetterling (1992). *Numerical Recipes. C: The Art of Scientific Computing*. Cambridge University Press.

Rust, R.T. (2006). From the editor: the maturation of marketing as an academic discipline, *Journal of Marketing*, 70: 1–2.

Shaw, M.J., C. Subramaniam, G.W. Tan, and M.E. Welge (2001). Knowledge management and data mining for marketing. *Decision Support Systems*, 31: 127–137.

Shen, D., J. He, and H.R. Chang (2005). In silico identification of breast cancer genes by combined multiple high throughput analyses. *International Journal of Molecular Medicine*, 15(2): 205–212.

Sowa, J.F. (1999). Conceptual Graphs: Draft Proposed American National Standard, International Conference on Conceptual Structures ICCS-99, *Lecture Notes in Artificial Intelligence*, Springer, p. 1640.

Steyvers, M. and J.B. Tenenbaum (2005). The large-scale structure of semantic networks: statistical analyses and a model of semantic growth. *Cognitive Science*, 29(1): 41–78.

Swanson, D.R. and N.R. Smalheiser (1997). An interactive system for finding complementary literatures: a stimulus to scientific discovery. *Artificial Intelligence*, 91: 183–203.

Thakur, S., K. Mane, K. Börner, E. Martins, and T. Ord. (2004). Content coverage of animal behavior data. In *Visualization and Data Analysis*, San Jose, CA, SPIE-ISandT, 5295: 305–311.

*The Gene Ontology Project*. [http://www.geneontology.org/].

Tsumoto, S., T.Y. Lin, and J.F. Peters (2002). Foundations of data mining via granular and rough computing. *Proceedings of Computer Software and Applications Conference 2002*, 1123–1124.

Tukey, J.W. (1977). *Exploratory Data Analysis*. Addison-Wesley, Reading, MA.

Van den Berg, J. and M., Schuemie (1999). Information retrieval systems using an associative conceptual space. In M. Verleysen (Ed.), *Proceedings of the 7th European Symposium on Artificial Neural Networks (ESANN '99)*. Brussels, Belgium: D-Facto Publications, pp. 351–356.

Van der Eijk, C., E. Van Mulligen, J.A. Kors, B. Mons, and J. van den Berg (2004). Constructing an associative concept space for literature-based discovery. *Journal of the American Society for Information Science and Technology*, 55(5), 436–444.

Van Raan, A.F.J. (2003). The use of bibliometric analysis in research performance assessment and monitoring of interdisciplinary scientific developments. *Technikfolgenabschätzung, Theorie und Praxis,* 12(1): 20–29.

Van Bruggen, J.M., E. Rusman, B. Giesbers, and R. Koper (2006). Latent semantic analysis of small-scale corpora for positioning in learning networks. Working paper from Open Universiteit Nederland. Retrieved October 14, 2006, from: http://dspace.ou.nl/handle/1820/561

Velicer, W.F. and D.N. Jackson (1990). Component analysis versus common factor-analysis — Some further observations. *Multivariate Behavioral Research*, 25(1): 97–114.

Voss, A., K. Nakata, and M. Juhnke (1999). Concept indexing, *Proceedings of the International ACM SIGGROUP Conference on Supporting Group Work*, Phoenix, AZ, pp. 1–10.

Wang, Y. (2000). Web Mining and Knowledge Discovery of Usage Patterns. CS 748T Project (Part I), February 2000, 25 pp.

Wiemer-Hastings, P. (1999). How latent is latent semantic analysis? *Proceedings of the Sixteenth International Joint Congress on Artificial Intelligence*, Morgan Kaufmann, San Francisco, pp. 932–937.

Wiemer-Hastings, P. (2004). Latent Semantic Analysis. In *Encyclopedia of Language and Linguistics*, Elsevier, Oxford, U.K.

Wiemer-Hastings, P. and A.C. Graesser (2000). Select-a-Kibitzer: a computer tool that gives meaningful feedback on student compositions 34. *Interactive Learning Environments,* 8(2): 149–169.

Wiemer-Hastings, P., K. Wiemer-Hastings, and A.C. Graesser (1999). Improving an intelligent tutor's comprehension of students with Latent Semantic Analysis. In Lajoie, S. and M. Vivet (Eds.), *Artificial Intelligence in Education*, IOS Press, Amsterdam, pp. 535–542.

Wikipedia (2006a). *Force-based algorithms*. Last visited August 13, 2006: http://en.wikipedia.org/wiki/Force-based_algorithms

Wikipedia (2006b). *High-throughput screening*. Last visited September 28, 2006: http://en.wikipedia.org/wiki/High_throughput_screening

Winarko, E. and J.F. Roddick (2005). Discovering richer temporal association rules from interval-based data. *Data Warehousing and Knowledge Discovery 2005*, pp. 315–325.

Wild, F. (2005). *An open source LSA package for R. CRAN*. Retrieved July 7, 2006, from http://cran.at.r-project.org/src/contrib/Descriptions/lsa.html

Xie, Y. and V.V. Raghavan (2002). Probabilistic logic-based characterization of knowledge discovery in databases. *Proceedings of IEEE International Conference on Data Mining Workshop on Foundations of Data Mining and Knowledge Discovery*, pp. 107–112.

Yang, Q. and X. Wu (2006). 10 Challenging problems in data mining research. *International Journal of Information Technology and Decision Making*, 5(4): 597–604.

Yao, Y.Y. (2000). Granular computing: basic issues and possible solutions, *Proceedings of the Fifth Joint Conference on Information Sciences*, 186–189.

Yao, Y.Y. (2001). On modeling data mining with granular computing, *Proceedings of the 25th Annual International Computer Software and Applications Conference (COMPSAC 2001)*, pp. 638–643.

Yao, Y.Y. (2003). A step towards the foundations of data mining. In *Proceedings of SPIE: Data Mining and Knowledge Discovery: Theory, Tools, and Technology*. V. Belur and V. Dasarathy, Eds., 5098: 254–263.

Yao, Y.Y. (2006). On conceptual modeling of data mining. In Wang, J., Zhou, Z.H. and Zhou, A.Y. (Eds.), *Machine Learning and Applications*, Tsinghua University Press, Beijing, pp. 238–255.

Yen S.J. and Y.S. Lee (2006). An efficient data mining approach for discovering interesting knowledge from customer transactions. *Expert Systems with Applications*, 30(4): 650–657.

Zadeh, L.A. (1965). Fuzzy sets. *Information and Control*, 8(3): 338–353.

Zhan, J.Z., S. Matwin, and L.W. Chang (2005). Privacy-preserving collaborative association rule mining. *Proceedings of 19th Annual IFIP WG 11.3 Working Conference on Data and Applications Security*.

Zhi-qiang, J., F.U. Han-guang, and L. Ling-jun (2005). Support vector machine for mechanical faults classification. *Journal of Zhejiang University Science*, 6A(5): 433–439.

Zyngier, S., F.V. Burstein, and J. McKay (2004). Knowledge management governance: a multifaceted approach to organizational decision and innovation support. *Proceedings of the 2004 IFIP International Conference on Decision Support Systems (DSS2004)* held July 1–3, 2004, Prato, Italy.

*Chapter 15*

# A Classification Model for a Two-Class (New Product Purchase) Discrimination Process Using Multiple-Criteria Linear Programming

Kenneth D. Lawrence, Dinesh R. Pai,
Ronald K. Klimberg, Stephan Kudyba,
and Sheila M. Lawrence

**Contents**

## 15.1 Introduction

Discriminant analysis differs from most statistical techniques because the dependent variable is discrete rather than continuous. One might assume that this type of problem could be handled by least squares regression by employing independent variables to predict the value of a discrete dependent variable coded to indicate the group membership of each observation. This approach will involve two groups.

    This chapter reports results of a numerical simulation for a new financial product service. The example has two explanatory variables — income and savings — and it classifies purchasers and non-purchasers of the new financial product service. The example compares weighted linear programming (WLP), logistic regression, and discriminant analysis (Mahalanobis method).

## 15.2 Methods of Estimating a Classification Method

### 15.2.1 Linear Discrimination by the Mahalanobis Method

The objective of discriminant analysis is to use the information from the independent variables to achieve the clearest possible separation or discrimination between or among groups. In this respect, the two-group discriminant analysis is not different from multiple regression. One uses the independent variables to account for as much of the variation as possible in the dependent variable.

    For the discriminant analysis problem, there are two populations that have sets of $n_1$ and $n_2$ individuals selected from each population. Moreover, for each individual, there are $p$ corresponding random variables $X_1, X_2, \ldots, X_p$. The basic strategy is to form a linear combination of these variables:

$$L = B_1 X_1 + B_2 X_2 + \cdots + B_p X_p$$

One then assigns a new individual to either group 1 or group 2 on the basis of the value of $L$. The values of $B_1$, $B_2$, $\ldots$ , $B_p$ are close to provide a maximum discrimination between the two populations. The variation in the values of $L$ should be greater between the two groups than the variation within the groups (Wiginton, 1980).

## 15.2.2 *Linear Discrimination by Logit Regression*

Both logit choice regression models and discriminant analysis use the same data (a single dependent variable.)

In discriminant analysis, the objective of the Mahalanobis approach is to construct a locus of points that are equidistant from the two group centroids. The distance, which is adjusted for the covariance among the independent variable, is used to determine a posterior probability that can be used as the basis for assigning the observation to one of the two groups. Thus, although the discriminant function is linear in nature, the procedure also provides a probability of group membership, that is, a nonlinear function of the independent variables in the model. When this probability of group membership corresponds to the probability of choice, effectively one has a choice model with a different functional form.

The multiple logistic response function is given by:

$$E(Y) = \frac{e^{B'X}}{1 + e^{B'X}}$$

where $Y_i$ are independent Bernoulli random variables with expected values $E(Y_i) = \Pi_i$

and

$$E(Y_i) = \prod_i = \frac{e^{B'X}}{1 + e^{B'X}}$$

The X observations are considered known constants. To fit this model, the method of maximum likelihood estimates is used to estimate the parameters of the multiple logistic response function. The fitted logistic response function is fit by $\Pi_i = [1 + e^{-B'X_i}]^{-1}$ (Kumar et al., 1995).

## 15.2.3 *Linear Discrimination by Goal Programming*

The approach is based on the development of the so-called linear discriminant function, where this function is expressed as:

$$f(x) = w_1 x_{i1k} + w_2 x_{i2k} + \cdots + w_m x_{ink} + b$$

where

$x_{ijk}$ = Score achieved by object $i$, of class $k$, on attribute $j$
$x_j$ = Weight given to attribute $j$
$b$ = Constant (and unrestricted in sign)

Let us now discuss how one may employ linear programming (LP) to develop this function by means of solving for the unknown weights.

The formulation of the LP model employed to represent the pattern classification problem depends on the measure of performance selected. This choice is usually a function of the characteristics of the particular problem encountered. However, two of the most typical measures of performance are those of (1) the minimization of the sum or weighted sum of the misclassifications and (2) the minimization of the single worst misclassification. To keep the discussion simple, we restrict the focus to training samples from just two classes. Thus, the general formulation of the first LP model (i.e., as used to generate a function that will serve to minimize the use of all misclassifications) is as follows.

## *Model I*

Find $w$ to

$$MIN \; Z = \sum_{i=1}^{p} p_i + \sum_{p+1}^{m} \eta_i$$

$$S.T.$$

$$\sum_{j=1}^{n} w_j x_{ijk} + b - p_i \leq -r \qquad \forall i = 1, ..., p$$

$$\sum_{j=1}^{n} w_j x_{ijk} + b - \eta_i \geq r \qquad \forall i = p+1, ..., m$$

$$x_{ijk}, p_i, \eta_i \geq 0 \quad \forall i, j, k$$

where

$w_j$ = Weight assigned to score (attribute) $j$ (and unrestricted in sign)
$x_{ijk}$ = Score achieved by object $i$, of class $k$, on attribute $j$
$b$ = Constant (and unrestricted in sign)
$r$ = Small positive constant (a value of 0.1 is employed here)
$\qquad -1 \leq w_j = \leq 1$
$i = 1, ..., p$ represents the indices of the objects in the first class
$i = p + 1, ..., m$ represents the indices of the objects in the second class

The second model (i.e., to develop a function that will minimize the single worst misclassification) is then given as follows.

## Model II

Find $w$ so as to

$$MIN\ Z = \delta$$

$$S.T.$$

$$\sum_{j=1}^{n} w_j x_{ijk} + b - p_i \leq -r \qquad \forall i = 1, \ldots, p$$

$$\sum_{j=1}^{n} w_j x_{ijk} + b - \eta_i \geq r \qquad \forall i = p+1, \ldots, m$$

$$x_{ijk}, p_i, \eta_i \geq 0 \quad \forall i, j, k$$

where all notation, as well as the restriction on the upper and lower limits on the weights, is the same as previously defined except that $\delta$ denotes the amount of misclassification. Thus, $\geq 0$ (Joachimsthaler and Stam, 1990).

### 15.2.4 Weighted Linear Programming (WLP)

This chapter employs the WLP method to classify the new product purchasers into two groups. The method does not make any rigid assumptions that some of the statistical methods make. The method utilizes constrained weights, which are generated using the standard evolutionary solver. The weights are used to develop a cut-off discriminant score for each observation to classify the observations into two groups. The objective is to minimize the apparent error rate (APER) of misclassification (Koehler and Erenguc, 1990). The advantage of the WLP method in classification is its ability to weight individual observations, which is not possible with statistical methods (Freed and Glover, 1981).

$$Min\ Z = \delta$$

$$S.T.$$

$$w_1 x_{ij} + w_2 x_{ik} \geq c \quad \forall i \in G_1$$

$$w_1 x_{ij} + w_2 x_{ik} \leq c \quad \forall i \in G_2$$

$$w_1 + w_2 \leq 1$$

$$w_1 + w_2 \geq 0$$

$$0 \leq c \leq M$$

$$x_{ij} \geq 0 \qquad \forall i, j$$

$$x_{ik} \geq 0 \qquad \forall i, k$$

where

$w_1, w_2$ = Weights generated by the standard evolutionary solve
$x_{ij}$ = Income for the observation $i$
$x_{ik}$ = Savings for the observation $i$
$C$ = Discriminant cut-off score use to classify the observations into two groups
$M$ = Maximum of the total of income and savings for a dataset

## 15.3 Evaluating the Classification Function

One important way of judging the performance for any classification procedure is to calculate its error rates or misclassification probabilities. The performance of a sample classification function can be evaluated by calculating the actual error rate (AER). The AER indicates how the sample classification function will perform in future samples. Just as the optimal error rate, it cannot be calculated because it depends on an unknown density function. However, an estimate of a quantity related to the AER can be calculated.

There is a measure of performance that does not depend on the form of the parent population, and which can be calculated for any classification procedure. This measure is called the apparent error rate (APER) and is defined as the fraction of observations in the training sample that are misclassified by the sample classification function.

The APER can be calculated easily from the confusion matrix, which shows actual versus predicted group membership.

For $n_1$ observations from $\Pi_1$ and $n_2$ observations $\Pi_2$, the confusion matrix is given by the following (Morrison, 1969):

**Predicted Memberships**

|  |  | $\Pi_1$ | $\Pi_2$ |  |
|---|---|---|---|---|
| Actual | $\Pi_1$ | $n_1c$ | $n_1m = n_1 - n_1 c$ | $n_1$ |
| Membership | $\Pi_2$ | $n_2m = n_2 - n_2 c$ | $n_2c$ | $n_2$ |

where
$n_1c$ = Number of $\Pi_1$ items correctly classified as $\Pi_1$ items
$n_1m$ = Number of $\Pi_1$ items misclassified as $\Pi_2$ items
$n_2c$ = Number of $\Pi_2$ items correctly classified as $\Pi_2$ items
$n_2m$ = Number of $\Pi_2$ items misclassified as $\Pi_1$ items

The apparent error rate is thus

$$\text{APER} = \frac{n_1m + n_2m}{n_1 + n_2}$$

or, the proportion of items in the training set that are misclassified.

The APER is intuitively appealing and easy to calculate. Unfortunately, it tends to underestimate the AER, and the problem does not appear unless the sample sizes of $n_1$ and $n_2$ are very large. This very optimistic estimate occurs because the data used to build the classification is used to evaluate it.

One can construct the error rate estimates so that they are better than the apparent error rate. They are easy to calculate, and they do not require distributional assumptions. Another evaluation procedure is to split the total sample into a training sample and a validation sample. One uses the training sample to construct the classification function and the validation sample to evaluate it. The error rate is determined by the proportion misclassified in the validation sample. This method overcomes the bias problem by not using the same data to both build and judge the classification function. There are two main problems with this method:

1.  It requires large samples.
2.  The function evaluated is not the function of interest because some data is lost.

## 15.4  An Example Problem for a New Product Purchase

This chapter focuses on the development of a classification procedure for a new financial product service. It is based on a data set that groups purchasers and non-purchasers of the new financial product service. The explanatory variables are income level and saving amount. The data include the training set for developing the discriminant classification model and the validation set for evaluating the model. Three methods of the classification model development are:

1.  Discriminant analysis by the Mahalanobis method
2.  Logistical regression analysis
3.  Discriminant analysis by mathematical programming

These methods and the classification function of each can be evaluated by the error rate they produced.

The future direction of this research will be to employ various multiple criteria linear programming models of the two-class discrimination model in terms of their effectiveness in terms of error rates.

The basic objectives of such models include:

1.  Maximize the minimum distance of data records from a critical value (MMD).
2.  Minimize the sum of the deviations from the critical value (MSD).

While the results of these objectives are usually opposite of one another in terms of results, a combination of these two objectives could provide better results. Various forms of multi-criteria methods will be employed. They will include both preemptive and weighted methods, as well as a compromise solution method. The basic data set will consist of a training set of data and a validation set of data. Moreover, the simulation process based on the original data sets of the data set will add to the effectiveness of the study. The classification will be either a purchase or a non-purchase.

### 15.4.1 Data and Methodology

To evaluate how the model would perform, a simulation experiment was conducted. We chose discriminant analysis — Mahalanobis method, logistic regression, and weighted linear programming (WLP) — as the three discriminant models (West et al., 1997). The discriminant analysis (Mahalanobis method) model and logistic regression model approaches were developed using Minitab software. We used Evolutionary solver to develop the WLP model with an objective to minimize the classification error (misclassification rates). The solver determines weights for the explanatory variables and a cutoff point, c, so that we can classify an observation into two groups, that is, purchasers and non-purchasers of the new financial product service.

The data was generated from multivariate normal distribution using three different $2 \times 2$ covariance matrices (correlations). The three covariance matrices corresponded with high ($\rho = 0.90$), medium ($\rho = 0.70$), and low ($\rho = 0.50$) correlations between the two explanatory variables (i.e., income and savings) (Lam and Moy, 2003).

Fifty replications were generated for each of the three cases. Sixty observations were generated as the training sample for each replication. Another forty observations were generated as validation sample for each replication. All three approaches were used in all replications of the three cases. The APER (percentage of incorrectly classified observations) in both the training and validation samples and their standard deviations are reported in Table 15.1.

## 15.5 Results

We used paired $t$-tests to test the difference between the average APER of all three approaches. We also used $F$-tests to test the ratio of the two population variances of the average APER of the three approaches. In general, the classification performances of discriminant analysis (Mahalanobis) and logistic regression model are similar but they were shown to be inferior to the WLP model, as seen in Table 15.1. For all three correlations cases, WLP model performance on the training set was clearly high. However, its performance on the validation set was somewhat inferior to the logistic regression model. The WLP model is comparatively more robust than the other models in this experiment, as evidenced by its low APER standard deviations in most cases.

The results of the WLP model are encouraging for several reasons. First, the methodology achieved lower APERs than the others for training sets in all

**Table 15.1  Apparent Error Rates (APER)**

| Case | | Discriminant Analysis (MM) | | Logistic Regression | | Weighted LP | |
|------|---|------|------|------|------|------|------|
| | | mean | stdev | mean | stdev | mean | stdev |
| $\rho = 0.9$ | Training | 7.7% | 3.1% | 7.1% | 2.6% | 5.9% | 2.1% |
| | Validation | 15.3% | 6.6% | 14.0% | 5.8% | 14.1% | 4.9% |
| $\rho = 0.7$ | Training | 10.4% | 2.8% | 10.5% | 2.7% | 7.2% | 1.9% |
| | Validation | 8.1% | 3.8% | 5.3% | 3.0% | 5.2% | 2.5% |
| $\rho = 0.5$ | Training | 8.5% | 2.7% | 8.8% | 3.3% | 6.5% | 2.3% |
| | Validation | 12.8% | 4.5% | 12.3% | 4.0% | 12.5% | 3.8% |

Paired *t*-tests were used to compare the average number of APER between WLP and the other two approaches with *Ho*: $\mu_{WLP} = \mu_i$, where $i = _1$. Discriminant Analysis, and 2. Logistic Regression, and *Ha*: $\mu_{WLP} < \mu_i$

*F*-tests were used to test the ratio of two population variances of the average APER between WLP and approach 1, with *Ho*: $\sigma^2_{WLP}/\sigma^2_i = 1$ and *Ha*: $\sigma^2_{WLP}/\sigma^2_i < 1$. The significance level used in both tests: $\alpha = 0.01$

three cases. Because lower APERs on the validation set are deemed as a good check on the external validity of the classification function, we feel that the WLP model performance was comparable to the logistic regression model on this count. Second, these results were achieved with relatively small samples. Finally, the model makes no rigid assumptions about the functional form and did not require large datasets.

# 15.6  Conclusions

This chapter examined the mathematical properties of the WLP, discriminant analysis (Mahalanobis method), and logistic regression for classifying into two groups purchasers and non-purchasers of the new financial product service. Presented was a general framework for understanding the role of three methods for this problem. While traditional statistical methods work well for some situations, they may not be robust in all situations. Weighted linear programming models are an alternative tool when solving problems like these.

This chapter compared three approaches: weighted linear programming and well-known statistical methods such as discriminant analysis (Mahalanobis method) and logistic regression. We found that WLP provides significantly and consistently lower APERs for both the training set and validations sets of data.

We used a simple model with only two explanatory variables. Future research could be extended to include more explanatory variables in the problem. Furthermore, it was assumed that the variables follow normal distribution. This assumption can be relaxed to judge the performance of the WLP and other statistical methods.

# References

Freed, N. and Glover, F. (1981), Simple but powerful goal programming models for discriminant problems, *European Journal of Operational Research*, 7, 44–66.

Joachimsthaler, Erich A. and Stam, A. (1990), Mathematical programming approaches for the classification in two-group discriminant analysis, *Multivariate Behavioral Research*, 25(4), 427–454.

Koehler, G.J. and Erenguc, S.S. (1990), Minimizing misclassifications in linear discriminant analysis, *Decision Sciences*, 21, 63–85.

Kumar, Akhil, Rao, V.R., and Soni, H. (1995), An empirical comparison of neural network and logistic regression models, *Marketing Letters*, 6(4), 251–263.

Lama, K.F. and Moy, J.W. (2003), A simple weighting scheme for classification in two-group discriminant problems, *Computers & Operations Research*, 30, 155–164.

Morrison, D.G. (1969), On the interpretation of discriminant analysis, *Journal of Marketing Research*, 6, 156–163.

West, Patricia M., Brockett, P.L., and Golden, L.L. (1997), A comparative analysis of neural networks and statistical methods for predicting consumer choice, *Marketing Science*, 16(4), 370–391.

Wiginton, J.C. (1980), A note on the comparison of logit and discriminant models of consumer credit behavior, *The Journal of Financial and Quantitative Analysis*, 15(3), 757–770.

# Index

## A

AdaBoost, 42
  algorithm for ensemble, 47
AKS. *See* Associative keyword space (AKS)
Analytic warehouse department, 6–7
Association Analysis, 19
Associative keyword space (AKS), 259, 260,
  262, 270
  of DM literature, 271, 272, 283
  interpretation, 271–273
  keyword clustering within, 273, 281
Automated detection of model shift
  characteristic report, 13–14
  stability report, 14
AutoRegressive Integrated Moving-Average
  (ARIMA) model, 19

## B

Bagging predictors, 42
Bioinformatics, 274–278, 285
Bootstrap aggregation, 42
Business process management, 185, 190–195
  dashboards, 191
  data flows, 192
  forecasts of KPIs, 192
  key capabilities, 192
  metrics,192–195
    invoices paid with purchase order number, 195
    invoices paid without purchase order
      reference, 194–195
    number of invoices from suppliers, 194
    number of transactions per system user, 194
    size of invoice, 195
    users for each vendor, 195
  process changes, 192

## C

CHAID. *See* Chi-squared Automatic
     Interaction Detector (CHAID)
Chi-squared Automatic Interaction Detector
     (CHAID), 232, 236
Chronic health conditions
  data mining for prediction of, 175–182
    analytic methods and procedures, 178–179
     logic regression, 178
     neural networks, 178–179
    discussions and conclusions, 181
    modeling results, 179–181
    as resource allocation tool, 176
    study data, 177–178
Churn model timeline, 10
Cross-validation neural network (CVNN)
     ensemble
  generalization error, 46
  origins, 41
  single neural network model *vs.*, 47, 49–51
  strategies, 43
CVNN ensemble. *See* Cross-validation neural
     network (CVNN) ensemble

## D

Data mining, 15, 153
  algorithms, 118
  applications in higher education, 123–147
    early ventures, 135
    end-to-end solution to, 127
    enrollment, 125–126
    hazard for, 133
    model assessment, 126–127
    predictive models, 126–127
    software for, 127

Printed and bound by CPI Group (UK) Ltd, Croydon, CR0 4YY

17/10/2024

01775690-0007